Normativity in Legal Sociology

Reza Banakar

Normativity in Legal Sociology

Methodological Reflections on Law and Regulation in Late Modernity

Springer

Reza Banakar
Sociology of Law
Lund University
Lund
Sweden

ISBN 978-3-319-09649-0 ISBN 978-3-319-09650-6 (eBook)
DOI 10.1007/978-3-319-09650-6
Springer Cham Heidelberg New York Dordrecht London

Library of Congress Control Number: 2014956568

Printed on acid-free paper

Springer is part of Springer Science+Business Media (www.springer.com)

Acknowledgements

The parts of this book which were previously published have been revised and updated before being reproduced here. In some cases, these revisions have been extensive, while in others only minor changes were deemed necessary. The author acknowledges the following for their kind permissions to use previously printed material from:

'Whose Experience is the Measure of Justice?' in (2008) *Legal Ethics* 10(2): 209–222; 'Law Through Sociology's Looking Glass: Conflict and Competition in Sociological Studies of Law' in Denis, A and Kalekin-Fishman, D (eds) (2009) *The New ISA Handbook in Contemporary International Sociology: Conflict, Competition, Cooperation*, London: Sage; 'Poetic Injustice' in (2008) *Retfærd: The Nordic Journal of Law and Justice* for volume 31(3): 69–90; 'The Politics of Legal Cultures' in (2008) *Retfærd: The Nordic Journal of Law and Justice* 31(4): 37–60; 'Power, Culture and Method in Comparative Law' in *International Journal of Law in Context* (2009) *International Journal of Law in Context* 5(1): 69–85; 'Having One's Cake and Eating It: The Paradox of Contextualisation in Socio-Legal Research' in (2011) *International Journal of Law in Context* 7(4): 487–503; 'Sociology of Law' in (2011) *Online Journal of International Sociological Association: Sociopedia.ISA* 1–14; 'Driving Dangerously: Law, Culture and Driving habits in Iran' in (2012) *British Journal of Middle Eastern Studies* 39(2): 241–257; 'In Search of Heimat: A Note on Franz Kafka's Concept of Law' in (2010) *Law and Literature* 23(3): 463–490; 'Can Legal Sociology Account for the Normativity of Law' in Baier M (2013) *Social and Legal Norms*. Farnham: Ashgate, pp. 15–38; and 'Law and Regulation in Late Modernity' in Banakar R and Travers M (eds) (2013) *Law and Social Theory*. Oxford: Hart, pp. 305–324.

The author is indebted to Mark Jones for his invaluable assistance in editing the first draft of this book. Mark's editorial contributions have raised the clarity of many discussions in this book. He is also indebted to Ann Williams for painstakingly proofreading and checking the references.

Contents

Chapter 1
Introduction: Emerging Legal Uncertainty

Abstract This introductory chapter begins by outlining the themes which run through the pages of this book before it explains how they are related to each other and why they lead us towards a deeper understanding of socio-legal theory and research. The overarching question guiding this inquiry is how legal sociology can produce an empirically valid and theoretically sound insight into the development of forms of law and legality in our contemporary global society. To answer this question we need to conceptualise law and legality, on the one hand, and elaborate on the properties of our contemporary society, on the other. The former involves engaging with debates on law and comparing various understandings of legality—among other things asking if the law is a rational system of norms, a field of practice or a form of experience. The latter entails comparing social conditions of a contemporary global society with earlier forms of social organisation.

The field of socio-legal research[1] has encountered three foundational challenges over the last three decades. Internally, it has been criticised for paying insufficient attention to legal doctrine and for failing to develop a sound theoretical foundation.[2] Could 'socio-legal research say anything about justice?' asked Cotterrell (1995, p. 297), and could it engage forcefully in legal debates? Externally, it has been forced to reconsider its concepts of law and legality, which had been overtaken by the changing makeup of law and regulation (Santos 1995; Gessner 1995; Twining 2000). In the wake of globalisation, the understanding of law as a nationally based body of legal rules, sources and institutions has come to be contested by forms of law and legality originating from multiple sources inside and outside nation states.

[1] "Socio-legal studies" has been used in the UK to refer to policy-oriented or applied empirical research about law. Moreover, it has been defined in contrast to the "sociology of law," which refers to more theoretically-oriented studies (see Chap. 3). However, "socio-legal research" shall be used in this chapter to refer to all social scientific studies of law, including legal sociology, sociological jurisprudence, legal anthropology and the Law and Society movement.

[2] See Hunt (1978), Abel (1980), Abel and Lewis (1989), Travers (1993), Cotterrell (1995), Nelken (1998), Simon (1999), and Banakar (2003).

R. Banakar, *Normativity in Legal Sociology*, DOI 10.1007/978-3-319-09650-6_1

The internal critique, which highlighted the theoretical shortcomings of the field, indicated the coming of age of socio-legal research, whereas concern with the changing character of law and regulation was a response to the social consequences of globalisation and the gradual move away from an industrial to a post-industrial (information) society.

Globalisation has reconfigured the social landscape of modernity by intensifying economic exchanges and trading interconnections across the world, which in turn have interlocked social, economic and cultural activities and processes amongst nations and beyond nation states, thereby bringing about a number of interrelated societal and ideological changes. Furthermore, it has compressed time-space, eroded socio-cultural borderlines, thus creating hybrid cultural and legal spaces, and brought about a gradual transformation of the nation state. At the same time, it has cast doubt on the viability of the welfare ideology, undermined traditional forms of regulation and subsequently recast the relationship between law, state and society. The socio-cultural consequences of globalisation, maintains Twining (2000, p. 10), revive and recast old issues 'such as those surrounding sovereignty and war', make familiar concerns regarding the environment and the regulation of multinational corporations more urgent and create new challenges, many of which concern the form and the role of law in society. Surprisingly, the role of globalisation in prompting new forms of law and legality at the national and international levels has not been explored sufficiently within mainstream legal studies. One of the reasons for this lack of attention to the implications of globalisation lies, according to Michaels (2013, p. 291), in legal theory's unwillingness to abandon the nation state as 'the ultimate point of reference for both domestic and international law'. Not even international law scholars, according to Berman (2007, p. 1159), have paid attention to the significance of legal pluralism and hybrid legal spaces which are created as a result of globalisation. Instead, these scholars have placed emphasis on:

> [F]ormal state-to-state-relations, the creation of overarching universal norms, or the solution of disputes by locating them territorially in order to choose a single governing law to apply. All of these approaches attempt to eliminate hybridity altogether by imagining that disputes can and should be made susceptible to a single governing normative authority. (Berman 2007, p. 1159)

Notwithstanding mainstream legal theory's 'methodological nationalism' (Michaels 2013, p. 291), we have been observing an emerging global legal pluralism and the rise of what Berman (2007, p. 1157) calls 'multiple normative communities' and 'hybrid legal spaces', which are propagated by several overlapping developments, including (1) the socio-cultural diversification of modern societies, e.g. the spread of diaspora laws such as migrant groups' legal practices in the host country that are based on their home countries' religion and customs, (2) the proliferation of law-generating centres at the 'regional' level, e.g. EU and ECHR, (3) forms of law and regulation at the "transnational" level, e.g. *lex mercatoria* and the internal governance of multinational corporations, and (4) the expansion of cyberspace as a multi-jurisdictional arena.[3] Emerging legal pluralism, which we have been witnessing over the last three decades, has been "decentring" the law, causing legal fragmentation and normative uncertainty. 'At the dawn of the 21st century', writes Dermas-Marty (2009, p. 1), 'the legal landscape's primary characteristics are imprecision, uncertainty and instability'. Furthermore, the anarchic forces of globalisation are 'ordering multiplicity, without reducing it to sameness, admitting pluralism without giving up on building a common law with a common measure for fair and unfair…' (Dermas-Marty 2009, p. 1). Douglas-Scott (2013, p. 146) goes further, warning against the expanding legal pluralism which has been largely celebrated as if 'only benefits could spring from its complex nature'. 'On the contrary', she continues, 'privatisation, technicisation and greater flexibility may threaten human well-being, by removing state benefits or failing sufficiently to regulate certain measures' (2013, p. 146).

This book engages with both the internal and external challenges posed to the study of law in society from a methodological standpoint. It will address the first two challenges concerning the relevance of socio-legal research to the law, by demonstrating that legal sociology has much to say about justice as a kind of social *experience* and that it has always engaged with forms of normativity, albeit on its own empirical terms rather than on legal theory's analytical terms. It will explore the third challenge, which was posed by the changing nature of society, in light of the ongoing "transition" from an industrial to a late modern, post-industrial information society. It will further argue that "transition," understood as moving from one long-term state of affairs, such as the agrarian society, to another durable state of affairs, such as the industrial society, is no longer a feasible future scenario with which we can work. Constant change, instead, is to be viewed as the permanent property of the relationship between law and society—and thus also the focal point of socio-legal inquiry. As we leave behind the durable social conditions of early modernity, which were shaped by industrial relations, and move towards late modernity, which is characterised by the socio-cultural implications of globalisation and the spread of digital technology, the focus of our analysis has to shift from the study of social change (as an event) to the examination of the rate of ongoing change (as an unceasing process) in society. Under late modern conditions, constant change is paradoxically the only empirically consistent property of society. This book partly aims at exploring what happens to law and regulation when the structural and institutional relations which uphold and mediate legal and policy measures over time change faster than it takes law and regulation to consolidate new norms and values. Can law and regulation step outside 'the river of flux', to borrow from Heraclitus (cf. Kirk 1954), and supervene on material flux and reshape the flow of the constantly changing social life, or do they become an integral part of

[3] Twining (2009, p. 70) identifies seven levels of law and legality, ranging from 'global', 'international', 'regional' and 'transnational' to 'inter-communal', 'territorial state' and 'sub-state'. 'Which of these orders should be classified as "law" or "legal"', he writes (2009, p. 70), 'is essentially contested within legal theory and also depends on the context and the purpose of the discourse'.

the unrelenting changes? What if they also join the flux and, as Douzinas and Warrington suggested (1994, p. 3), become 'open, decentred, fragmented, nebulous and multiform'? To rephrase Bauman (2005, p. 1) liberally, how can the type of law and regulation which cannot keep its own social and legal form or 'stay on the course for long' exert a normative force on society?

The chapters in this book were initially conceived as discrete research papers and essays in legal sociology engaging with the three challenges outlined above. They have been revised and developed before being presented here in one volume as interrelated studies of the role of normativity in socio-legal research, on the one hand, and the challenges posed to modern law by the socio-cultural implications of globalisation, on the other. Nevertheless, it is important to emphasise that they remain, and should be read, as separate studies which map some of the central debates of the socio-legal research against the changing relationship between law and society. As we make our way through the chapters, we shall note a gradual shift of focus from the study of "certainty" associated with the long-term relations of industrial society, which represents the ideal conditions of early modernity, to "uncertainty" caused by the acceleration of the rate of social change, which captures a growing trend in our contemporary forms of social organisation. The case will be made that greater attention to the growing contingency of social actions and processes, the increasing reflexivity of the individual vis-à-vis social structures and the subsequent rise in insecurity, risk and discontinuity provide an empirically more fruitful description of societal developments in contemporary society. It will also provide an empirically sound point of departure for constructing forms of regulation which respond to how the social reality around us *is* changing, instead of seeking to revitalise outmoded images of social organisation. Many of these outdated images belong to the early stages of modernity, defined by the enduring relations of industrialisation which allowed for experimenting with social engineering but once applied to present conditions fail to grasp the transitory dynamics of the late modern digital/network society. The concern with uncertainty is developed and articulated progressively as our analysis is repeatedly, albeit inadvertently, drawn to the transformation of the seemingly solid relations and durable institutions of early modernity into fleeting interactions and transient networks which increasingly define present-day society.

There will be occasional overlaps between discussions in some chapters and on certain topics, such as the duality of law, the doctrinal method, socio-legal methodology and risk management. Moreover, concepts such as rationality, power, normativity, contextualisation, community, identity, reflexivity, risk and security will be discussed in more than one chapter. Nonetheless, by viewing these topics and concepts from different standpoints, and analysing them in different contexts, we deepen our understanding of the methodological issues of socio-legal research, generally, and the role of law in contemporary society, in particular. To borrow a metaphor from Wittgenstein, the occasional overlaps represent separate attempts to traverse the same streets as part of different journeys through the same city (Gasking and Jackson 1967, p. 51). Each time we approach and walk through the same street from a different direction, we see it from a different angle and learn not only more about it, but also about how the various parts of the city are interconnected. Needless to say, the streets through which we shall pass more than once have been carefully selected, as they are amongst the more important thoroughfares in our little town.

I shall begin this introductory chapter by outlining the main themes which run through the pages of this book, before I move on to explain how issues raised in various chapters are related to each other and lead towards a deeper understanding of the same set of issues. The complex set of problems at hand concerns how legal sociology can produce an empirically valid and theoretically adequate insight into the ways in which forms of law and legality are developing in our contemporary global society. This in turn requires a conceptualisation of law and legality, on the one hand, and an elaboration on the properties of our contemporary society, on the other. The former involves engaging with debates on law and comparing various understandings of legality—among other things asking if the law is a rational system of norms, a field of practice or a form of experience. The latter entails comparing social conditions of a contemporary global society with earlier forms of social organisation.

1 Methodology

1.1 Socio-Legal Methodology

A broadly conceived concern regarding socio-legal methodology runs through the pages of this book, serving as one of the three leitmotifs of the studies presented herein. "Methodology" captures the interaction between theoretical assumptions and methods (or techniques) of research. Expressed differently, methods of inquiry are always founded on certain epistemological assumptions about social reality. Sociology of law consists of many methodological approaches which, to a large extent, reflect various paradigms within mainstream sociology (for a comprehensive discussion, see Banakar and Travers 2005, 2013). Notwithstanding this diversity of approaches, the socio-legal field as a whole distinguishes itself not only from mainstream legal studies, but also from Critical Legal Studies (CLS), which is on the whole sympathetic to legal sociology, by deploying an empirical epistemology which requires the use of social scientific methods in the study of law. By reflecting on socio-legal methodology we can tease out some of the conflicting epistemological assumptions and social-theoretical suppositions about the study of law, which are otherwise taken for granted.

Methodological deliberations take centre stage in some of the chapters, while they indirectly inform debates in the others. How can we employ social theory and methodology to study the law, legal thinking, legal ideas, legal practice, legal institutions and the legal system? What is "law" or "the law" from a social-theoretical standpoint, and how (and why) does it differ from the concept of law used within jurisprudence and legal theory? What do we gain—and what do we sacrifice—by describing and analysing the law not on its own terms but through the lenses of social theory? Every chapter in this book engages with some aspect of these questions by examining the tension between the social-theoretical and legal discourses which constitute the disciplines of sociology and law, respectively.

The first two chapters following this introduction aim jointly at providing an overview of some of the main research themes and debates within the field of socio-legal research. Briefly, Chap. 2 unfolds the general methodological approaches of socio-legal research by comparing them with those employed within traditional legal studies. It also highlights how "sociological imagination," which drives a great deal of sociological theorising and research, differs from the 'authority paradigm' (cf. Samuel 2009) which informs traditional legal scholarship. These debates are then placed in the context of globalisation, the "methodological nationalism" which has dominated both legal thought and much of social theory, and the transformation of the state. Chapter 3 presents the diverse approaches among sociological studies of law by distinguishing between the "sociology of law," "Law and Society," "sociological jurisprudence" and "socio-legal studies." It then contrasts top-down and bottom-up studies of law in society as two basic methodologies which cut across disciplinary divisions within the field, consequently offering an alternative view of how the socio-legal research is conducted. We then discuss critically the so-called "gap" problem by reassessing the significance of studies of the discrepancy between the law as a body of rules with a degree of autonomy and the law as an institutionalised form of practice. This concluding section argues that the gap between 'law in the books' and 'law in action' and conceptual separation of law from justice, are brought on by the modern law's "disembeddedness", i.e. dislodging from its societal context.

The disembeddedness of modern law is never total and the legal system's autonomy from other social domains and processes is always a question of degrees rather than an either/or issue. We might separate law from justice conceptually, but empirically, people's experience of law and legality remains in various ways linked to justice. Chapter 4 expands on this point by examining the debate between Alexy (2002) and his critics on how positive law and justice are related. It also contrasts normative philosophical approaches, which describe law and justice at the level of legal systems, with an empirical approach which seeks to capture how justice is experienced at the mundane level of everyday reality. However, the empirical approach to the study of law, which employs social theoretical constructs to describe and analyse legal phenomena, is not without its critics and its ability to grasp the law's normativity has been questioned by legal scholars. Chapter 5 engages with one aspect of this critique by examining Denis Galligan's argument that adopting a social scientific approach to the study of the law, which describes the law in extra-legal terms, amounts to losing sight of law's distinctiveness. This chapter also identifies three ideal typical methods of contextualising the law, which seek to *re-embed* the law in its societal context, arguing that each approach reverses the de-contextualisation effects of modern law to different degrees.

One of the points made in this book is that attempts to "re-embed" the law while preserving its system autonomy amounts to a contradiction in terms, but a contradiction which is generated in the first place by modernity and its emphasis on rationality (we shall expand on this point below—see Sect. 1.3). From Chap. 6 onwards we begin to explore the limits of modernity in constructing the relationship between law and society in a rational manner. Chapter 6 uses Franz Kafka's office writings and some of the cases he processed as an insurance lawyer, on the one hand, and images of law, bureaucracy, hierarchy and authority in his fiction, on the other, as a starting point for introducing his rhetoric as a method for highlighting the resilience of the lifeworld in the face of rational attempts to order human conduct (cf. Travers 2009). This chapter demonstrates how the everyday experience of reality subverts efforts to regulate life through formal measures, thus articulating a critique of modernity as a rational project, a notion which is expanded in the subsequent chapters. Franz Kafka's concept of law and his images of legality take us beyond the rational (instrumental) understanding of the law advanced by various schools of legal positivism, revealing it as a form of experience involving more than a grain of contradiction and irrationality. Chapter 7 explores the disciplinary tensions between law and sociology, by focusing on the duality of norms and facts in the context of the debate between Hans Kelsen and Eugen Ehrlich. Following up on the role of rationality in modernity, this chapter also highlights legal positivism's neglect of the role of the non-rational (i.e. those qualities of modernity which do not lend themselves to calculations and predictions) and its imperative need to conceptualise law's fragmentary and contradictory bundle of rules, decisions and practices as a coherent whole. Chapter 8 broadens the scope of the debate on the methodological issues of socio-legal research by reflecting on the challenges facing comparative law. It argues that a contextual understanding of laws should be regarded as the indispensable methodological characteristic of all comparative studies of law that aspire to transcend the understanding of thereof as a body of rules and doctrine. It argues further that although the cultural perspective facilitates the contextualisation of the law, a cultural understanding is neither a precondition for undertaking comparative legal research nor necessarily the correct approach under all circumstances, for certain aspects of law and legal behaviour need not be conceptualised in cultural terms. The chapter concludes by proposing that the combination of top-down and bottom-up approaches could provide a meta-methodological framework within which specific comparative techniques can be employed. Such a framework will enable comparatists and socio-legal researchers to account for how law interacts with and simultaneously manifests itself at the macro, micro and intermediary meso levels of society over time.

Chapter 9, on Iranian legal culture, was also conceived initially as an interest in methodology. When studying non-Western legal systems, we can easily forget that assumptions regarding the autonomy of the legal system, i.e. the need to demarcate the boundaries of the adjudicative and legislative organs and legal rules they generate from other social institutions, are products of Western legal cultures. Expressed differently, it is conceivable that legal sociology is not promoted in certain non-Western countries because it is not historically or culturally in tune with their conceptions of law and society. This chapter serves as an example of how socio-legal theories, which have been developed through the study of Western legal systems, can fail to capture the complexity of late modern societies in non-Western settings. To understand Iranian law and its sense of legality, one must understand how the state and society have developed in Iran—a development which is fundamentally at odds with historical accounts of the relationship between law, society and the state in the West.

Chapter 10 does not engage directly with methodology as such, but it does discuss the UK's anti-terrorism legislation as a method of pre-empting threats. The role of this chapter is to exemplify the shift from the traditional paradigm of social control, where policymakers attempt to regulate behaviour by upholding desirable norms and values, to late modern forms of governance which try to manage risks and insecurities. This is a shift from a traditional form of regulation, which aims at safeguarding and enhancing continuity and security in human affairs, to a form of governance based on predicting, managing and eliminating the unforeseen dysfunctional outcomes of social developments. The traditional forms of regulation exert normativity on social processes by embedding norms and values in social relations and institutions. Risk management does not, however, require inserting norms and values into social structures and is uninterested in resolving social problems or reforming society. Nevertheless, Chap. 11 demonstrates that risk management strategies also exert normativity. It argues that normativity is not necessarily linked to the application of specific norms, but it may be generated nonetheless by the social context of everyday life. This point brings us back to one of the central methodological questions of legal sociology, which were developed in the first three chapters of the book, namely whether or not legal sociology can capture the normativity of law. These methodological discussions are then summed up in Chap. 12, where we ask if theories and methods which were developed to study social issues and conditions of law in the early stages of modernity can be used to study law and regulation in late modernity. Chapter 13 concludes the book by asking what kind of law is emerging de facto in response to the fluidity of late modernity, and how legal imagination envisages the future of law.

Taken together the chapters as a whole offer a sustained examination of academic discourses on legal studies and the field of legal sociology. They argue that academic disciplines are produced and institutionalised by excluding certain debates, ideas, concepts and methodologies from the scope of their inquiry and analysis. For example, theories of modernity, which were developed at the turn of the previous century and continue to inform much of the applied research on law and regulation, often exclude "uncertainty" from the scope of their analysis by seeking mechanisms which enhance certitude and security in social relations. Similarly, socio-legal research, inspired by the works of Durkheim (including structural functional analysis), has traditionally shied away from engaging with the normativity of the law,[4] while traditional approaches to legal theory have either

[4] Paradoxically, Durkheim was singularly interested in the study of morality and his analysis of the law may be regarded as part of his attempt to grasp morality in a sociological fashion. This point will be discussed in Chap. 11.

dismissed or ignored empirical methods prevalent in the social sciences (cf. Morris 2006 and Banakar 2010; this point is discussed further in several chapters, including Chap. 11). Not surprisingly, distinctions are made by academic lawyers as well as some legal sociologists between "is" and "ought," "facts" and "norms" and "normative analysis" and "empirical research," in order to justify the separation of legal from sociological analysis. This book challenges the sharp distinction made between the factual and the normative when studying law and legality, and it questions the separation between "is" and "ought" as it is employed by legal positivism (cf. Kelsen 2002; Tuori 2006; Raz 2007) and by certain schools of legal sociology (cf. Black 1972, 1998), to separate law from morality and legality from justice. It will do so partly by arguing that law and justice emerged historically in social and ethical unison as an integral part the moral constitution of human community and as the basis for social organisation (cf. Banakar and Lort Phillips 2014; Murphy 2012; Barden and Murphy 2011; Cotterrell 2006).

1.2 The "Separation Thesis"

The "separation thesis"—'the contention that there is no necessary connection between law and morals, or law as it is and law as it ought to be' (Hart 1983, p. 57, n. 2; also cf. Alexy 2002)—provides the foundation upon which various schools of legal positivism are constructed. The separation thesis may be regarded as part of legal positivism's method of reducing the conditions of legal validity to 'facts of non-normative type' (cf. Marmor 2011, p. 5). The validity of legal rules is therefore not derived from their contents but from their sources, which in turn are conceptualised in terms of a *social* actor or institution such as a "sovereign" (this argument is also known as the "pedigree thesis"). This topic is touched upon in Chap. 2, where it is presented in light of the "authority paradigm" and as the epistemological basis upon which the majority of legal studies rest. The notion is explored further in Chap. 4 as part of the debate on Robert Alexy's theory of legal argumentation and in connection with the problematic relationship between positive law and justice. However, the core of the separation thesis, i.e. the attempt to distinguish "is" from "ought," constitutes the second leitmotif of this book, which we return to and re-examine in different chapters within different contexts in an attempt to transcend the constraints it imposes on the socio-legal understanding of law, morality and justice.

1.3 Disembeddedness of Modern Law

Another recurring theme of this book concerns the rationalisation process which underpins modernity, generally, and the development of modern institutions, in particular. Modernity and rationality are employed here along the lines described by Kai Eriksson:

> Modernity has often been referred to as the industrial order that broke away from the agricultural system based on relatively self-sufficient localities and strong local government. However, it also refers to the emergence of a particular way of conduct, *defined by an obsession with rationalization, systematization, and control*. Centralized order, consistent meaning and the closed whole represented the principle ideals and goals of this mode of conduct. (Eriksson: 2011, p. 3; my emphasis)

Rationality, whether in its instrumental manifestation, which is concerned with calculating practical means-ends relationships (Weber 1978), or in its communicative form, which is concerned with reaching mutual understanding (cf. Habermas 1987), is either an attribute of social action or an imperative of social systems. However, its force lies in being context-independent.[5] By following certain procedures which enhance efficacy, or in the case of communicative rationality promote mutual understanding, we are expected to produce certain favourable outcomes. It also means that, at least in theory, rationality can produce normative coherence and empirical certainty. Legal philosophy, perhaps not surprisingly, is awash with attempts to justify law as a rational system of rules. From Plato to Kant, Rawls and Habermas, we also find an attempt to link rationality and morality, thus creating an ethically sound basis for law and legal argumentation.

The development of a modern rational approach to social organisation is amongst the main factors which have transformed the law into a formal system of legal norms capable of generating decisions based on *legal* authority, thus distinguishing modern law from the arbitrary exercise of power or decisions made on the basis of moral principles or political expediency. This bestows the legal order with system autonomy, making the separation of powers—which is the cornerstone of the democratic political order—possible. At the same time, the process of bestowing law with autonomy "disembeds" it, i.e. it dislodges the law and its institutions from the societal context within which they have grown historically, thus relieving the law of the burden of extra-legal considerations, e.g. from morally justifying legal decisions. Institutions of the law distinguish themselves from other spheres of action by developing certain properties, including formal procedural rules of legal proceedings, time limits, the involuntary participation of parties in a trial, an interest in discovering the truth and legal reasoning's dependency on valid law which excludes certain questions and forms of justification from the domain of debate and examination (cf. Melissaris 2005). These formal properties, as we shall see in Chap. 4, mould legal discourse into a distinctly autonomous

[5] Flyvbjerg (1998, p. 227) demonstrates in his empirical study how the exercise of rationality is often linked to the application of power. Max Weber described this kinship of power and rationality by coining concepts such as 'formal rational authority' (Weber 1978). Any attempt to discuss rationality without analysing its corresponding form of power, Flyvbjerg argues, will be misleading. This 'holds true for substantive as well as communicative rationality. Communication is more typically characterised by non-rational rhetoric and maintenance of interests than by freedom from domination and consensus seeking' (Flyvbjerg 1998, p. 227).

form of practical discourse. Thus, although legal argumentation might contain moral elements, the claim to correctness raised in the law is nonetheless distinct from claims to correctness raised in moral discourse (Alexy 2002).

To exemplify the social effects of the disembedding of the law, we can consider what happens to moral obligations and duties (moral rights) which ordinarily grow over time as part of the normative structures of everyday life, once they are "juridified," i.e. incorporated into positive law and expressed as legal entitlements (or *legal* rights) backed by the threat of violence. Once the moral imperatives underpinning obligations are expressed in terms of *legal* rules and rights, they cease to require moral justification for their validity or enforcement (cf. Smith 2002, p. 47). This not only enhances law's efficacy and autonomy, but it also turns it into a political instrument that may be employed to neutralise moral conflicts—a strategy which, as we shall argue in this book, only generates new conflicts. More importantly, the "juridification" of moral rights drains them of their moral force (Banakar 2010, p. 29; Smith 2002), without completely severing the ties between moral obligations and legal rights.

The law's disembeddedness can never become complete, as legal institutions retain much of their socio-historical properties.[6] Nonetheless, in order to present itself as a rational and autonomous system, and to operate efficiently and generate legal certainty, the law has to overlook its socio-historical context, wherein its values and socio-cultural source of legitimacy lie (treating it as an extra-legal factor). The purposive rationalisation of modern law, which compels the disembedding of the legal system, does not eliminate but rather only *displaces* moral concerns, thus giving rise to new conflicts (cf. Deflem 2013, p. 81). There is therefore a conflict built into the make-up of modern law, which in order to operate as a rational system of norms and decisions capable of enhancing continuity and certitude in various spheres of action (such as within the economy and polity) has to disavow the legal relevance of the socio-historical context out of which it was born and upon which it remains dependent.

1.4 The "Gap" Problem

The consequences of law's disembeddedness have been discussed in various works in reference to Alan Norrie's critical assessment of liberal law's contradictory and antinomial character (Norrie 2005; cf. Douzinas and Gearey 2005, p. 35). The

[6] In the context of *welfare law*, Habermas's solution was to describe the law both as an institution and as a medium (Habermas 1987, pp. 366–368). According to Deflem (2013, p. 81), 'law as an institution refers to legal norms that remain in need of justification on the basis of the intimate connection of law to morality', while 'law as a medium' refers to how legal regulations can 'operate effectively by means of a specified procedure, such as in the case of business and administrative law'. Deflem (2013, p. 81) adds that 'law as a medium can also concern areas of society that properly belong to the lifeworld'.

"separation thesis," the attempt to distinguish between "is" and "ought" and the subsequent disembedding of the legal system, has been studied by successive generations of socio-legal scholars as a *rational* shortcoming of positive law. It has also been discussed in relation to the so-called "gap" problem, i.e. the discrepancy between the claims of law (or the intentions of the legislature), on the one hand, and its *de facto* impact on social behaviour and societal conditions, on the other (Pound 1910; Nelken 1981; Tamanaha 1997, pp. 101–103 and 117–118). Studies of the gap have allowed socio-legal scholars to describe and analyse how law as a system of rules operates at the level of social organisation, or alternatively how legal rules are translated into normative practices. These studies, however, have often neglected the fact that the "gap" is an integral part of the empirical reality of modern law. Therefore, studies which aim at closing this "gap" are misguided insofar as their objective—attractive as it may be to policymakers—can be achieved at the expense of completely re-embedding the law, thereby depriving the legal system of its autonomy. Chapter 3 ends by discussing alternative approaches to the study of law which take us beyond the misconceptions inherent in the studies of the "gap."

2 Uncertainty and Irrationality

Certainty and uncertainty are two sides of the same coin insofar as the experience of one presupposes at least the awareness of the other as a pending possibility. Certainty suggests knowledge and security, while uncertainty correlates with unforeseen threats, anxiety, risk and insecurity. Social activities oscillate between these two poles, never reaching absolute certainty or uncertainty. However, describing and analysing social developments from the vantage point of certainty or uncertainty amounts to emphasising different aspects of social developments and ultimately painting two contrasting pictures of the society in which we live. We can analogously compare the social significance of certainty/uncertainty with the foundational role played by consensus/conflict in social theory. Concentrating on conflicts, we tend to depict social relations and institutions in terms of power disparity and domination, whereas focusing on consensus leads us to emphasise social integration and harmony. Thus, conflict and consensus provide two opposing paradigms.[7] Similarly, certainty and uncertainty indicate two major paradigms—the former highlights security, continuity, knowledge, truth and rationality, whereas the latter brings into focus the indeterminacy, insecurity, discontinuity and irrationality which are incorporated into our social activities and forms of social organisation. In that sense, emphasis on certainty may imply an understanding of

[7] Many social philosophers, such as Habermas, Bourdieu and Giddens, have tried to bridge the conflict and consensus divide by synthesising elements of conflict and consensus theories of classical sociology. For a discussion, see Banakar and Travers (2013).

consensus as the foundation of social development, whereas to study uncertainty highlights unresolved conflicts lurking under the surface of modernity.

I must hasten to add that the kinship between consensus/conflict and certainty/uncertainty does not allow us to treat these two sets of dichotomies as inseparable equivalents or functions of each other. As reflected in many social welfare programmes, one may recognise the decisive role of social conflicts, and even acknowledge that they are generated by structural relations, and yet search for stabilising social tools, such as legal regulatory solutions, which can produce certainty and stability in social processes. This approach often appeals to policymakers who seek regulatory mechanisms capable of enhancing certitude, without removing the structural causes of the problem they are addressing. The fact that such an approach to social regulation and reform, which addresses the symptoms of social problems while leaving their root causes intact, can generate new social conflicts—and thus new forms of uncertainty—is another debate which does not need to detain us at this juncture.

For our immediate purposes, it suffices to point out that while certainty is a prerequisite for the smooth and effective running of social institutions, uncertainty is an attribute of social conflicts, unforeseen problems, dysfunctions and system failures. Nevertheless, the distinction between certainty/uncertainty takes us beyond the consensus and conflict divide in social theory by contrasting the role of the rational and irrational in modern society. As we shall argue in Chap. 12, the rational/irrational distinction cuts across the traditional consensus/conflict paradigms, regrouping social theories according to their belief in whether modern society is ultimately a rational or an irrational construct. As a result, Kant, Hegel, Marx, Durkheim, Parsons and Habermas find themselves within the same paradigm, which assumes the rationality of modernity, while Schopenhauer, Nietzsche and Foucault find themselves together in an opposing paradigm (cf. Bendle 1996).

Law is amongst the few formal tools we can employ to enhance certitude in human affairs. Central to "the rule of law" (*Rechtssicherheit*) is the promise of certainty and uniformity in legal decision-making. Understandably, the focus of legal theory as well as socio-legal research has been traditionally on certainty, i.e. on the mechanisms which help to ensure law's internal operations and safeguard expectations and expectation of expectations in social relations and institutional activities. Attempts to close the gap between "law in books" and "law in action," which we discussed above, also belong to the search for legal certainty. Efforts to harmonise various categories of legal rules (commercial law is the best example) across national boundaries are also motivated by the belief that by increasing similarities between legal systems we enhance certitude, thus improving law's efficiency.[8] Uncertainty, on the other hand, has only negative connotations. At

[8] Assumptions about the desirability of harmonising laws are often based on "anecdotal evidence" rather than on observations about how contemporary global societies are developing and, as we shall argue in Chap. 8 which deals with comparative law methodology, remain in want of empirical verification.

best, it draws attention to areas of social life which are in need of control—where law should be brought in to create certainty by securing expectations—and at worst, it highlights the failures of the law. Talking about emerging uncertainties amounts to challenging orthodoxies and beliefs in the force of rationality, universal values and norms which continue to inform traditional social and legal theories.

As the social and cultural consequences of globalisation penetrate deeper into our daily lives, relationships and institutions, the pendulum of social organisation swings increasingly away from those factors and mechanisms which have traditionally fostered similarity and certitude towards processes which generate difference and uncertainty. Two developments, one micro and the other macro in character, hasten this swing towards uncertainty. At the micro level, it is the increased ability of social actors to reflect on structures (which have traditionally exerted a degree of control over their actions), in order to emancipate themselves from the constraints of social institutions in a way which, although not new in the context of modernity (for modernity, admittedly, has been partly about the liberation of human agency from the fetters of traditional authority, practices and institutions), is nevertheless unprecedented in its scope and societal consequences (Archer 2007, p. 2). The enhanced reflexivity of the social actor and its implications for law and regulation are explored in the two final chapters of the book, in which the development of legal sociology from an industrial to a post-industrial (information) society is discussed.

At the macro level, the sense of uncertainty grows as the centres of decision-making and normativity move from the municipal to the transnational level, where states have little control. As Beck (1999, p. 2) explains, territorially-based social relations, networks and communications, distinctive to a nation state, are undermined by 'a new kind of capitalism, a new kind of economy, a new kind of global order and a new kind of personal life'. As transnational and global forces emerge and reshape political and legal landscapes across nations, we observe a move from the welfare-oriented social and legal policies of the 1960s and 1970s, when an excessive juridification of the social sphere (Teubner 1987) was carried out in many Western countries in order to reform social conditions, to legal forms of regulation concerned more with managing risks than with addressing the causes of social problems. The shift to risk management strategies, which will be discussed over several chapters, is often explained by reference to the inability of late modern social systems and institutions (such as law, economy and polity) to respond fully to and control the increasing complexity of moral conflicts arising out of the 'unforeseen consequences of functional differentiation' through further functional differentiation (Beck 1999, p. 5). In parallel to this development, we witness the rise of global problems such as environmental pollution, climate warming, war, terrorism, famine and pandemics, to mention but a few. These are caused by anonymous transnational forces that do not lend themselves to simple risk calculations or policy regulation and, as pointed out by von Wright, lack an obvious unity or purposeful coordination, in that they 'do not form a unified system or order' and are subsequently difficult to identify (von Wright 1997, pp. 49–52). Hence, for Bauman (1998, p. 58), they represent the 'new world disorder', where 'no one seems to be in control'. A decade after Bauman made this remark, we would witness the unfolding of one aspect of the 'new world disorder' in the events leading to the recent global economic meltdown, the so-called "credit crunch." The financial crisis of 2008, and its socio-economic consequences for individuals, firms and companies, as well as multinational corporations and governments, demonstrates this trend in Chap. 13.

As a result of globalisation and the development of information technology, many relationships which were previously regarded as long term and stable have now become temporary and transitory. Over the last few decades, we have witnessed a gradual developmental trend towards growing uncertainty, insecurity and anxiety caused by what Bauman (2000, 2005) calls the 'liquefaction' of solid structures and relationships of modernity. The best example of this development is the family, traditionally the bedrock of society and the primary source of socialisation (Parke 2013). Although family continues to exist as one of the central institutions in contemporary societies—some even argue that it has gained in importance (Wyn et al. 2011, p. 4)—its role and functions have nevertheless undergone many transformations. Family has been transformed from a lifelong, more or less stable and enduring heterosexual institution to a transient partnership (cohabitation) which allows same-sex marriage. In tandem with this transformation, family law has changed from a normatively solid instrument for upholding the institution of marriage and ensuring security in marital relations into a flexible framework for accommodating uncertainties associated with short-term cohabitation. The spread of prenuptial agreements as a normal arrangement, which in effect amounts to a premarital plan for divorce, in certain jurisdictions is a case in point.[9] The other interesting development is the transformation of working life and labour relations (and subsequently labour laws) as employment law moves gradually towards accommodating the needs of employers—dictated by uncertain and volatile markets within which they can only plan their business in the interim—for short-term contracts and flexible dismissal rights. We discuss these matters in more detail in the concluding chapter of this book.

Thus, the emphasis on uncertainty and insecurity will be discussed and developed gradually in the following pages by highlighting the social conditions specific to late modernity. This emphasis does not suggest that we are gliding into a state of anarchy and perpetual anomie; instead, it draws attention to the transformation of our societies, communities and identities, asking what types of social order, law and legality emerge in response to growing uncertainty. Thus, interest in uncertainty and late modernity is one of the main features of the background against which the chapters of this book are presented.

[9] In Britain, for example, prenuptial agreements have been enforceable under British divorce law since 2010. See *Radmacher v. Grantino [2010] UKSC 42*.

3 Late Modernity

The notion of "late modernity" is used in three interrelated senses: first, to discuss how social norms, relationships and structures, which were previously considered as enduring and stable over time, are becoming rapidly unstable—thus giving rise to new, short-lived social formations which do not generate or require ethical commitments. Second, to explore the enhanced reflexivity of agency in respect to existing social structures and institutions, and third, to capture the disjuncture created between structural relationships, institutions and systems, which might in themselves be solid. For example, although the legal system might consist of solid institutions, such as courts and the police, its relationship with other institutions and systems (such as global finance and multinational corporations), or with sections of the general population (such as certain minority or religious communities), might have been destabilised by the forces of globalisation in ways which are new. This threefold understanding of late modernity helps to examine the transformation of the state under the conditions of globalisation. The question at the centre of our inquiry is how law fares under late modern conditions.

The idea of late modernity will be employed critically to tease out the novelty of ongoing social developments, albeit without endorsing the idea of a liquid society, advanced by Bauman (2007), as an adequate description of contemporary society. As I shall argue in Chap. 13, Bauman underestimates the power of domestic politics and the nation state—a flaw which is linked to his tendency to underrate the force of existing social structures and the continued "solidity" of many institutional relationships. Although the book will suggest that certain radical changes have taken place in the way we organise social activities and plan social developments—changes which are caused either by the social consequences of globalisation or by the advancement of digital technology—it nonetheless argues that we continue to find ourselves within the primary paradigm of modernity. More importantly, the overwhelming majority of people regard their daily lives and experiences, or at least aspects thereof, as "solid," a point which reflects the 'resilience of the lifeworld' (Travers 2009), while suggesting that the radical changes we referred to above have not permeated all walks of life (or all societies) to the same extent. As Raymond (2011, p. 656) has argued, 'liquid freedom' and the sense of disengagement, which characterises the late modern age, 'may only suggest the privileges concomitant with the new found wealth of the extraterritorial elites and their associates'. Alternatively, we may interpret Bauman's liquid modernity as a critique of 'the lifestyle of the affluent classes..., whose outlook on life is not immediately affected by the urges of daily survival' (Raymond 2011, p. 656). Although liquefaction and its consequences in terms of angst, insecurity, uncertainty, enhanced individualisation and disengagement may be discussed at the level of society, or as a societal development, any study of liquidity must necessarily take into consideration the persistence of solidity. This will also allow, in theory, the possibility of re-solidifying those relationships which have been disembedded, destabilised and liquefied as a result of globalisation and the conditions created by and for the benefit of mobile capital. As we shall argue, liquid conditions generated by highly unpredictable global markets translate into flexible labour and employment laws that undermine employee protection against unfair dismissal, which in turn liquefies the employer-employee relationship. The same development draws attention to the importance of global responsibility and gives rise to anti-globalisation and other protest movements which seek new, but solid, solutions to the problems of late modernity.

To sum up, late modernity is the third major leitmotif of this book, which will also take shape gradually in the second half of the book as the emphasis on uncertainty grows stronger. Thus, the studies presented herein also aim to interrogate the role and the significance of law for social organisation and the experience of legality under conditions of late modernity, which itself sharpens our focus on the consequences of globalisation and the rise of new technologies which not only facilitate forms of communication but also give rise to a risk and surveillance society (Bauman 2000; Beck et al. 1994; Giddens 1994). In a relatively short time these new technologies have become an integral part of how people interact with each other. Technologies such as social media (Twitter and Facebook) cross the traditional public/private distinction and suggest the rise of a new form of life and social organisation.

Do recent developments, which are described broadly in terms of 'liquid modernity' (Bauman 2000), 'reflexive modernity' (Giddens 1994), 'risk society' (Beck 1992), 'network society' (Castells 2000) and 'surveillance society' (Lyon 2001), necessitate a re-examination of socio-legal research's concepts, priorities, focus and, ultimately, methodologies? What were the main puzzles which engaged the minds of the founders of legal sociology, and how were these developed and transformed by the second and third generations of socio-legal scholars? Furthermore, what was excluded from the discourses of socio-legal research, at what expense and why (cf. Constable 2005)? Finally, how do established methodological approaches meet the needs of socio-legal studies in a contemporary global society dominated by new surveillance technologies and characterised by a move away from the ideology of the welfare state towards risk management? These questions constitute the backdrop against which the chapters in this book are presented.

References

Abel, R. L. (1980). Redirecting social studies of law. *Law and Society Review, 14*, 803–829.

Abel, R. L., & Lewis, P. S. C. (1989). Putting law back into the sociology of lawyers. In R. L. Abel & P. S. C. Lewis (Eds.), *Lawyers in society, vol 3: Comparative theories* (pp. 80–153). Berkeley: University of California Press.

Alexy, R. (2002). *The arguments from injustice: A reply to legal positivism*. Oxford: Clarendon.

Archer, M. (2007). *Making our way through the world: Human reflexivity and social mobility*. Cambridge: Cambridge University Press.

Banakar, R. (2003). *Merging law and sociology: Beyond the dichotomies of socio-legal research*. Berlin/Wisconsin: Galda and Wilch.

Banakar, R. (2010). Law, rights and justice in late modern society: A tentative theoretical. In R. Banakar (Ed.), *Rights in context: Law and justice in late modern society*. Farnham: Ashgate.

Banakar, R., & Lort, P. A. (2014). Law and community in the 2011 London riots. In R. Nobles & D. Schiff (Eds.), *Law, society and community: Socio-legal essays in honour of Roger Cotterrell* (pp. 169–87). Farnham: Ashgate.

Banakar, R., & Travers, M. (2005). Law, sociology and method. In R. Banakar & M. Travers (Eds.), *Theory and method in socio-legal research* (pp. 1–25). Oxford: Hart.

Banakar, R., & Travers, M. (Eds.). (2013). *Law and social theory*. Oxford: Hart.

Barden, G., & Murphy, T. (2011). *Law and justice in community*. Oxford: Oxford University Press.

Bauman, Z. (1998). *Globalisation: The human consequences*. Cambridge: Polity.

Bauman, Z. (2000). *Liquid modernity*. Cambridge: Polity.

Bauman, Z. (2005). *Liquid life*. Cambridge: Polity.

Bauman, Z. (2007). *Liquid time: Living in the age of uncertainty*. Cambridge: Polity.

Beck, U. (1992). *Risk society: Towards a new modernity*. London: Sage.

Beck, U. (1999). *World risk society*. Cambridge: Polity.

Beck, U., Giddens, A., & Lash, S. (1994). *Reflexive modernisation: Politics, tradition and aesthetics in the modern social order*. Cambridge: Polity Press.

Bendle, M. F. (1996). Logics of integration and disintegration in contemporary social theory. *Journal of Sociology, 32*(3), 70–84.

Berman, P. S. (2007). Global legal pluralism. *Southern California Law Review, 80*, 1155–1237.

Black, D. (1972). The boundaries of legal sociology. *Yale Law Journal, 81*(May), 1086–1100.

Black, D. (1998). *Sociological justice*. Oxford: Oxford University Press.

Castells, M. (2000). *The rise of the network society, the information age: Economy, society and culture* (Vol. I). Oxford: Blackwell.

Constable, M. (2005). *Just silences: The limits and possibilities of the modern law*. Princeton: Princeton University Press.

Cotterrell, R. (1995). *Law's community*. Oxford: Oxford University Press.

Cotterrell, R. (2006). *Law, culture and society: Legal ideas in the mirror of social theory*. Farnham: Ashgate.

Deflem, M. (2013). The theory of Jürgen Habermas. In R. Banakar & M. Travers (Eds.), *Law and social theory* (pp. 75–90). Oxford: Hart.

Dermas-Marty, M. (2009). *Ordering pluralism: A conceptual framework for understanding the transnational legal world*. Oxford: Hart.

Douglas-Scott, S. (2013). *Law after modernity*. Oxford: Hart.

Douzinas, C., & Gearey, A. (2005). *Critical jurisprudence: The political philosophy of justice*. Oxford: Hart.

Douzinas, C., & Warrington, R. (1994). *Justice miscarried: Ethics, aesthetics and the law*. London: Harvester Weatsheaf.

Eriksson, K. (2011). *Communication in modern social ordering*. New York: Bloomsbury.

Flyvbjerg, B. (1998). *Rationality and power: Democracy in practice*. Chicago: The University of Chicago Press.

Gasking, D. A. T., & Jackson, A. C. (1967). Wittgenstein as a teacher. In K. T. Fann (Ed.), *Ludwig Wittgenstein: The man and his philosophy* (pp. 49–55). Sussex: Harvester.

Gessner, V. (1995). Global approaches in the sociology of law. *Journal of Law and Society, 22*(1), 85–95.

Giddens, A. (1994). *Reflexive modernity*. Cambridge: Polity.

Habermas, J. (1987). *The theory of communicative action, volume 2: System and lifeworld: A critique of functionalist reason*. Boston: Beacon.

Hart, H. A. L. (1983). Positivism and the separation of law and morals. In H. A. L. Hart (Ed.), *Essays in jurisprudence and philosophy*. Oxford: Oxford University Press.

Hunt, A. (1978). *The sociological movement in law*. London: Macmillan.

Kelsen, H. (2002). *Introduction to the problems of legal theory*. Oxford: Oxford University Press (original publication 1934).

Kirk, G. S. (1954). *Heraclitus: The cosmic fragments*. Cambridge: Cambridge University Press.

Lyon, D. (2001). *Surveillance society: Monitoring everyday life*. Buckingham: Open University Press.

Marmor, A. (2011). *Philosophy of law*. Princeton: Princeton University Press.

Melissaris, E. (2005). The limits of institutionalised legal discourse. *Ratio Juris, 18*(4), 464–483.

Michaels, R. (2013). Globalisation and law. In R. Banakar & M. Travers (Eds.), *Law and social theory* (2nd ed., pp. 287–304). Oxford: Hart.

Morris, L. (2006). Sociology and rights: An emerging field. In L. Morris (Ed.), *Rights: Sociological perspectives* (pp. 1–16). London: Routledge.

Murphy, T. (2012). Living law, normative pluralism and analytic jurisprudence. *Jurisprudence, 3* (1), 177–210.

Nelken, D. (1981). The gap problem in the sociology of law: A theoretical review. *Windsor Yearbook of Access to Justice, 1*, 35–61.

Nelken, D. (1998). Blinding insights? The limits of a reflexive sociology of law. *Journal of Law and Society, 25*, 407–426.

Norrie, A. (2005). *Law and the beautiful soul*. London: GlassHouse.

Parke, R. D. (2013). *Future families: Diverse forms, rich possibilities*. Chichester: Wiley.

Pound, R. (1910). Law in books and law in action. *American Law Review, 44*(1), 12–36.

Raymond, L. M. L. (2011). Modernity, solidity and agency: Liquidity reconsidered. *Sociology, 45* (4), 650–664.

Raz, J. (2007). The argument from justice, or how not to reply to legal positivism. In G. Pavlakos (Ed.), *Law, rights and discourse: The legal philosophy of Robert Alexy* (pp. 17–35). Oxford: Hart.

Samuel, G. (2009). Interdisciplinarity and the *Authority Paradigm*: Should law be taken seriously by scientists and social scientists? *Journal of Law and Society, 36*(4), 431–459.

Santos, B. S. (1995). *Toward a new common sense: Law, science and politics in the paradigmatic transition*. London: Routledge.

Simon, J. (1999). Law after society. *Law and Social Inquiry, 24*, 143–194.

Smith, C. (2002). The sequestration of experience: Rights, talk and moral thinking in 'Late Modernity'. *Sociology, 36*(1), 43–66.

Tamanaha, B. Z. (1997). *Realistic socio-legal theory: Pragmatism and a social theory of law*. Oxford: Clarendon.

Teubner, G. (Ed.). (1987). *Juridification of social spheres*. Berlin: de Gruyter.

Travers, M. (1993). Putting sociology back into the sociology of law. *Journal of Law and Society, 20*, 434–451.

Travers, M. (2009). *Crime, governance and the resilience of the lifeworld: Is it time to re-think the concept of risk?* Paper presented at Crime and Governance: Risk, Resilience and Beyond, TASA Workshop on Crime and Governance, Brisbane, 9 September

Tuori, K. (2006). Self-description and external description of the law. *Foundations: Journal of Extreme Legal Positivism, 2*, 27–43.

Twining, W. (2000). *Globalisation and legal theory*. London: Butterworths.

Twining, W. (2009). *General jurisprudence: Understanding law from a global perspective*. Cambridge: Cambridge University Press.

von Wright, G. H. (1997). The crisis of social science and the withering away of the nation state. *Associations, 1*, 49–52.

Weber, M. (1978). In G. Roth & C. Wittich (Eds.), *Economy and society, 2 vols*. Berkeley: University of California Press.

Wyn, J., Lantz, S., & Harris, A. (2011). Beyond the 'transitions' metaphor: Family relations and young people in late modernity. *Journal of Sociology, 48*, 13–22.

Chapter 2
Conflict and Competition Between Law and Sociology

Abstract Notwithstanding the kinship between legal and social theory, law and sociology remain two separate disciplines whose encounters are often characterised by rivalry rather than partnership. This chapter explores the roots of this rivalry and separation by describing some of the conflicts and competitions which arise out of—and impede—attempts to integrate legal and sociological understandings of law. It starts by juxtaposing sociological and legal epistemes, before discussing similarities and differences between various approaches to the study of law by focusing specifically on the (inter)disciplinary conflicts and competitions between them. This approach will be employed as a method for highlighting the discourses which constitute the sociological studies of law. The chapter concludes by reflecting on the potential of law and sociology to learn from one another.

Law is a multifaceted and multi-layered phenomenon with countless normative, academic, professional and institutional manifestations. All of these manifestations are intrinsically "social," i.e. products of collective thoughts and actions,[1] which is why they fall within the scope of sociological inquiry. It is thus not surprising to know that some sociologists and jurists have tried to bring the benefits of sociological ideas to legal thought and practice. However, introducing sociological insights into law, a feasible and useful project in theory, has been accomplished only marginally in practice. Despite the social make-up of law and the kinship between legal theory and social theory,[2] the former being a branch of the latter, and

This chapter has borrowed material from 'Law through Sociology's Looking Glass: Conflict and Competition in Sociological Studies of Law', published in Denis and Kalekin-Fishman (2009).

[1] "Social" refers to the quality of perceptions, actions, interactions, relationships, institutions, structures, collective events and processes. As we shall discuss in Chap. 10, the continued role and significance of the "social" has been questioned by postmodern theorists (cf. Baudrillard 1983; Rose 1996).

[2] According to Ehrlich (2002, p. 25), since 'the law is a social phenomenon, every kind of legal science (*jurisprudenz*) is a social science'. Kelsen (1945, pp. 24–28) did not share this view. Moreover, it is not unlikely that his understanding of sociology as relevant to the science of law only in a very limited fashion (if at all) might indeed be responsible for marring the view on the subject for several generations of jurists. We discuss the dispute between Kelsen and Ehrlich in Chap. 7.

R. Banakar, *Normativity in Legal Sociology*, DOI 10.1007/978-3-319-09650-6_2

despite the efforts of socio-legal scholars over the past 100 years to integrate legal and sociological ideas, law and sociology remain separate. Moreover, when they meet, their disciplinary encounter is often characterised by rivalry rather than by partnership. This chapter explores the roots of this rivalry and separation by describing some of the conflicts and competitions which arise out of—and impede—attempts to integrate legal and sociological understandings of law.

Although the study of law played a significant role in the formation of classical sociology, the subject has become conspicuous only by its absence from recent mainstream sociological research and teaching. Beyond its immediate concern, this chapter hopes to draw attention to law's normative role in guiding action and shaping relationships, a role which increases in sociological significance as societies become ethno-culturally more diverse and socio-politically more complex. Moreover, as the chapters in this book demonstrate, law continues to partake in, while registering and reflecting, the transformation of modernity at various levels. "Reflections" always involve degrees of distortion, but the law and legal systems provide as useful a mirror of social developments as sociology can hope. This chapter may also be read as an attempt to show that mainstream sociology has more to learn from studying law in contemporary society than when Durkheim (1984, p. 24) famously described it as the 'visible symbol' of social solidarity.

1 Law and Sociology

> It is surprising that social philosophers and sociologists feel able to offer explanations of society which do not assign a central place to law. It is surprising that legal philosophers and lawyers can speak about law as if legal phenomena were self-contained and capable of being isolated from social phenomena in general.
>
> Law seems to have a special status among social phenomena by reason of its forms, its rituals, its specialised language, its special rationality even, and its specific social effects. But, on the other hand, law is clearly embedded in the totality of the social process which is its cause, and on which it has a substantial determinative effect, not least in providing the continuing structure of society, its hardware programme. Allott (2002, p. 36)

1.1 Jurisprudence, Legal Studies and Legal Practice

Law manifests itself simultaneously in different forms and at different levels of social reality (cf. Gurvitch 1947). It is a formal instrument of regulation (i.e. a tool in the hands of policymakers); a body of rules, doctrines and decisions (i.e. a normative system with a distinctive social form and identity); a field constituted by the actions of lawyers, the judiciary and other practitioners of law (i.e. an institutionalised form of practice); an occupational setting (i.e. a profession with a well-established code of practice, identity and interest); an academic discipline (i.e. *scientia iuris*, legal studies and jurisprudence) and a form of learning, teaching and training (i.e. legal education). Focusing on any aspect of law, we discover further layers of meaning and the diversity of legal forms. For example, looking at law as a system of rules we find that some rules are substantive while others are procedural, some regulate private transactions whereas others confer powers or impose duties, and so on (Galligan 2006, p. 6). Similar diversity can be found in respect to the legal profession, which consists of many groups and individuals with different working conditions and forms of experience as well as legal tasks and aims. The working conditions and daily tasks of lawyers who work at large international law firms, for example, are a world apart from those of the sole practitioners who provide legal services for local communities (Cotterrell 1992, pp. 184–187).

In addition, law is often seen, experienced and employed differently by different groups in society. Some see it as a source of justice, while others experience it as a form of oppression. Some use it to reform social conditions, whereas others employ it to promote personal interests (for a discussion, see Banakar 2010). Some regard it as an arena where marginalised groups can struggle for their rights (Banakar 2004), while others perceive it as an ideology implicated in perpetuating racial, gender and class violence (Tuitt 2005). Still another group sees the law as an expression of social organisation aimed at facilitating interpersonal and inter-institutional interactions and exchanges (Stjernquist 2001). The list of the ways law is seen, depicted, employed and/or experienced by various people could be made much longer, but none of these images of law by itself captures it in its entirety. Fragmented as the reality of law might be, the legal order still presents itself as a unified corpus capable of interacting with other normative orders, such as custom and religion, without apparently compromising its distinctive normative force or identity.

The problems associated with the multifaceted character of law, which make it sociologically impossible to generalise about its nature, are hardly alien to jurisprudence (I use the term to refer to both legal theory and legal philosophy), which is concerned with clarifying the general framework of legal ideas and formulating general and abstract descriptions of legal systems (for a discussion, see Galligan 2006, pp. 7–12). Within jurisprudence we find many orientations and schools of thought that implicitly or explicitly recognise the social and institutional character of law (Raz 1979, p. 41). Yet, the image of law as a highly rationalised, rule-based activity, i.e. as a system of rules, norms, decisions, doctrines and principles designed to direct action, guide legal analysis and justify decisions in an "objective" manner, pervades juristic discourses and creates the cornerstone of legal education. Rule-based thinking is an integral part of the legal method and what Samuel (2009) describes as the 'authority paradigm', i.e. a paradigm which relies on authoritative sources and justifies its decisions and arguments by referring back to legislation, previous legal decisions and doctrine.

1.2 Law as a System of Rules

The significance of the rule-based understanding of law can be observed in theories which subscribe to "legal positivism" and see it as consisting in rules (Hart 1998; Kelsen 2001; Raz 1979). The tradition of legal positivism, which continues to provide the most influential modern account of law, has its roots in the Enlightenment and emerged in the nineteenth century as a reaction, in part, to natural law theories which sought a permanent and universally valid basis for law in nature and/or divine reason.[3] Various schools of legal positivism share three fundamental assumptions: firstly, law is a system of rules, norms or principles, secondly, it is a matter of "social fact" and its sources of authority and validity are empirically verifiable and thirdly, there is no *necessary* link between law and morality. This means that the validity of a legal rule is not derived from its content but from its source, which in turn is conceptualised in terms of a *social* actor or institution such as the "sovereign." There are many schools of legal positivism, and thus many versions of the relationship between law and morality (the so-called "separation thesis," which we will discuss in detail in Chap. 4) and positive law's validity and the significances of legal sources (the so-called "pedigree thesis").

Although legal positivism recognises the social nature of the sources of law and employs a broadly conceived empirical approach to determine the validity thereof, it nevertheless pays little, if any, attention to the social constitution of this agency. As a result, we find H.L.A. Hart (1907–1992), who is one of the most influential legal philosophers of the twentieth century, recognising the importance of "officials" of the law but nevertheless neglecting to consider how the social constitution of these "officials" may influence the way law is formulated, promulgated, interpreted and enforced (Cotterrell 2003, pp. 210–211). Hart also argues that law consists of various rules which are essentially social, but again he stops short of analysing for whom law speaks and 'whose voices and expressions are excluded from legal expressions' (Cotterrell 2003, pp. 210–211). The most fundamental category of rules in any particular legal system, according to Hart (1998), is 'the rule of recognition', which enables officials of the law to determine if a rule is a "valid" rule of law.[4] Legal positivism's unwillingness to discuss the constitution of the "social" is a reflection of the objectives of much of jurisprudence—obvious

[3] Due to lack of space I limit my discussion of jurisprudence and legal positivism to the English analytical tradition of Austin and Hart.

[4] The 'rule of recognition' is the 'primary' rule of the legal system (Hart 1998). It establishes a test for determining what the valid law is in any particular legal system. Considered from a standpoint "external" to the operations of the law, the rule of recognition may be described as a "social" rule which needs to be acknowledged and employed as such by officials of the law (it is "social" in the sense that it may be observed empirically as it is employed and applied by officials). Moreover, it confers validity on other legal rules and ensures coherence within the law as a system of rules. Thus viewed "internally," the rule of recognition imposes duties on officials of the law to apply those rules that are generated in a particular manner and pass the validity test. Herbert Hart's internal and external perspectives are discussed in Chaps. 5 and 11.

exceptions being legal realism, critical legal studies and schools of legal feminism. Legal positivism tries to provide an adequate account of law as it *is*, in contrast to how law *ought* to be, but it wishes to achieve this analytically and at the level of general theory, i.e. by clarifying the basic concepts and frameworks through which we observe, describe and understand law rather than through empirical investigation of the mundane practices and experiences of men and women who produce and reproduce the law and its institutions.

To give a more recent account, Gardner (2001, p. 201) defines legal positivism as a broad intellectual tradition which advances and enforces the proposition that 'in any legal system, whether a given norm is legally valid, and hence whether it forms part of the law of that system, depends on its sources, not its merits (where its merits, in the relevant sense, include the merits of its sources)'. According to legal positivism, studies of the law must begin by considering what constitutes valid law, which in turn requires an understanding of how legal actors (or the social agencies and institutions of the legal system, such as officers of the law or the court) identify and describe the sources of the law and their hierarchy. It is noteworthy that Gardner's definition, which is in line with Hart's concept of law, makes no reference to the state (or the sovereign, as Austin and Bentham did) and thus avoids concerns raised about the centrality of the state as the source of law. The sovereign, however, is still a source of law, but a one which is identified as such by the rule of recognition. Moreover, Gardner's officials of the law and their 'rule of recognition' remain locally embedded, demonstrating the difficulty of legal positivism to break with its 'methodological nationalism' (Michaels 2013), which we shall discuss below.

1.3 Rule-Based Reasoning

According to various schools of legal positivism, which continue to dominate legal theory and legal education, legal systems are not only made up of rules, but they are also founded on and operate through them. It is therefore hardly surprising if we discover that rule-based thinking and reasoning perform a vital role in the reproduction of modern legal systems. They are part of the method through which law distinguishes legal from extra-legal events, while at the same time it appears to be deciding cases on an all-or-nothing basis, which in principle leaves little or no space for general moral or sociological considerations (Luhmann 1985). More importantly, rule-based thinking impedes "reflexivity"[5] by narrowing down the

[5] Somewhat simplistically, the concept of reflexivity refers to the ability to have an internal conversation with oneself, evaluate the constraints of one's social situation, to think unthought thoughts and act accordingly (which might amount to acting unconventionally). Reflexivity is the essence of modernity and what enables the social actor to break free from the yoke of tradition. It is not, however, a new phenomenon and has already been discussed by ancient philosophers. According to Archer, it is the type of internal conversation which is 'mediated between the

alternative ways of thinking about the law and acting legally, although I should hasten to add that it does not, and cannot, eliminate reflexivity. Law, indeed, is deployed "imaginatively" or "strategically" by individuals and groups to serve their specific ends. Those who employ the law in new and imaginative ways often do not submit blindly to its rules and subvert its internal logic by forcing it to reconsider its operations in view of new circumstances. "Strategic litigation", for example, plays an important role in common law jurisdictions where precedence is a source of law. Litigating strategically in order to develop the scope of the existing law, or to challenge how public bodies exercise their legal powers, can require a degree of reflexivity and ability to think outside the law's existing normative structures. Strategic litigation does not, admittedly, belong to the routine or "normal" operations of the law, but nevertheless demonstrates the possibility and the limits of acting reflexively within the law.

As argued in the Introduction, reflexivity is enhanced at the level of agency by social consequences of globalisation (which also means that traditional institutions exert less control over the individual's actions). The legal implications of this development may be discussed in at least three ways. First, we may argue that as the individual actors' reflexivity is enhanced vis-à-vis social structures, the law gains in normative importance. Once traditional institutions, such as family, school and local community, lose their normative force and ability to provide means of social integration, control and identity, or where society is fragmented into a multiplicity of incompatible beliefs and value systems, then the legal system becomes perhaps the only institution capable of providing a coherent and independent set of guidelines for action and codes of conduct vital for upholding a degree of continuity and certainty in relationships. Second, we may take the opposite view and argue that law and legal thought are badly out of tune with social developments (which is the point made by Ralf Michaels in the next section). The question we should ask is whether our search for continuity and our need for certainty, combined with the constraints of rule-based thinking (which conceptualises law as a coherent system of rules), are not delimiting our legal imagination and distracting us from considering alternative forms of regulation. This brings us to the third point that under late modern conditions, where societies are socio-culturally diversified, the state is undergoing transformation and many sources of normativity and law-making are moved outside its reach, we necessarily have more than one system of valid law. Under these conditions, nationally-based laws cannot be applied to all equally (not even in theory), while alternatives to formal rules of the legal system (such as religious laws of various groups and "soft laws" generated by multinational corporations and other international bodies) proliferate.

---

objective structural and cultural shaping of the contexts confronting agents. . ., who activated their properties, as *inter alia* constraints and enablements, by the particular projects they deliberatively sought to pursue in order to realize their personal concerns. Reflexive deliberation accounts for subjects' evaluations of their situations in the light of their personal concerns, and their re-evaluation of their projects in the light of their situations' (Archer 2010, p. 8).

Let me reiterate that rule-based thinking impedes, but does not eliminate, reflexivity. Legal enforcement, generally, and applying the law to the facts of a case, in particular, might appear as rational, formal processes based on a mechanical method of decision-making. In practice, however, they are mediated through interpretive processes, where the same rule can be interpreted by various authorities and lawyers in different ways, thus reflecting an array of legal standpoints, legal contexts, interests and social situations. Nevertheless, legal reasoning and argumentation are never free from the normative constraint of the legal sources from which positive law ultimately gains its validity and authority. Therefore, legal rules may be regarded as standards for action, or as one among many resources used to *negotiate* the boundaries of law. The interpretive and contextual nature of legal rules indicates that law consists not only of rules alone, but also communicative processes through which the interpretation and application of rules are realised in various social and legal contexts. Sociologically, these communicative processes, rather than legal rules, are the units of analysis. From a sociological point of view, the rule-based approach exhibits law's attempt to rationalise the chaos of social life by internally redefining events and ideas outside the legal system in its limited vocabulary and by confining complex social processes to the conceptual boundaries of legal rules and standards.

1.4 The Consequences of Globalisation

The traditional conception of law's source of authority (or its understanding of "valid law") is founded on the Westphalian Model and, to borrow from Michaels (2013, p. 291), operates on the basis of 'methodological nationalism', i.e. on the assumption that the state represents 'the ultimate point of reference for both domestic and international law'. The acceleration of globalisation has been undermining the importance of national boundaries and the role of nation states while simultaneously generating new regulatory challenges. Globalisation has been promoted by organised economic interests such as multinational corporations in an attempt to expand their markets by developing international production networks, 'dispersing production facilities among different countries', fragmenting ownership, making production process flexible and so on (see Snyder 1999, p. 335). However, according Snyder (1999), this globalising economic process has entailed a number of political and legal implications:

> [G]lobalization has witnessed the rise of new political actors such as multinational firms, non-governmental organisation and social movements. It has tended to weaken, fragment and sometimes even restructure the state, but has not by any means destroyed or replaced it. Globalisation has also altered radically the relationship to which we have become accustomed in recent history between governance and territory. It has thus blurred and splintered the boundaries between the domestic and external spheres of nation-states and of regional integration organisations.... (Snyder 1999, pp. 335–336)

Since Snyder wrote these lines in 1999, globalisation has been enhanced further—some would say revolutionised—by the development of new information technology, which further undermines the traditional forms of law and regulation. For example, the multi-jurisdictional architecture of cyberspace, in that it transcends national borders or overlaps several jurisdictions at the same time, means that our traditional forms of regulation either become redundant or lose their efficacy once they are applied to online behaviour. We are also confronted with the growing significance of transnational law, which refers to forms of law, legal regulation and ordering, which not only exist alongside traditional domestic and international law, but also extend beyond the traditional boundaries of nation states. Moreover, the socio-cultural diversification of modern societies and the increased interaction between legal traditions has made us aware of the fact that we are living in legally pluralistic environments. This has led many to argue that there are no longer any self-contained legal systems or normatively-closed legal orders of the kind which is assumed by the "authority paradigm." Not only legal systems, but also legal traditions are instead defined as 'hybrids' (Örücü 2007). Twining (2000, p. 10) summarises the impact of globalisation on law by asking the following question:

> Can one... give an adequate account of law in the modern world which does not give some attention to the significance of transnational non-governmental organisations (Amnesty International, Green Peace, the Catholic Church, transnational women's networks, international trade union organisations) to peoples that are nations without states (the Maoris, the Welsh, gypsies, the Native Peoples of North America and Australia), to organised crime, liberation movements, multinational companies, transnational law firms, and significant classes such as the vast herds of displaced persons (both refugees and internally displaced)?

Today, legal problems increasingly transcend the traditional national boundaries and jurisdictions of sovereign states begging for a new understanding of the role of law in society and a new approach to regulatory challenges, an approach which is in tune with the new reality of the global (network) society in which we live. The conventional understanding of the legal system, i.e. a juridical order defined in terms of the nation state, is giving way to the hegemony of meta-legal orders, such as the EU, and the transnational sources of private law-making, including multinational corporations and NGOs which exist outside the traditional jurisdiction of nation states. The law is thus increasingly characterised through a pluralism which reflects a normative landscape fragmented by the socio-cultural forces of globalisation. Notwithstanding the consequences of globalisation for law and regulation, legal theory and much of legal education proceed with business as usual. As Michaels (2013, p. 286) points out, 'legal thought has so far reacted to globalisation not with a true paradigm shift but instead by more and more inapt attempts to adapt the methodological nationalism that has provided its paradigm for the last two hundred years or so'. Methodological nationalism, adds Michaels, continues to prevail in all areas of law:

> Discussions in public law assume the existence of one government (unitary or not). Private law has been nationalized – not just formally, as codes (in civil law countries), but also in

> our understanding of it. Even law that is not national law is understood within such methodological nationalism. Thus, international law, understood as law between states, perpetuates the idea of the state as the only relevant reference point. Even where law is moved to the supranational level – as is the case for the law of the European Union – it remains caught in the perspective of the state. More, even where non-state law is described as law, the concept of law used is typically borrowed from the model of state law. Conflicts between legal systems are, in such a perspective, viewed as an exception; the dominant solution in private international law is to allocate international transactions to one state. (Michaels 2013, p. 286)

The tension between the empirical reality of law, i.e. how it operates through socio-cultural processes and institutions and how it changes in response to social developments over time, on the one hand, and the ideal descriptions of the law, i.e. how law ought to operate and develop, on the other, constitutes one of the main concerns of this book. We shall therefore return to this issue in the coming pages. Let us now return to our discussion of the traditional legal method which, as pointed out, continues to dominate much of legal thought and legal education, and examine how it distinguishes itself from the general approach of sociology.

1.5 Doctrinal Methodology

Bartie (2010, p. 350) describes doctrinal research as the 'lingering core of legal scholarship', whose traits include:

> [F]ocusing on legal principle (largely that generated by courts but also the legislature); basing argument and prescription on a normative premise which is not unpacked or explained; reacting to events comprising of changes to the law by judges or legislatures; and, looking for deficiencies in legal principles, suggesting ways to improve them or clarifying the law so that judges or legislatures can better understand their development. The methodology adopted is likened to that of the courts with primary focus resting on the internal logic of judgments or statute.

The 'conventional legal approach to the law is all about doctrine', write Tiller and Cross (2006, p. 518), and it represents the standards or principles which 'can generate outcomes in conventional disputes independent of the political or economic ideology of judges'.[6] A basis for a doctrine is laid when a court outlines a specific framework—a set of rules, procedures and other legal techniques—to decide a case. The doctrine becomes established once other courts follow the same procedure and form of reasoning to decide similar cases. This type of reasoning requires an understanding of substantive rules, their origins (legal sources), how they have developed over time, their scope and underlying policy.

---

[6] This understanding of law is questioned by critical legal scholars and various schools of feminism as a smoke screen for concealing the class, racialised and gendered nature of the law and legal reasoning. Even assuming that the judge can and does apply the law objectively, he or she applies a law which is tilted in favour of a specific group's interests and values.

It can also require an analysis of the relationship between the rules within the same substantive category of law and how these overlap with other legal categories.

It is simpler to grasp doctrinal studies by describing how black letter scholars carry out their research. According to Tiller and Cross (2006, p. 518), the role of the doctrinal researcher is to examine 'the content of legal opinion to evaluate whether it was effectively reasoned or to explore its implications for future cases'. Doctrinal scholars' 'principle or even sole aim', write Dobinson and Johns (2010, p. 19), 'is to describe a body of law and how it applies' to various cases. They 'may also provide an analysis of the law to demonstrate how it has developed in terms of judicial reasoning and legislative enactment' (Dobinson and Johns 2010, p. 19).

There have been occasional attempts to redefine and adapt the doctrinal approach to empirical "sciences." Ross (1958, p. 40), for example, argued that the 'doctrinal study of law must be recognised as an empirical social science'. When it is used as a form of textual analysis, and as part of the process of searching for causal relations between legal rules and decisions, on the one hand, and juridical practice, on the other, its results should lend themselves to scientific evaluation (Ross 1958). Nevertheless, it remains a primarily hermeneutic and argumentative activity, the thrust of which, as Dobinson and Johns (2010) argue, remains 'normative' and its general approach 'purely theoretical'. In the final analysis, it is based on an authoritative form of reasoning, i.e. its usefulness, validity and correctness are largely the functions of legal sources.

It is important to note that what we just described is a specific *methodology*.[7] In contrast to social scientists, who are constantly engaged in methodological debates and disagreements, doctrinal scholars do not normally discuss methodology. It is only recently that the scientific validity of the doctrinal method has been highlighted and debated among certain academic lawyers. van Hoecke (2011, p. 2) suggests that this change of attitude was brought about by 'the research assessment procedures and the repartition of public money among "scientists"'. However, conventional approaches to the study of law have traditionally taken doctrinal methods for granted, and even today only a small group of academic lawyers, who are often interested in interdisciplinary research, engage in such debates. By not reflecting on their methodology, doctrinal scholars take for granted their research technique and its underlying epistemological assumptions and, by implication, treat it as the only valid approach to the study of law. In fact, they automatically exclude methodological alternatives, thus laying the ground for what we shall describe below as the "judicial gaze."

As Vick (2004, p. 177) has pointed out, in contrast to their counterparts in other disciplines such as sociology, doctrinal scholars 'do not usually "produce" new knowledge', and what they generate is often parasitical upon the work which has already been done by others. Doctrinal studies use jurisprudence, legal history and comparative law as auxiliary sources of knowledge or tools of analysis. Although a

---

[7] "Methodology" refers not only to research techniques, but also to the theoretical assumptions behind the choice of such techniques. See the Introduction.

large part of such studies remain descriptive, black letter lawyers can—and do—engage in prescriptive work which aims to influence the developmental direction of the law. However, they often shy away from social theorising or addressing the broader societal issues which arise out of legal practice, legal doctrine or legal developments. This is in part because they treat the law as 'a sealed system which can be studied through methods which are unique to the "science of law"' and believe that 'legal developments can be interpreted, critiqued, and validated by reference to the internal logic of this sealed system' (Vick 2004, pp. 178–179). In short, doctrinal studies use their own method of reasoning and analysis to collect the specific rules and decisions of the existing legal system, reduce them to their essential statements of rules and exceptions, systematise them and, at times, even evaluate them. Sources from which they collect their raw material are limited to 'a finite and relatively fixed universe of authoritative texts' such as statutes, legal opinions and legal cases (Vick 2004, p. 178).

Admittedly, legal knowledge produced through the exegesis of legal texts is of a special kind, but its esoteric character should not conceal its social nature. Forms of knowledge and "truth" that law produces are dependent on communicative processes which are inherently social and fall within the scope of social theory. As pointed out by Cotterrell (2006, p. 45), law has no "truth" of its own, and sociology is in principle capable of grasping the essence of legal doctrine and providing it with a form of insight which is 'not only useful but *necessary* for legal studies'. Why sociological ideas are not adopted to enrich doctrinal analysis is another matter which will be addressed in Sect. 3.

Legal doctrine can therefore be described as the prevailing methodology within the 'authority paradigm' (Samuel 2009). Its widespread application creates the normative context in which lawyers acquire their "juridical gaze," i.e. it sets the backdrop against which they learn to identify relevant questions and to read and criticise legal texts by paying close attention to textual contexts while avoiding the broader social and political contexts of legal arguments.[8] 'A question which cannot be legitimately answered by reference to a statute or judgment', writes Bradney (1998, p. 76), 'lies outside the doctrinal gaze'. However, knowledge of legal rules and doctrine does not by itself provide a sufficient basis for legal practice. Much of lawyers' day-to-day work concerns dealing with clients, interviewing witnesses or drafting documents, all of which require the use of non-legal knowledge and social skills. Furthermore, practicing lawyers have a pragmatic understanding of law, which is aimed at settling cases to their advantage. Legal rules and doctrine are only two among a number of devices (or "resources") that the practicing lawyer employs if, and in so far as, they serve to negotiate the boundaries of the law in his or her favour. Legal doctrine is abandoned in favour of other measures (for

[8] The notion of "gaze" is borrowed from Foucault (1997) and refers to an impersonal way of observing which does not belong to any individual person and can operate as a general principle of surveillance (even monitoring one's own activities) while unifying diverse practices.

example, delay tactics) when it no longer serves to bring about the desired end (Banakar and Travers 2005, p. 9).

Most scholars agree that doctrinal studies are *of* the law, i.e. they are born out of the practical needs of the law and serve certain normative needs of legal practice. However, we find little agreement on how jurisprudence, which appears to be *about* the law, is related to legal practice. Some theorists see much of it as "theory-talk," which at best conveys a better understanding of the context in which law is practiced, albeit without helping to shape those practices (cf. Haplin 2001, p. 12). Others see jurisprudence as a practical inquiry which is interpretive, normative and ultimately action-guiding (Coyle and Pavlakos 2005, p. 6). In this latter sense, there is a dialectical relationship between theory and practice which brings together conceptual, normative and empirical descriptions and understandings of law. Nonetheless, there is little doubt that jurisprudence observes and learns from legal practice while influencing it indirectly. In that sense, the boundary between "what is *of* the law" and "what is *about* the law" becomes blurred. Various assumptions about the nature of law which are elaborated by jurisprudence can exert, for example, a normative force over legal education and doctrinal studies. Moreover, legal philosophical discussions can engage more directly with legal issues by clarifying certain legal concepts, ideas or relationships (for an example, see Hoefeld's typology of rights in Hoefeld 1923).

2 The Sociological Imagination

Besides interacting and competing with legal studies and jurisprudence, the sociological studies of law have benefitted from the exchange of ideas and competition with branches of social sciences and humanities with invested interest in the study of law and social order. Restricting our presentation to sociology in the strict sense of the word will exclude some of the best empirical studies of law which are conducted by non-sociologists within other interdisciplinary areas.[9] From Bronislaw Malinowski's *Crime and Custom in Savage Society* (1926) to Sally Falk Moore's 'semi-autonomous social fields' (1973) and Franz and Keebet von Benda-Beckmann's study of living law in Indonesia (2009), social and legal anthropology have been sources of methodological inspiration for legal sociology. This has not, however, been a one-sided affair, and legal anthropology has in return gained from legal sociology and other social sciences (cf. von Benda-Beckman 2008, p. 86). Similarly, historical studies such as *Law and Economic Growth: A Legal History of the Lumber Industry in Wisconsin, 1836–1915* by Hurst (1964), *A*

[9] Robert Ellickson's *Order without Law* (1991) is an example of a study carried out by a non-sociologist in reference to a law and economics debate, which nevertheless may be regarded as sociological. Also see Strahilevitz's discussion, which in a way builds on Ellickson's study on loose-knit communities growing in cyberspace (Strahilevitz 2003).

History of American Law by Friedman (1973) and *Whigs and Hunters: The Origin of the Black Act* by Thompson (1975) have left a lasting impression on legal sociology. This list can be made much longer to include works produced within criminology, political science, psychology, comparative law and legal philosophy, which are either potentially socio-legal or have in various ways benefitted socio-legal research. To grasp the mutually beneficial exchange of ideas between the sociology of law and the areas mentioned above, we need to consider the disciplinary boundaries of mainstream sociology which in the final analysis determine the scope of socio-legal field. Admittedly, sociology has its own specific way of looking at the world and selecting what to study (Erikson 1997), which distinguishes it not only from legal studies, but also from other neighbouring social science disciplines.

Sociology does not consist of rules, if by a "rule" we mean a binary method of making decisions or a set of standards for guiding action. Instead, it consists of assumptions, concepts, ideas and methods, none of which is treated in a formalistic manner or as an element of a normatively sealed system. Sociology's constitutive concepts and methods are understood and applied *reflexively* and in accordance with the general criteria of social scientific enquiry. That is also why, in contrast to doctrinal studies, sociology allows many competing sets of theoretical and methodological approaches, while at the same time it constantly questions and re-examines its own assumptions and critically scrutinises the intellectual foundations of its own discipline. Sociology's "reflexivity" transforms it into a subversive creature that refuses to be contained intellectually—that cannot but constantly challenge all intellectual constraints—and which stands in stark contrast to the "authority paradigm" of the traditional legal studies we described above.[10]

Sociology finds itself between science and literature (or arts generally), and it uses both but belongs to neither (Lepenies 1988). Its "oscillations," or "hesitations" as Boudon (2002) calls them, between science and the arts ensure its disciplinary openness. Smelser (1997, p. 18) also sees sociology as an intellectual tradition between art and science and describes it in terms of its 'proximity to *three* intellectual outlooks that simultaneously constitute part of its environment and part of itself'. These are: the *scientific* orientation (the search for natural laws, construction of logical theoretical frameworks, the application of causal analysis and so on), the *humanistic* orientation (a 'preoccupation with the human condition including human suffering') (Smelser 1997, p. 19) and the *artistic* orientation (an aesthetic orientation towards sociology's subject matter combined with 'an

[10] Since the 1950s, sociology seems to have been moving from one disciplinary crisis to another. As Deflem (2013) points out, it has been criticised for being too conservative, too radical, generally in decline or too politicised. Sociology's intellectual subversions, i.e. its incessant need to re-examine its scientific status and validity and question its public and professional commitments, can also explain why it appears to be in a state of permanent crisis. However, Deflem arguably states that sociology's crisis has now ended, since an 'underdeveloped group of sociologists', who mainly do quantitative research and are highly politicised, have come to dominate the rank and file of sociology.

emphasis on the application of knowledge, such as the art of medical practice' (Smelser 1997, p. 19). Sociology, 'having differentiated in complex ways out of *all three* of these orientations, still maintains connections with all of them', which is why it 'has never tried to seal itself into a closed paradigm' (Smelser 1997, p. 19), has developed as an epistemologically diverse discipline consisting of a number of competing paradigms and perspectives on society and has always borrowed and adapted ideas, concepts and methods from other disciplines such as history, social anthropology, economics, law, linguistics and psychology. Sociology is at its best when it looks 'at the world through a variety of conceptual lenses, draws on a variety of research techniques, and measures the data [it gathers] against a variety of explanatory frameworks' (Erikson 1997, p. 11). It is in this intellectually open sense that the sociology of law is related to sociology and has developed to comprise many perspectives on the relationship between law and society. The multi-paradigmatic make-up of the sociology of law and its reflexive character distinguish it from traditional (doctrinal) legal studies—the former is based on an investigative approach, while the latter on authoritative sources (Samuels 2009)—and ensure its openness towards other fields of research within social sciences and humanities. This disciplinary openness admittedly comes at a price (see Banakar 2003), but it nevertheless remains perhaps the most important single property of the sociology of law.

Sociology has become professionalised (although not in the sense of law and medicine, whose professional identity is linked to their monopoly on legal and medical practice), and sociologists' public duties are a matter of internal debate. However, the core of sociology is the "sociological imagination" which, according to Wright Mills (1970), consists of the awareness ("self-consciousness") that one's experience of daily life and reality, as well as one's trajectory and biography, are related to and must be understood in terms of the wider society and the course of history:

> Sociological imagination enables its possessor to understand the larger historical scene in terms of its meaning for the inner life and the external career of a variety of the individuals. It enables him to take into account how individuals, in the welter of their daily experience, often become falsely conscious of their social positions. (Wright Mills 1970, p. 11)

Sociology is driven ultimately by sociologists' curiosity about social life, as reflected in their attempts to explain and understand social reality. The most valuable asset of a sociologist, to use Erving Goffman's words, is 'the bent to sustain in regard to all elements of social life a spirit of unfettered, unsponsored inquiry and the wisdom not to look elsewhere but to ourselves and our discipline for this mandate' (Goffman 1983, p. 5). This does not mean that sociologists do not have civic commitments, or that sociology is free from all forms of pragmatism and instrumentalism, and neither is it implied that all sociological studies are driven by the desire to enlighten. Sociology has become increasingly pragmatic over the years, and a growing number of sociologists tend to see their role as the providers of scientific knowledge to decision-makers (Halliday and Janowitz 1992). Still, what bestows on sociology a unique understanding of social phenomena and transforms it into "a form of life" will remain reflexive curiosity about social life and the urge to reveal the hidden social structures and the taken-for-granted assumptions which guide our actions and decisions. This means that a sociologist is often not satisfied with the self-descriptions of law, behind which he or she searches for layers of meaning, social functions and power structures.

In contrast to the lawyer, who thinks pragmatically, sees law as an instrument with which to do things and reasons "authoritatively" (i.e. justifying his or her arguments by reference to valid sources of law such as legislation or previous legal decisions) to decide individual cases, the sociologist is often interested in the general characteristics of social phenomena and looks for repeated patterns of social behaviour. This is in turn directed at producing a general knowledge of society, i.e. social theories. Individual cases *in themselves* and *for themselves* are often of little value to the sociologist. Even when sociologists and other social scientists conduct "case studies," they try to go beyond the specific properties of that particular case by connecting it to some broader social concern. Thus, sociology and law are founded on two different approaches or epistemes, which can also be said about the relationship between sociology and medicine; nonetheless, there is less tension between the sociology of medicine and the medical profession than there is between law and sociology. Sociologists of medicine have much to say about the social roots of health and illness, but they do not suggest that medical doctors use sociological theories and concepts in their diagnosis and treatment of physical disorders and disease. In contrast, the sociology of law can appear to be claiming that it understands law better than law understands itself and to be telling lawyers how they should understand, conceptualise, apply and practice law (Nelken 1998; Banakar 2000).

The sociology of law is thus a meeting place for two different standpoints on the role of law in society. These two standpoints can be described at the level of social action by focusing on how an *ideally typical* lawyer and sociologist would perceive the relationship between law and society. At this level the question becomes if, and how, a legal image derived through processing individual cases and shaped by a pragmatically-oriented practice of law can be integrated with a sociological image aspiring towards generalisable knowledge of society and formed through social-scientific reflexivity. Alternatively, we can compare the two standpoints from an institutional level by exploring their discourses. In its extreme form, the legal standpoint regards the state (or the "the rule of recognition") as the primary source of law, and it conceptualises the law as a sealed system consisting of successive layers of rationally interconnected rules, decisions and principles which can and should be studied in reference to its internal logic (Kelsen 2001). In contrast, the sociological standpoint views legal rules as a sub-category of social norms and the legal system as a set of socially constructed institutional practices which, like knowledge, permeate all walks of social life and, directly or indirectly, form all collective social action. In its radical form, the sociological standpoint rejects the primacy of the state as a source of law and argues that the centre of gravity of law has always been in social relations and processes (Ehrlich 2002; Griffiths 1986;

Gurvitch 1947).[11] Irrespective of how we compare the epistemes of law and sociology, the socio-legal field appears as being constituted by tension between a legal and a sociological image of society. Epistemic tension causes disputes between sociology, legal studies and jurisprudence on how to view and study law, but it also forms debates within the socio-legal field on, for example, how to understand, conceptualise and study law sociologically. As we shall see in Sect. 2, some sociological studies adopt a "legal centralist" view and conceptualise law in terms of positive or state law, while other research approaches adopt a broader perspective, or a legal pluralist view, by treating it as a special form of social organisation.

Recognising the diversity of forms of law has always been the cornerstone of the sociology of law and marks the place where it diverges from and challenges traditional legal scholarship and a great deal of jurisprudence. However, even those socio-legal schools which adopt a pluralistic concept of law continue to interact with and be influenced by positive (state) law through their rejection of the state as the main source thereof (Griffiths 1986). Admittedly, this concern with official forms of law links the sociology of law with jurisprudence and legal studies, on the one hand, and with legal practice, on the other, but nevertheless it does not bring them together. This is partly because socio-legal approaches, jurisprudence and legal studies articulate their concerns differently. What is captured by these different understandings of law is the tension between a "juridical gaze," which is gained through legal training devoted to the reading of cases and law reports and searching for, interpreting and applying legal rules, and an inquiring approach which uses sociology's looking glass to see beyond the self-descriptions of law and the legal profession. How this tension has been utilised, and to what extent these two images are brought together, is discussed in the next section, wherein various orientations within the sociological studies of law are discussed.

3 Can Law and Sociology Learn from Each Other?

As we argued earlier, legal practice is dependent not only on knowledge of legal rules and doctrine, but also on tacit know-how about the social relationships and processes which produce and reproduce legal institutions. Jurisprudence is not interested in the day-to-day mundane practices of lawyers and officials, so instead it seeks to elucidate the general characteristics of legal thought, clarify legal concepts and produce general descriptions of legal systems. But it still requires data on how law operates and interacts with its social environment, in order to

---

[11] Traditional legal sociology's understanding of the law without the state (ideas developed by Ehrlich and Gurvitch) is gaining currency as transnational law spreads across the globe. Transnational law refers to all forms of law, legal regulation and ordering which exist alongside traditional domestic and international law but extend beyond the traditional boundaries of nation states (cf. Cotterrell 2012).

produce such general descriptions, and it also needs methods for verifying the empirical validity of these general descriptions. Therefore, both legal practice and jurisprudence, in principle, should be open to the types of insight that sociology and other social sciences can provide. Sociological accounts of how law works as an institution can provide legal practice with an insight into law's social processes, while social science methods can help jurisprudence to examine whether or not its concepts and frameworks are grounded in the reality of law or need to be modified or disregarded (Galligan 2006, p. 18).

Sociology, in return, can gain from the study of how sets of formal norms, principles and ideas are linked dialectically to patterns of institutional practices, which in turn reproduce the normative backbone of modern society. Sociology can also learn from jurisprudence about the internal mechanisms of the law, about how those who participate in legal processes understand and define their participation and about the "softer" interpretive expressions of law which are found in legal doctrine and legal reasoning and which are not readily available to those who view the law from the outside. In short, sociology is equipped and placed strategically to observe and analyse law's interaction with its social environment, whereas jurisprudence is best equipped to explore its internal operation and realities. This can also mean that neither jurisprudence nor sociology is equipped sufficiently to provide an adequate description and analysis of the role of law in society. As pointed out by Gurvitch (1947, p. 241), the sociology of law and philosophy of thereof, without mutual contact, are doomed to 'sterility, dogmatism, and impotence' (Gurvitch 1947, p. 241; for a similar conclusion, see Habermas 1996, p. 66).

If sociology and jurisprudence can complement each other, however, why do they not join forces to establish *the* science of law? Possible answers to this question can be found by examining, as we did above, sociological and legal epistemes and by demonstrating that law and sociology make sense of and orient themselves towards the social world by using different sets of concepts and ideas. Irreconcilable as these sociological and legal ideas might appear on the surface, they all represent forms of knowledge acquired by observing and examining social (rather than physical or supernatural) conditions. Why is it then that epistemic tensions nonetheless appear to pose insurmountable obstacles to bringing together law and sociology? To answer this question, we need to consider the politics of academia in addition to epistemic differences. For example, why could H.L.A. Hart not admit that he had read Max Weber in *Economy and Society* and was indebted to Weber for his internal account of legal rules (Lacey 2004)? Also, why do some prominent philosophers of law, such as Dworkin, regard sociological and historical studies which view the law from without as 'perverse' while failing to recognise that internal studies of the law which ignore questions about its social properties external manifestations are also 'impoverished and defective' (Dworkin 1986, p. 14)? I suggest here that the answers to these questions reveal as much about the construction and distribution of 'scientific stakes' in academia (Bourdieu 1975) as about the theoretical make-up of sociology, legal studies and jurisprudence. The tension between law and sociology is thus as much about academic competition between disciplines and fields of research as it is about epistemic conflicts.

Academic competition should be viewed in the context of power relations in academia and as a means of obtaining or maintaining access to financial resources, such as funding, grants, posts, contracts, etc. This type of professional interest is a powerful incentive for individual researchers in academic fields such as law and sociology, but it leads to disciplinary isolation once each discipline has developed its own "stakes" and internal 'structure of the distribution of the specific capital' (Bourdieu 2004, p. 59). Law and sociology have long established their own academic forms of capital that exist independently of the "stakes" in other fields of research, which in turn relieves them of the need to compete with each other. The preoccupation of academic lawyers and mainstream sociologists with their own "scientific stakes" has been at the expense of paying sufficient attention to the epistemological debates and exchanges which form the interdisciplinary lifeline of socio-legal research.

Socio-legal research appears to have no alternative but to create and establish its own forms of capital, which will potentially transform it into a discrete discipline independent of law and sociology. However, the most valuable asset of socio-legal research lies in its ability to offer an added value to both law and sociology by highlighting issues that neither law nor sociology can articulate or study alone. Moreover, it can provide this added value as long as it remains an interdisciplinary space which offers relief from the methodological constraints of other disciplines (Banakar and Travers 2005). Thus, socio-legal research finds itself in a paradoxical situation, in that it needs to create its own "scientific stakes," in order to become independent of both law and sociology, which are no longer interested in epistemological confrontations, while at the same time it needs to safeguard its interdisciplinary character, in order to continue the epistemological debates which law and sociology no longer pursue. This paradoxical situation brings uncertainty to socio-legal research, discouraging those who seek the academic security and identity of established disciplines but posing an exciting challenge to those who wish to explore the socio-legal issues which lie beyond the disciplinary boundaries of law and sociology. Socio-legal research is still in its initial stages of its development, and the realisation of this paradox signals its move to a new stage when the socio-legal field has to reconsider its relationship with both law and sociology.

References

Allott, P. (2002). *The health of nations: Society and law beyond the state*. Cambridge: Cambridge University Press.

Archer, M. (2010) 'Reflexivity', Sociopedia.ISA. http://cdh.epfl.ch/www.isa-sociology.org/publ/sociopedia_isa.htm

Banakar, R. (2000). Reflections on the methodological issues of the sociology of law. *Journal of Law and Society, 27*(2), 273–295.

Banakar, R. (2003). *Merging law and sociology: Beyond the dichotomies of socio-legal research*. Berlin/Wisconsin: Galda and Wilch.

Banakar, R. (2004). When do rights matter? In S. Halliday & P. Schmidt (Eds.), *Human rights brought home* (pp. 165–184). Oxford: Hart.
Banakar, R. (Ed.). (2010). *Law in context: Law and justice in late modern society*. Farnham: Ashgate.
Banakar, R., & Travers, M. (2005). Law, sociology and method. In R. Banakar & M. Travers (Eds.), *Theory and method in socio-legal research* (pp. 1–25). Oxford: Hart.
Bartie, S. (2010). The lingering core of legal scholarship. *Legal Studies, 30*(3), 345–369.
Baudrillard, J. (1983). *The death of the social*. New York: Semiotext(e).
Benda-Beckmann, F. (2008). Riding or killing the centaur? Reflections on the identities of legal anthropology. *International Journal of Law in Context, 4*(2), 85–110.
Benda-Beckmann, F., & Benda-Beckmann, K. (2009). The social life of living law in Indonesia. In M. Hertogh (Ed.), *Living law: Reconsidering Eugen Ehrlich* (pp. 177–197). Oxford: Hart.
Boudon, R. (2002). Sociology that really matters. *European Sociological Review, 18*(3), 371–378.
Bourdieu, P. (1975). The specificity of the scientific field and the social conditions of the progress of reason. *Social Science Information, 14*(6), 19–47.
Bourdieu, P. (2004). *Science of science and reflexivity*. Cambridge: Polity.
Bradney, A. (1998). Law as a parasitic discipline. *Journal of Law and Society, 25*(1), 71–84.
Cotterrell, R. (1992). *The sociology of law: An introduction*. London: Butterworths.
Cotterrell, R. (2003). *The politics of jurisprudence: A critical introduction to philosophy of law*. London, UK: LexisNexis.
Cotterrell, R. (2006). *Law, culture and sociology*. Aldershot: Ashgate.
Cotterrell, R. (2012). What is transnational law. *Law and Social Inquiry, 37*(2), 500–524.
Coyle, S., & Pavlakos, G. (Eds.). (2005). *Jurisprudence and legal science*. Oxford: Hart.
Deflem, M. (2013). The structural transformation of sociology. *Sociology, 50*, 156–166.
Denis, A., & Kalekin-Fishman, D. (Eds.). (2009). *The new ISA handbook in contemporary international sociology: Conflict, competition, cooperation*. London: Sage.
Dobinson, I., & Johns, F. (2010). Qualitative legal research. In M. McConville & W. H. Chui (Eds.), *Research methods for law* (pp. 16–45). Edinburgh: Edinburgh University Press.
Durkheim, E. (1984). *The division of labour in society*. London: Macmillan (original publication 1903).
Dworkin, R. (1986). *Law's empire*. London: Fontana.
Ehrlich, E. (2002). *Fundamental principles of sociology of law*. New Brunswick: Transaction Publications (original publication 1913).
Ellickson, R. C. (1991). *Order without law*. Cambridge, MA: Harvard University Press.
Erikson, K. (1997). *Sociological visions*. Maryland: Rowman and Littlefield.
Foucault, M. (1997). *The birth of clinic*. London: Routledge (original publication 1963).
Friedman, L. M. (1973). *A history of American law*. New York: Simon and Schuster.
Galligan, D. J. (2006). *Law in modern society*. Oxford: Oxford University Press.
Gardner, J. (2001). Legal positivism: 5 ½ myths. *American Journal of Jurisprudence, 46*(1), 199–227.
Goffman, E. (1983). The interaction order. *American Sociological Review, 48*(1), 1–17.
Griffiths, J. (1986). What is legal pluralism. *Journal of Legal Pluralism and Unofficial Law, 24*, 1–55.
Gurvitch, G. (1947). *Sociology of law*. London: Routledge & Kegan.
Habermas, H. (1996). *Between facts and norms*. Cambridge: Polity.
Halliday, T. C., & Janowitz, M. (1992). *Sociology and its public: The forms and fates of disciplinary organisation*. Chicago: The University of Chicago Press.
Haplin, A. (2001). *Reasoning with law*. Oxford: Hart.
Hart, H. L. A. (1998). *The concept of law*. Oxford: Oxford University Press.
Hoefeld, W. (1923). *Fundamental legal conceptions*. New Haven, CT: Yale University Press.
Hurst, J. W. (1964). *Law and economic growth: A legal history of the lumber industry in Wisconsin, 1836–1915*. Cambridge, MA: Harvard University Press (original publication 1964).
Kelsen, H. (1945). *General theory of law and state*. New York: Russell & Russell.

Kelsen, H. (2001). *Introduction to the problems of legal theory*. Oxford: Clarendon (reprint, original publication 1934).
Lacey, N. (2004). *A life of H.L.A. Hart: The nightmare and the Noble dream*. Oxford: Oxford University Press.
Lepenies, W. (1988). *Between literature and science: The rise of sociology*. Cambridge: Cambridge University Press.
Luhmann, N. (1985). *A sociological theory of law*. London: Routledge & Kegan Paul.
Malinowski, B. (1926). *Crime and custom in savage society*. London: Kegan Paul.
Michaels, R. (2013). Globalisation and law. In R. Banakar & M. Travers (Eds.), *Law and social theory* (2nd ed., pp. 287–304). Oxford: Hart.
Moore, S. F. (1973). Law and social change: The semi-autonomous social fields as an appropriate subject of study. *Law and Society Review, 7*(4), 719–746.
Nelken, D. (1998). Blinding insights? The limits of a reflexive sociology of law. *Journal of Law and Society, 25*(3), 407–426.
Örücü, E. (2007). A general view of "Legal Families" and "Mixing Systems". In E. Örücü & D. Nelken (Eds.), *Comparative law: A handbook* (pp. 169–188). Oxford: Hart.
Raz, J. (1979). *The authority of law*. Oxford: Clarendon.
Rose, N. (1996). The death of the social? Re-figuring the territory of government. *Economy and Society, 25*(3), 327–356.
Ross, A. (1958). *On law and justice*. London: Stevens and Sons.
Samuel, G. (2009). Interdisciplinarity and the authority paradigm: Should law be taken seriously by scientists and social scientists? *Journal of Law and Society, 36*(4), 431–459.
Smelser, N. (1997). Sociology as science, humanity and art. In K. Erikson (Ed.), *Sociological visions* (pp. 17–30). Maryland: Rowman and Littlefield.
Snyder, F. (1999). Governing economic globalization: Global legal pluralism and European Union. *European Law Journal, 5*(4), 334–374.
Stjernquist, P. (2001). *Organised cooperation facing law: An anthropological study*. Stockholm: Almqvist & Wiksell.
Strahilevitz, L. J. (2003). Social norms from close-knit groups to loose-knit groups. *University of Chicago Law Review, 70*(1), 359–360.
Thompson, E. P. (1975). *Whigs and hunters: The origin of the Black Act*. London: Allen Lane.
Tiller, E. H., & Cross, F. B. (2006). What is legal doctrine. *Northwestern University Law Review, 100*(1), 517–533.
Tuitt, P. (2005). *Race, law, resistance*. London: GlassHouse.
Twining, W. (2000). *Globalisation and legal theory*. London: Butterworths.
Van Hoecke, M. (Ed.). (2011). *Methodologies of legal research: Which kind of method for what kind of discipline*. Oxford: Hart.
Vick, D. W. (2004). Interdisciplinarity and the discipline of law. *Journal of Law and Society, 31*(2), 163–193.
Wright Mills, C. (1970). *The sociological imagination*. London: Penguin (original publication 1950).

Chapter 3
Social Scientific Studies of Law

Abstract This chapter presents the diverse approaches among sociological studies of law by distinguishing between the "sociology of law," "Law and Society," "sociological jurisprudence" and "socio-legal studies." It then contrasts the top-down and bottom-up studies of law in society as two basic methodologies which cut across disciplinary divisions within the field, thereby offering an alternative view of how the field is organised. In the final section of this chapter, we critically reconsider the "gap" problem, i.e. the significance of studies of the discrepancy between the law as a body of rules and as an institutionalised form of practice. The chapter concludes by discussing alternative approaches to the study of the "gap."

1 Approaches to the Study of Law in Society

Sociological studies of law are similar in one respect to the sociologies of medicine and religion, in that they accommodate two *ideal typical* approaches—one which is informed in the first place by the theoretical concerns and objectives of mainstream sociology and one which reflects the concerns of their subject matter, i.e. law and legal behaviour (for a comparative study of sociologies of law, religion and medicine, see Banakar 2000), on the one hand, and the relationship between law and policy, on the other (Nelken 1981). We can call the former "pure" and the latter "applied" socio-legal research. Each "pure" and "applied" approach can in turn be divided into different orientations, depending on the extent to which it is influenced by the concerns of sociology, other social sciences, law or policy.

Figure 3.1 helps to visualise the relationship between the social scientific studies of the law, but it also gives the wrong impression that a sharp line may be drawn between pure and applied research. As Nelken (1981, p. 38) has pointed out, 'the notion of an "applied" sociology existing in isolation from theoretical problems and developments is a difficult one to defend. The same is true of the claim that socio-legal studies is merely concerned with describing the law in action. . .'. This figure also fails to demonstrate the impact of policy-oriented research, which is funded

This chapter has borrowed material from 'Law through Sociology's Looking Glass: Conflict and Competition in Sociological Studies of Law', published in Denis and Kalekin-Fishman (2009).

R. Banakar, *Normativity in Legal Sociology*, DOI 10.1007/978-3-319-09650-6_3

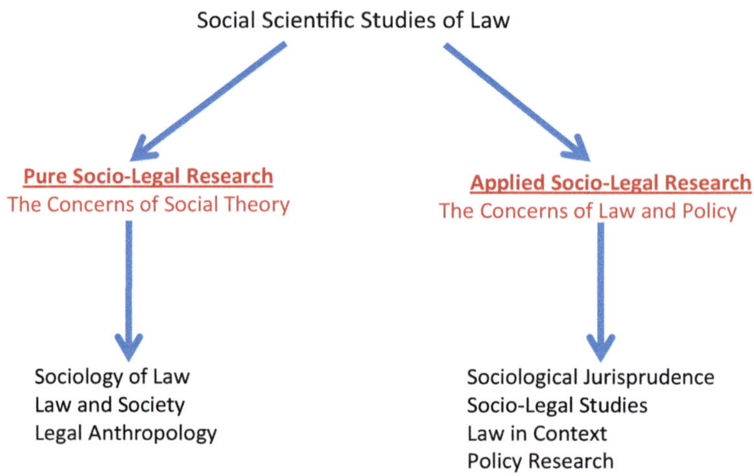

Fig. 3.1 The relationship between socio-legal approaches

more readily by government agencies than pure research in the field (Sarat and Silbey 1988). In addition, it does not do justice to the important role played by legal anthropology and political science in the development of the field as a whole. While the sociology of law and sociological jurisprudence are influenced primarily by mainstream sociology, Law and Society, Socio-Legal Studies and policy research are influenced by both sociology and other social science disciplines. Finally, the figure is based on a British view of the sociology of law, in the sense that it distinguishes sharply between Socio-Legal Studies and the sociology of law (Banakar and Travers 2005; Campbell and Wiles 1976).[1] Such a division would not automatically apply, for example, to the Scandinavian situation, where there has not been a socio-legal movement within law schools.

In the remaining part of this section, we shall briefly describe how the various research approaches within the field are informed by social sciences and shaped by their specific interests in the study of the law.

1.1 The Sociology of Law

The sociology of law distinguishes itself from, for example, philosophy of law or legal history, by fulfilling three interrelated and broadly defined criteria. Firstly, it borrows its concepts and theoretical frameworks from sociology. Secondly, it conceptualises law in terms of social systems, institutions, processes, practices,

[1] Let me reiterate that I distinguish between "Socio-Legal," which refers to the British movement within law schools that is influenced by social theory, and "socio-legal," which refers to all social scientific studies of law, including sociology of law.

actions and experiences, thus treating it either as a socially dependent or independent *variable*. Thirdly, it adopts an empirical approach to collecting the data it requires in order to conduct its analysis (Ferrari 1989, p. 9). The notion of "empirical," as it is used here, should be understood in broad terms. Some research orientations have adopted a strict positivistic interpretation of what empirical data means, i.e. they study only what can be measured through, for example, surveys and structured interviews, while other orientations use more interpretive methods, such as participant observation, open interviews and discourse analysis. These two approaches generate different definitions of law and understandings of the role of the sociology of law. For example, Baumgartner (2000, p. 406), who is influenced by Black's (Black 1976) positivistic approach, defines the sociology of law as 'the scientific study of legal behaviour', a study which deals only with what is 'observable and measurable' while aiming to 'predict and explain legal variations of every kind'. Sutton (2001, p. 8), describes law as 'a group activity' and the sociology of law as the study of 'the legal behavior of human groups'. Sutton's definition appears to be the broadest in terms of the theoretical and methodological constraints to which it subscribes. Not only does Sutton avoid specifying how sociological studies of law should proceed methodologically, but he also avoids subscribing to any concept of law. At least in principle, Sutton allows the possibility of a form of "legal behaviour" which exists independently of positive law and thus of the state. Baumgartner, on the other hand, adopts a strictly positivistic approach, which methodologically recognises only what is "observable and measurable" as its proper subject matter, and theoretically equates law with positive (state) law. These two definitions show that the sociologists of law can—and often do—differ on how the subject should be conceptualised and studied. These disagreements should be viewed against the backdrop of the multifaceted nature of the law and the epistemic tension we discussed in the previous chapter.

The sociology of law studies legal behaviour, institutions and systems in the tradition of Durkheim and Weber, who used the study thereof as a means to investigate the underlying social mechanisms of modernity. Law provides sociologists with a standpoint from which they may view and study a range of theoretical and substantive issues such as social differentiation, socio-cultural integration, forms of authority, legitimacy, the role of rationality, the exclusion or criminalisation of groups, the rise of professions, equality of access to wealth and resources or the significance of gender, sexuality and race in social organisation. As Cotterrell (2005, p. 504) explains, Durkheim seemed to 'approach legal materials mainly for their capacity to provide, in the documentary form of ancient and modern codes, "visible symbols" of social solidarity; an "index" or measure of this elusive phenomenon'. Durkheim's analysis of law is thus 'a methodological device for examining something that is, apparently, of greater sociological significance than law itself' (Cotterrell 2005, p. 504). To give a concrete example, if a sociologist of law decides to study unlawful gender or ethnic discrimination, it is most probably not because he or she wishes to explore judicial interpretation, or how doctrine is employed in the process of legal reasoning to decide discrimination cases; instead, it is more likely that he or she seeks to understand how the interpretation and application of anti-discrimination laws help to constitute race and gender-related social inequalities in society (Banakar 2004). Expressed differently, how law views and treats unlawful discrimination provides the sociologist with a vantage point from which to study (1) how law internally reconstructs social inequalities in society and (2) how society copes with conflicts of values, interests and worldviews by using formal methods of dispute resolution.

Most sociological studies of law focus on its external manifestations, for example on the rate of litigation in a specific jurisdiction, asking why one group is more likely to litigate than another, or they examine the attitudes of ordinary citizens to new legislation, asking how the introduction of a new law influences behaviour. Such studies often ignore concepts and ideas which are internal to law and legal reasoning and through which law constructs its images of society and impacts on social relations. This tendency has caused a great deal of misunderstanding in regard to the sociology of law's potential to grasp and study law's normativity (this point is discussed in detail in Chap. 11). Looking at the sociologist's neglect of legal ideas in a positive light, we could argue that it frees him or her from the internal culture of the legal system and the normative and epistemological assumptions about the law and legality, which are often taken for granted by officers of the law and academic lawyers, as well as by many laymen. Bourdieu (1987) treats these taken-for-granted assumptions as the 'symbolic power' of the law (for a discussion see Chap. 11). The sociologist's method of questioning the way law is conceptualised internally, enables him/her to identify the sources of law in social formations and associations which have come about and exist independently of the state (Ehrlich's 'living law' exemplifies this point). It also makes it possible to ask questions which fall outside the paradigm of legal studies regarding, for example, the objectivity of legal reasoning. This is partly why many sociologists and social anthropologists regard social interactions and relations as the primary focus of their study while treating the law as a 'residual category' (Sarat 2000, p. 195). This can lead them to emphasise the interests and experiences of ordinary men and women in general, and marginalised groups in particular. As a result, the majority of socio-legal research appears to foster a "critical" rather than a "neutral" understanding of the ideology of law, thus highlighting issues related to social justice, 'marginalised groups, peripheral institutions [and] deviant behavior' (Abel 1987, p. 827) and generally depicting law in a negative light.

However, freedom from the constraints of law's internal culture can mislead the sociologist into assuming that the legal system's *modus operandi* is of no importance to the studies conducted from a vantage point external to the legal system. As a result, the sociologist can be hoodwinked into treating one manifestation of the legal system, such as the rate of litigation in one jurisdiction or the attitude of certain groups to a particular law, as representing the totality of law in action. A more complete picture of the relationship between law and society emerges once the sociologist recognises that law's internal operations and processes are in constant interaction with and inseparable from the extra-legal factors which constitute its social environment. Law's normativity—the intangible quality central to law which creates the sense of obligation and duty, rights and entitlements, emerges out of the interplay of operations which constitute the inside and outside of the law. As we shall demonstrate in the coming chapters, the sociology of law is capable of studying law's normativity, but it does that on its own empirical terms, rather than on mainstream legal studies' analytical terms.

1.2 Law and Society Studies

"Law and Society," as I employ the term here, is primarily an American movement which was established after the Second World War mainly through the initiative of sociologists who had a vested interest in the study of law (Friedman 1986; Garth and Sterling 1998). The major difference between the sociology of law and Law and Society is that the latter does not limit itself theoretically or methodologically to sociology and tries instead to accommodate insights taken from all social-science disciplines. Not only does it provide a home for sociologists, social anthropologists and political scientists with an interest in law, but it also tries to incorporate psychologists and economists who study the subject.

Although Law and Society has in principle relied on and used all social sciences, it has nonetheless received more input from mainstream sociology, social anthropology and political science than from other disciplines. Psychology or economics, in particular, have had only a marginal impact on the development of the movement, partly due to the fact that early on they formed their own "law and psychology" and "law and economics" associations and journals. An excellent example of research in the law and society tradition is to be found in *Order Without Law*, where Ellickson (1991) uses different social scientific ideas, including economic theories, to study how residents of Shasta County, a rural area in California, resolve a variety of disputes that arise from trespassing by cattle and fence-tending.

Law and Society, according to Simon (1999, p. 144), has brought about 'change in legal education, judicial administration, and political discussion of law. It [has also] helped complete the realist shift of law school textbooks from cases to material and notes [and] achieved recognition in the law through the creation of the significant social science functions within the court system'. Having said that, Simon (1999, p. 144) admits that the Law and Society project still 'finds itself not only incomplete but also increasingly uncertain about its identity or future'. This uncertainty is not limited to the development of Law and Society, though, as it affects social and legal sciences equally. To borrow from Simon (1999, p. 146) again, it is caused largely by the collapse of 'the sense of confidence associated with establishing social science as a critical grammar of power', which in turn is linked to 'a sense of crisis and decline whenever you find the term social...'. We shall return to the crisis of the 'social' in Chap. 12 when we discuss the transformation from an industrial to a post-industrial society and its corresponding ideological move from welfare to market capitalism.

1.3 Sociological Jurisprudence

Sociological jurisprudence is also linked closely with the sociology of law and Law and Society studies. It is, however, much older than the Law and Society movement and more interested in legal theory and legal education (see Ehrlich 1936; Gurvitch 1947; Petrazycki 1955; Pound 1943; for an authoritative overview see Treviño 2013). It is also often associated with Roscoe Pound (1870–1964), who is also known as a prominent philosopher of law, and through him with the American legal realist movement. However, there are historical and theoretical reasons for including a number of European scholars, such as the Polish-Russian jurist Leon Petrazycki (1867–1931) and the Austrian jurist Eugen Ehrlich (1862–1922), under this rubric, as these scholars were critical of analytical jurisprudence for its conceptual formalism and neglect of empirical facts such as the role of social forces in creating the legal order and shaping legal behaviour. They also argued that legal research, legal education and judicial decision-making should adopt the methods and insights of social sciences, in order to counterbalance this shortcoming. Moreover, they were "jurists"—the jurist concept is used here as an *ideal type* to refer to lawyers who are committed to promoting law's general "well-being." Law's "well-being," Cotterrell (2013, p. 511) points out, is a variable socio-historically determined idea which differs significantly in time and place and thus does not lend itself easily to a clear definition. Furthermore, it represents attempts made internally to uphold law's central values of justice and order, which are both technical and cultural at the same time. Cotterrell (2013, p. 511) explains:

> The jurist's focus could be said to be on law as a practical idea in general, or as embodied in the legal system (or type of legal system) which the jurist serves. The focus is on the worth of law, its *meaningfulness* as a social institution. To this extent, a juristic perspective goes beyond the everyday practice of law in courts or lawyers' offices, but is one of *committed*, not disinterested analysis or observation of law, its coherence, fairness, consistency, reputation, accessibility, enforcement and effectiveness. That suggests a theoretical sensibility, but not necessarily adherence to any wide-ranging theoretical system.

The founders of sociological jurisprudence were jurists in the sense described above by Cotterrell (2013, p. 518), in that they looked 'beyond law's technical efficacy to its existence as an idea embodying cultural expectations'. The group of jurists we are concerned with here favoured empirical social sciences (rather than analytical or moral philosophy) as their primary vehicle for enquiries. Nevertheless, they distinguished themselves from mainstream sociologists, such as Emile Durkheim and Max Weber, by directing their intellectual efforts towards developing the law, to which they were committed, rather than towards advancing sociology as a discipline. While mainstream sociologists used law to study social developments and issues arising out of the rise of modernity, Petrazycki, Ehrlich and Pound employed social sciences to transform legal education and practice and to devise a scientific concept of law. At the centre of this transformative legal project, we find theories and concepts which are empirically tuned and broader in scope than what most practicing and academic lawyers recognise as the law proper.

Pound criticised and challenged the legal formalism (which used strict conceptual logic) that dominated American legal thought of his day for being mechanical, artificial and out of touch with the needs of society. He argued instead for a jurisprudence which placed the human factor and condition—rather than logic—at the heart of its analysis. He borrowed insights from the philosophy of pragmatism and the new discipline of sociology to develop a new approach to law, legal research and legal education, which led him to argue that it was 'law in action' and not 'law in the books' which constituted the basis of law and legal institutions. In addition, Pound criticised the individualist theories and standards of 'legal justice' to which lawyers adhered, and instead he urged both legal scholars and practitioners to work towards a concept of 'social justice' which was informed by the standards of sociologists.

European scholars went further than Pound by directly challenging the underlying ideology of legal positivism. They urged lawyers to recognise the vital role played by the informal and unofficial mechanisms of social control in creating legal institutions and moulding legal behaviour. In this way they confronted the jurisprudence of their time by presenting the social forms of law, rather than the rules posited by the state, as the basis of legal order. For them the state could not be the primary source of law for the simple reason that its existence presupposed a form thereof. Petrazycki and Ehrlich argued, each in his own way, for an empirically-based concept of law which was broader than state law and existed independently of any outside authority.

Using our example of unlawful discrimination, a sociologist working within this tradition would begin his or her study by analysing anti-discrimination laws. He or she would recognise and take into consideration the internal point of view of lawyers by studying legal cases and court decisions to settle disputes based on gender or ethnic discrimination. However, he or she would not limit the sphere of inquiry to positive law and its application by the courts but would also pay attention to how these disputes are settled by extra-legal means, sometimes outside the courts and in the shadow of law. If the sociology of law tends to view law from the outside, by emphasising how it interacts with other social factors and institutions, sociological jurisprudence tries to view how it is seen from both inside, i.e. how it is experienced by legal practitioners and others who participate in its processes, and outside. The dialectical interaction between the internally and externally produced concepts, ideas and images of law lies at the heart of many studies which fall within this tradition (Banakar 2003).[2]

To sum up, the sociology of law, Law and Society and sociological jurisprudence began somewhat differently, in different times and places and with different aims in mind; nonetheless, there is more which unites than separates them. As a result, many of the individual studies couched within these three orientations are

[2] Distinguishing between the legal system's internal and external points of view, or the "inside" and "outside" of law, is problematic and misleading. For a discussion, see Banakar (2003). Also see Norrie (2005), whose idea of antinomies of law will be discussed in Chap. 4.

hardly distinguishable from each other. These three orientations demonstrate the diversity of aims, theory and methods within sociologically-inspired studies.

1.4 Socio-Legal Studies and Legal Policy Research

Socio-Legal studies in the UK have grown mainly out of the interest of law schools in promoting interdisciplinary studies of law. Whether regarded as an emerging discipline, sub-discipline or a methodological approach, the subject is often viewed in light of its relationship to and oppositional role within law (Thomas 1997, p. 3). It should therefore not be confused with the legal sociology of many western European countries or the Law and Society scholarship in the US, which foster much stronger disciplinary ties with social sciences. In the past, it has been presented as the applied branch of the sociology of law and criticised for being empiricist and atheoretical (Campbell and Wiles 1976; Travers 2001). Travers (2001, p. 27), for example, regards Socio-Legal studies as a subfield of social policy, 'mainly concerned with influencing or serving government policy in the provision of legal services', adding that it 'has given up any aspirations it once had to develop general theories about the policy process' (Travers 2001, p. 26).

Looking more closely at the work which has been produced by Socio-Legal researchers in more recent years,[3] we detect two general approaches (both *ideal types*). The first approach, which I call the study of Law in Context, uses social theory and a broadly conceived notion of what empirical research amounts to, in order to study issues which are internal to the processes and operations of law (cf. Twining 1999).[4] Studies of Law in Context are neither empiricist nor sociological, yet they are conducted against the backdrop of social theory. According to the second approach, the "socio" in Socio-Legal studies does not refer to sociological theory or to an empirical understanding of the broader context of social development; instead, it represents 'an interface with a context within which law exists' (Wheeler and Thomas 2002, p. 271). The second approach consists largely of what Travers calls "Policy Research," which is concerned with social policy, regulation, enforcement and implementation issues, i.e. how law affects social behaviour or social conditions. It can also consist of studies of the legal profession, legal education, legal services and access to justice as well as forms of dispute resolution (Boon et al. 2005; Boon and Webb 2008; Webley and Duff 2007). These studies can indeed employ social theories, either to underpin their arguments or to interpret their empirical data, but they are not interested in developing theories of

[3] Papers published in journals such as *Journal of Law and Society*, *Modern Law Review* and *Social & Legal Studies* provide fairly reliable indicators of the type of work produced by the Socio-Legal community in Britain.

[4] This could also mean that the rise of legal feminist scholarship and postmodern legal research has brought Socio-Legal studies (SLS) closer to Critical Legal studies (CLS). While SLS has gone from strength to strength, CLS has somewhat shrunk in size and lost its ideological momentum.

their own or engaging in social-theoretical debates. They might, however, draw attention to the gap between the intentions of legislatures and the reality of law once it is interpreted and enforced by officials, though alternatively they might study the real impact of certain policies on social conditions. Policy research is not committed to theory development either, but it is nevertheless more empirically-oriented than studies of Law in Context.

Again, using gender or ethnic discrimination as an example, a study of Law in Context could focus on the discrepancy between anti-discrimination legislation and the empirically verifiable reality of unlawful discrimination through a closer scrutiny of the legal instruments themselves, asking questions concerning the goals and intentions of the legislation, the substantive provisions constituting said legislation or its remedial structures (Fredman 2002, pp. 1–2). According to this standpoint, whenever a law fails to bring about its intended effects, one should begin to re-evaluate its goals, substantive provisions and remedial structures. In other words, if a law is ineffective and does not deliver the policy goods, it must be *technically* flawed. Thus, a closer examination, for example, of who bears or should bear the burden of proof in discrimination cases, or how the law distinguishes between direct and indirect discrimination, becomes of paramount importance. From the sociologist's point of view, the difference between studies of Law in Context and mainstream legal studies is insignificant, for they both seek no generalisable knowledge about social conditions or relations underpinning discrimination, or about how law sees and relates to racial violence or gender discrimination. We find, however, a significant difference between Law in Context and the approach adopted by black letter scholars who focus on legal doctrine, in that the former does not treat the law as a sealed system of rules and doctrines to be studied on its own terms alone. Unlike doctrinal studies, Law in Context recognises the important role played by—and can seek the causal analysis of—extra-legal factors and relations. More importantly, studies of Law in Context seek and produce new knowledge on law, its limits and potentials.

Policy research can share many of the assumptions held by the sociologist about law and still take a more pragmatic view of its impact on social conditions, without engaging with the broader social theoretical issues surrounding such an impact. Furthermore, it sees law more in terms of legislation, i.e. as a measure aimed at realising policy objectives, than as a set of technical or doctrinal legal issues which might preoccupy some lawyers. Policy researchers will be more interested in asking questions about the efficacy of enforcing anti-discrimination provisions. Enforcement here is not necessarily defined in terms of how the law is interpreted by the courts, but how legal institutions facilitate, or alternatively discourage, the examination of race- or gender-related discrimination. Policy researchers, for example, would use surveys to assess knowledge of a piece of anti-discrimination legislation among employers and employees, and to form an idea about the attitude of employers to the law and to what extent various groups perceive that they are the victims of unlawful discrimination. Policy researchers could also try to establish what sort of legal aid is available to those who seek compensation for unlawful discrimination (for references to various studies, see Banakar and Travers 2005).

The two applied socio-legal approaches discussed here treat the social sciences largely as a tool for gathering empirical data on the role of law in society. Admittedly, regarding social sciences as an auxiliary method for collecting legal data makes them somewhat acceptable to some academic lawyers, but it nevertheless impairs their reflexive properties which enable researchers to identify and explore the taken-for-granted social and cultural values of the law. Why socio-legal research stops short of adopting the reflexive approaches of the social sciences in general, and of sociology in particular, is a question which takes us back to the epistemic conflicts and institutional competitions that define the relationship between legal practice, jurisprudence and sociology and which we discussed at some length in the previous chapter.

2 Top-Down and Bottom-Up Approaches

There is another way of viewing, describing and classifying socio-legal research, which cuts across the disciplinary divisions we described above. This alternative description is based on two ideal types of research often employed within socio-legal research. The first ideal type consists of research conducted against the backdrop of an omnipotent nation state and in response to the need to devise effective public policies. These studies often start their inquiries by exploring the effects of "the law" on society, which they conceptualise in terms of positive rules or policies which are introduced from above to change behaviour or to regulate a specific activity. Such studies might deal with the "gap" between the intentions of the legislature or policymakers and the de facto effects of the law on social conditions (the "gap" will be discussed in the next section). They might also be critical of the law or simply provide data on how it operates in a socio-cultural environment. In either case, unintentionally as it might be, many of these studies treat the state as the source of law and legality and take the attitudes and concepts of law's officials and administrators, i.e. those responsible for the interpretation, implementation and enforcement of legal rules, as the point of departure for exploring the effects of legislation on social patterns of behaviour and social conditions. This means that they perceive, describe and analyse the relationship between law and society from a *top-down* perspective. A classic example of this type of research is found in Vilhelm Aubert's pioneering study of the impact of the Norwegian Housemaid Act 1948 on the behaviour of housemaids and their employers (Aubert et al. 1952). This Act was introduced to improve the working conditions of domestic help through precise provisions regulating their working hours, termination of contract, wages, days off, vacations, etc. To enhance its impact, the Act limited the freedom to set the law aside contractually. Aubert, Eckhoff and Sveri studied the behavioural effects of this Act in 1952, which was achieved through interviews aimed at evaluating knowledge about the provisions of the Act among a representative sample of housewives and housemaids in Oslo (see Aubert et al. 1952; Aubert 1977, p. 117). Although Aubert and his collaborators departed from legislation, they nonetheless paid close attention to the social context of law and studied the relationship between the legal knowledge of ordinary people and how they used the law. This is perhaps why this study continues to be of methodological interest after more than half a century. More recently, a strong case was made by Denis Galligan for this type of top-down research, which we shall discuss in detail in Chap. 5. Galligan (2006, p. 36) argued that socio-legal research should start with those features of law which are 'relevant to the actions of citizens and officials... and examine meanings attributed to such features by citizens and officials, and the actions that follow'. Failing to do so, according to Galligan (2006, pp. 3–4), we might run the risk of abandoning any sense of law as a distinctive formation, i.e. we could overlook those social properties of the law which make it different from norms of social organisation. This ideal and typical top-down research is often deductive and proceeds with implicit or explicit assumptions about law and society.

The second type of study is carried out using a bottom-up perspective, i.e. by departing from the social and institutional contexts in which law is employed by the citizenry. Macaulay's (1963) study of non-contractual relations in business is a classic example of this type of research. This study found that businessmen frequently ignored the legal aspects of their contracts and agreements. When they succeeded in reaching an agreement during informal social exchanges, they kept their word as if they were bound by a formal contract. When a dispute arose as a consequence of the breach of a formal contract, they frequently settled it without reference to the contract or legal sanctions. Business people actively sought to avoid legal formality and the use of law and lawyers in their affairs, because in their opinion it was bad for business. In most situations a contract was not needed and could have negative consequences, mainly because its functions were often served by other mechanisms. This also meant that the business community could avoid most of its problems without resorting to legal sanctions. Moreover, it was observed that there were many effective non-legal sanctions which made the use of law unnecessary. Galanter's (1974) study of 'why the "haves" come out ahead' is another classic example. Galanter's methodology is described from the outset in simple and clear terms:

> Most analyses of the legal system start at the rules end and work down through institutional facilities to see what effect the rules have on the parties. I would like to reverse that procedure and look through the other end of the telescope. Let's think about the different kinds of parties and the effect these differences might have on the way the system works. (Galanter 1974, p. 97)

The focus of bottom-up studies could be on how law is deployed and experienced by various groups within a given social or cultural space and what "law," understood broadly to include "living law" and "the law," i.e. state law, means to them (Ewick and Silbey 1998; Nielsen 2000; Kurkchiyan 2011).

The bottom-up model lends itself to qualitative research and can produce 'grounded theory' (Glaser and Strauss 1967). In addition, it portrays law and legality not as an autonomous system consisting of rules and formal procedures but as an integral and constitutive element of the cultural life of a modern society. How ordinary people use law to organise their daily life, or how social institutions and organisations condition the way it is employed and legality realised, rather than how it is interpreted and enforced by legal system officials, is taken as the starting point for the second type of study (also see Selznick 1949; Santos 1977; Stjernquist 2001; Silbey 2005). The first type, the top-down approach, adheres to the concept of state (official) law, whereas the second type, the bottom-up approach, employs a broader (often pluralistic) concept of law akin to Petrazycki's 'intuitive law' (see Podgórecki 1991) or Ehrlich's 'living law' (1936). For the bottom-up approach, the domain of law and legality could not be restricted to official sources of state law, for law is regarded as sociologically "thicker" (or more complex) than state law but "thinner" (or sociologically less complex) than the social interactions and institutional arrangements which lay the basis for social order (cf. Carbonnier 1965; quoted in Olgiati 1998, p. 91). 'Semi-autonomous social fields', to borrow from Moore (1973), are fields of social interaction that lie outside the realm of state law. When focusing on the law we lose sight of the fact that these fields 'have their own customs and rules and the means of coercing or inducing compliance' (Moore 1973, p. 721). Not surprisingly, policymakers have traditionally preferred to promote top-down research, which equates law with state law and regulation, thereby giving rise to 'the pull of the policy audience' (Sarat and Silbey 1988).

3 The "Gap" Problem

> [The] mere evidence of a gap between law-in-action and law-in-theory would not in itself overwhelm all resistance to change. Who can imagine a study, after all, that would not dis-cover such a gap? Little is more predictable about the law than that these gaps exist. (Black 1972, pp. 1089–1090)

Studies of the so-called "gap," aimed at exploring discrepancies between the law as a system of rule and the law as a form of practice, have played an important role in the development of the sociology of law (cf. Nelken 1981). Since similar studies continue to be produced by socio-legal researchers, we conclude this chapter by critically revaluating the "gap" problem and highlighting alternative approaches to the study of law, which successfully avoid this "gap."

3.1 Various Forms of the "Gap"

The "gap" has a long history, and as Tamanaha (1997, pp. 101–103) has demonstrated, it appears in at least two forms: in Ehrlich's (1936) study of living law and in Pound's (1910) emphasis on the importance of 'law in action'. The awareness of a discrepancy between official state law and the norms used by ordinary people to decide disputes and organise society motivated Ehrlich to search for a form of law more in tune with the normative make-up of society, i.e. a form of ordering which reflects how people de facto organise their relationships and activities over time, rather than how they ought to organise themselves (Ehrlich 1936; for a recent collection of essays on Ehrlich's work, see Hertogh 2009). Pound (1910) was also concerned with the "gap," but in his case it was conceptualised in terms of the distinction between 'law in books' and 'law in action'. For Pound, valid law consisted of legal rules and principles laid down by authorities, and the distinction between law in books and law in action served to highlight the social nature of the legal process, a process which, once grasped sociologically, could be engineered to manufacture a tighter fit between law and the social reality it tried to regulate. For Ehrlich, a norm could acquire a sense of legality even though it had not been lain down by the state. Instead, a norm gained legal authority when it dominated 'life itself even though it has not been posited in legal propositions' (Ehrlich 1936, p. 496). He called these social norms 'living law' (for a comparison between Ehrlich and Pound's concepts of law, see Nelken 1984).

How socio-legal scholars have conceptualised and studied the "gap" has been determined by at least four factors:

1) Their concept of law: whether they have understood law strictly in terms of official state law, or have described it broadly to include norms of social organisation;
2) Their understanding of how society is constituted and reproduced: if they have viewed conflict or consensus as the driving force behind social developments;
3) Their conceptualisation of how law and society are related: if they have regarded them as independent variables, one dependent of the other, or as interdependent;
4) Finally, their methodological approach: by the methods of inquiry they have employed. Have they used qualitative methods to study micro processes and social action, or applied quantitative methods to explore macro processes, structural relationships and social systems? The choice of method may be determined partly by the researcher's concept of law and even guide them to study law top-down (starting with the law and asking how it impacts upon society) or bottom-up (starting with people's experience of law and legality).

The scope of the gap problem has been extended over time to include new areas of inquiry. It has moved from the study of how laws are interpreted by courts and other authorities to the implementation of public policy and welfare measures, and more recently to the study of aspects of the information society and globalisation. One recent study (Svensson and Larsson 2009) explores the discrepancy between copyright laws, which through international treaties and conventions have become uniformly established in most countries, and actual social behaviour in cyberspace, which deviates radically from the rules of copyright. The "gap" has also linked the concerns of legal sociology and comparative law (see Chap. 8), which demonstrates a continuity of research interest which stretches from the classical works of Ehrlich and Pound, through debates and research on industrialisation and the welfare state, to current debates on the possibility of law and legal institutions "travelling" between jurisdictions (Nelken 2001, pp. 8–9) and unifying or harmonising laws across various legal systems (Legrand 2001).

Many inquiries into the "gap" problem (understood as the disparity between law's intentions and its actual impact on social conditions) depart from the assumption that discrepancies between law in books and law in action are caused by an organisational shortcoming within the modern legal system. These studies often assume that the "gap" can—and should—be closed, in order to ensure correspondence between the ideal (normative) aspects of the law, on the one hand, and its empirical manifestations and the reality of legal practice, on the other. Alternatively, they could be guided by the belief that a legal system informed by the reality of the law in action—what the courts do in actual fact and how lawyers and laymen reason using the law—and designed in view of law's limits of efficacy would deliver greater certitude and consistency. However, these studies often neglect the historical dimension of the gap that it is generated by conflicts which are built into modernity in general and modern law in particular and which reveal themselves as dualities, antinomies and dichotomies (these points will be developed in the next chapter). The "gap" is thus part of the reality of modern law—part of its definition. It is therefore suggested here that the focus of socio-legal research should be shifted away from attempts to close the "gap" and moved towards the examination of the *interplay* between law as a system of legal rules, practices, doctrines and decisions, on the one hand, and as a form of experience, a specific sphere of social action and an institutionally-based form of socio-cultural practice, on the other (cf. Banakar 2003).

More significantly, it is argued that positivism (the ideology of modernity as a rational project) has concealed the extent to which social and legal practices and institutions are fragmented, disconnected and internally inconsistent. Attempts to resolve the "gap" problem also draw our attention away from an understanding of the antinomial make-up of modern law. These are familiar discussions within Critical Legal Studies (CLS), but whereas CLS uses a broadly philosophical and social-theoretical approach to examine these issues, this book uses an empirical methodology and explores these questions against the backdrop of the rise of "late modernity." Finally, although studies of the "gap" have generated a great deal of data pertaining to law's operations, they do not break new theoretical grounds.

3.2 Alternatives to the "Gap"

Emphasis placed here on the role of the "gap" should not mislead us into concluding that legal sociology consists only of studies of discrepancies between law in books and law in action. Studies of legal cultures have been used, for example, to make sense of law as a cultural artefact and to describe and understand how it manifests itself as a form of experience in everyday life (Kahn 1999). For some researchers, they have provided a method with which to circumvent the ideological dominance of legal studies and to create distance from one's own taken-for-granted values, attitudes and beliefs.[5] Other socio-legal approaches, for example, have explored how law creates images of society internally, images which in turn impact upon society at a discursive level and influence the way we think about and experience law. The question becomes how law constitutes society:

> The constitutive approach sees law more as a pervasive influence in structuring society than as a variable whose occasional impact can be measured. Law is seen as a way of organizing the world into categories and concepts, which while providing spaces and opportunities, also constrains behaviour and serves to legitimate authority. (Garth and Sarat 1998, p. 2)

Most studies which concern dispute resolution also avoid the "gap" by acknowledging the discrepancy as a normal phenomenon, i.e. a characteristic of the way modern law operates in society as a *disembedded* social system. Seen from this standpoint modern law can operate as an autonomous system (independent of systems of polity, economy and religion), but only by employing formal rationality and viewing and describing the world through its own limited concepts and ideas. Socio-legal research, for example, has shown that law's ability to resolve social conflicts is restricted by its modus operandi in general, but by the internal formal rationality of its concepts and operations in particular (Shamir 1996, p. 235). When a social conflict is recognised as legally relevant and is brought before the law, it is transformed into a legal dispute and resolved by imposing law's formal categories onto the conflict. Sociologically, law avoids dealing with the conflict at hand by redefining it in its own terms, using concepts which might have nothing to do with the original cause of the conflict (Niklas Luhmann describes this process in terms of 'complexity reduction'; see Luhmann 2004). 'In this way law confirms the normality of its own categories and reconstructs society in its own image' (Banakar 2005, p. 149). This does not mean that law has no impact on social conditions, does not generate change or has no effect on how social conflicts are managed; instead, it means that its impact is often different from what policymakers have intended and the public has envisaged. Law might not provide the most effective way of resolving social conflicts, but various studies show that it can be used to cope with disputes (Felstiner et al. 1981; Felstiner 1974). There is also a new wave of interest in the relationship between law and development, which acknowledges that reforming substantive areas of law does not necessarily lead to social development, and yet it is argued that enhancing the quality of institutions responsible for the administration of law can have positive social impacts (Davis and Trebilcock 2001). More recent debates on legal transplants show that the belief in law as an instrument of social reform lives on, albeit in new forms.

To sum up, the law can function as a relatively autonomous social system as long as it is disembedded from its societal context and allowed to follow its own system logic. The disembeddedness of the law—which is never complete—shields it to a degree from the normative force of cultural and moral values and political interests

---

[5] However, even researchers who choose to study law from a cultural standpoint might do so to identify obstacles to social engineering, i.e. to discover how the internal and external legal cultures of a group create a "gap" (Nelken 2007, p. 111).

prevalent in society, but it also creates dichotomies, such as law in books and law in action, and generates contradictions inside and outside of the law. These dichotomies and contradictions provide the point of departure for the discussions in the next chapter.

References

Abel, R. (1987). Redirecting social studies of law. *Law and Society Review, 14*(3), 805–829.

Aubert, V. (1977). *Sociology of law*. London: Penguin.

Aubert, V., Eckhoff, T., & Sveri, K. (1952). *En lov i søkelyset (A law in the searchlight)*. Oslo: Akademisk forlag.

Banakar, R. (2000). Reflections on the methodological issues of the sociology of law. *Journal of Law and Society, 27*(2), 273–295.

Banakar, R. (2003). *Merging law and sociology: Beyond the dichotomies of socio-legal research*. Berlin/Wisconsin: Galda and Wilch.

Banakar, R. (2004). When do rights matter? In S. Halliday & P. Schmidt (Eds.), *Human rights brought home* (pp. 165–184). Oxford: Hart.

Banakar, R. (2005). Studying cases empirically. In R. Banakar & M. Travers (Eds.), *Theory and method in socio-legal research* (pp. 141–159). Oxford: Hart.

Banakar, R., & Travers, M. (2005). Law, sociology and method. In R. Banakar & M. Travers (Eds.), *Theory and method in socio-legal research* (pp. 1–25). Oxford: Hart.

Baumgartner, M. P. (2000). The sociology of law. In D. Patterson (Ed.), *A companion to philosophy of law* (pp. 406–420). Oxford: Blackwell.

Black, D. (1972). The boundaries of legal sociology. *The Yale Law Journal, 81*(6), 1086–1100.

Black, D. (1976). *The behavior of law*. New Haven, CT: Yale University Press.

Boon, A., & Webb, J. (2008). Legal education and training in England and Wales: Back to the future? *Journal of Legal Education, 58*(1), 79–121.

Boon, A., Flood, J., & Webb, J. (2005). Postmodern professions? The fragmentation of legal education and the legal profession. *Journal of Law and Society, 32*(3), 473–92.

Bourdieu, P. (1987). The force of law: Towards a sociology of the judicial field. *Hasting Law Journal, 38*(5), 805–853.

Campbell, C. M., & Wiles, P. (1976). The study of law in society in Britain. *Law and Society Review, 10*(4), 547–578.

Carbonnier, J. (1965). Le grandi ipotesi della sociologia teorica del diritto. *Quaderni di Sociologia, XIV*, 267–283.

Cotterrell, R. (2005). Durkheim's Loyal Jurist: The sociological theory of Paul Huvelin. *Ratio Juris, 18*(4), 504–518.

Cotterrell, R. (2013). The role of the jurist: Reflections around Radbruch. *Ratio Juris, 26*(4), 519–522.

Davis, K. E., & Trebilcock, M. J. (2001). Legal reforms and development. *Third World Quarterly, 22*(1), 21–36.

Denis, A., & Kalekin-Fishman, D. (Eds.). (2009). *The new ISA handbook in contemporary international sociology: Conflict, competition, cooperation*. London: Sage.

Ehrlich, E. (1936). *Fundamental principles of the sociology of law*. Cambridge: Harvard University Press (original publication 1912).

Ellickson, R. C. (1991). *Order without law*. Cambridge, MA: Harvard University Press.

Ewick, P., & Silbey, S. (1998). *The common place of law: Stories from everyday life*. Chicago: University of Chicago Press.

Felstiner, W. L. F. (1974). Influences of social organization on dispute processing. *Law and Society Review, 9*, 631.

Felstiner, W. L. F., Abel, R. L., & Sarat, A. (1981). The emergence and transformation of disputes: Naming, blaming, claiming .... *Law and Society Review, 15*, 631–54.

Ferrari, V. (1989). Sociology of law: A theoretical introduction. In V. Ferrari & P. Uusitalo (Eds.), *Two lectures on the sociology of law*. Helsinki: University of Helsinki (Sociology of Law Series, no. 6/101, pp 7–31).

Fredman, S. (2002). *Discrimination and human rights: The case of racism*. Oxford: Oxford University Press.

Friedman, L. M. (1986). The law and society movement. *Stanford Law Review, 38*(3), 763–780.

Galanter, M. (1974). Why the "Haves" come out ahead: Speculations on the limits of legal change. *Law and Society Review, 9*, 95–160.

Galligan, D. J. (2006). *Law in modern society*. Oxford: Oxford University Press.

Garth, B. G., & Sarat, A. (Eds.). (1998). *How does law matter?* Illinois: Northern University Press.

Garth, B., & Sterling, J. (1998). From legal realism to law and society: Reshaping law for the last stages of the social activist state. *Law and Society Review, 32*, 409–471.

Glaser, B. G., & Strauss, A. (1967). *Discovery of grounded theory: Strategies for qualitative research*. Chicago: Aldine Publishing Company.

Gurvitch, G. (1947). *Sociology of law*. London: Routledge & Kegan.

Hertogh, M. (Ed.). (2009). *Living law: Reconsidering Eugen Ehrlich*. Oxford: Hart.

Kahn, P. W. (1999). *The cultural study of law: Reconstructing legal scholarship*. Chicago: The University of Chicago Press.

Kurkchiyan, M. (2011). Perceptions of law and national order: A cross-national comparison of collective legal consciousness. *Wisconsin International Law Journal, 29*(2), 366–392.

Legrand, P. (2001). What "Legal Transplants"? In D. Nelken & J. Feest (Eds.), *Adapting legal cultures* (pp. 55–69). Oxford: Hart.

Luhmann, N. (2004). *Law as a social system (trans: Ziegert K)*. Oxford: Oxford University Press.

Macaulay, S. (1963). None-contractual relations in business. *American Sociological Review, 28* (1), 55–67.

Moore, S. F. (1973). Law and social change: The semi-autonomous social fields as an appropriate subject of study. *Law and Society Review, 7*(4), 719–746.

Nelken, D. (1981). The gap problem in the sociology of law: A theoretical review. *Windsor Yearbook of Access to Justice, 1*, 35–61.

Nelken, D. (1984). Law in action or living law? Back to the beginning in sociology of law. *Legal Studies, 4*, 152–174.

Nelken, D. (2001). Towards a sociology of legal adaptation. In J. Feest & D. Nelken (Eds.), *Adapting legal cultures* (pp. 7–54). Oxford: Hart.

Nelken, D. (2007). Defining and using the concept of legal culture. In E. Örücü & D. Nelken (Eds.), *Comparative law: A handbook* (pp. 109–132). Oxford: Hart.

Nielsen, L. B. (2000). Situating legal consciousness: Experiences and attitudes of ordinary citizens about law and street harassment. *Law and Society Review, 34*, 1055–1090.

Norrie, A. (2005). *Law and the beautiful soul*. London: GlassHouse.

Olgiati, V. (1998). The paradigm shift of a key concept: Norm production in contemporary sociology of law in Europe. *Journal of Legal Pluralism, 41*, 89–109.

Petrazycki, L. (1955). *Law and morality*. Cambridge, MA: Harvard University Press.

Podgórecki, A. (1991). *A sociological theory of law*. Milano: Dott. A. Giuffre Editore.

Pound, R. (1910). Law in books and law in action. *American Law Review, 44*, 12–36.

Pound, R. (1943). Sociology of law and sociological jurisprudence. *University of Toronto Law Journal, 5*(1), 1–20.

Santos, B. S. (1977). The law of the oppressed: The construction and reproduction of legality in Pasargada. *Law and Society Review, 12*, 5–125.

Sarat, A. (2000). Pain powerlessness, and the promises of interdisciplinary legal scholarship. *Windsor Year Book of Access to Justice, 18*(1), 187–212.

Sarat, A., & Silbey, S. (1988). The pull of the policy audience. *Law and Policy, 10*(2), 97–166.

Selznick, P. (1949). *TVA and the Grass Roots: A study in the sociology of formal organization*. Berkeley: University of California Press.

Shamir, R. (1996). Suspended in space: Bedouin under the law of Israel. *Law and Society, 30*, 231–257.
Silbey, S. (2005). After legal consciousness. *Annual Review of Law and Social Science, 1*, 323–368.
Simon, J. (1999). Law after society. *Law and Social Inquiry, 24*(1), 143–194.
Stjernquist, P. (2001). *Organised cooperation facing law: An anthropological study*. Stockholm: Almqvist & Wiksell.
Sutton, J. (2001). *Law/society: Origins, interaction, and change*. London: Pine Forge.
Svensson, M., & Larsson, S. (2009). Social norms and intellectual property: Online norms and the European legal development. *Research Report in Sociology of Law*, Vol. 1, Lund University. SSRN: http://ssrn.com/abstract=1598288.
Tamanaha, B. (1997). *Realistic socio-legal theory: Pragmatic and social theory of law*. Oxford: Clarendon.
Thomas, P. (1997). Socio-legal studies: The case of disappearing fleas and bustards. In P. Thomas (Ed.), *Socio-legal studies* (pp. 1–22). Dartmouth: Aldershot.
Travers, M. (2001). Sociology of law in Britain. *American Sociologist, 32*(2), 26–40.
Treviño, A. J. (2013). Sociological jurisprudence. In R. Banakar & M. Travers (Eds.), *Law and social theory* (pp. 35–51). Oxford: Hart.
Twining, W. (1999). *Law in context*. Oxford: Clarendon.
Webley, L., & Duff, L. (2007). Women solicitors as barometer for problems within the legal profession. *Journal of Law and Society, 34*(3), 374–402.
Wheeler, S., & Thomas, P. (2002). Socio-legal studies. In D. J. Hayton (Ed.), *Law's future(s)* (pp. 267–280). Oxford: Hart.

Chapter 4
Whose Experience Is the Measure of Justice?

Western liberal law is essentially contradictory and antinomial, so that legal concepts, troubled and oppositional, generally hunt in pairs.

Norrie (2005, p. ix)

Abstract The previous chapters highlighted the epistemic tensions between the approaches of traditional legal scholarship and jurisprudence, on the one hand, and sociology and socio-legal research, on the other. They also described some of the sharply defined distinctions made between 'law in books' and 'law in action', 'positive law' and 'living law', 'facts' and 'norms' and the 'internal' and 'external' operations of the law. This chapter continues to probe the dual conceptualisations of the law by examining Robert Alexy's theory of legal argumentation and his idea of 'law's claim to correctness', which represent an attempt to bridge one the intractable dichotomies of the law, namely the gap between positive law and justice.

Alexy's (1978, 1985, 2000, 2002) theory of legal argumentation is amongst the notable contributions made to mainstream jurisprudence in the last decades. Remaining true to its rational discursive mission, it engages with both analytical positivism and natural law theories. This chapter attempts to examine some of the legal philosophical debates surrounding Alexy's work from a socio-legal standpoint. Moreover, by examining the complexity of the relationship between law and justice, it presents and critiques the 'separation thesis' that informs various schools of legal positivism. Therefore, in the following pages special attention is paid to positive law's attempts to separate facts from values, law from morality and legal certainty from justice. The roots of these dichotomies, or antinomies as they are also called, in order to highlight their one-sided oppositional character (cf. Norrie 2005),

---

This chapter is a revised and updated version of 'Whose Experience is the Measure of Justice?' In: (2008) *Legal Ethics* 10(2): 209–222.

R. Banakar, *Normativity in Legal Sociology*, DOI 10.1007/978-3-319-09650-6_4

can be traced back to the Enlightenment and beyond (Barton 1998).[1] Using the debate on Alexy's thesis that Western liberal law cannot help but raise claims to moral correctness, this chapter will bring into focus the continued efforts of mainstream jurisprudence to employ antinomies to organise itself—a task which it performs not so much by studying the empirical manifestations of the law but more so by conceptually containing the duality of positive law within an essentially rationalistic discourse.

Before we turn to the specifics of Alexy's thesis, it is perhaps helpful to gain a general conception of the theoretical assumptions that inform the approach of this chapter. Therefore, Sect. 1 presents the theoretical background against which I have read the debate on Alexy's theory of legal argumentation. I have explored the role of dichotomies in socio-legal research elsewhere (cf. Banakar 2003), but in the following pages I shall employ Alan Norrie's critical examination of antinomies to throw light on some of the shortcomings of Alexy's theory and also to discuss the concerns of mainstream jurisprudence. Thus, this chapter presents both Norrie's study of antinomies and Alexy's thesis on 'law's claim to correctness,' using the former to assess the latter critically. Section 2 brings into focus Alexy's central thesis, while Sect. 3 discusses the duality of law, exemplified by the attempts of mainstream jurisprudence to cope with the tension between the positivist notion of law and the idea of justice. Section 4 concludes the chapter by reflecting on some of the implications of Alexy's thesis.

1 The Ethical Form of Judgement

In *Law and the Beautiful Soul* (2005, p. 5), Alan Norrie recognises Western liberal law's progressive ethical capacity, acknowledging that despite its failings it has the potential to provide 'a limited and ambivalent experience of justice'. He also argues that the law has 'significant structural limits and complexities' (Norrie 2005, p. ix) which make it oblivious to its flaws, thus undermining its ethical force. Being 'antinomial', positive law differentiates itself conceptually into parts which, once viewed from a historical standpoint, are inseparable from each other. That is why liberal law establishes a *legal* foundation for 'the right', which does not necessarily need to be ethically valid.[2] Expressed differently, 'the good' is no longer treated as

[1] Dichotomies of this kind can also be found in the ancient philosophers' reflections on the structure and order of things, the best known example of which is Aristotle's distinction between corrective and distributive justice. However, the dichotomies discussed in the coming pages were brought on as part of the attempt to establish law and politics as autonomous spheres of social action, which is why it is more fruitful to explore them in the context of the Enlightenment. For a discussion see Barton (1998).

[2] We touched on this point briefly in the introductory chapter and discussed it from a different standpoint. Once moral rights are imported into the legal system, they cease requiring moral justification for their validity.

the necessary attribute of the legality of rights. Yet, paradoxically, the promise of 'the good', ethically correct judgement and, ultimately, the expectation of justice remain an integral part of the way law is perceived by most people. It is also, as Alexy would maintain, an important part of law's claim whereby it is part of law's self-identity and the way in which it organises and presents itself. Admittedly, modern law does not live up to the ethical standards of the Beautiful Soul, but it does not refute the promise of ethically-based judgements either. To dismiss law's promise of 'the good' and its claim to justice as part of its rhetoric (or its ideological domination) misses the role these judgements play in challenging its operations and subverting its 'objective' methods of decision-making. To deliver the promise of 'the good' enshrined in liberal law, the law has no alternative but to go beyond its own normative boundaries, objective methods and institutional constraints.

In Chap. 11, we shall discuss how law, morality and justice have developed historically as a fundamental part of the normative structures of human community (cf. Barden and Murphy 2011). It suffices here to point out that law and justice have emerged hand in hand as the normative elements of social organisation, and their interdependence continues to be reflected in ordinary men and women's conflation of law and morality and their expectation that legal processes deliver justice. It was first through the rise of positivism that law and justice were separated from each other conceptually and treated as different categories. This process of forced separation, which took shape as law was transformed into a modern rational system, may be examined as an integral part of the separation of the system from the lifeworld, to borrow a pair of concepts from Habermas (1984), which by itself is unproblematic until the instrumental rationality of the former dominates the latter and reshapes human relations. The rise of modern social systems as autonomous spheres of social action therefore generates a series of one-sided, often false oppositions which invade the sphere of law as a set of antinomies, instances of which are found in legal theory in the separation of the universal from the particular, the formal from the informal, the factual from the ideal and the individual from the collectivity to which he or she belongs (cf. Norrie 2005, p. 183). In essence, these antinomies expose the conflicts that are embedded in the socio-historical constitution of modernity, and although liberal law is ethically constrained by them, it nevertheless 'plays a central role in structuring, shaping and limiting the ethical possibilities in Western liberal societies' (Norrie 2005, p. ix).

The contradictory elements of law are generated partly by attempts to guide action in various contexts by reference to abstract ahistorical criteria, while the institutions of law remain tied up to socio-historically-defined social relations. Law has to ignore and deny the relevance of its socio-historical ties, especially if it is to appear as an internally coherent system of rules, doctrines and decisions capable of operating autonomously. That is why theories of legal positivism describe the totality of law in terms of legal rules and doctrine, which are employed to guide the practice of law, while ignoring the broader social contexts in which rules and doctrine need to be interpreted before they are transformed into legal practice. By overlooking the significance of the broader social and historical context out of which not only legal practice but also institutions of law have emerged, legal positivism obscures and mystifies the relationship between legal practice and the societal context of law (Norrie 2005, pp. 20–31). To unpack this notion, Norrie refers to the idea of the 'legal subject as a responsible agent,' which is represented by doctrines such as *mens rea* and *actus reus*. He argues that liberal theory, which underpins the subjective principles of criminal law, 'affirming the need for intention, foresight, knowledge and belief concerning actions and their consequences,' is highly individualistic and atomistic (Norrie 2005, p. 53). Not even the atomised liberal understanding of human action can completely ignore society, which is why the above account of social action is restricted by recognising the need for mutual cooperation. Liberal law abstracts agency from 'the context of social conflict and deprivation which generates crime' and excludes 'that context from the judicial gaze' (Norrie 2005, p. 30). Furthermore, it provides a partial and mystified image of the individual and society that allows and justifies an individualised relationship between legal and moral judgement. According to Norrie (2005, p. 149), we need to take into consideration 'both mediation of agency by structure and the reproduction and transformation of structure by agency,' while recognising the intractably interwoven empirical manifestations of this (structuration) process. In other words, structure and agency are produced and reproduced through the same complex social process.

The notion of justice, as it is deployed in the following pages, is also linked to Norrie's general approach and refers to the ethical form of judgement that lies beyond the domain of positive law. This understanding of the concept of justice is in turn informed by the figure of the Beautiful Soul, a product of the European Enlightenment, which raised the 'possibility of combining moral virtue and aesthetic value in the perfection of lived human being' (Norrie 2005, p. 2). Somewhat oversimplified, it is the leading ethical ideal of the Enlightenment that morality necessarily requires a rational basis, the unification of emotion and reason. However, this ideal of ethical perfection and 'the possibility in the here and now of attaining the morally good life' (Norrie 2005, p. 2) was soon suspected of accommodating latent negative properties. In the early writings of Hegel (1948, p. 240), the figure of the Beautiful Soul represents 'boldness and confidence of decision about fullness of life,' capable of maintaining 'a loving heart in the face of the conventional existence of one's people' (Norrie 2005, p. 3). Hegel changed his view of the Beautiful Soul from 'admiration to outright rejection,' from the idea of a 'morally full life' to a life which was 'empty,' 'hollow' and 'impotent' (Norrie 2005, p. 3). We observe this shift of attitude in the ambiguous assessment of the Beautiful Soul in contemporary society. Modern society, on the one hand, looks down on the virtuous action, dismissing and suppressing it as dangerous, fanatical, hypocritical or unrealistic, while, on the other hand, praises it for its principled conviction. The figure of the Beautiful Soul assumes an ideal metaphysical form—the promise of things to come—and persists against all odds because the institutions of modernity, such as private property and law, 'cannot sustain or actualise its radical moral implications' (Norrie 2005, p. 180).

By separating and compartmentalising 'the right' or forms of freedom from 'the good' or the radical form of ethics, liberal law embodies and reproduces the rise and demise of the Beautiful Soul. The promise of 'the good' and human perfectibility, the most radical promise of the Enlightenment, which the liberal law embodies is constantly contained and repressed at the expense of the attempt to produce a legally valid modern notion of 'the right':

> This work of expression on the one hand and repression on the other is signposted by the pathologies of antinomialism that bedevil liberal thought and which reach into the finest points of its law. The chain of antinomies begins at the edge of law, in opposition between "the ideal" and 'the actual', and between "social" and 'the individual' justice. It reaches into law's foundations, through lines drawn between the "internal" and the "external", the 'formal' and the "substantive", and the "universal" and the "particular"... [W]hat these antinomies bespeak, I argue, is confusion and dis-ease in thought, in practice, in law. (Norrie 2005, p. x)

In short, liberal law 'contains and represses a radical sense of "the good" in order to produce a modern sense of "the right"' (Norrie 2005, p. X), which causes a disjunction between the political and ethical basis for 'the right' that modern liberal law establishes and 'the good' that it promises. In order to deliver 'the good', Norrie argues, law has no alternative but to go beyond itself, beyond its own structural limits and complexities. Legal positivism responds to this challenge by containing conceptually the contradictory concepts and ideas embedded in liberal law. Norrie, on the other hand, seeks a middle way, using a dialectical approach in order to not only avoid reproducing the antinomies, but also to go beyond their decontextualising effects.

This is the theoretical background against which I have explored the legal philosophy of Robert Alexy in an attempt to maintain a semblance of the Beautiful Soul.

2 Law's Claim to Correctness

Although there are similarities between Alexy and Norrie, there are also differences separating their viewpoints. While Norrie's dialectical approach is rooted in the Hegelian tradition, Alexy's emphasis on rational discourse is a neo-Kantian construct which we also find in the works of his German contemporaries such as Habermas (1984). Alexy was also deeply influenced by Gustav Radbruch's famous 'formula', which brought into focus the conflict between positive law and justice (cf. Radbruch 1946), or the requirements of legal certainty, on the one hand, and the needs of justice and expediency, on the other (Bix 2011, p. 48). According to Radbruch, when conflict arises between the principle of justice and positive law, the court should maintain legal certainty and security (ultimately opting for social order) by applying the rules of law, even when their application results in injustice. The logic underpinning this position is deceptively simple: there can be no justice without social order. For Radbruch justice is the core value of law, which means that positive law cannot be granted total primacy over the requirement of justice and yet, paradoxically, social order must be prioritised if justice is to be realised. Therefore, law is best described as the search for the balance between justice, security and certainty (order), and social utility (cf. Cotterrell 2013, p. 516). In his 'reflections around Radbruch', Roger Cotterrell explains this point:

> Even where the judge cannot do justice through law, there is an obligation to serve the value of order which demands certainty in legal doctrine and predictability in legal decisions. Doing justice and pursuing aims through law presupposes law's stability. To that extent, providing order is the first task of the law. (Cotterrell 2013, p. 516)

However, Radbruch also maintains that extreme injustice is not law. If the applicable rule of law diverges considerably from the needs of justice, thus causing grave suffering, law's requirements of order, which is the prerequisites for justice, cannot be upheld. It also means that the law in question is flawed and lacks the essence of legality (Radbruch 1946, p. 107 and Radbruch 1990). Bix (2011, p. 50) clarifies how this point informs Alexy's legal theory:

> Radbruch's Formula(s), and his conception of law, are based on the notion that people may not expect their legal system to be uniformly just and fair, but there *is* an expectation of minimal justice that comes with the notion of "legality." This view—especially as it appears in the less well known second version of Radbruch's Formula (that to be legal the rules must at least "make an attempt at justice")—could be translated into Robert Alexy's well-known assertion: "Every legal system lays claim to correctness".

When in its deliberation the law intentionally disregards any consideration of equality—the core of justice—it invalidates itself as a legal system. Thus, the occasional failures of the legal system to deliver justice do not legally invalidate it per se, as long as it has attempted to achieve just outcomes and does not generate extreme forms of injustice or cause grave suffering. As Bix has observed, Alexy's theory may be viewed as the defence of a version of Radbruch's formula:

> [. . .] offering arguments for it that are different from and more sophisticated than those that were adduced by Radbruch himself. Alexy also placed Radbruch's formula within a larger context of conceptual analysis and theories about the nature of law. Both Radbruch and Alexy claim that their positions are incompatible with legal positivism, and therefore count as a rejection (and perhaps refutation of it). (Bix 2006, p. 139)

Alexy's work attracted attention outside Germany in the 1980s with the publication of the English translation of his doctoral thesis on legal argumentation (see Alexy 1985). His starting point—that legal discourse is a special case of moral discourse—is neither new nor original in itself. However, Alexy adds that moral correctness is an intrinsic property of the law and legal argumentation, and it exists at the level of the legal system and legal institutions and at the level of individual laws and decisions which constitute the legal order (cf. Mcilroy 2013). This idea should be explored against the backdrop of Radbruch's legal theory (1946) and Jürgen Habermas's discourse ethics (1984). Both Radbruch and Habermas, each in his own way, regard law to be necessarily connected with justice. Radbruch explained the link between justice and legal certainty by arguing that 'every legal system contains a legal rule, which overrides all others, which directs judges to disregard unjust rules even if they are law' (Raz 2007, p. 29).[3] This means, firstly,

[3] This interpretation is based on Raz's reading of Alexy and Radbruch. See Raz (2007).

that positive law which produces grossly unjust results is not valid and, secondly, that the application of positive law requires making moral judgements as to the content and consequences of the law. However, Radbruch does not necessarily discard the basic assumptions of legal positivism, including the 'separation thesis', concerning moral judgements which can be expressed in terms of legal norms that override other norms.

Alexy also argues that law necessarily raises a claim to correctness. This proposition suggests a theoretical affinity with Karl-Otto Apel and Jürgen Habermas's primary thesis that the speech act raises various validity claims.[4] As Alexy (2007a, p. 358) explains to one of his critics:

> Discourse theory is an essentially universalistic theory. It claims, first, that all human beings participate (apart from unusual circumstances) in the practice of asking, asserting and arguing; secondly, that this practice necessarily presupposes universals of reasoning that can be expressed by rules of discourse; and, thirdly, that the practice of discourse is oriented towards truth or correctness as regulative ideas.

Both Alexy and Habermas share the conviction that 'law consists of more than pure facticity of power, orders backed by threats, habits, or organized coercion' (Alexy 2000, p. 138). Besides possessing a factual side, law also comprises 'a critical or ideal dimension,' which is defined by a 'claim to correctness'[5] or, to borrow Habermas' terminology, a 'claim to legitimacy' (Cooke 2007, p. 225),[6] a claim which when made by law also entails making a claim to justice, operating as the defining property of a legal system. A normative system that fails to raise the claim to correctness, according to Alexy, is not a legal system but a system of 'power, force and coercion beyond the categories of correct and wrong, and just and unjust' (Alexy 2000, p. 144). This is why the 'claim to correctness' becomes an integral part of the method of identifying and defining the law. We should note that the 'critical dimension' that indicates law's ability to make moral judgements is internal to its operations and, as I shall argue, amounts to an indecisive break with the central tenet of legal positivism, hence Peter Goodrich's description of Alexy as 'the apologist or polemicist in defence of the law' (Goodrich 2008, p. 105).

Alexy argues that 'there are moral elements active in law,' whereby adjudication (at least in hard cases) requires making moral judgements, and that 'legislation

[4] Bongiovanni et al. (2007, p. 277) argue that, according to Alexy, Habermas's claim to correctness oversimplifies the structure of the regulative speech act by constructing it as fulfilment of norms. Therefore, Alexy distinguishes between 'normative speech acts' and a 'normative statement (a judgement of value or obligation).'

[5] The claim to correctness raised by legal acts can be denied, a fact which does indeed cause theoretical difficulties for Alexy. As Bulygin (2000) pointed out, the claim to correctness cannot be the necessary defining requirement of a legal system, if it is possible not to raise the claim. Alexy, however, explains that legal systems which fail to fulfil the claim to correctness are 'faulty legal systems,' and legal norms which fail to raise the claim are 'faulty legal norms' (Alexy 2000, p. 146).

[6] According to Cooke (2007), Alexy and Habermas differ in their understanding of the context-transcending components of law, which opens law up to internal criticism.

claims to be morally justifiable even in case of political compromise' (Alexy 2000, p. 143). In addition he maintains that there is no one single objective morality and sense of justice that is shared by all lawmakers and officials of law; different legal systems can and do give expression to different forms of justice (Alexy 2000), and the claim to correctness raised in law is not the same as the claim to correctness raised in morality. Claims raised by law are embedded in the institutional context of the law and thus are of a higher order of complexity (Alexy 1985, pp. 214ff). Legal discourse is moulded by the institutional constraints of the legal system and can be regarded as a distinctly autonomous form of practical discourse.[7] As Vassiloyannis (2007, p. 109) explains, Alexy's legal theory distinguishes itself from other approaches by arguing that 'the claim to correctness of legal argumentation can only be fulfilled within the institutional framework of an existing legal order.' Since Alexy does not subscribe to a relativist standpoint, this 'claim to correctness' which is raised in legal argumentation must depend on the extent to which positive law can satisfy the criterion of correctness. This opens up his theory to criticism from a number of standpoints. For example, MacCormick (2007, p. 60) regards it as a 'category mistake,' whereas others, such as Sieckmann (2007, p. 199), try to show that 'such a claim cannot be supposed to be necessary.'

MacCormick (2007, p. 60) criticises Alexy's 'law's claim to correctness' (as well as Raz's 'law's claim to legitimate authority') by arguing that institutional normative orders such as law are 'state of affairs[...] incapable of performing speech acts;' consequently, saying that 'law claims anything, meaning this literarily, is a category mistake.' Cooke (2007, p. 277), who also questions aspects of Alexy's thesis, inadvertently replies to MacCormick by pointing out that although the claim to correctness is realised through the actions of the functionaries of the legal system, such a claim is, nonetheless, 'not a private matter' and has an 'objective character' reaching beyond its immediate addressees. Alexy (2007a, p. 334) also replies in a similar vein, pointing out that the 'claim' raised by those who participate in the legal system is not a private or personal matter, but is rather a claim that they necessarily have to raise.

In the process of demonstrating that law's claim to moral correctness is based on a category mistake, MacCormick distinguishes sharply between law as an institution and as an ideal. He therefore reproduces a dichotomy which, as mentioned above, is the recurrent theme of contemporary jurisprudence. MacCormick can argue in this manner because he individualises social action, treating it in isolation from its socio-historical context, which frees him from considering the dialectical relationship between social agency and institutions. MacCormick's standpoint reflects liberal law's atomistic understanding of human agency and rejects any

[7] These constraints include the strictly formal procedural rules of legal proceedings, time limits, the involuntary participation of parties in a trial, their interest in discovering the truth and, not to forget, legal reasoning's relationship with valid law which excludes certain questions from the domain of debate and examination (cf. Melissaris 2005).

socially constructed phenomenon, such as law's claim to correctness, which cannot be attributed directly to individual action.

Alexy (1998, p. 206) argues that legal acts 'are always connected to the non-institutional act of asserting that the legal act is substantially and procedurally correct.' The legal system is obliged to meet and satisfy its claims to correctness, which in turn involves the '*guarantee* of justifiability' (Alexy 1998, p. 3). Moreover, there is an 'expectation that all the addressees of the claim will accept the legal act as correct, as long as they take the standpoint of the respective legal system and so long as they are reasonable' (1998, p. 3). Correctness therefore entails justifiability and acceptance, but as Sieckmann (2007, pp. 197–198) points out, it is unclear what 'justifiability' means:

> If only legal correctness in the sense of compatibility with the legal norm is meant, then only justification and acceptance of a decision as legally correct would be required. This, however, would not suffice to establish a claim to moral correctness. If a claim to moral correctness and, accordingly, the normative implications of such a claim are to be proven necessary, a stronger concept of correctness must be used. (Sieckmann 2007, p. 198)

The only way to make the normative implications of the claim to correctness 'stronger' is by ensuring that the justification and acceptance of legal decisions are not only raised and guaranteed internally and with respect to substantive and procedural norms of law, but also considered with respect to external (extra-legal) assertions, interests and social processes. This is, however, easier said than done, for, as I shall argue below, modern liberal law operates by excluding interests and opinions which it defines internally as legally irrelevant.

A comparison with Norrie's conception of the link between law and morality will help us to better assess Alexy's contribution. Whereas the critical 'context-transcending' potential identified by Alexy is realised internally through law's claim to correctness, Norrie's Beautiful Soul is an ideal external element to the law. It is in fact 'a metaphysical ethics beyond here and now,' as Norrie explains (2005, p. 16), requiring law to transcend its limits to realise the promise of morally-based forms of judgements. This requires the transformation of law as we know it, an idea to which Alexy is not willing to subscribe, but also a transformation which, although it might sound appealing to the critical ears of those not engaged in obscuring law's contradictions, relies and builds on metaphysical faith. On this point, on law's possibility of moving towards an ethically more responsive state, Alexy's claim to correctness, which is similar to Habermas's idea of validity claims raised by speech acts, provides a sociologically more promising approach. The problem with Alexy's notion of a claim to correctness is that it wishes to remain faithful to positive law's institutional framework. I shall explore the consequences of this issue in the concluding section of this chapter.

3 The Separation Thesis

In *The Arguments from Injustice: A Reply to Legal Positivism*, Alexy (2002) writes that 'the separation thesis', according to which law is defined, without including any moral element in its definition, constitutes the common feature of all theories of legal positivism. Alexy goes on to say that '[t]he separation thesis presupposes that there is no conceptually necessary connection between law and morality[. . .]. The great legal positivist Hans Klesen captured this in the statement, 'thus the content of the law can be anything whatsoever" (Alexy 2002, p. 3). The core of the separation thesis is thus a fairly simple one in so far as it maintains that 'no moral concepts feature in the definition of law' (Raz 2007, p. 19). For Raz (2007, p. 35), however, this is an 'unpromising' way to identify legal positivism, for it overlooks how the discourse of legal theory has advanced the discussion of the nature of law beyond the point where legal positivism may be used as 'an illuminating category' (2007, p. 35). More specifically, Alexy's separation thesis ignores the fact that 'many normative and evaluative concepts are common to moral and non-moral discourse,' and he suggests that there is a simple method of demarcating the line between the moral and non-moral domains and concepts (Raz 2007, p. 19). In addition, Raz (2007, p. 19) argues that when he maintains 'that necessarily the law claims to have legitimate authority, and that that claim is a moral claim,' it does not mean or prove that he believes in a definition of law which includes moral concepts, for he has not formulated a concept thereof. Raz is troubled by what he regards to be the underlying structure of Alexy's argument, which, according to him, misleads us into labelling legal theories in terms of positivist or non-positivist and, as he points out, even classifies Raz's work, which regards 'legitimate authority' as an essential feature of law, as non-legally positivist. Raz is also puzzled by Alexy's distinction between the participant and the observer's perspectives. According to this distinction, the former participates in normative deliberations within the legal system—for example, a lawyer arguing a case before the court—while the latter asks how decisions are made in a certain legal system—for example, an academic lawyer explaining how the court actually decided a case (Raz 2007, p. 23). Raz finds no significant difference between these two perspectives, for both the participant and the observer are expected to be faithful to the law in their deliberations or descriptions. In other words, they share the same conception of law.

In his reply Alexy explains that, in spite of what Raz may think, the distinction between positivist and non-positivist theories helps to highlight an important property of law. Alexy (2007b, p. 37) writes:

> The divide between legal positivist and non-positivist theories of the nature of law will be an illuminating category for as long as law exists. The reason for this lies in the dual nature of law, which stems from the fact that law is, on the one hand, factual in nature and, on the other, ideal. The relationship between law as facts and law as ideal is the most important issue in explaining its nature. Non-positivists claim that the factual dimension is internally connected with the ideal dimension; positivists—in any case today, and in considerable numbers—do not grow tired of stressing the important relations between the real and the ideal, but they insist that the ideal remains essentially external to what the law is.

Following this line of reasoning, Alexy adds that while positivist definitions of law 'refer only to facts,' non-positivist definitions 'refer to both facts and ideals' (2007b, p. 37). By way of reference to Radbruch's formula (see Sect. 2 above), Alexy goes on to argue that 'the law as it is' must be connected to 'law as it ought to be.' Concerning his distinction between participant and observer perspectives, which was dismissed by Raz, Alexy explains that the former seeks and adduces arguments which he or she considers to be the correct legal answer, whereas the latter asks and adduces arguments 'that reflect how legal questions are actually decided in that legal system' (Raz 2007, p. 45). I shall return to the dichotomy between the participant and the observer's standpoints, which in my view reveals limitations to Alexy's theoretical and methodological approach, in the concluding section of this chapter.

4 Reflections

The exchange between Alexy and Raz, which was sketched hastily above, represents a 'landmark philosophical debate,' according to Pavlakos (2007, p. 3). Such debates arguably help to clarify various positions and perhaps break new ground in legal research. Yet, despite all their analytical sophistication they appear to achieve very little beyond restating what seems to be fixed positions in an ongoing debate. This type of mainstream jurisprudential debate appears circular, self-referential, too concerned with conceptual analysis and nonchalant towards debates about law which are advanced by researchers within social sciences and humanities. The only point of interest here is the unwillingness of the new versions of legal positivism to be associated with the narrow version of the separation thesis. Justice is knocking at the door of legal positivists, and although it has not been allowed entry into the realm of law, it has made its voice heard.[8]

The duality of law, in general, and the separation thesis, in particular, should also be examined in relation to the socio-historical properties of modernity. Social theorists have described the advent of modernity in dichotomous terms such as system/lifeworld (Habermas 1984), Gemeinschaft/Gesellschaft (Tönnies 1971) or organic solidarity/mechanic solidarity (Durkheim 1984). Modernity concerns the transformation from a form of society organised around a sense of tightknit community and a relatively enduring perception of moral bonds, to a new form of social organisation based on ephemeral, impersonal and instrumental bonds or transitory networks of interests, dictated by the dominance of capitalism and the advance of urbanisation, industrialisation, information technology and increased social mobility. Modernity empowers human agency, thus enhancing the social

[8] The resemblance with Franz Kafka's sketch 'Before the Law' is more than accidental. In Kafka's sketch, 'the man from the country', who is seeking justice, wastes a lifetime awaiting the permission of 'the doorkeeper' to gain entry into law (cf. Kafka 1992, p. 165).

actor's reflexivity which enables her to free herself from the normative power of traditional institutions. This freedom, however, comes at a price, which we will discuss in the coming chapters. From this sociological standpoint, though, modernity is synonymous with increased reflexivity, on the one hand, and the functional differentiation of society, on the other, which combined together translate into the increased complexity of social systems and the growing contingency (uncertainty) of social action. Most social theorists, such as Habermas, regard this transformation which severs connections between the moral foundations of modern society, and its macro organisational characteristics and imperatives, as highly problematic and seek ways of bridging the gap between the social spheres of action in order to minimise the negative side-effects of modernity.[9] However, while social theorists tend to see law as one of the instruments which can be deployed to maintain and perhaps even enhance social cohesion, i.e. to re-connect system and lifeworld or Gemeinschaft and Gesellschaft, mainstream legal positivists continue to insist on the separation of the spheres of law and morality. According to legal positivists, the rationality, objectivity and system integrity of law depends on its normative closure and separation from other spheres of social action. Such assumptions rest uncomfortably with social theoretical analyses of law, which often see it as a socio-historical institution and a form of practice linked to various spheres of social action.[10] This stance was articulated in Alan Norrie's search for a dialectical method which brings the factual and the ethical dimensions of law together. In the remaining section of this chapter, I will argue that Alexy finds himself torn between these two standpoints: he neither decisively rejects the assumptions regarding the normative closure or the unity of law, nor does he completely adopt the social scientific standpoint that places law's operations in a broader societal context.

[9] Habermas is concerned with the way the system, i.e. the steering media of money and power, penetrates into the fabric of the lifeworld, i.e. the intersubjectively shared background taken for granted by participants in communicative action, reifying human relations. This reification destroys the potential of the lifeworld to organise social action around shared values, giving meaning to social life and integrating highly differentiated and pluralistic modern societies. This leads Habermas to argue for procedural rationality in law, i.e. a type of rationality that is not embedded in any particular value system but rests on the procedural character of the law. In this sense, the legal system becomes an instrument for coordinating social action and reproducing the modern state and economy that are anchored in, but uncoupled from, the lifeworld. Law is therefore given the double task of adapting to and surviving in a complex society while coordinating social action by mediating between the system and lifeworld (cf. Habermas 1984).

[10] Niklas Luhmann is among the few social scientists who have sought to construct a sociological theory which supports the separation thesis. According to Luhmann, law is normatively closed, constituting itself self-referentially by referring to its own previous communications. At the same time, it is cognitively open and in interaction with its environment, which includes other social systems such as politics and economy. Indeed, Luhamann stresses that law's normative closure is a condition for its cognitive openness. Although it is normatively closed and thus separate from other spheres of social action, it can nevertheless observe other systems and address their concerns within its own normative structure (Luhmann calls this 'structural coupling') (cf. Luhmann 2004).

By locating a 'context-transcending' potential in law, Alexy demonstrates the indivisibility of law and morality. It is, however, unclear if he has overcome the one-sidedness of antinomies which, to borrow a phrase from Norrie, 'bedevil legal thought' (Norrie 2005, p. x). The critical and ideal dimensions which Alexy discovers are internal to the system of law, suggesting that the antinomial distinction between the internal and external continues to lurk in the background, awaiting the opportunity to introduce new contradictions into the system. As mentioned above, Alexy's claim to correctness (1) requires the institutional framework of an existing legal system and (2) depends on the ability of positive law to satisfy the criterion of correctness.[11] In that sense, Alexy does not break completely with legal positivism. In his reconciliatory reply to MacCormick, he plays down the ideological differences between the atomised conception of the individual action and a social scientific understanding of society as an entity which cannot be reduced to individual actions. It is therefore understandable that he is criticised for providing 'a positivistic distinction between law and morality,' amounting to 'a mere apology' instead of constructing 'a moral bridge that would take us from moral to legal argumentation' (Vassiloyannis 2007, p. 110).

As mentioned above, Alexy's claim to correctness, which reminds us of Habermas's idea of validity claim, provides a sociologically informed approach that defines law in terms of the social practices of rational discourse. An understanding of law in terms of rational discourse also requires exchanges between the domains of law and morality. This appropriation of the idea of validity claim is, however, hampered by Alexy's unwillingness to break free from legal positivism. When positive law is regarded as the medium through which legal argumentation must be conducted in a rational (correct) manner, then the outcome of such argumentation becomes dependent on positive law's institutional constraints and standards which are, in part, organised around a dual perception of law. Somewhat oversimplified, Alexy searches for the link between law and morality within a framework which is organised around separating the two entities. This means that legal argumentation, which is aimed at realising the promise of justice, is tied to and thus restricted by the institutional arrangements and boundaries of positive law. This approach becomes more problematic once we consider that ethical judgements which satisfy the criteria of justice are external to the domain of positive law. As a result, the form of justice that Alexy's model can offer will be necessarily watered down, no more than an apology for positive law's shortcomings.

When discussing justice, Alexy appears to see the experience of law's officials as the yardstick for measuring justice, which is why his primary concern is whether participants (such as law's officials) and observers (such as legal academics) share the same concept of law. It is perhaps not surprising that Alexy's concept of justice does not reflect the actual experience of injustice or unjust treatment ('experience', being an empirical concept, falls outside this type of self-referential conceptual reasoning). That is why, following Radbruch (1946), Alexy can argue that the

[11] The notion of positive law as it is used here is the same as Norrie's modern liberal law.

principle of legal certainty must override the requirement of justice, as long as the law is not 'grossly unjust.' As Alexy (2007b, p. 50) puts it, 'extreme injustice is not law'. Admittedly, he uses this argument to uncover flaws in the separation thesis underpinning legal positivism, for the judge who refuses to apply an unjust law does so partly by referring to ethical reasons outside the law. Nevertheless, it does not explain why Alexy appears to be oblivious to the other side of this equation, which states that a law or a legal decision might be valid even when it appears as 'mildly' or to a 'reasonable degree' unjust to officials of law.

According to Alexy (2007b, p. 53), the 'extreme injustice thesis presupposes that it is possible to know that a law is, or is not, extremely unjust.' Taking his 'argument from injustice' at face value, the notion of 'grossly unjust' or 'extreme injustice' assumes the existence of a universally valid standard of justice which can be applied irrespective of the interest of law's officials, in order to determine whether a decision is legally valid. Alexy does not consider that, irrespective of whether people share the view of law's officials or not, they experience the justice of law, legal processes and legal regulation in different ways; rather, their experience is the function of a range of social, economic, political and cultural factors which exist independently of any specific theory or concept of law. Ordinary men and women might indeed share the same concept of law as that held by judges, lawyers and legal academics such as Alexy, but this does not mean that they experience legal processes and the relationship between law and morality in the same way as a high court judge or a law professor.

Let me elucidate this point by giving an example. The Code of Practice under the Police and Criminal Evidence Act 1984 (PACE) 'allows an officer to stop and search a person or a vehicle in a public place where there are reasonable grounds for suspecting that there are stolen goods, weapons or articles for use in offences such as theft or burglary and criminal damage' (Davies et al. 2005, p. 155). In addition, 'authorisations made under section 44 of the Terrorism Act 2000 allow officers to stop and search vehicles and persons within vehicles (section 44(1)), and pedestrians (section 44(2)).' 'Authorisation may be given only if the authorising officer considers it expedient for the purposes of preventing acts of terrorism. The power conferred allows an officer to search for articles of a kind that could be used in connection with terrorism, whether or not there are grounds for suspecting the presence of such articles' [section 45(1) and (2), *Home Office Circular* 2008]. The official statistics collected by the police and the Home Office show that the use of these powers has been targeted disproportionately towards young black and British Asians, who are 'six times more likely to be stopped by the police than white people' (*The Guardian* 2008). The Home Office revealed in 2004 that the number of Asians being stopped and searched under the 2000 Terrorism Act had gone up by more than 300 %: from 744 to almost 3,000 (Dodd 2005). In practice, stop and search powers have come to rely on racial profiling and the targeting of primarily blacks and other ethnic minorities in deprived areas of large cities. This law may be experienced as 'just' or perhaps as 'occasionally mildly unjust' from the standpoint of law's officials and policymakers, who for reasons of race (they are mainly white), economy and social status (they do not reside in the deprived areas) never experience the 'discretionary' effects of the enforcement of this law.[12] Evidence to this effect can be found in the recent proposal by the Conservative Party to broaden the application of stop and search powers (*The Guardian* 2008). The same law can, however, be experienced as grossly unjust by those minority groups and individuals who find themselves on the receiving end. 'Sus' laws of the late 1970s and 1980s, which empowered the police to arrest any person suspected of loitering with intent to commit an arrestable offence, are regarded by many as one of the main causes of the race-related conflicts which led to the 1981 Brixton riots. Whose experience of stop and search powers can provide us with the standards we need to measure the justice of this provision? In short, Alexy's 'argument from injustice' has no concept of human experience, i.e. how agents experience legal processes.

Alexy's neglect of experience brings us to another puzzling aspect of his approach, namely his participant/observer dichotomy, which was criticised by Raz as nonsensical. I argue here that law's observers and participants are not, as Alexy suggests, necessarily insiders to law, as they can be—and often are—outsiders to law's processes and operations. Alexy's insistence on limiting his analysis to what is internal to law deceives him into omitting the experiences of occasional participants of the legal system, such as juries and plaintiffs, and disregarding the descriptions of legal processes which are provided by outside observers such as social scientists, journalists and lay people. As I have argued elsewhere (Banakar 2003), we can distinguish at least four standpoints, each capable of producing specific forms of legal knowledge and interest: (1) inside participants, e.g. judges and practicing lawyers, who participate in and reproduce legal processes and various institutional practices associated with law; (2) inside observers, e.g. legal advisors or legal academics, who observe legal processes without necessarily participating in them; (3) outside participants, e.g. plaintiffs, defendants, juries, lay judges and witnesses, who for a limited period of time participate in legal processes and have no professional affiliation with the inside participants; and (4) outside observers, e.g. policy researchers studying law's effects or journalists reporting on trial proceedings, who observe legal processes and institutional practices of the law from the outside, but without necessarily participating in the actual processes themselves.

The four perspectives described above reflect the institutional properties of law and can be used to study the structure/agency relationship. Nonetheless, they exist independently of any individual social actor in the sense that the same person can entertain more than one such perspective in a day's work. A lawyer, for example, can act as an inside participant in one setting, by taking part in the process leading up to a legal judgment, and as an outside observer in another setting, by providing legal advice. In the same day's work, the same lawyer might even act as an outside

[12] According to Bowling and Phillips (2007, pp. 936–937), 'the concept of 'reasonable suspicion' is frequently absent in many instances of the use of police stop/search powers.' Instead, decisions to use such powers are often based on 'generalisations and stereotypes, particularly where levels of discretion are highest.'

participant, by appearing before a court as a plaintiff or defendant. The important characteristic of these perspectives is that they interact with and inform each other, transcending the conception of law based on its internal and external characteristics. The totality of what we perceive as law is the outcome of the interaction of such perspectives at any given time and place. Such a dialectical approach would allow us to study law in its social context and avoid the constraints placed on our analysis by the dichotomies that modern law employs to organise itself and to cope with its internal contradictions. What does this mean for Alexy's theory of legal argumentation? It means that 'claim to correctness' cannot be constructed internally, and any theory of law which is concerned with justice requires overcoming the internal/external divide. Law's claim to correctness cannot provide an adequate basis in itself and has to be explored and evaluated in relation to claims which are raised by 'outsiders' to law in respect of its operations. Law's image of society, its definitions of individual responsibility and autonomy, is constantly interacting with socio-historical processes and structures which lie outside its boundaries.

To sum up, it is not enough for law, whether defined in terms of practices, a body of rules or legislation, to 'cohere' internally, where coherence refers to raising and justifying a claim to the correctness of legal acts. For law to function effectively, i.e. with sensitivity and in response to its social environment, it needs to 'cohere' internally as well as externally, responding to claims which are raised within and without its institutional boundaries. But coherence, which is simultaneously external and internal to law, amounts to a contradiction in terms, revealing the problematic nature of concepts of law which are based on the internal/external divide. For law to 'cohere' internally and externally simultaneously, it needs to adopt a different form of rationality, that which already lies at the heart of Alexy's 'claim to correctness', i.e. communicative rationality, which would not allow the practical discourse that underpins it to be limited to how officials of law discuss and define a problem which has implications for other people and social events. In that sense, modern liberal law can never fulfil simultaneous internal/external coherence, for it works on the basis of abstracting actions from their social context and excluding what it internally defines as legally irrelevant (including affected people's interests and experiences of justice) from the scope of its analysis. At least when theorising about law and legal institutions, we could acknowledge that in order for law to be based truly on communicative rationality, it must transcend the internal/external dichotomy which mainstream jurisprudence employs to place the contradictory outcomes of legal operations outside the juridical gaze.

References

Alexy, R. (1978). *Theorie der juridischen Argumentation. Die Theorie des rationalen Diskurses als Theorie der juridiscen Begründung*. Suhrkamp: Frankfurt am Main.

Alexy, R. (1985). *A theory of legal argumentation: The theory of rational discourse as theory of legal justification*. Oxford: Clarendon.

Alexy, R. (1998). Law and correctness. *Current Legal Problems, 51*(1), 205–221.
Alexy, R. (2000). On the thesis of a necessary connection between law and morality: Bulygin's critique. *Ratio Juris, 13*(2), 138–147.
Alexy, R. (2002). *The arguments from injustice: A reply to legal positivism*. Oxford: Clarendon.
Alexy, R. (2007a). Thirteen replies. In G. Pavlakos (Ed.), *Law, rights and discourse: The legal philosophy of Robert Alexy* (pp. 333–366). Oxford: Hart.
Alexy, R. (2007b). An answer to Joseph Raz. In G. Pavlakos (Ed.), *Law, rights and discourse: The legal philosophy of Robert Alexy* (pp. 37–58). Oxford: Hart.
Banakar, R. (2003). *Merging law and sociology: Beyond the dichotomies of socio-legal research*. Berlin/Wisconsin: Galda & Wilch.
Barden, G., & Murphy, T. (2011). *Law and justice in community*. Oxford: Oxford University Press.
Barton, T. D. (1998). Troublesome connections: The law and post-enlightenment culture. *Emory Law Journal, 47*(1), 163–236.
Bix, B. (2006). Robert Alexy, Radbruch's formula, and the nature of legal theory. *Rechtstheorie, 37*, 139–149.
Bix, B. (2011). Radruch's formula and conceptual analysis. *The American Journal of Jurisprudence, 56*(1), 45–57.
Bowling, B., & Phillips, C. (2007). Disproportionate and discriminatory: Reviewing the evidence on police stop and search. *Modern Law Review, 70*(6), 936–961.
Bulygin, E. (2000). Alexy's thesis of the necessary connection between law and morality. *Ratio Juris, 13*(2), 133–137.
Cooke, M. (2007). Law's claim to correctness. In G. Pavlakos (Ed.), *Law, rights and discourse: The legal philosophy of Robert Alexy* (pp. 225–248). Oxford: Hart.
Cotterrell, R. (2013). The role of the jurist: Reflections around Radbruch. *Ratio Juris, 26*(4), 519–522.
Davies, M., Croall, H., & Tyrer, J. (2005). *Criminal justice: An introduction to the criminal justice system in England and Wales* (3rd ed.). London: Pearson/Longman.
Dodd, V. (2005, August 17). Asian men targeted in stop and search. *Guardian*. http://www.guardian.co.uk. Accessed 28 Jan 2008.
Durkheim, D. (1984). *The division of labor in society*. New York: Free Press (original publication 1893).
Giorgio Bongiovanni, G., Rotolo, A., & Roversi, C. (2007). The claim to correctness and inferrentialism: Alexy's theory of practical reason reconsidered. In G. Pavlakos (Ed.), *Law, rights and discourse: The legal 634 philosophy of Robert Alexy* (pp. 275–300). Oxford: Hart.
Goodrich, P. (2008). Alexy Ad Iustitium. *Social and Legal Studies, 17*(1), 105–108.
Guardian. (2008). Stop and search. 31 January 2008.
Habermas, J. (1984). *The theory of communicative action* (Vol. I). Boston: Beacon.
Hegel, G. W. F. (1948). *Early theological writings*. Chicago: University of Chicago Press.
Home Office Circular HPAN-628GM4. (2008). http://www.knowledgenetwork.gov.uk/HO/circular.nsf. Accessed 28 Jan 2008.
Kafka, F. (1992). *The transformation ('Metamorphosis') and other stories*. Harmondsworth: Penguin.
Luhmann, N. (2004). *Law as a social system (trans: Ziegert K)*. Oxford: Oxford University Press.
MacCormick, N. (2007). Why law makes no claims. In G. Pavlakos (Ed.), *Law, rights and discourse: The legal philosophy of Robert Alexy* (pp. 59–68). Oxford: Hart.
Mcilroy, D. H. (2013). When is a regime not a legal system: Alexy on moral correctness and social efficacy. *Ratio Juris, 26*(1), 65–84.
Melissaris, E. (2005). The limits of institutionalised legal discourse. *Ratio Juris*, 18(4), 464–483.
Norrie, A. (2005). *Law and the beautiful soul*. London: GlassHouse.
Pavlakos, G. (Ed.). (2007). *Law, rights and discourse: The legal philosophy of Robert Alexy*. Oxford: Hart.
Radbruch, G. (1946). Gesetzliches Unrecht und übergesetzliches Recht. *Süddeutsche Juristenzeitung, 1*, 105–108.

Radbruch, G. (1990). In A. Kaufman (Ed.), *Rechtsphilosophie III*. Vol 3 of the Gustav Radbruch Gesamtaugsgabe. Heidelberg: CF Mueller.

Raz, J. (2007). How not to reply to legal positivism. In G. Pavlakos (Ed.), *Law, rights and discourse: The legal philosophy of Robert Alexy* (pp. 17–35). Oxford: Hart.

Sieckmann, J. (2007). Human rights and the claim to correctness in the theory of Robert Alexy. In G. Pavlakos (Ed.), *Law, rights and discourse: The legal philosophy of Robert Alexy* (pp. 189–206). Oxford: Hart.

Tönnies, F. (1971). The concept of Gemeinschaft. In W. J. Cahnman & R. Heberle (Eds.), *Ferdinand Tönnies on sociology* (pp. 62–72). Chicago: University of Chicago Press.

Vassiloyannis, P. (2007). Discourse ethics, legal positivism and the law. In G. Pavlakos (Ed.), *Law, rights and discourse: The legal philosophy of Robert Alexy* (pp. 109–130). Oxford: Hart.

Chapter 5
On the Paradox of Contextualisation

Abstract We continue our discussions on the relationship between law and social sciences in this chapter by focusing more closely on socio-legal methodology. We use Denis Galligan's main argument in Law in Modern Society as our starting point. According to Galligan (Law in modern society. Oxford: Oxford University Press, 2006), adopting a social scientific perspective which describes and analyses the law in extra-legal terms can easily entail losing sight of the law as a distinct social formation. To avoid this pitfall, socio-legal research should contextualise those features of the legal system which are relevant to the actions of citizens and officials of the law. This chapter argues that since the 'relevant' features described by Galligan are related ultimately to legal rules, his approach amounts to a top-down method of contextualising the impact of law on society, and as such he loses sight of law's fluidity and societal embeddedness. Using Galligan's methodology as its backdrop, this chapter sketches the contours of three ideal typical approaches to the contextualisation of law. The first approach examines how social institutions absorb law within their existing networks of rules and relations, the second reverses law's method of dislodging actions from their socio-historical context and the third uncovers the socio-cultural and historical embeddedness of the legal system. This chapter concludes by arguing that these three approaches reverse the de-contextualising effects of modern Western law in different ways and to certain degrees. Scholars who employ the second and third approaches often do so as part of their search for alternative forms of law and legality. What is identified by Galligan as losing sight of the distinctiveness of the law should, in their case, be explored in light of the ongoing struggle for law, rather than as the failure of social sciences to account for the specificity of positive law.

Robert Alexy's notion of 'law's claim to correctness,' which we discussed in the previous chapter, asserted that legal discourse possessed a unique property. The claim to correctness raised in law is mediated through the institutional settings of the legal system and recast by the procedural and material constraints of positive law. As a result, it becomes distinct from a claim to correctness raised in, for

This chapter is a revised version of 'Having One's Cake and Eating It: The Paradox of Contextualisation in Socio-Legal Research' in (2011) *International Journal of Law in Context* 7(4): 487–503.

R. Banakar, *Normativity in Legal Sociology*, DOI 10.1007/978-3-319-09650-6_5

example, moral discourse. As we shall see in this chapter, Denis Galligan, whose take on law is different from that of Alexy, also argues that there is something qualitatively unique about the law. In addition, Galligan asks if describing the law in social scientific terms would not amount to losing sight of what makes the law a unique social formation. Before we take this point further and examine Galligan's thesis in more detail, we must return to the discussions in Chap. 2 concerning the limits of the traditional methods of legal studies. Why do we need to resort to social scientific methods and concepts—which are not *of* the law, but *about* the law—to describe the law? Are law's own methods not sufficient for this purpose?

Traditional doctrinal scholarship provides an important service to practicing lawyers by analysing legal rules and decisions, clarifying ambiguities within rules, structuring them in a logical and coherent manner and describing their inter-relationship (Chynoweth 2008). The systematisation and formulation of the law in terms of doctrine creates a conceptual basis for constructing a *legal context* that helps to determine which rules should be applied in a particular situation. In this sense, doctrinal studies emerge out of the study of legal texts (or black-letter law), which are generated by legislature, courts and other legal authorities and feed back into legal practice once they are used in deciding cases.[1] As pointed out in Chap. 2, the method of doctrinal research, being functional to legal practice, dominates academic law and legal education. Notwithstanding its role in supporting legal practice, the doctrinal approach is criticised for conveying a normatively closed image of law (Cotterrell 1995, pp. 50–53), for constructing the legal context narrowly, for presenting the legal system as a body of rules which can be studied in isolation from the broader societal context of the legal system by the exegesis of authoritative texts (Bradney 1998, p. 76; Vick 2004), for 'not being self-conscious about its assumptions' (Twining 1999, p. 44) and for cultivating what Samuel (2009) calls the 'authority paradigm.' Internally, i.e. from the standpoint of the legal system and its functionaries, this paradigm (or legal context) is produced by way of self-reference and normative closure, continually reaffirming the authority of legal sources such as legal texts, previous legal decisions and/or legislation, and prioritising definitions and methods based on what William Twining called 'practical insider attitudes' (Twining 2000, p. 129; for a discussion, see Banakar 2003, p. 8). Externally, i.e. from the standpoint of policymakers and citizenry, it is upheld through the threat of violence against non-compliance, backed by the authority of the modern state. The authority paradigm's normative closure and its dependency on coercion encourage 'rigidity and introspection rather than an open-minded

[1] 'Context' is an open-ended notion (cf. Twining 1999, pp. 43–44) that refers to a network of ideas, concepts, practices, relationships and situations, which together determine the meaning and applicability of a particular phenomenon (for discussions, see Twining 1999; Burke 2002; Nelken 2009) and overlap with the concept of paradigm (cf. Samuel 2009). Nevertheless, in relation to the law, the idea of a *legal* context helps to identify the elements upon which positive law relies for its operations, for its authority, for its legal meaning and for positioning itself in time and space. The legal context also allows the identification of phenomena which do not belong within the sphere of the law, i.e. which fall outside law's focus (cf. Burke 2002, p. 174).

attitude to academic methods and pursuits' (Samuel 2009, p. 432). Moreover, it fosters an understanding of the law as a system which exists independently of societal forces. In order to escape the intellectual constraints of the authority paradigm, many academic lawyers turn to social theory and social sciences, which in contrast to law are based on the 'perspective of enquiry' (Samuel 2009, p. 432).[2] These scholars place the law in the broader socio-cultural context of the legal system and study legal phenomena in relation to societal forces, which are the prerequisite for the existence of the legal system and the production of the narrow legal context of the law. However, such an evasive strategy often comes at a price.

In *Law in Modern Society* (henceforth *LMS*), Denis Galligan draws attention to the price paid for evading the disciplinary confines of the law, and he argues that adopting a social scientific perspective, which describes and analyses the subject in terms other than those of the law such as power, domination, culture or morality, can easily entail losing sight of the law as a distinct social formation with its own specific character, features and architecture. He writes:

> The step into society in the first place is taken to escape the confines of legal analysis and the certainties of legal professionals by considering law as a social formation and the way in which it interacts with other social formations. From there it is a short step to abandoning any sense of law as distinctive, and to re-conceive it at best as one set of rules among many, at worst as of slight social relevance... The most notable and culpable failure is to assume that law is a mask for something else, for some more basic categories which are discovered by stripping away the mask. If such ideas have had their heyday, only slightly less culpable is the notion that law, being superficial or super-structural, has no social significance, and can be collapsed, deconstructed, or reduced to something else: power, economics, gender, race, political hegemony, ideologies or whatever. (*LMS*, pp. 4–5)

Had law not been a social formation distinct from the other social phenomena with which it interacts, and had it not possessed its own very specific social properties and mechanisms, it would have long collapsed into politics, economy, religion, morality or culture. This is a powerful argument that requires those interested in the 'strong' versions of legal pluralism,[3] as well as those who see law primarily as a cultural artefact or a function of custom, religion, politics or economic relations, to reconsider many of their fundamental assumptions.

What follows is an attempt to present and examine the thesis in Denis Galligan's *LMS*. The first section of this chapter outlines his project and then describes the author's central concern. Section 2 explores his proposed methodology, according to which socio-legal research should take law seriously by studying those features

[2] In the UK, interdisciplinary studies of law have improved their standing within law schools in recent years (Bradney 2003, pp. 9–10; Cownie 2004, pp. 197–198). In particular, the area of socio-legal studies 'has gone from strength to strength' (Wheeler and Thomas 2002, p. 274). In spite of the rising popularity of interdisciplinary research, doctrinal studies of law continue to set the framework within which law students are taught to read and criticise legal, moral and policy arguments. For a discussion see Chap. 2.

[3] The strong version of legal pluralism rejects all legal centralist and formalist models of law, as 'a myth, an ideal, a claim, an illusion' (Griffiths 1986, p. 4). For a critical discussion, see Tamanaha (1993).

of the legal system that are relevant to the actions of citizens and officials of the law in the context of what Galligan calls the 'social sphere.'[4] In the final section of this chapter, Galligan's approach is confronted with mainstream law-and-society research,[5] and the contours of three ideal typical approaches to contextualisation are sketched. The first approach studies the extent to which the implementation and enforcement of legal rules are contingent upon social and institutional factors such as socio-cultural norms and conventions, and how social institutions absorb law within their existing network of social rules and relations. The second approach throws light on how positive law examines social actions and relationships in isolation from their socio-cultural and historical settings. The third approach uncovers the societal embeddedness of the legal system. The second and third approaches are largely interrelated and differ only in respect to their scope—while the former aims at reversing law's method of dislodging actions from their socio-historical context, the latter concerns itself with the totality of the law and tries to 're-place'[6] the legal system in its socio-historical context.

This chapter concludes by arguing that these three approaches reverse the de-contextualising effects of modern Western law in different ways and degrees. Scholars who use the first approach try to have their cake and eat it, too. They take the constitution of the legal system for granted, and thus by and large they safeguard the specificity of positive law while contextualising legal rules. They cannot, however, completely avoid 'contaminating' the legal context with extra-legal concepts and insights. In contrast, researchers who resort to the second and third approaches are not concerned with preserving the constitution of positive law and are often searching for alternative forms of law and legality. What is identified by Galligan as losing sight of the distinctiveness of the law should, in their case, be explored in light of the ongoing struggle for the law rather than the failure of social sciences to account for the specificity of positive law.

---

[4] The social sphere is the social setting of the institutions, practices, rules and conventions where legal rules are interpreted and enforced. According to Galligan, 'organisation' refers to a group of people who are united by a common purpose, whereas 'institution' refers to the rules which govern their common pursuit. The term 'social sphere' brings together organisational arrangements and institutional conditions, while envisaging 'an environment of conventions and understandings including but going beyond rules' (*LMS*, p. 108). Although at first glance the social sphere appears to be conceived broadly, on closer inspection it becomes quite structured, solid, ordered and rule-based. Rules are always in sight and help to bring order to social life.

[5] In the following, 'socio-legal research' and 'law-and-society' will be used interchangeably.

[6] Following Burke (2002), I shall use the verb 're-place' to refer to the process of putting actions and events back into their original contexts.

1 Galligan's Project

1.1 Developing Hart's Concept of Law

Galligan is influenced deeply by Herbert Hart's work, and *LMS* may be read, partly, as his attempt to uncover, describe and clarify the potential of Hart's legal theory for socio-legal research. To achieve this end, Galligan pilots Hart's *The Concept of Law* (1961) in the direction of socio-legal theory and research through what remain for many social scientists the uncharted waters of analytical jurisprudence. For example, Hart places officials of the law at the centre of his legal system, arguing that the minimum requirements for the existence of a legal system are satisfied 'as long as officials accept the law as binding and act accordingly,' thus implying that law is not in the first place dependent on support from and recognition of citizens who must obey the law (*LMS*, p. 128). Hence, for the legal system to operate, we only need to ensure that its officials *accept* and adopt the internal view of secondary rules, while citizens *obey* the primary rules. As a result, Hart relegates 'citizens to the sidelines' (*LMS*, p. 121). Being concerned about the democratic and analytic implications of neglecting the role that citizens do play—and ought to play—in legal processes, Galligan takes on the challenge of empowering them and restoring them to their proper position (*LMS*, p. 122). Without abandoning Hart's legal theory, Galligan sets out to demonstrate that the analytical distinction between the attitudes of officials and those of the people does not withstand close scrutiny (*LMS*, p. 128). It is not only officials but also often ordinary people who *accept* the law and treat it as binding on their own and other people's actions. The notion of obedience becomes inappropriate when parties use the law voluntarily, for example to establish contractual relationships. Their very choice and use of law is in itself evidence of their acceptance thereof, which is how Galligan unpacks many of his ideas concerning Hart's distinction between the internal and external perspectives on law, demonstrating their relevance to socio-legal research and making them receptive to socio-legal analysis. However, it is important to add that Hart admitted many of these points during his lifetime, especially when meeting with the critique directed at *The Concept of Law* by legal theorists such as Raz (1980) and McCormick (1981). In addition, as Cotterrell (2003, p. 97) explains:

> Various passages in *The Concept of Law* might suggest that Hart assumed all along that the internal view of rules was one that could be understood by a hermeneutic observer (a legal theorist, for example) as well as by an official or citizen adopting the rules as guides for his and others' conduct.

1.2 From Rules to Rulings

As part of his attempt to bring Hart's ideas to bear on socio-legal theory, Galligan uses a handful of anthropological and historical studies (mainly of Roman law) to venture beyond the analytical boundaries of Hart's jurisprudence. At the risk of oversimplification, Galligan's theoretical framework may be described in terms of six consecutive levels of analysis:

1) Law is made up of rules, but it is more than rules and did not start historically as a collection of rules.
2) Systems of positive rules belong to advanced legal orders—traditional societies, on the other hand, are based on conventions and shared understanding. By moving 'backwards from rules to rulings,' we can identify 'law in its most elemental sense... as the expression of primary relations among the members of society' (*LMS*, p. 47).
3) Certain acts such as marriage and contract are simply legal and recognised as legal acts in all societies, including primitive communities.
4) Law started when 'rulings' were made in regard to these legal acts.
5) Rules were then eventually deduced from these 'rulings' (legal rules are rationalised versions of the original 'rulings'). In that sense, legality is an intrinsic characteristic of all societies, but it is manifested as a social fact once 'rulings' are made in respect to legal acts.
6) The original legal act is a social act and continues to provide the basis for interpreting and enforcing legal rules. Hence, the 'social' context in which law should be analysed consists of its original legal context.

This theoretical framework perhaps explains why Galligan starts his book by unfolding Hart's views on legal rules. Starting with rules, he moves on to search for the social context of law, developing the notion of the 'social sphere' which, besides containing rules, conventions and practices, provides the basis for meaningful social action. The concept of the social sphere should not be confused with what is broadly understood as 'social context'[7] in the contextual studies of law. 'A social sphere may be described,' writes Galligan, 'as an area of activity in which the participants share understandings and conventions about the activity, and which influence and guide the way they engage in it' (*LMS*, p. 103). While social context is defined deliberately in an open-ended fashion (see Twining 1999, p. 40), the social sphere is constructed as a well-structured and institutionalised environment, capable of providing a high degree of certitude (i.e. it is 'solid' in the sense of early modern institutions).[8] Galligan then goes on to discuss issues related to the reception and coercion of law, and he explains how the architecture of law, 'the detailed manner in which laws are expressed' (*LMS*, p. 139), interacts with social spheres and how this interaction is decisive for making sense of the mechanisms of implementation and compliance.

---

[7] See the discussion on 'context' above, n. 1.

[8] This definition is significant, as it demonstrates that Galligan is not concerned with the increased 'liquidity' of social relations and structures debated by sociologists such as Bauman (2000) or Beck (1992). Instead, he continues to work with the solid concepts and structures of early modernity. Also see above, n. 4.

From a methodological standpoint, socio-legal research should, according to Galligan, start with those features of law 'relevant to the actions of citizens and officials... and examine meanings attributed to such features by citizens and officials, and the actions that follow' (*LMS*, p. 36). On top of the list of such features we find legal rules,[9] but there are other normative factors, such as law's contribution to 'social goods,' which might direct actors' actions. This does not mean that socio-legal research should limit the scope of its analysis to the study of individual actions; rather, it needs to examine how various social spheres interact with different aspects of the law while paying special attention to its moral and pragmatic foundations. Galligan does not describe his approach in terms of contextualising the law, yet he discusses the contextual contingency of social and legal rules (*LMS*, p. 53) in some detail and his methodology was devised specifically to contextualise the law without dislodging legal rules from their legal context (or from their 'authority paradigm'). The next section explains how Galligan achieves this goal by allowing the legal context to determine what is socially relevant.

1.3 The Social Context of Rules

Starting our analysis with rules is justified because, according to the theoretical framework sketched above, not only does law consist of rules, but also rules are one of the features of modern legal orders that we can identify as relevant to the actions of citizens and officials. Judges, officials and others who participate in legal processes express themselves in terms of or by reference to rules. More importantly, Galligan argues that rules defined as 'conventions' are constitutive of many organised activities. This does not mean that activities such as chess, tennis or law consist of rules exclusively, but once you decide to play chess or tennis, or get involved in law, whatever your reason for doing so, you commit yourself to the conventions that make up these activities. Rules in general, whether social or legal, are standards which guide action in a specific manner. They are also standards against which action can be assessed and judged. Legal rules especially provide 'a general standard which is applied in particular cases without having to reassess the merits in each case; predictability and stability result' (*LMS*, p. 50). However, they are expressed in language and therefore have an open texture which allows outside factors to affect their interpretation and application. Thus, even clear and precise rules are contingent upon surrounding considerations and require contextualisation (*LMS*, pp. 54–55).

The recognition that all rules need to be interpreted before they make an impact on social life is of little value if it fails to consider the full extent and significance of

[9] The significance of legal rules for the aspects of the law which are relevant to the actions of citizens and officials will be discussed further and developed in Sect. 2.

their contextual contingencies. Social and legal rules often signal that 'a certain kind of deliberative process has to be gone through, a process of which the rule is a vital but not conclusive part' (*LMS*, p. 57). Deliberations are required to determine if a specific rule is applicable in a particular situation and, if it is, what it means; for example, 'it may require consideration of related rules, the weighing of presumptions and the consideration of factors to take into account' (*LMS*, p. 57). In short, rules are the starting point of deliberations and, as such, they neither dictate fully what action should be taken 'nor exhaust the range of actions that may be properly taken' (*LMS*, p. 57).

What happens to legal rules, whether they are adopted, enforced, alternatively modified or marginalised, depends to a great extent on the institutional settings in which they are used. Institutions not only consist of rules, but also of values, standards, dispositions, etc., which are created once people 'come together to carry out some activity' (*LMS*, p. 106). Galligan explains that 'where an activity is itself created by legal rules, as in the case, say, of administrative agencies, informal rules often emerge in order to interpret the legal rules, or even to modify or marginalise them' (*LMS*, p. 108). This point is in line with what Selznick (1949) demonstrated over half a century ago in his study of the Tennessee Valley Authority.[10] To go beyond Selznick's classical wisdom, Galligan turns to Niklas Luhmann to explain that practices which underpin specific social spheres and activities can become self-contained, in other words normatively closed. This means that once social systems import ideas from their environment, they translate them into their own operational logic:

> Law, for instance, can influence what happens within psychiatry, *but only if* [legal activities which take place in the environment of psychiatry] are translated into its [psychiatry's] language, meanings, conventions, and understandings. (*LMS*, p. 110)

Galligan is by implication helping us to make a subtle distinction between two approaches to contextualisation: (1) where law and its legal context are integrated into other social systems, thus broadening their contexts by inserting legal rules and considerations into their institutional make-up and (2) where the legal context is broadened to incorporate socio-cultural or psychological processes—as in the case when it is argued that legal reasoning reproduces 'the maleness of the law' (see Smart 1995), or legal doctrine can operate as a vehicle of racial violence and domination (Tuitt 2004)—which is the form Galligan wishes to avoid, for it dilutes the law's context. The first approach preserves the integrity of law's legal context and authority and assesses how legal rules fare as they are brought to bear on social spheres and applied to social conditions. The second approach involves reconstructing the legal context by redefining legal concepts and operations in extra-legal terms. But why is Galligan so concerned about preserving the distinctiveness of the law? Why should we not expand the legal context to better represent the inter-relatedness of law and other social forces?

---

[10] This type of reasoning is rooted deeply in the sociology of law and can be traced back to Roscoe Pound and Ehrlich (1936).

1.4 Why Do We Need Legal Rules?

If law consists of norms of organisation which precede state law and remain of greater social significance to legal order, as suggested by strands of legal pluralism, why do we need legal rules to coordinate social relations (*LMS*, p. 193)? Only once we take law seriously, when we recognise that 'law is itself a distinct social formation with its own character and features,' which 'in the course of its interaction with other parts of society... neither collapses into them nor becomes part of them' (*LMS*, p. 6), can we start to discover the added value that state law brings to social norms of organisation. This is one of the more compelling arguments for re-examining the relevance of 'strong' versions of legal pluralism, which regard law in terms of norms of social organisation or cultural norms and values,[11] and for questioning social theories which treat the law as a function of culture or social structure, custom or tradition. But what exactly is this unique property of the law to which Galligan is referring? To answer this question, we need to consider how he describes the foundation of the modern legal system, first in terms of the authority of law (that citizens and officials recognise and obey the law) and second as the configuration of a set of social relations 'between citizens as private parties, between citizens and officials nationally (and internationally), among officials nationally (and internationally)' (*LMS*, p. 244). The distinctive feature of law emerges out of the specific configuration of these relationships once its legitimate authority, i.e. an authority which descends from the people and not from above, is recognised by both citizenry and officials:

> The main background factor is a high level of regard on the part of both citizens and officials for the authority of law, a factor that at once separates modern orders from other systems where it is lacking. From this background the special features of social relations [distinctive of law] emerge. In the relationship between citizens, freedom to enter into arrangements and transactions is prized; once entered into, their security and stability is expected. Relations between citizens and officials have several aspects, the first and most important being that officials hold authority in accordance with the *ascending* model, meaning that authority originates in the people rather than descends from on high. Secondly, officials are expected to provide the legal framework for security and stability of private arrangements among citizens. Thirdly, officials are empowered actively to direct society in order to achieve social goods, either by their positive provision or by restricting citizens' activities. Fourthly, officials hold power on trust and are accountable for their actions. Fifthly, the terms of trust include obligations to maintain the legal order.... (*LMS*, p. 244)

This suggests a certain level of affinity between Galligan and Weber's concepts of law, an affinity which is recognised perhaps somewhat indirectly in various parts of *LMS* (see, for example, the notes on *LMS*, pp. 44–45), but which are largely mediated by Hart's legal theory and embedded in the distinction between the internal and external aspects of legal rules (*LMS*, p. 48) and the role of officials—Weber (1978, p. 34) called them 'special staff holding themselves ready to ensure

[11] Also see above, n. 3.

the authority of law by avenging transgressions'—on the one hand, and the exercise of legitimate force, on the other.[12]

Taking law seriously, we can examine how it contributes to 'positive pursuits of social goods' (*LMS*, p. 196) by, on the one hand, facilitating private arrangements, imposing criminal sanctions and regulating private activities (*LMS*, p. 194) and, on the other, by removing discrimination, protecting human rights and creating a global order (*LMS*, p. 196). Galligan mentions in passing that law is an instrument of power and can 'fall into the hands of special interest or be the engine of cruelty and oppression' (*LMS*, p. 193), but he does not explain why it has been implicated historically in perpetuating inequalities by acting as the vehicle of slavery, apartheid, ethnic cleansing and genocide (see Tuitt 2004). He instead focuses on how law is used 'to advance the good of society' (*LMS*, p. 193), and he goes on to discuss the limits of implementation and compliance in terms of officials who take action to bring about compliance (*LMS*, p. 229) and the design of legal regimes (*LMS*, p. 299), although he does not ask why abuses of human rights and racial, ethnic and gender discrimination continue to persist in modern societies, despite the fact that they have been prohibited in national and international law. By not asking such questions, which ultimately concern the connection between law and justice, and treating them as extra-legal and socio-historically contingent, he avoids considering the possibility that the internal operations of a modern legal system can generate forms of racial and gender violence.[13] In his enthusiasm to expose the weakness of legal pluralism and critical strands of law-and-society, which supposedly do not take law seriously in so far as they focus on social processes and institutional practices of law rather than legal rules, Galligan forgets that many of these 'social

---

[12] According to Lacey (2004), Hart's annotations in the margins of a volume of *Max Weber on Law in Economy and Society* reveal that he had carefully read Weber's work. She writes: 'On one occasion John Finnis consulted one of Herbert's volumes of Max Weber and found it heavily annotated… Finnis later asked him on two separate occasions about Weber's influence on his account of 'internal aspects of rules'. Herbert denied that any such influence existed, ascribing the origins of the idea instead to Peter Winch's *The Idea of a Social Science*. Finnis felt unable to respond to his denial by saying that he had seen the counter-evidence in his copy' (Lacey 2004, p. 230). The copy in question is now kept at the Library of the Hebrew University in Jerusalem and, according to Lacey (Lacey 2004, p. 230), it 'suggests strongly that there was a Weberian undertone in the concept of law'.

[13] Let me give an example. According to Tuitt (2004, p. 42), the concept of reasonable man is, in part, founded on what amounts to 'racial knowledge' and embodies 'a white, middle-class and aged judiciary'. It emphasises conformity with standard practice norms and ideals, and by doing so it leaves little space for the recognition of 'difference'. This 'difference' does not refer to the multiplicity of choices or the diversity of practices of competent experts, but to the possibility of challenging 'the core of reasonable man,' which defines reasonableness as what is commonly practised. Hence, the concept of reasonable man, which is central to tort, reflects a particular ideology which is neither gender- nor racially-neutral. The concept of reasonable man is constructed in opposition to the 'Other.' In fact, Tuitt argues that 'racially inscribed practices and ideologies endure in the reasonable man' (2004, p. 47).

goods' remain largely unfulfilled promises.[14] The importance of this last point can be appreciated fully once Galligan's approach and proposed methodology are examined against the backdrop of law-and-society.

2 Taking the Law Seriously

2.1 Two Points of Disagreement

On two points Galligan might find himself at odds not only with Critical Legal Studies and legal pluralism, but also with mainstream law and society scholarship. The first point concerns the tendency of law-and-society to conceptualise law, to borrow a term from Sarat (2000, p. 195), as a 'residual category.' To explain this point we should compare the position taken by Galligan regarding the approach adopted by scholars such as Lawrence Friedman.[15] Part of Friedman's scholarship engages with the minute details of law, demonstrating his insider's knowledge and understanding of legal processes, while other parts of his work reveal his sophisticated sociological and historical grasp of the law and the legal system. Soifer (1988, p. 998) sums up Friedman's understanding of law and society in the following way:

> Repeatedly, in forceful metaphors, Friedman argues that society—the puppeteer—pulls the strings and law responds. Law may be a dialect, but social and economic forces create and develop the language for law's development.

Friedman (1985, p. 148) must be taking the law seriously when he writes that the 'structures of law and government, at least in the short run, exert a powerful influence on the way demands and attitudes become concrete', and yet he regards law as a 'dialect' rather than a 'language.' This has two implications: (1) Friedman emphasises the impact of social development on the formation of law, rather than the reverse, and (2) he sees law as a social phenomenon embedded in society.[16] Schools of legal positivism, on the other hand, have been working towards transforming the dialect of law into an independent language in its own right,

---

[14] In 'After Legal Consciousness', Silbey (2005, p. 323) draws attention to a similar issue. She asks how the law sustains 'its institutional power despite a persistent gap between the law on the books and law in action. Why do people acquiesce to a legal system that, despite its premises of equal treatment, systematically reproduces inequality?' The gap between Galligan and Silbey's approaches could not be wider. Whereas Galligan answers this question in terms of law's ability to deliver social goods, Silbey sees this as a function of law's hegemony. It is also worth noting that Silbey does not start her examination with the law and its officials, but with how ordinary people might contribute to 'the law's systematic effects, as well as to its ineffectiveness' (Silbey 2005, p. 326).

[15] Lawrence Friedman is one of the founders of the Law and Society movement and a scholar with a cautiously optimistic view of law's potential for good.

[16] Friedman elaborated on these insights through a number of impressive studies of American law and legal culture (see, e.g. Friedman 2002).

hence the conceptual separation of law from morality and other extra-legal forces, which we discussed in the previous chapters. This de-contextualising process, which requires dislodging of the dialect from the context of the language out of which it was born, is linked intimately to the rise of modernity and can be traced back to the Enlightenment (this point will be developed further in the final section of this chapter; see Burke 2002). Whereas Galligan sees law as a distinct formation separate from social spheres, and wishes to preserve its autonomy when contextualising it, Friedman insists that law cannot be adequately understood in isolation from the broader and sociologically more foundational social context upon which it is dependent.[17]

This brings us to the second point, which concerns law-and-society scholars' commitment to social justice. In the minds of most people the images of law and justice are intertwined, that is to say most people continue to entertain a concept of law which is closer to natural law than to legal positivism, whereby law is expected to be just and unjust law is seen as a travesty thereof. Modern Western law often refers to justice at the symbolic and operational levels, but its form of reasoning is not based on ensuring substantive justice. This is in line with one of the central tenets of legal positivism, which regards law and justice as separate entities[18]: 'The existence of law is one thing,' wrote John Austin famously, 'its merit and demerit another' (1832/1985, p. 157). Instead, modern law sees itself as the source of legality or legal order, which in turn upholds a form of social order. Within legal philosophy, however, we find many definitions of justice aimed at explaining, but not necessarily justifying, the separation of law from morality. For example, justice is defined as a moral standard, or an ethical form of judgement, which lies beyond the scope and internal operations of positive law (Norrie 2005). This means that to deliver justice, legal reasoning and decision-making must transcend the boundaries of positive law and mere legality to satisfy an ethical form of judgement (for a discussion, see Chap. 4).

As argued in the previous chapter, there is an irresolvable conflict between modern law's modus operandi and ethics, a conflict which ultimately is built in to the project of modernity. According to Douzinas and Gearey (2005, p. 28), modern law uses rational means to calculate and thematise people 'by turning them into legal subjects,' whereas ethics uses 'an indeterminate judgement without criteria'. Justice is then defined as 'the bringing together of the limited calculability and determinacy of law with the infinite openness of ethical alterity' (Douzinas and

[17] This point is disputed by some socio-legal scholars and comparatists. The fact that certain legal institutions and ideas can travel between jurisdictions demonstrates a degree of independence for legal constructs. For a discussion, see Nelken (2009). However, this is not an issue with which Galligan engages.

[18] Constable (2005) points out that positive sociology and socio-legal positivism are also implicated in spreading the image of modern law in terms of the separation of law and justice. She argues that 'law has not always been empirical, or, broadly speaking, sociological. Nor need law always be so' (Constable 2005, p. 10).

Gearey 2005, p. 28).[19] Seen from a different angle, justice in its absolute form deals with universal moral conceptions and standards. To do justice, however, law needs to recognise and respond to the singularity and specificity of the socio-cultural contexts that form various groups' and individuals' actions and experiences. There is therefore tension between the universal claims of justice, which overlook the contextual significance of actions and experiences, and its particularistic claims, which require the contextualisation of those actions and experiences. Positive law tries to contain this tension by conceptually divorcing law from morality and by enhancing the autonomy of the legal system with social systems such as polity and economy. Part of this process necessitates developing a method for examining actions and relationships in isolation from their socio-cultural settings and circumstances (cf. Norrie 2005, p. 53). Mainstream jurisprudence sidesteps the tension by emphasising the universal aspect of justice at the expense of its context-specific conditions. Many socio-legal researchers, however, stress its particularistic dimension, which requires re-placing actions and experiences in their socio-cultural and historical contexts. This is in line with the second approach to contextualisation, which was described in the introduction. Essentially, it reverses (or deconstructs) the legal method of abstracting agency from the socio-cultural and historical contexts of the agent's action (cf. Norrie 2005, p. 53) and brings these contexts back into the juridical gaze.

The Law and Society movement, especially as it has developed in North America, addresses issues of justice often by focusing on 'marginalised groups, peripheral institutions, deviant behaviour' (Abel 1987, p. 827), whose perspectives on and experiences of justice are often overlooked in the legal system and theoretical discourses of law professors on the relationship between law and justice. The movement's commitment to social justice has led many of its scholars to question law's hegemony and its internally generated values such as belief in the rule of law and the objectivity of legal reasoning. It has also led them to conduct bottom-up studies of law in society, where the starting point for research is the experience and social realities of those who are at the receiving end of law and legal regulation, rather than the normative assumptions of policymakers or the attitudes and behaviour of the officials of the law (cf. Galanter 1974). What might appear to some lawyers as losing sight of the specificity of the law is but the attempt of mainstream law-and-society researchers to generate a new understanding thereof, which better reflects its role in society and can help to produce more effective modes of social reform.

---

[19] Modern law does generate a sense of justice internally, but this is either in terms of formal equality before the law, due process and the claims of objectivity in decision-making (cf. Douzinas and Gearey 2005, p. 135) or by making claims to correctness (Alexy 2000). Moreover, as Douzinas and Gearey argue (2005, p. 136), 'the justice of law is negative', i.e. a form of justice which is observed only when it is breached, rather than one which is urged and encouraged as a positive guideline for action. This internally produced sense of justice is on positive law's terms—it is couched in, and constrained by, the formalism and normative closeness of the legal system, and thus it is limited in form and content. See also Luhmann's (2004, p. 213) description of justice as 'a programme of (all) programmes'.

2.2 Are Legal Rules the Focal Point of Legal Experience?

According to the methodology proposed by Galligan, socio-legal research should start with analysing the features of law *relevant* to the actions of citizens and law's officials, before considering the role of the social sphere where laws are interpreted, implemented and enforced. Galligan does not specify what makes a feature of the law 'relevant' to various patterns of social action, but the emphasis he places on legal rules, and the space he devotes to expounding the connection between them and other aspects of social and legal action, suggests that the rules of law are the cornerstone of his methodology and the standpoint from which the issue of 'relevancy' is determined. Galligan implies this connection in one place by stating that 'how citizens and officials regard legal rules, the meaning they attribute to them, and how they then deal with them, are vital pieces of the legal landscape' (*LMS*, p. 36). Elsewhere he adds:

> We should agree with Hart's claim that to miss the way legal rules feature in the actions of officials – and we should add citizens – would be to miss an important aspect of social behaviour. In taking this approach, we implicitly accept the sense in which legal rules are part of the social context.... (*LMS*, p. 79)

Law is more than legal rules, Galligan tells us repeatedly, but in his scheme of things legal rules are nevertheless 'the focal point of legal experience' (*LMS*, p. 74). It is noteworthy that following Galligan's proposed methodology, socio-legal research will consist of top-down studies. It will:

1) Depart from an aspect of law which citizens or officials have identified as relevant to their actions—note that treating citizens and officials together in this way emphasises the similarities rather than the differences between their experience of law;
2) Use this aspect to identify relevant legal rules—note that this step links the legal experiences of both officials and citizens to legal rules;
3) Address issues of enforcement, implementation and compliance by placing legal rules in the context of social spheres where they are employed and interpreted—note that this step potentially takes us out of the legal context. As I will argue, Galligan minimises the risk of losing touch with the legal context by defining the social sphere narrowly in terms of rules and conventions, i.e. categories which are central to his concept of law; and
4) End by returning to the law to confront the contextualised conclusions of our study, i.e. our observations of how legal rules fare when interacting with social spheres, with the intentions of the law or the aims of legislature.

This could be a useful method for conducting policy analysis and studying the 'gap'—the discrepancy between 'law in the books' and 'law in action' (Pound 1917)—but it does not capture the variety of methodological approaches and theoretical concerns of law-and-society. Moreover, it does not distinguish clearly between the insider perspectives and experiences of the functionaries of the law, which are often embedded in its internal culture (or in the narrow legal context of the judicial system) and the outsider viewpoints and experiences of ordinary citizens, which are often embedded in the broader context of society (see Banakar 2003). Therefore, it neither elaborates on the interaction between officials' legal culture and the general legal culture of citizens (cf. Friedman 1987) nor recognises that this cultural interaction is not necessarily reducible to specific legal rules. Moreover, starting with legal rules, as Galligan's method does, we are more likely to take the assumptions and concerns of the legal system—which are formed either at the macro level of legislation and policymaking or at the level of legal institutions, i.e. at the level of courts and other legal authorities—as our point of departure. Starting with the law and finishing with the law also increases the likelihood that our analysis stays within the 'authority paradigm', which prioritises the 'practical insider attitudes' (Twining 2000, p. 129) and assumptions of the law and its officials. It also means that our contextualisation of legal rules will be carried out in terms of what makes sense to law's officials and other insiders. Subsequently, how law is formed at the micro level through social interaction, and how citizens recognise, employ and experience law and legal processes, is overlooked.

To capture the formation of law at the micro level we need to conduct our study bottom-up, starting by investigating what aspects of law and legal institutions are taken seriously and employed or avoided by ordinary people to organise their lives. We also need to recognise that sometimes these aspects are not employed or conceived in terms of legal rules. The Swedish scholar Per Stjernquist, to give an example, also emphasises the role of legal rules (understood in terms of state law) and defines the sociology of law as 'the study of the interaction between legal rules and measures, on the one hand, and political, economic and social processes on the other' (Stjernquist and Widerberg 1985, p. 7—*my translation*). He also admits that citizens occasionally take legal rules into consideration when planning their everyday cooperation and transactions. Nevertheless, he maintains that social cooperation, rather than legal rules, is the keystone in social and legal order. Expressed differently, cooperative undertakings are not generated by law but by citizens, and legal measures at best only support and facilitate cooperation (Stjernquist 2000, p. 5). As regards citizens, he sharply distinguishes them from law's functionaries, because their interests are distinct from those of policymakers, legislature and law's officials.

According to Stjernquist, social or customary norms growing out of the activities of communities and the associations of people are central to law-and-society research. These customary norms, which remind us of Galligan's social sphere, define patterns of behaviour and set the bases for the future interactions and organised activities of individuals and social groups. Legal rules are often introduced intentionally to protect and assist these patterns of action, which emanate from informal and often spontaneous attempts to organise social life. However, unlike Galligan, he does not take the analysis of legal rules as the basis for his methodology. Even when legal rules loom large, as in his study of the Swedish Sale of Goods Act 1905, Stjernquist begins by interviewing elderly smallholders in the woodlands of southern Sweden to discover how they understand and in what terms they express legal issues at the turn of the century (Stjernquist 1950, 2000). He conducts these interviews without a preconception of how the smallholders' legal concerns and understanding of legal issues should (or should not) be related to the rules of the legal system.[20] Thus, his starting point is the way in which ordinary men and women perceive, conceptualise and use law, how they participate in legal processes, how they interact with officials and thus partake in producing and reproducing legal institutions. This approach ensures that he is working with concepts and ideas which emerge out of the everyday social reality of those people he studies, and that he maintains a critical distance from the normative assumptions and claims of the law and its officials. The recognition that law should be studied as an integral part of the culture, conventions and socio-historical conditions of ordinary people takes Stjernquist beyond the second approach to contextualisation, to where law in its entirety becomes the object of contextualisation. This is in line with what scholars such as Ehrlich (1936) accomplished at the turn of the previous century, what legal pluralism as a school has tried to achieve and what many comparative lawyers argue for today (cf. Menski 2007).

2.3 *The Plurality of Experiences*

More recent theorising within the sociology of law shows greater awareness of the diversity of forms, expressions and experiences in contemporary (late modern) societies. Cotterrell (2006), for example, uses the concept of 'community' as a basis for explaining the plural and fragmented nature of law.[21] The concept of community helps us to go beyond the idea of association or cooperation, which was used by socio-legal scholars of Stjernquist's generation, and allows us instead to consider the role of law among groups that are no longer necessarily united by a single society, culture or nation state. While Stjernquist's cooperation was based primarily on the structural and functional dependency of individuals and groups, community can potentially highlight the social psychological relationships which produce the normative force of late modern collectivities. For Cotterrell, community represents a:

---

[20] This study demonstrated that the conception of legal issues relevant to the lives of smallholders, especially pertaining to the sale of goods, diverged significantly from Swedish law (Stjernquist 2000, p. 19). Social customary norms regulating the sale of goods, which incidentally varied from region to region, existed prior to legal rules. Thus, when the Swedish Sale of Goods Act 1905, which emphasised the requirement of formal agreement between contracting parties, was introduced, it had to recognise as valid law current commercial customs, when no formal agreement existed. As a result, legal rules were merely adapted to, rather than superimposed upon, their corresponding social norms. According to Stjernquist (1950, 2000), social norms and legal rules each formed consistent, albeit separate, systems of rules, existing side by side over a long period of time. This study also explains why some people may have an understanding of legal issues which are not in terms of or related to the valid rules of the legal system.

[21] The legal concept of community, as used by Cotterrell, is related closely to, though not the same as, Ferdinand Tönnies' *gemeinschaft* (1955).

> [. . .] vital kind of social relations that take the form of networks or groups not necessarily bounded by a "society"; fluctuating, forming and reforming, crossing national or political boundaries, having overlapping memberships, conflicting, cooperating or merely coexisting. (Cotterrell 2006, p. 7)

These relationships are, in turn, based on intersubjectivity or, to use Cotterrell's (2006, p. 77) words, they consist of 'networks of shared understanding that characterize contemporary social life'. Community consists partly of networks of interactions and relationships 'imbued with a high degree of trust, which, in general, can only be securely built over time, with the accumulated experiences of past interactions' (Cotterrell 2006, p. 73). Law is, consequently, a regulatory aspect of the social makeup of community, an aspect of the interpersonal mutual trust which is but the basis for a stable community life. Cotterrell stops short of explaining what the unit of analysis for socio-legal research must be, but on the basis of his overall presentation it can be concluded that legal rules or doctrine are not the basic elements of community law; instead, its building blocks consist of the network of shared understanding, ultimately of interaction, communicative action or practices which aim at creating reciprocal, binding relationships of trust.

Using a legal concept of community, like Cotterrell, or using the notion of association or cooperation, like Stjernquist, does not imply a denial of the importance of state law in modern society, and nor does it suggest an invitation to take law lightly. Rather, it offers a social theoretical framework for conceptualising and exploring the distinctive character of law in pluralistic communities that constitute late modern societies. More importantly, it ensures that our view of the law is not limited to or shaped primarily by an internal viewpoint that reflects the concerns, attitudes, perceptions and expectations of its officials. Ordinary people interact with the law and its institutions in many different ways and in many different social settings, and thus they experience law in many different lights.

A recent comparative study of legal consciousness, based on data collected through focus groups in England, Poland, Bulgaria and Norway, illustrates that the majority of people in England, Poland and Bulgaria (but not in Norway) perceive law in terms other than written texts and legal regulation (Kurkchiyan 2011; see also Kubal 2010, p. 217). According to this study, as many as 71 % of the English cohorts understand the law in terms of order, discipline, law-making or other factors not related to rules, as against 29 % who regard law as texts and regulations (which we can relate to legal rules).[22] This study draws our attention to the plurality of legal experiences. Ordinary people define and experience law in many different ways, depending on a range of factors such as their social positioning (some people are more exposed to the law and its institutions than others), the legal culture to which they belong (i.e. the external legal culture which reflects the general attitude of groups of people to law and differs from society to society) and

[22] A larger percentage of the Bulgarians (41 %) and the Poles (43 %) who partook in this study linked law with legal texts and rules than the English (29 %). I should hasten to add that 83 % of Norwegians perceived law in terms of written laws and regulations (Kurkchiyan 2011). The Norwegian data was not, however, analysed in this study.

the legal tradition and history on which their legal system is based. For example, some of the differences between the attitude of the English and the Poles might have been caused by differences between English common law and Polish civil law traditions, on the one hand, and their recent political history, on the other.

Even if I agreed with Galligan that socio-legal research should start with the study of those features of the law which are relevant to the actions of citizens or law's officials, I would still have to argue that these features do not necessarily need to be expressed in terms of or identified in connection with legal rules. Studies of law in society can also begin by exploring the way ordinary people interact with law's officials, use (or avoid) legal institutions, employ legal processes to further their projects, are affected by the legal order and view and experience law and legal regulations. The *experience* of the law and legal processes does not necessarily have to be in terms of specific rules of the legal system.

3 Having One's Cake and Eating It

Modern Western law strives to enhance its autonomy and maximise its efficacy as a social system by freeing its institutions and practices from the societal context out of which they have emerged historically and upon which they continue to rely socio-culturally. Its de-contextualising efforts—its attempts to abstract social actions and relationships from their social, cultural and historical contexts—were originally necessitated by the growing functional differentiation of modern society,[23] and they can be traced back to the Enlightenment's intellectual and institutional separation of humans from nature, individuals from groups, facts from values, reason from belief, etc. (Barton 1998; cf. Burke 2002; cf. Norrie 2005).[24] At the same time, the autonomy of law cannot be achieved or maintained without preserving its modus operandi, the method of abstracting actions from their context, which uses formal concepts and rational bureaucratic procedures to constrain its view of social events, relationships and processes and delimits its interface with its social environment. This means that any attempt to contextualise law, whether through the application of social scientific or other methods, cannot help but to reverse, partially as it might be, modern law's de-contextualising mechanisms (what we called "disembeddedness"). This reversal entails broadening the interface between the legal system and society, which in turn opens up avenues of critical inquiry not desirable within the normative framework of Galligan's project. For example, it can lead to the uncovering of modern law's internal contradictions, highlighting its unfulfilled promises (Norrie 2005) and, ultimately, questioning its

[23] Social theorists have described this historical process in different terms. Habermas (1984), for example, explains it in terms of the separation of system from lifeworld, while Tönnies (1955) describes it as the separation of *Gessellschaft* from *Gemeinschaft*.

[24] This means that de-contextualisation itself has a socio-historical context (cf. Burke 2002).

claim to autonomy, objectivity and rational authority. The question is not if, but rather to what extent, any particular effort to contextualise law will deconstruct its specific form of authority and reasoning.

Contextualising, or "re-embedding", the law while safeguarding its modus operandi (which is one of the main sources of positive law's distinctiveness as a social formation) amounts to trying to have one's cake and eat it. Galligan writes at length about enforcement, implementation and compliance, which compels him to contextualise the law by using his notion of the social sphere to examine the institutional and organisational conditions which create the environment of the legal system. His social spheres, however, are carved out of the broader socio-cultural setting of the legal system in such a way as to emphasise rules and conventions, i.e. the 'solid' structural aspects of the social context, and play down the aspects of human action and interaction which do not fit into the rationalistic model of social organisation. Admittedly, this allows him to minimise the conceptual contamination of law's own narrow legal context and to avoid questioning the self-images of the law. Nonetheless, by confronting the law with social spheres, he sanctions chipping away at the edges of law's conceptual formal rationality. In addition, Galligan pays another price—in my view a much higher one—for his attempt to safeguard the specificity of the law's context: he loses sight of the fluidity of law and fails to account for the growing 'liquidity' of contemporary society (Bauman 2000; for discussion, see Banakar 2010).

There is a range of interrelated reasons why socio-legal scholars contextualise law. Some resort to contextualisation to capture its fluidity and to show how it permeates social structures, processes and experiences. Others use it to demonstrate that despite the efforts of the modern legal system to enhance its autonomy, parts of the law always remain embedded in the broader societal and historical processes from which it tries to separate itself. Linked closely to this second group we find those who use contextualisation to bring into light law's taken-for-granted assumptions and values. Others use it to explain why its actual effects are often different from the intentions of the legislature, yet others contextualise it to demystify the methods through which it upholds its authority and hegemony. This list can be made much longer, but irrespective of our reasons for re-placing the law in a broader socio-cultural or historical perspective, contextualisation will involve dislodging the law out of its narrow legal context. Since what is specific about the law is integral to its legalistic context, contextualisation will necessarily amount to losing sight of and/or deconstructing certain aspects of the law. In short, at the heart of contextualisation of positive law lie the desire and the need to deconstruct law's autonomy and specificity. Some of the insights generated through contextualisation will not be of any use to practicing lawyers and will not fit into the self-understandings and self-descriptions of the law (cf. Nelken 2009, p. xvii). Not only might these insights be primarily sociological and aimed at expanding and deepening our understanding of social developments, but they might also be concerned with devising alternative concepts of law. This takes us back to the very beginning of the sociology of law, to the theories of 'living law' (Ehrlich 1936), 'intuitive law' (Petrazycki 1955; Podgorecki 1991) and 'social law' (Gurvitch 1947), which challenged the claims of legal positivism as well as those of natural law, and employed social sciences to transform the law and legal regulation. For these scholars, law-and-society could not be restricted to how institutions absorbed and deployed the law in accordance with their internal mechanisms, rules and conventions. Socio-legal research, instead, involved re-placing either parts of the law, or the law in its entirety, into its socio-cultural and historical contexts. Socio-legal research, understood as such, is part of the political struggle for determining the content, form and scope of law.

References

Abel, R. (1987). Redirecting social studies of law. *Law and Society Review, 14*, 805–829.
Alexy, R. (2000). On the thesis of a necessary connection between law and morality: Bulygin's critique. *Ratio Juris, 13*, 138–147.
Austin, J. (1985). *The province of jurisprudence determined.* Cambridge: Cambridge University Press (original publication 1832).
Banakar, R. (2003). *Merging law and sociology: Beyond the dichotomies of socio-legal research.* Berlin/Wisconsin: Galda and Wilch.
Banakar, R. (Ed.). (2010). *Rights in context: Law and justice in late modern society*. Aldershot: Ashgate.
Barton, T. D. (1998). Troublesome connections: The law and post-enlightenment culture. *Emory Law Journal, 47*, 163–236.
Bauman, Z. (2000). *Liquid modernity*. Cambridge: Polity.
Beck, U. (1992). *Risk society: Towards a new modernity.* London: Sage.
Bradney, A. (1998). Law as a parasitic discipline. *Journal of Law and Society, 25*, 71–84.
Bradney, A. (2003). *Conversations, choices and changes: The liberal law school in the twenty-first century*. Oxford: Hart.
Burke, P. (2002). Context in context. *Common Knowledge, 8*, 152–177.
Chynoweth, P. (2008). Legal research. In A. Knight & L. Ruddock (Eds.), *Advanced research methods in the built environment* (pp. 28–38). Oxford: Wiley/Blackwell.
Constable, M. (2005). *The limits and possibilities of the modern law.* Princeton: Princeton University Press.
Cotterrell, R. (1995). *Law's community: Legal theory in sociological perspective*. Oxford: Clarendon.
Cotterrell, R. (2003). *The politics of jurisprudence* (2nd ed.). Oxford: Oxford University Press.
Cotterrell, R. (2006). *Law, culture and society: Legal ideas in the mirror of social theory.* Aldershot: Ashgate.
Cownie, F. (2004). *Legal academics: Culture and identities*. Oxford: Hart.
Douzinas, C., & Gearey, A. (2005). *Critical jurisprudence: The political philosophy of justice.* Oxford: Hart.
Ehrlich, E. (1936). *Fundamental principles of the sociology of law.* Cambridge: Harvard University Press (original publication 1913).
Friedman, L. M. (1985). *Total justice*. New York: Russell Sage.
Friedman, L. M. (1987). *The legal system*. New York: Russell Sage.
Friedman, L. M. (2002). *American law in the 20th century*. New Haven: Yale University Press.
Galanter, M. (1974). Why the "Haves" come out ahead: Speculations on the limits of legal change. *Law and Society Review, 9*, 95–160.
Galligan, D. J. (2006). *Law in modern society*. Oxford: Oxford University Press.

Griffiths, J. (1986). What is legal pluralism. *Journal of Legal Pluralism and Unofficial Law, 24*, 1–55.
Gurvitch, G. (1947). *Sociology of law*. London: Routledge & Kegan.
Habermas, J. (1984). *The theory of communicative action, volume 1, reason and the rationalization of society*. Boston, MA: Beacon.
Hart, H. L. A. (1961). *The concept of law*. Oxford: Clarendon.
Kubal, A. M. (2010). *Socio-legal integration of Polish post-2004 EU enlargement migrants into the United Kingdom* (Doctoral thesis). Faculty of Law, Oxford University, Oxford.
Kurkchiyan, M. (2011). Perceptions of law and national order: A cross-national comparison of collective legal consciousness. *Wisconsin International Law Journal, 29*(2), 366–392.
Lacey, N. (2004). *A life of H.L.A. Hart: The nightmare and the Noble dream*. Oxford: Oxford University Press.
Luhmann, N. (2004). *Law as a social system*. Oxford: Oxford University Press.
McCormick, N. (1981). *H.L.A. Hart*. London: Edward Arnold.
Menski, W. (2007). Beyond Europe. In E. Örücü & D. Nelken (Eds.), *Comparative law: A handbook* (pp. 189–216). Oxford: Hart.
Nelken, D. (2009). *Beyond law in context* (pp. 255–285). Aldershot: Ashgate.
Norrie, A. (2005). *Law and the beautiful soul*. London: GlassHouse.
Petrazycki, L. (1955). *Law and morality*. Cambridge, MA: Harvard University Press.
Podgorecki, A. (1991). *A sociological theory of law*. Milano: Dott: A. Giuffre Editore.
Pound, R. (1917). The limits of effective legal action. *International Journal of Ethics, 27*(2), 150–167.
Raz, J. (1980). *The concept of a legal system: An introduction to the theory of legal system*. Oxford: Oxford University Press.
Samuel, G. (2009). Interdisciplinarity and the authority paradigm: Should law be taken seriously by scientists and social scientists? *Journal of Law and Society, 36*(4), 431–459.
Sarat, A. (2000). Pain, powerlessness, and the promises of interdisciplinary legal scholarship: An idiosyncratic, autobiographical account of conflict and continuity. *Windsor Year Book of Access to Justice, 18*(1), 187–212.
Selznick, P. (1949). *TVA and the Grass Roots: A study in the sociology of formal organization*. Berkeley: University of California Press.
Silbey, S. (2005). After legal consciousness. *Annual Review of Law and Social Science, 1*, 323–368.
Smart, C. (1995). *Feminism and the power of law*. London: Routledge.
Soifer, A. (1988). Beyond mirrors: Lawrence Friedman's moving pictures. *Law and Society Review, 22*(5), 995–1016.
Stjernquist, P. (1950). *Föreningsfirmans funktion*. Lund: Gleerups.
Stjernquist, P. (2000). *Organised cooperation facing law: An anthropological study*. Stockholm: Almqvist & Wiksell.
Stjernquist, P., & Widerberg, K. (1985). *Rätten i Samhällsbyggandet*. Stockholm: Nordstedt.
Tamanaha, B. Z. (1993). The folly of the "Social Scientific" concept of legal pluralism. *Journal of Law and Society, 20*(2), 192–217.
Tönnies, F. (1955). *Community and association (Gemeinschaft und Gesellschaft)*. London: Routledge and Kegan Paul.
Tuitt, P. (2004). *Race, law, resistance*. London: GlassHouse.
Twining, W. (1999). *Law in context*. Oxford: Clarendon.
Twining, W. (2000). *Globalisation and legal theory*. London: Butterworths.
Vick, D. W. (2004). Interdisciplinarity and the discipline of law. *Journal of Law and Society, 31*(2), 163–193.
Weber, M. (1978). In G. Roth & C. Wittich (Eds.), *Economy and society: An outline of interpretive sociology*. Berkeley: University of California Press.
Wheeler, S., & Thomas, P. (2002). Socio-legal studies. In D. J. Hayton (Ed.), *Law's future(s): British legal developments in the 21st century* (pp. 267–279). Oxford: Hart.

Chapter 6
A Note on Franz Kafka's Concept of Law

Much of Kafka's greatness as an analyst of modern life—of the fusion of bureaucracy and technology as its governing principle—is owed to his office job.
(Corngold et al. 2009, p. 9)

Abstract The focus of this chapter is on Franz Kafka's office writings and the images of law and legality in his fiction. Notwithstanding the fact that Kafka lived during early modernity (1883–1924), his writings highlight the role of uncertainty, insecurity, transience and the unknowable. His contemporaries included Hans Kelsen, who during the same period was elaborating the foundations for his Reine Rechtslehre, which is amongst the rationalistic modern theories of the law (Kelsen, *Reine Rechtslehre: Einleitung in die Rechtswissenschaftliche Prohlematik*. Leipzig, Vienna: Franz Deuticke, 1934). By contrast, Kafka's concept of law was sensitised to those aspects of the modern project, which were marginalised in the discourse of modernity. In Kafka's descriptions of events, efforts to employ rational means to control human conduct are continually undermined by a sense of uncertainty, which is lurking just under the surface of everyday life threatening to disrupt the order of things. Expressed differently, rational organization is constantly subverted by the unpredictability of human conduct. The sense of uncertainty and unpredictability is caused by the resilience of the lifeworld in the face of rational attempts at regulating the everyday life .

This chapter is based on 'In Search of Heimat: A Note on Franz Kafka's Concept of Law'. In: (2010) *Law and Literature* 23(3): 463–490.

R. Banakar, *Normativity in Legal Sociology*, DOI 10.1007/978-3-319-09650-6_6

When reading Franz Kafka's novels, short stories and parables, notes Koelb (1989, p. 1), one cannot help wondering: 'Whatever made him think of that?' The answer to this question involves, according to Koelb (1989, p. 1), 'an investigation into rhetoric,' i.e. into Kafka's attempt to 'understand a particular discourse as fully as possible as if one were certain that all its elements were saturated with meaning'. This chapter examines Kafka's 'rhetoric' while paying special attention to his day job as an insurance lawyer and a bureaucrat and to his legal and clerical writings, which show he borrowed material from the cases he was involved in to develop some of the characters, settings and images in his fiction. Joseph K. and his inexplicable experience of the law in *The Trial*, for example, were born out of an actual legal case, while Gregor Samsa and his bizarre transformation into an insect in *Metamorphosis* were inspired by Kafka's daily work experience. Would Kafka have thought the way he did, constantly striving 'to interpret discourse that looks like one thing but might well be another' (Koelb 1989, p. 65)—often its opposite—had he not been leading a dual life,[1] practicing law during the day and producing fiction during the night? His day job as an insurance lawyer and his nighttime preoccupation as a fiction writer both involved creative writing, one belonging to the world of modern work, the other to art (cf. Gross 2003). In Kafka's fiction these two separate worlds merge to uncover the inner contradictions of modernity. In *The Trial*, the priest whom Joseph K. encounters in the cathedral tells him that 'The right perception of any matter and a misunderstanding of the same matter do not wholly exclude each other' (Kafka 1978, pp. 238–239). I will argue in the following pages that conflating the 'right' perception of a matter and the reverse of its everyday logic, the hallmark of Kafka's 'rhetoric', needs to be explored in the discursive context of his work as a lawyer. The legal aspects of Kafka's work, admittedly, do not explain his 'linguistic imagination' (Corngold 1970, p. 106, cited in Koelb 1989, p. 1) but instead throw new light on the link between law and his images of legality. They also challenge some of the previous readings of Kafka's work which emphasise the theological, psychoanalytical, ontological, historical, metaphysical and existential interpretations of his fiction at the expense of exploring the role of law in his narratives (cf. Sontag 1966; Litowitz 2002, pp. 113–114). It might indeed be true, as noted by Camus (2004, p. 599), that Kafka's novel *The Trial* is 'the diagnosis,' while '*The Castle* imagines a treatment.' This should not, however, distract us from also considering the significance of Kafka's choice of criminal proceedings when making 'the diagnosis', or private law when searching for a 'treatment'.[2] Is his choice of law arbitrary, or does it resonate a concern with

[1] Kafka probes the duality of his identity and daily experiences in several places. In 'My Neighbour,' for example, he reveals the tension between his two types of work/writing and in 'A Crossbreed' he examines his split personality: half kitten, half lamb. See Kafka (1979).

[2] Josef K., the protagonist in *The Trial*, is subjected to criminal proceedings according to the Austro-Hungarian law of the time, while the Land Surveyor K., in *The Castle*, is engaged in what amounts to a civil law dispute with the castle authorities, who have allegedly summoned him.

the rise of modernity which engaged legal and social theorists of the time? More importantly, does Kafka offer an insight into the complexity of the relationship between modern law, justice and bureaucratic forms of organisation, notions left unexplored by his contemporaries and by later legal scholars?

This chapter is divided into seven sections. It starts by briefly introducing the notion of *Heimat* before moving on to sketch the contours of the existing debate on Kafka's literary work. Next, it argues that his office writings, training and daily work as a lawyer, as well as his career as a bureaucrat, have significance for his fiction. It then explores the ways in which Kafka's legal work shaped his ideas about law and legality, focusing on his unfinished novel *The Castle*. Like Josef K. in *The Trial*, the protagonist in *The Castle*, known only as 'K.', is subjected to an ethical form of judgement that lies beyond the scope and jurisdiction of positive law. This ethical form of judgement, which is regarded ordinarily as the sphere of justice, delivers in Kafka's world what appears as an incomprehensible form of injustice. Shifting the focus of the discussion to *The Trial*, the chapter shows that Kafka's law is not only dissimilar to positive law, but also defies categorisation as religious law, natural law or customary law. The chapter ends by making three interrelated points. First, Kafka's notion of law takes us beyond a Weberian concern with the rise of bureaucracy and the rationalisation of modern society. Second, his office writings illustrate that the images of law portrayed in his fiction, which are regarded as his 'ambivalence about the law' (Litowitz 2002, p. 106), are based on his experience of working with it as an insider and an outsider at the same time, which allowed him to observe contradictions intrinsic to the internal and external operations thereof. Third, Kafka describes the role of 'non-rational'[3] elements in the formation of modern law and legal institutions. This, however, needs to be studied in the context of his overall writing as a search for *Heimat,* for the peaceful and harmonious hometown or community to which one can belong and with which one can identify oneself.

1 Heimat

German discourse on *Heimat* at the turn of the nineteenth century had a romantic undertone lamenting the loss of the idyllic 'organic' community brought about by the rise of modern 'mechanical society'.[4] Ferdinand Tönnies (1855–1936) described modernity as the passage from a form of society dominated by *Gemeinschaft* (community) to one dominated by *Gesellschaft* (association), i.e. from a

[3] I am using the notion of 'non-rational' intentionally as a type of rationality which, although it does not comply with the instrumental rationality of Weber, is not necessarily irrational. It might, for example, refer to 'communicative rationality' as developed by Habermas. Thus, in the following, 'non-rational' does not necessarily imply irrational.

[4] For a discussion on the relationship between *Heimat* and Kafka's novel *The castle* see Boa (2003), pp. 61–79.

social order based on spontaneous and tacit common understandings, close emotional ties, sameness and a strong sense of belonging to a place, to one based on impersonal bonds intrinsic to modern, industrialised urban life (Tönnies 1955). It is also a transformation from a form of social organisation based on interpersonal trust and unofficial sanctions to one based on formal contract and official sanctions. The modern individual, who in the course of this passage remains dependent on both the community and the association, inevitably becomes caught up in the tension between the forces of *Gemeinschaft* and *Gesellschaft*. The consequences of this tension for the individual are depicted in many of Kafka's works. The dilemma of the modern individual in respect to *Gemeinschaft* is presented against the rural backdrop of *The Castle*, where K. is neither welcomed nor needed by the village community to which he hopes to belong, and the alienating effects of the impersonal relations of *Gesellschaft* are portrayed in the urban setting of *The Trial*, where Joseph K. is virtually an exile in his hometown.

In his short piece 'Homecoming' (also translated as 'I Have Returned'), Kafka sheds *Heimat's* artificially romantic and idyllic attributes by conflating the everyday sense of community and belonging with its reverse:

> I have returned, I have crossed the front yard and I look round me. It is my father's old farmstead... Do you feel you belong, do you feel at home? Yes, it is my father's house, but each object stands cold beside the next, as if each was preoccupied with its own affairs, which I have partly forgotten, partly never known... And I dare not knock at the kitchen door, I only listen from a distance... And since I am listening from a distance, I can catch nothing; all I hear, or perhaps just imagine I hear, is the faint chiming of a clock that floats across to me from my childhood. (Kafka 1979)

Like *Gemeinschaft*, *Heimat* is a place of taken-for-granted relations, assumptions, worldviews, intuitively shared values and sentiments—it is not a place for conscious critical reflection, and only outsiders possess the external vantage point required for viewing it critically from a distance. In Kafka's world, *Heimat* is described from without, from the standpoint of the outsider, as an estranged space and an alienating experience, and yet the search for its harmony, security and warmth continues in his fiction. This continued search for *Heimat* may imply the impossibility of redemption, but it may also denote the inescapable dilemma of modern man who, on the one hand, values his personal autonomy and, on the other, needs the security, support and the sense of belonging that only *Gemeinschaft* can provide. Retaining one's autonomy as an individual is in conflict with the need to enjoy the 'warm circle' of the community, for membership of the community may only be gained at the expense of compromising one's autonomy (cf. Bauman 2001). The search for *Heimat* continues also because *Gemeinschaft*, or the community, is the paradise lost of modernity, a place not available to us but 'which we would dearly wish to inhabit and which we hope to repossess' (Bauman 2001, p. 3).

2 Chewing Sawdust

Many attempts have been made to examine Kafka's legal background and the role of law in his fiction (cf. Umphrey and Sarat 2007; Litowitz 2002; Ziolkowski 2003; Dargo 2006–2007; Glen 2007; Heidsieck 1994; Minkkinen 1994; Robinson 1982). These attempts remain, nevertheless, relatively few in number compared to the vast collection of literature devoted to the study of his life and works, and they are somewhat marginal to legal scholarship (for biographies of Kafka see Brod 1995; Wagenbach 2003; Murray 2004; Robertson 2004). Mainstream studies of Kafka's works normally present his fiction as an engagement with absurdity, a critique of bureaucracy or a search for redemption, failing to account for the images of law and legality which constitute an important part of 'the horizon of meaning' in his fiction.[5] Many of his descriptions of the legal proceedings in *The Trial*[6]—metaphysical, absurd, bewildering and 'Kafkaesque' as they might appear—are, in fact, based on accurate and informed descriptions of German and Austrian criminal proceedings of the time (Corngold et al. 2009, p. 230; also see Robinson 1982). The significance of law in his fiction is also neglected within legal scholarship, for as Posner (1986) pointed out in some of his earlier writings on law and literature, most lawyers do not consider writings about law in the form of fiction of any relevance to the understanding or the practice thereof.[7] Regardless of the concerns of mainstream studies of Kafka with redemption and absurdity, and what lawyers such as Judge Posner might think relevant to law and legal practice, the fact remains that Kafka was an insurance lawyer who, besides being involved in litigation, was also 'keenly aware of the legal debates of his day' (Ziolkowski 2003, p. 224).

After receiving his law degree in 1906, Kafka worked for 2 years at the Italian insurance firm Assicurazioni Generali, before joining the Prague-based Workmen's Accident Insurance Institute for the Kingdom of Bohemia, a quasi-governmental agency that managed the local administration of the Austrian Empire's compensation system. Although because of his Jewish background he was promoted slowly, he eventually did rise 'to a high-ranking position (*Obersekretär*)' and became 'a

[5] No author can claim monopoly over the interpretation of his/her text, and they cannot be fully conscious of all possible connections between thoughts and images which his/her text might offer. Admittedly, any text has its 'horizon of meaning,' yet the readers of the text may legitimately contextualise it within their own universe of meaning and personal experiences in order to make sense of it. In fact, readers have no alternative but to interpret the text against their pre-understanding of the world. The process of interpretation, to borrow from Gadamer (2006), is the reader's dialogue with the text, bringing the text's horizon of meaning face to face with the reader's preconceptions of the world in general and the text in particular. This also means that the meaning of a text is never fixed, never complete; a text is always open to reinterpretation and its meaning is continuously subject to negotiation and constantly evolving.

[6] *The Trial* is a mistranslation of the original German title *Der Prozeß*, which means 'The Proceeding'.

[7] Posner's argument holds only if we regard law as 'positive law' and legal practice as a rule-based activity predicated on legal doctrine. For a discussion see West (1985). For a critique of Posner's concept of law and literature see Weisberg (1992, pp. 201–210).

significant innovator of modern social and legal reform in the Crown Land of Bohemia' (Corngold et al. 2009, p. ix). The Institute was responsible for determining and collecting insurance premiums covering work-related injuries for all types of industrial settings. Kafka remained at the Institute until his resignation in 1922 on the grounds of ill-health, 2 years before his death in the Kierling sanatorium near Vienna.

Over the years Kafka served as an insurance lawyer, he produced a large number of office documents ranging from reports and briefs to speeches and newspaper essays. Eighteen of these documents have been selected, translated into English, edited by Stanley Corngold, Jack Greenberg and Benno Wagner, equipped with commentaries which contextualise and analyse each document separately, and published in a single volume. This collection reveals the extent to which Kafka used material and ideas from his office work to develop his fiction, and how his legal writings were influenced by his general literary style. Greenberg (2009) provides several examples of how Kafka used material from his office writing in his fiction:

> In Kafka's professional writing about insuring quarries, we find what may be a one-to-one correspondence with the location of the ultimate scene in *The Trial*... The 1914 report on quarry safety described a quarry in which there was "a loose stone block 1m^3" and accompanied the text with a photograph. That year Kafka began writing *The Trial*, which ends in a chilling execution scene in a quarry. (Greenberg 2009, p. 357)

> Not as congruent as the quarry of the insurance report and the quarry of the execution site, but suggestive nevertheless, is the relationship between wood planing machines insured by Kafka's Institute and the torture machine of *In the Penal Colony*. Planing machines caused many injuries that required workmen's compensation. In a report directed at technical experts, mechanical engineers and business owners, Kafka wrote of finger joints and entire fingers cut off by square shaft planing machines, presenting a lengthy argument, illustrated with drawings that advocated replacing them with much safer cylindrical-shaft planing machines. (Greenberg 2009, p. 358)

Official documents often carry more than traces of Kafka's style as a fiction writer—we hear in them what his office writing editors aptly call 'Kafkaesque echoes' (Corngold et al. 2009, p. xii). For example, his brief on 'Risk Classification and Accident Prevention in Wartime (1915)' ends with the following reference to a German case:

> A prisoner of war was employed as an operator of a large overhead crane. One day, for no good reason, he set the crane's hoist motor at full power. When the hoist cable broke, the pulley block shot up into the air and flew into the work place behind, without, as it happened, hitting anyone.
>
> There was no doubt that the prisoner of war's principal intention had been to disable the crane and to disrupt the flow of work. The German authorities recommended that any firm employing prisoners of war make certain that these are not called upon to perform tasks on which the welfare of the operation depends. (Kafka 2009, pp. 332–333)

This ending not only reminds us of Kafka's story *The Penal Colony*, but also highlights in Kafka's special style the precariousness and vulnerability of the normality of daily life.

A number of people, including Kafka himself and Max Brod his friend, biographer and editor of his works, have been responsible for drawing the attention of critics away from Kafka's legal work. Brod writes, for example, that 'Franz had always looked on his legal profession solely as a makeshift, and dreamed of other activities' (Brod 1995, p. 7). Kafka often complained in his diaries and letters that his day job was unbearable and conflicted with his only desire and calling, which was literature (Kafka 1973, p. 279 also see Gross 2003, p. 82). In a letter to his father, he belittled his legal career by writing that he studied law only by default after he failed to find something which was compatible with his 'self-absorption' and 'vanity' (Kafka 2008, pp. 62–63). In the same letter he famously described his experience of studying law in terms of chewing sawdust: 'For the few months before the final university exam, my mind was fed with intellectual sawdust which had been chewed by a thousand mouths before' (Kafka 2008, p. 63). This does not mean that Kafka was not exposed to ideas which were emerging out of the jurisprudence of his day during his studies at the German-speaking Ferdinand Karl University of Prague. Besides taking courses in Roman law, Austrian civil law, constitutional law, economics and trade law and administrative law, Kafka took 'four courses with Hans Gross, who was a professor in Prague from 1902–1905 – three in criminal law and one on the history of philosophy of law' (Ziolkowski 2003, p. 225). It is therefore likely that Kafka was familiar with Gross's idea that 'it is not the crime but the criminal who is the proper object of punishment' (Ziolkowski 2003, p. 225), an idea based on criminal psychology which, arguably, later shaped the fate of Joseph K. in *The Trial*.[8]

The same idea can be discerned in *In the Penal Colony*, where a man, who has been condemned to death for falling asleep on duty, is to be executed by 'the remarkable piece apparatus,' in reality a deadly and barbarous torture instrument inspired, as noted above, by the dangerous wood-planing machines insured by Kafka's Institute (Greenberg 2009, p. 358). The condemned man has had no opportunity to defend himself and has no idea about the sentence he is about to receive. The officer in charge of the torture machine, who is incidentally also the judge, explains to 'the explorer', who is a stranger on a visit to the penal colony, that 'There would be no point in telling him. He'll learn it corporally on his person' (Kafka 1977, p. 174). The officer nostalgically recalls the days under the Old Commandant when executions brought the community together: '[a] whole day before the ceremony the valley was packed with people; they all came to look on' (Kafka 1977, p. 183) and to celebrate justice being done. To the officer's regret, the New Commandant is influenced by the women around him, and thus it does not favour this method of punishment, which is why no one attends the executions any longer. Although the New Commandant is powerful enough to stop this brutal

[8] Heidsieck (1994, 2008) sketches the intellectual environment of the law faculty and shows that Kafka was taught by several prominent academics of the time. In particular, the legal philosopher Oskar Kraus played an important role in giving him 'a firm grasp of how modern law emerged from the Aristotelian, Roman, and Judeo-Christian concepts of natural law and rational law.'

practice, he nonetheless does not dare to bring about its demise. In this story, we see how Kafka employs his linguistic imagination to transform the wood-planing machine, which mutilated the fingers of workers who operated them, into a torture instrument. At the same time, he links the idea of a criminal as the object of punishment to a romantic, albeit through his 'rhetoric' perverted, sense of justice and the community, lost as the result of the passage from the Old to the New form of social order—a New order which disapproves of the violence of the Old system, but dares not end it. The perversion of justice in the colony mirrors the working conditions of workers operating the planing machines, who, like the condemned man, are kept unaware of their sentence and the punishment they are to receive. It also suggests the inability of the Workmen's Accident Insurance Institute, presented as the New order in the colony, to put an end to the old practices which might put workers at risk of serious injury. Admittedly, this is not the only interpretation of *The Penal Colony*, but nevertheless it is one which gains credibility once we place Kafka's fiction into the context of his office writing and his legal background.

To explore the relationship between Kafka's concept of law, his overall concern with the human condition and modernity's search for the community lost, I will focus in the next section on one of his major novels, *The Castle*, which is often overlooked by those who are interested in his legal ideas in favour of *The Trial*. I will also make use of *The Trial* in Sect. 4, where I explore Kafka's notion of law as a non-state form of legality.

3 The Castle

Kafka's novel *The Castle* starts with the late-night arrival of the land surveyor, K., to a village blanketed by snow (Kafka 1998, p. 1).[9] On his arrival, K. takes up refuge in a local inn for the night, where he is rudely awakened by the son of a castellan who challenges K.'s right to stay the night in what is the property of the castle. When K. explains that he is the land surveyor summoned by the castle,[10] the castellan makes a phone call to the castle to confirm K.'s claim. The castle official first replies that no such person has been summoned, but he calls back a minute later to confirm K.'s story. K. is thus allowed to stay. The next morning, K. leaves the inn, making his way through the snowy streets towards the castle and hoping to get there to clarify the confusion surrounding his visit, but more importantly to assume the duties for which he has been summoned. The castle appears sharply outlined in

[9] Kafka's *The Castle* (1998) was originally published as *Das Schloß* in Munich by Kurt Wolff Verlag in 1935. In the following I shall use the new translation of *The Castle* translated by Mark Herman (1998).

[10] There is a suggestion in the text that K. might indeed not know where he is, for when he is woken up in the inn he wonders: 'What village is this I have wondered into? Is there a castle here?' (*The Castle*, p. 9). This suggests that K. might be a self-appointed land surveyor.

clear daylight as an untidy and miserable heap of low-lying village houses on the hill. With his eyes fixed on the castle—for nothing else matters to K. but reaching it—he sets off. However, his journey proves to be long:

> The street he had taken, the main street in the village, did not lead to the castle hill, it only went close by, then veered off as if on purpose, and though it did not lead any farther from the castle, it didn't get any closer either. K. kept expecting the street to turn at last toward the castle, and it was only in this expectation that he kept going.... (Corngold 2009, p. 10)

Exhausted by his futile attempt to reach the castle, he takes a sleigh back to the inn. At this point a messenger appears with a letter from a castle official by the name of Klamm,[11] notifying K. that he needs to report to the village mayor. The mayor informs K. that he has been summoned by the castle as a result of confused communications between castle authorities; otherwise, they do not need a land surveyor.

K. is neither granted permission to enter the castle nor given direct access to its officials. The castle, nonetheless, acknowledges K.'s presence, apparently facilitates his stay by finding him a position as the janitor in the local school and assigns Barnabas, a messenger from the castle, as the go-between. This proves hardly satisfactory, for K. realises before long that Barnabas does not receive the letters from Klamm but from a clerk; he goes to 'the offices', but it is not certain if these are in the castle. Moreover, although he is at the service of the castle, he is uncertain of his messenger status and not sure if the high official, who is referred to as Klamm, is in fact Klamm or only someone who looks like Klamm.

The villagers are alarmed by K.'s defiant attitude towards the rules and conventions that create their community and govern their relationship with the castle, and they view K. with suspicion. He violates the local mores by questioning normal procedures and by endlessly seeking to contact Klamm. For the villagers, especially for the landlady of the inn, who had been briefly Klamm's mistress, such an important official cannot be approached by a stranger such as K. In a meeting which takes place in the presence of Momus,[12] one of Klamm's village secretaries, who wishes to take a deposition in order to complete the gap in the official records of the castle, the landlady tells K. that 'Klamm will never speak to anyone he doesn't want to speak to, no matter how strenuously a certain individual exerts himself and no matter how insufferably he pushes himself to the fore...' (*The Castle*, p. 109). However, there is still slight hope for K. Admittedly, the fact that Klamm does not wish to speak to K. is sufficient for continuing to deny K. permission even to come face to face with Klamm, but K. may establish some

---

[11] In Czech, 'Klam' means 'illusion'. Although Kafka's works are all written in German, he could also speak and write in Czech. His choice of the name Klamm for K.'s official contact with the castle is therefore most probably not accidental, particularly since Klamm turns out to be a shadowy figure who regularly visits the village, and the letter brought by the messenger indicates Klamm as K.'s point of contact with the castle.

[12] The choice of the name 'Momus' shows Kafka's sense of humour. Momus is the Greek god of mirth, but whenever he speaks in *The castle* everyone becomes serious. See Robertson (2004), p. 40.

form of official connection with Klamm through his secretary's deposition. She tells K.:

> In your case the only path leading to Klamm passes through the secretary's depositions. But I don't wish to exaggerate, perhaps this path doesn't lead to Klamm, perhaps it ends long before it reaches him; that decision is made by the secretary at his own discretion. Anyhow, for you this is the only path that does at least lead in Klamm's direction. (*The Castle*, p. 112)

K. employs all the means at his disposal to contact Klamm, in order to obtain an audience with him, hoping that Klamm can unlock the doors of the castle for him. All his efforts fail. Towards the end of the novel, K. does come across a castle official by the name of Bürgel at the Herrenhof Inn, in the early hours of the morning while waiting to see one of Klamm's village secretaries. Bürgel tells him many important things about the inner workings of the world of the castle, about the strange opportunities that can arise and which are almost never utilised, but K. falls asleep during this meeting. Kafka never finished *The Castle* and the manuscript ends here, but he told Max Brod that he had envisaged the ending as:

> The ostensible land surveyor was to find partial satisfaction at last. He was not to relax in his struggle, but was to die worn out by it. Round his deathbed the villagers were to assemble, and from the castle itself the word was to come that though K.'s legal claim to live in the village was not valid, yet, taking certain auxiliary circumstances into account, he was permitted to live and work there.[13]

The Castle is heavily indebted to *The Grandmother*, a realist novel by Božena Němcová, a female Czech writer, who lived between 1820 and 1862. Němcová's tale is about the people of a Czech village who have no access to their overlord in the castle, where German is spoken. Kafka must have read this novel at school where, according to Brod (1995, p. 251), it was used 'as the basis for instruction in the Czech language'. Although Kafka has borrowed some of the main themes and characters of *The Castle* from Němcová's village tale, his story unfolds differently from hers. In Němcová's version the protagonist, 'the grandmother', succeeds against all odds to make contact with the duchess who rules the village, thus obtaining justice. In Kafka's version, not only justice but also the authority of the village remain out of reach of K., who is, incidentally, a character born out of a report on 'Fixed Rate Insurance Premiums for Small Farms Using Machinery (1909)' (Corngold 2009, pp. 74–79). This report deals, among other things, with land surveying and invalid surveys, as well as unsuccessful attempts made by the Institute to mediate the world of farmers (the village) and the ministry in Vienna (the castle).

Borrowing material from his office work allows Kafka to retain a vital link with the 'real world'; the fact that the 'real world' appears to be 'without anchor' (Weisberg 1992, p. 135), and the link chosen by Kafka is legal and formalistic and thus constrained in relation to life and inclined to 'misreading', is part of the irony which defines Kafka's existence. He employs this material in the same way as

[13] Kafka (2005a), p. 7. Quoted in Willa and Edwin Muir's translation of *The Castle*.

dreams use daytime objects, experiences and images from the dreamer's immediate life context and waking thoughts. The material is transformed by Kafka's 'rhetoric' (his specific style of 'verbal imagination' (cf. see Koelb 1989, p. 1), which we will discuss as 'double thoughts' in the next section) as it is incorporated into his fiction in such a way as to make a broader connection between various thoughts, images, texts and events inevitable, connections which might not have been intended by the author. As a result, Kafka expresses with a different voice, and perhaps even unwittingly, many of the concerns of modernity which preoccupy contemporary social sciences. This transformation and integration of legal material into Kafka's fiction also explains why his critics have too readily neglected law as a significant element in the interpretation of his texts.

Kafka wrote *The Castle* over a period of 9 months, between January and September of 1912, while recovering from a nervous breakdown. His writings are reminiscent of those of Max Weber's *Economy and Society*, published 10 years later in 1922, in so far as bureaucracy, domination and authority loom large in both tomes. Kafka's writings are, at the same time, very different from Weber's work, for not only do they choose the medium of fiction, and thus nurture no social scientific aspirations, but they also demonstrate that bureaucracy, despite its formal rational properties, does not eliminate the unpredictable and arbitrary elements in social organisation. The 'irrationality' of modern rational organisation, which is only hinted at in Weber's notion of the 'iron cage', plays a key role in Kafka's writings. The meeting between K. and Momus, where the latter wishes to take a deposition in order to fill the gap in the archives, which most probably no one will ever read, is an excellent example of Kafka's concern with the spread of bureaucracy as an end in itself. *The Castle* represents a timeless bureaucracy which is irrational in its arbitrariness and unpredictability. As Warner points out, 'the rules change every time he [K.] seeks confirmation of what is expected of him in his post of Land Surveyor. He is confronted by an unpredictable 'personnel bureaucracy' that first appears to hire him and then seems to find ways of evading this commitment' (Warner 2007, p. 1025).

4 Subversion

The Castle is written in Kafka's usual style: the events are described in a sober, pedantically detailed, formal, at times legalistic but above all realistic manner. At the same time, an unmistakable sense of dreamlike unreality presides over the description of events. The borderline between everyday, taken-for-granted reality and unreality is disturbingly blurred in Kafka's writing. The dichotomy of real/unreal does not withstand his descriptions—he shows the 'unreal' as a poorly concealed, integral part of the taken-for-granted reality. His descriptive realism, for example when K. leaves the inn in the morning with the intention of walking to the castle, which clearly appears in front of him in the daylight, is subverted by K.'s failure to get any nearer to the castle by walking towards it. In this way, Kafka challenges the surface logic of everyday life, laying bare its non-rational elements and fragmented structures at two levels. First, he subverts the reality in his fiction externally, i.e. at the level of the reader, by conflating realistic and unrealistic elements of his narrative, leaving the reader bewildered and confused.[14] Second, he subverts the reality of his fiction internally, a move achieved in *The Castle* through K.'s actions, which violate the rules and the social norms of the village community, such as when he refuses to give a deposition to Klamm's village secretary and instead brusquely walks out of the door, thus questioning the normal state of the village's affairs. K. subverts the reality of the village community by provoking the hostility of the villagers and unveiling the non-rational constituents of their seemingly peaceful and harmonious existence. Expressed differently, by exposing the inner contradictions and hidden conflicts within a seemingly harmonious village community, K. threatens the foundations of the villagers' *Heimat* to which he wishes to belong.

Petty village officials such as the schoolmaster, with whom K. is in direct contact, express their concerns simply by treating K. with open contempt.[15] K. is in a sense challenging them directly when, through his actions, he questions the authority of the castle upon which the village officials' status is dependent. The villagers are also challenged, and therefore they react with hostility. A villager tells K. that their lack of hospitality, which might surprise him, only reflects the fact that they have no need for guests (*The Castle*, p. 12). It might be the case that the castle has indeed summoned K., the villager explains, in which case the castle probably needs him, and 'this may be an exception, but we little people go by the rule' (*The Castle*, p. 12). The 'rule' is the rule of the castle, which in turn is the village's source of authority and social order. It is important to note that the castle is as inaccessible and incomprehensible to ordinary villagers as it is to K. Unlike K., however, the villagers have learnt to take the legitimacy of the castle and its source of authority for granted. This interpretation does not make K. a 'pilgrim-hero,' as the editors of *The Office Writings* suggest (Corngold 2009, p. 2); if anything, K. is a non-believer among those who have seen the 'light', and this 'light' is not necessarily divine, but simply another social psychological form of domination. What sort of authority and source of order would the castle possess if it needs a stranger such as K.? K. thus not only poses a threat to the identity of the villagers and their social order through his ignorance of the rules and customs, but also his very presence in the village is a constant and disturbing reminder of the fallibility of the authority of the castle and the uncertainty of the social order it represents. Whether by necessity or by official

[14] To give another example, Gregor Samsa, a travelling salesman, wakes up one morning to find himself transformed into a monstrous insect. Instead of panicking as a result of this inexplicable transformation, Gregor stays in bed feeling melancholic due to the rainy weather outside, bemoaning his exhausting job which forces him to be 'on the move, day in and day out' (Kafka 1992, p. 76).

[15] This sounds like a caricature of petty bureaucrats in action, a parody of 'the little cogs,' to borrow a phrase from Max Weber: '[T]hose little cogs, little men clinging to little jobs' (quoted in Zeitlin 2001, p. 323).

error, K. was summoned by the castle—in either case, his presence undermines the authority of the castle. K. is therefore the embodiment of the villagers' anxiety and the signifier of the irrevocable tension between *Gemeinschaft* and *Gesellschaft*.

Why does K. remain where he is not needed, not welcomed and treated with scorn and hostility? The hostility which confronts and obstructs him does 'cause for a slight attack of despair,' but he is not there accidentally—he is there on a mission (*The Castle*, p. 14). Only by accessing the castle and clarifying matters with Klamm, whose name, as mentioned above, means 'illusion', can he hope to vindicate his right as a citizen of the village community and thus obtain justice. Paradoxically, he is vindicating his right of entry into the village community by breaking its basic rule, i.e. trying to contact Klamm. In a sense, K.'s relentless effort to enter the castle represents modern man's search for *Heimat* without compromising his/her autonomy—a search which is motivated rationally by the need for safety and security and conducted irrationally by appealing to the inaccessible and impersonal authority of *Gesellschaft* to open up the doors of *Gemeinschaft*. Two interrelated issues are thus brought into sharp focus: first, the paradoxical conditions of modern man, as captured by Kafka's 'rhetoric', and, second, the kinship between the search for *Heimat* and the desire for justice as revealed in *The Castle*.

5 Paradoxes

Throughout Kafka's fiction, and occasionally also in his clerical writings, the rational is conflated with the non-rational, the mundane with the extraordinary. For example, the way he ends his brief on 'Risk Classification and Accident Prevention in Wartime (1915)', by reference to a German case (quoted above in Sect. 1), underlines the precarious and vulnerable nature of the normality of daily life. Kafka can explain, for example, why the prisoner of war endangers his workmates—he obviously wished to disrupt the flow of work—yet Kafka adds that this was 'for no good reason.' Admittedly, he might be suggesting that there is no good reason which could justify disrupting the flow of work or endangering other people's lives, but the way he tells this story also suggests that the prisoner acted impulsively to express an inexplicable and suppressed feeling. In the scheme of Kafka's fiction, this conflation of the 'rational' and the 'non-rational'—or the 'real' and the 'unreal'—is, however, an obvious twist which diverts our attention away from his subversion of our powerful images and cogent experiences of life at a more foundational level. According to Michael Wood, Kafka 'invites' us to think contrary thoughts, what Wood calls 'double thoughts':

> "It is certainly an excellent arrangement," the official says, "always unimaginably excellent, even if in other respects hopeless." We can easily picture, or even recall, arrangements that are excellent for some and hopeless for others, and that is what the phrase "in other respects" invites us to do. But the larger rhythm and grammar of the sentence asks us to go beyond this option and think both contrary thoughts at once, taking excellence and hopelessness as partners in an intricate dance, each calling for implying the other; as if

> the arrangement is excellent because it is hopeless, hopeless because it is excellent. (Wood 2008, p. 1)

In fact, Kafka is not 'inviting' us to think double thoughts; instead, he is only holding up to us a mirror, which consists of his linguistic imagination and works through his 'rhetoricity,' as Koelb called it (1989, p. 10). Furthermore, it 'allows for two incompatible, mutually self-destructive points of view' (de Man 1979, p. 131 quoted in Koelb 1989, p. 10), one asserting while the other denies its own illocutionary mode. Kafka's mirror reveals that our thoughts and actions often contain contradictory elements as well as rational and non-rational components, even when we believe we are thinking logically and acting normally. It reveals the extraordinary nature of the mundane. From where does this awareness of the conflation of contrary thoughts and images originate? Would Kafka express himself in this way had he not been trained as a lawyer to bring order to the chaos which constitutes everyday life by selecting elements out of it, dislodging them from their context and then reconstructing them through a formal style which claims to be factual, objective, conceptually exact, coherent and concise? Kafka's office writings show that he mastered and practiced this formal, rational style of writing. His fiction, on the other hand, bears the scars of a continual battle with law's reductionist tendencies, its artificiality and conceptual limitations, its denial of subjectivity and, finally, the terror of its arbitrariness.[16] Weisberg describes Joseph K.'s terror in *The Trial*, 'his misreadings of reality,' that threaten to become the reader's terror (Weisberg 1992, p. 136). These 'misreadings' are as much necessitated by law's reductionism [what Luhmann (1986) conceptualises as law's normatively closed self-reproductive limits] as by Kafka's 'rhetoricity', i.e. his ability to capture and reproduce the openness of discourses 'to radically divergent interpretations' (Koelb 1989, p. 10). In the well-known parable *Before the Law*, the door of the law is kept open specifically for the man from the country, who is paradoxically refused entry into the law by its doorkeeper. The door itself is 'dreadful and intoxicating' at the same time, while the word 'before' lends itself to several interpretations: 'Standing outside of something spatially, preceding it temporally, awaiting something, or being on display before something or someone' (Umphrey and Sarat 2007, p. 6). Would Kafka use this type of formal language, which through its ostensibly logical construction only in vain conceals the illogical makeup of the whole situation, had he not been familiar with legal forms of 'double thought'?

Kafka's 'rhetoric', which exploits the openness of discourses to divergent interpretations, allowing him to identify and employ 'double thoughts' in his narratives, places him in the company of critical and postmodern writers and legal scholars, whose works often highlight the fragmentary, contradictory and

[16] Kafka's letters and diaries show that he struggled with the limits of his language as a medium of communication and a tool for obtaining understanding and grasping the truth. The more he sharpened his language to enhance his descriptions and better dissect the complexity of social reality, the more apparent the shortcomings of the language became.

paradoxical nature of modern law.[17] Kafka came to law thinking rhetorically and in terms of 'double thoughts'. As Koelb shows, in Kafka's name (Franz Amschel Kafka[18]) resides already 'an enormous narrative potential' and 'a powerful stimulus toward a recognition of the rhetorical possibilities' (Koelb 1989, p. 20) across languages, cultures and religions. His legal training and practice as an insurance lawyer in a bureaucratic and hierarchically organised company could only enhance his rhetorical style and his sensitivity to the 'double thoughts' which pervade our thoughts and actions. 'Double thoughts' also reflect Kafka's experience of leading a double life, not to mention his feeling of being a 'crossbreed' (part kitten and part lamb). Both his day and night jobs involved creative writing, but as Gross points out, these two types of writing belonged to two different worlds—one to the world of work, the other to art. Like Poseidon, the God of the Sea, who instead of ruling the seas spent his time 'going over the accounts,' Kafka's day job also ostensibly prevented him from realising his true calling. Kafka therefore had no alternative but to merge these two worlds and 'to balance his *Brotberuf* with his *Beruf*—the two sides of his calling as a writer' (Gross 2003). In the remaining part of this chapter, I will concentrate on Kafka's understanding of law, in order to show the extent to which it is permeated by the interplay of contradictory thoughts.

6 The Desire for Justice

Arnold Heidsieck points out that Kafka's fiction demonstrates an interest 'in the interrelationship of constitutional, civil, administrative, and criminal law with the history of law and moral thought.'[19] Josef K., in *The Trial*, wonders about the men who arrested him, asking himself 'What authority could they represent? K. lived in a country with a legal constitutional state... all the laws were in force; who dared seize him in his own dwelling?' (Kafka 1978, p. 10) K. is fully aware of his rights; he also possesses a working knowledge of law (he is 'virtually a lawyer')[20] and yet

[17] For example, in *Force of Law*, Derrida (1990, p. 941) describes the juridical ideology as superstructures which 'both hide and reflect the economic and political interests of the dominant forms of society.' Norrie (2005), thinking along similar lines, writes that 'legal discourse is essentially contradictory,' or, as he prefers to call it, 'antinomial in its form' (see Chap. 4).

[18] Kafka's parents gave him the Hebrew name of Amschel, derived from Anslem (blackbird), which may be translated into Czech as *kavka*. According to Koelb (1989, p. 19), Kafka's first lessons in rhetoric began when he was an infant: 'The name bore and concealed in its few syllables an abundance – an overabundance – of meanings, not all of which sat comfortably with the others. The lesson must have been repeated on numerous occasions throughout Franz's childhood, as he was unnecessarily reminded over and over again that he bore the name of a comical and not altogether respectable bird.'

[19] According to Heidsieck, Kafka was taught by several prominent academics of the time. In particular, the legal philosopher Oskar Kraus played an important role in giving him 'a firm grasp of how modern law emerged from the Aristotelian, Roman, and Judeo-Christian concepts of natural law and rational law' (Heidsieck 2008, p. 1; 1994).

[20] Quoted in Ziolkowski (2003), p. 229.

he appears as a complete outsider to the law and its processes, declaring that he does not understand the court system. When K. meets his lawyer, Herr Advokat Huld, he is surprised that a lawyer such as Huld, who works 'at the court in the Palace of Justice and not at the one in the attic,'[21] moves in such 'legal circles' where his case is discussed (Kafka 2007, p. 91). Later he asks Block, a businessman who also is a client of Advokat Huld:

> "Does the lawyer take on ordinary legal cases too?"... K. found this alliance between court and jurisprudence profoundly reassuring. "Of course," the businessman said, and then whispered to K., "They say that he is better at the ordinary legal cases than the others". (Kafka 2007, p. 156)

In a passage that had been crossed out of the original manuscript of *The Trial*, when Josef K. is dragged to his death in the final part of the novel, he happens to see a policeman and thinks 'The state is offering me its help... what if I shifted my case over to the jurisdiction of the state law?' (Ziolkowski 2003, p. 229). This leads Ziolkowski to conclude that 'K. has been caught up in a different jurisdiction all together' and we are dealing with the 'parallel existence of a dual law,' which, like Roman civil law and Church canon law that functioned side by side effectively throughout centuries, derives 'from a common source in Justinian's *Corpus Iuris Civilis*—shared procedures that often betrayed their kinship' (Ziolkowski 2003, p. 229). The law applied to Josef K.'s case is similar, albeit only in certain respects, to state law—it uses such concepts as a legal proceeding, case, court, defendant, lawyer and judge—otherwise, it is unlike state law in that courts or legal proceedings are 'distorted' beyond everyday recognition and, perhaps more significantly, represent a system against which 'one cannot defend oneself; one must make confessions' (Kafka 2007, p. 126). It is highly bureaucratic in a modern rational sense, but overtly arbitrary and non-rational in respect to its substantive outcomes and judgments. (As we shall see in the concluding section of this chapter, this parallel legal system is the quasi-legal framework of Austrian insurance law). As Block tells K., 'Many people claim that they can predict the outcome of the trial from the defendant's face, especially the shape of his lips. And these people claimed that, judging from the expression of your lips, you were certain to be convicted, and soon' (Kafka 2007, p. 158). The unfolding of *The Trial* shows that these people predicted the outcome of Josef K.'s trial correctly.

While law in *The Trial* is couched in the procedural form of criminal law, with the intent to punish Josef K., the law of *The Castle* is understood as an aspect of private law, in that it is conciliatory in tone and restitutive in effect. There is no need for state intervention in *The Castle* because the land surveyor K. appears as if he has already been condemned and sentenced to exile in a village which neither

[21] In *The Trial*, Josef K.'s Court of Inquiry is not held in the Palace of Justice on a weekday, but in the attic of a building in the suburbs on a Sunday morning. As Robinson points out, such descriptions of legal proceedings in *The Trial* provide a parody of the legal system. Robinson (1982), pp. 134–135. See Minkkinen (1994) for a discussion of 'reversals' in Kafka's descriptions of the law.

welcomes nor needs him. Seen from a different angle, the tension between him and the castle appears to have been caused by a prima facie contractual dispute. The castle acknowledges the presence of K. in the village, but it does not recognise the existence of a binding contract to employ him as a land surveyor. The problem arises once K. insists on a point of principle that he should confront the castle directly, to clarify matters. He is driven by an inexplicable urge to vindicate his right and to satisfy his desire for justice. His desire may, admittedly, be interpreted as a metaphor for the search for God and (the impossibility of) redemption. He might indeed be the 'sacred man' (*homo sacer*) who, as Umphrey et al. argue in reference to Joseph K. in *The Trial*, 'has been abandoned by law' (Umphrey and Sarat 2007, p. 7). I suggest, however, that K.'s desire for justice should be seen above all as another double thought, which captures the tension between the individual and his/her community: to satisfy his desire for justice, he must gain an audience with the castle authorities and convince them of the need to recognise his particular situation and circumstances. The only medium of action available to K., however, is through the impersonal bureaucracy of the castle, through Momus's deposition, i.e. by way of submitting to procedures which establish their objectivity precisely by way of disregarding the singularity of his position and by a 'misreading' of the events creating his case. This paradox lies at the heart of the relationship between modern law, which strives towards *generality* and *universality*, and justice, which requires the recognition of *singularity* and *specificity*.[22] In this context, K.'s rights function as a mediating element between the universalistic drive of law, represented by the timeless bureaucracy of the castle, and his particularistic need for justice. Kafka expressed this paradox not only in his fiction, but also in his legal writing, for example in 'The Scope of Compulsory Insurance for The Building Trades' (1980), where he recognises the tension between 'a 'top-down' bureaucracy based on centralised power and a 'bottom-up' model based on the voices of the individuals' (Corngold 2009, p. 71). This is once again suggestive of the tension between *Gesellschaft* and *Gemeinschaft* discussed in previous sections.

In short, two forms of law can be identified in Kafka's work. One is the law of criminal proceedings exemplified in *The Trial*, which appears to run parallel to state law, whilst the other is the private law of *The Castle*, which does not need the direct intervention of the state for its enforcements. The former indicates a form of law which is predicated on punishment, the latter a form concerned with restitution.[23] Both are independent of state law, yet they are highly bureaucratic and patriarchal and exercise their power in an arbitrary fashion. Why is Kafka insisting on using the formal bureaucratic vocabulary of state law if he is referring to a form of law other

[22] Ethical paradoxes emanating from legality and the rule of law are, of course, not unique to modern law. Cicero noted a similar paradox when he said that 'we are slaves of the law' in order that 'we might be free,' as quoted in Hayward (1986, p. 19).

[23] Similarly, Durkheim (1933) used different forms of law to represent stages of social solidarity and moral cohesion, suggesting that it evolved from repressive forms (punishment offences) to restitutive form (using, for example, compensation) as society became more socially differentiated.

than state law? It has been argued that he was perhaps thinking in terms of religious law, canon law or Talmud, which existed during certain periods alongside state law. However, this explanation—intriguing as it might sound in view of his troubled relationship with his father, his Jewish background and his feeling of exclusion from the Jewish, German and Czech cultures—is not sufficiently convincing, for it fails to account for the procedural character and institutional references in his fiction which belong to modern law—more specifically to the German and Austrian legal systems of the time—rather than to canon law or Talmud. Moreover, the inaccessibility of justice and the obscurity of the source of authority, on the one hand, and the indeterminacy of the outcome of cases, on the other, distinguish Kafka's law not only from religious laws, but also from traditional natural law.

An answer to the above question regarding Kafka's fusion of forms of laws, mixing strict procedures with arbitrary outcomes, may be found by returning to his office writing, and more specifically to the voluminous case of Josef Franz Renelt,[24] the 'owner of an orchard and a quarry in the northern Bohemian village of Pömmerle,' who was suspected by the Institute of 'incomplete wage declaration' (Corngold et al. 2009, pp. 225–248). According to the Institute, Renelt defrauded the authorities by listing some of his employees who worked at the quarry, and whom he was required by law to insure, as orchard workers, who were exempt from insurance. Kafka was involved in the litigation of this case, which took some 9 years and was brought before insurance tribunal, criminal and administrative courts, before it was finally settled. In an extended commentary to this case, the editors of *The Office Writings* explain that although Renelt won this case on a procedural point (the Institute had, in breach of the rules of insurance law, interviewed Renelt's employees without his knowledge), he was vigorously pursued (almost persecuted) by the Institute in an attempt to make of him an example. In the concluding part of *The Office Writings*, Greenberg sums up the case in this way:

> The Institute sued Renelt repeatedly. Evidence was difficult to gather, witnesses recanted, memories failed, and Renelt's side used physical force to wrest records from investigators.
>
> The Renelt chronicles left traces in three of Kafka's major novels. In *The Man Who Disappeared*, or *Amerika*, written at the time Renelt's chronicles began, Karl Rossmann loses his job and runs into a policeman. After a short interrogation, he attempts escape and runs away again...
>
> Shortly afterwards, Kafka started writing *The Trial*. As Renelt encounters insurance law and criminal law, the accused Josef K. – who, like Renelt before the Aussig district court, "is not in custody" – tries to identify the jurisdiction he is dealing with. His later reflections on his strange trial could be regarded as a copy of Renelt's successful shift of focus from the factual to the procedural aspects of the legal dispute and its ensuing transformation into an out of court settlement: in a deleted passage of Kafka's last novel, *The Castle*, we find a comment on the vain struggle for physical possession of

[24] 'Criminal Charge against Josef Renelt for Illegal Withholding of Insurance Fees (1913)' in Corngold et al. (2009, pp. 225–248).

> written evidence that occurred in yet another phase of Renelt's matters. (Greenberg 2009, pp. 362–363)

Kafka's use of Renelt's case in *The Trial* and *The Castle* suggests that his protagonists are neither innocent nor victims of a bureaucratic system. They appear as victims only because Kafka is telling the story from their point of view and not from the standpoint of the court or the castle, which, being a part of a bureaucratic system, cannot have a personal point of view. This does not mean that justice was done in *The Trial*, in *The Castle* or in Renelt's case; however, it implies that Kafka's concept of law reaches beyond the understanding of law as an organising tool of *Gesellschaft* (i.e. top-down state law) and considers how law may be experienced by the modern individual.

7 Kafka's Law

Does Kafka have a concept of law? Such a question would have probably amused Kafka, whose descriptions and images of law and legality are diffused by the practice of double thoughts. His perpetual fusion of the rational with the non-rational, the mundane with the extraordinary, renders any concept of law (understood as a set of logically interrelated propositions about the nature and operations of law in modern society) obsolete. However, three interrelated insights can be gained from his work, which might serve as a basis for sketching an outline of a general concept of law.

First, Kafka's notion of law takes us beyond a Weberian concern with the rise of bureaucracy and the rationalisation of modern life. Admittedly, Weber did take into account the irrational; however, using his ideal types, he nonetheless distinguished sharply the rational (or the various forms of rational action) from the irrational elements in law and social organisation. In contrast to Weber's conceptual distinction, Kafka shows the rational and the non-rational as two sides of the same coin, as inseparable entities—as the inherent paradox of modernity.

Second, Kafka understands law not only in terms of a fusion of the rational and non-rational outcomes of bureaucratic procedures (which requires observing law's operations from outside), but also in terms of the non-rational elements contained in law's internal procedures. Kafka's jurisprudence is therefore not limited to an outsider's perspective (cf. Litowitz 2002, pp. 113–114), even though by telling the story from the point of view of his protagonists, who perhaps somewhat misleadingly appear as innocent victims, he creates that impression. Kafka's fiction reflects at the same time an insider's *awareness* of the paradoxical nature of law's internal operations. His office writings allow us to show that he did, in fact, combine internal and external views of the law. Kafka was not a functionary of law in the strict sense of the word, i.e. he was not an officer of the court and he did not work within the institutions of law. Instead, he was an insurance lawyer serving a quasi-official Institute. In this capacity, he was simultaneously an insider and an outsider in relation to legal processes and institutions. Renelt's case proves that he participated actively in litigation, and his other writings show that he reflected on the importance of how law was construed by the courts. Among his legal writings we find a concern with the interpretation of the law, which argues for continuity and uniformity in legal decision-making, even when the interpreter is not in favour of the substance of the rule which is interpreted, an issue which signals his position as an insider (for a discussion see Greenberg 2009, pp. 359–361). His awareness of the paradoxical nature of legal interpretation, the vehicle of law's internal operations that constructs its authority self-referentially, is then reflected in his parable on 'The Problem of Our Laws':

> Our laws are not generally known; they are kept secret by the small group of nobles who rule us. We are convinced that these ancient laws are scrupulously administered; nevertheless, it is an extremely painful thing to be ruled by laws that one does not know... For the laws are very ancient, centuries of work have gone into their interpretation and by now this has probably become law itself; there does indeed remain a certain possible latitude of interpretation but it is very limited. Besides, the nobility have obviously no call to let their personal interest sway them into interpreting the laws to our disadvantage, since these were drawn up in the interest of the nobility from the very beginning; the nobles stand above the law, and that seems to be the very reason why the law has been given over exclusively into their hands. Of course, there is wisdom in that – who doubts the wisdom of ancient laws? – but equally there is distress for us; probably that is unavoidable (Kafka 1979, p. 128)[25]

The first part of the passage quoted above, up to the point where Kafka argues that the interpretations of the laws have themselves become a source of law, indicates an insider's experience of the authority of law as it is constructed internally through self-reference. The second part, where he points out that 'the nobility have obviously no call to let their personal interest sway them into interpreting the laws to our disadvantage,' because the laws are already constructed to serve their personal interests, subverts any assumption which might regard law's self-referential operation as adequate in itself, by confronting it with an outsider's view of the same authority in terms of the hegemony of the 'nobility'. Kafka is almost suggesting that the internal paradox of the law—that it can operate self-referentially—is a function of the political domination of 'the nobles'. It is to his credit that his notion of 'the nobility' can be construed in so many different ways as to refer to a number of modern and postmodern legal ideas, ranging from Kelsen's *Grundnorm* (1934) to Derrida's 'originary violence' of law.

Third, as the 'principal compliance officer' (Greenberg 2009, p. 359), he used the threat of litigation and criminal prosecution as a means for implementing what amounted to a social policy aimed at distributing risks linked to work-related injuries. This type of regulation 'juridified' a socio-economic sphere between individual employers and the state, which had previously been organised informally (contractually) by employers. Kafka was, in effect, applying a form of social policy backed by insurance law, which strengthened the position of the employees. We must also remember that this type of welfare-oriented, top-down intervention was a

[25] For a slightly different translation of 'The Problem of Our Laws' see Kafka (2005b).

novel idea at the time. Wagner (2009, pp. 19–48) explains that the radical welfare policy which developed in Austria during Kafka's time disconnected civil and criminal law from insurance law. Arbitration tribunals were set up at each insurance institute, headed by a professional judge and four lay assessors, to decide a very large number of disputes concerning compensation payments to injured workers. Wagner (2009, p. 27) adds that since 'no central court for public insurance existed in Austria, no appeal was possible against the rulings of arbitration courts'. What appears in Kafka's fiction as a parallel jurisdiction to state law—a legal system against which one cannot defend oneself (Kafka 2007, p. 126)—could illustrate his outsider's view of *indirect* juridification, i.e. the regulation of a space between the state and the individual through policy measures implemented by bureaucrats rather than legal rules enforced by courts of law.

These insights into Kafka's conception of law, however, must be studied in the context of his overall writing as a search for *Heimat*—a search which in *The Castle* is combined with the desire for justice. The land surveyor K.'s abandonment by the castle authorities, his inability to enter the castle to confront the authorities and his estrangement from the village community paradoxically emancipate him from the rules, norms and traditions of the castle (i.e. from the external impersonal bonds of *Gesellschaft*) and the village (i.e. from the internal personal relations of *Gemeinschaft*), thus allowing him to retain his autonomy while defining his identity and his situation. At the same time, this freedom from internal and external constraints situates him in a seemingly hopeless and meaningless struggle. K. represents the figure of a modern immigrant freed from the socio-economic and political constraints of his *Heimat*, only to find himself in the impossible position of an unwelcome outsider who does not belong and is apparently not needed. He is the figure of the modern refugee who flees the tyranny of his countrymen, seeking his human rights in foreign lands, only to be caught up in dehumanising and degrading bureaucratic networks. He is an outsider despite the fact that he is not a member of any racial, ethnic, religious or linguistic minority group. Neither is he excluded on the basis of his gender or class. This leads Litowitz to argue that Kafka's protagonists are 'situational outsiders,' i.e. their outsider status is not a function of race, gender, religion or class but determined 'in relation to the dominant legal apparatus' (Litowitz 2002, pp. 127–128). Kafka himself was both an insider and outsider in relation to the law. The fact that he chooses to tell his stories from the standpoint of outsiders shows the alienating effect of the law at the level of the individual. But more importantly, K. represents the tension between the modern individual and his/her *Heimat*, i.e. the modern sense of alienation—the otherness—which turns all of us, to different degrees, into 'outsiders'.

A similar search for *Heimat* can be identified in the writings of socio-legal scholars of the time, such as Ehrlich (2002), a contemporary of Kafka and a citizen of the decaying Austro-Hungarian Empire, who devised the concept of 'living law' as the non-state law of social integration. Ehrlich's living law emerges spontaneously out of *Gemeinschaft* as people interact to form social networks and groups and, in contrast to state law, which operates top-down, operates bottom-up, shaping social relations. Similar ideas can be traced though Georges Gurvitch's 'social law'

(1932) to Roger Cotterrell's 'law's community' (1995), which is based on mutually binding interpersonal trust, a form of law which also operates bottom-up and independently of the state. The difference between Kafka's search for *Heimat* and a socio-legal search for a form of law, which is socially and culturally embedded and yet links the 'warm circle' of the community with the impersonal relations of modern society, is that the former regards the search as an end in itself (the search is all that exists), while the latter sees the search as part of the answer to the social malaise and fragmentation caused by the passage from a form of society organised around *Gemeinschaft* to a form of society dominated by *Gesellschaft*.

Unlike Ehrlich and scholars who have followed in his footsteps, Kafka neither challenges the supremacy of state law nor enters into confrontation with the proponents of legal positivism. By applying his 'rhetoric' to material from his office writing, and with the benefit of the insights gained from living a double life as a lawyer and a writer, he nevertheless succeeds in producing an imaginative understanding of law and legality as an integral part of the human condition under modernity. Without sociological or legal theorising, Kafka's fiction takes us beyond the understanding of law as an instrument of social control and reform and introduces us to law as a form of experience.

References

Bauman, Z. (2001). *Community: Seeking safety in an insecure world*. Cambridge: Polity.

Boa, E. (2003). The castle. In J. Preece (Ed.), *The Cambridge companion to Kafka* (pp. 61–79). Cambridge: Cambridge University Press.

Brod, M. (1995). *Franz Kafka: A biography*. New York: DA Capo Press.

Camus, A. (2004). *Hope and the absurd in the work of Kafka* (The Plague, the Fall, Exile and the Kingdom, and other essays, pp. 549–605). New York: Alfred Knopf.

Corngold, S. (1970). Kafka's *Die verwandlung*: Metamorphosis of the metaphor. *Mosaic, 3*, 91–106 (Summer).

Corngold, S. (2009). Kafka and the Ministry of Writing. In S. Corngold et al. (Eds.), *Franz Kafka: The office writings* (pp. 1–18). Princeton: Princeton University Press.

Corngold, S., et al. (Eds.). (2009). *Franz Kafka: The office writings*. Princeton: Princeton University Press.

Cotterrell, R. (1995). *Law's community: Legal theory in sociological perspective*. Oxford: Clarendon.

Dargo, G. (2006–2007). Reclaiming Franz Kafka, Doctor of Jurisprudence. *Brandeis Law Journal*, 45(Spring Issue), 495–526.

de Man, P. (1979). *Allegories of reading: Figural language in Rousseau, Nietzsche Rilke, and Proust*. New Haven: Yale University Press.

Derrida, J. (1990). Force of law: The mythical foundations of authority. *Cardozo Law Review, 11*, 991–1078.

Durkheim, E. (1933). *The division of labor in society*. New York: Free Press (original publication 1893).

Ehrlich, E. (2002). *Fundamental principles of the sociology of law*. London: Transaction Publishers (original publication 1913).

Gadamer, H.-G. (2006). *Truth and method*. London: Continuum (original publication 1975).

Glen, P. J. (2007). The deconstruction and reification of law in Franz Kafka's before the law and the trial. *Southern California Interdisciplinary Law Journal, 17*(22), 23–66.
Greenberg, J. (2009). From Kafka to Kafkaesque. In S. Corngold et al. (Eds.), *Franz Kafka: The office writings* (pp. 355–372). Princeton: Princeton University Press.
Gross, R. V. (2003). Kafka's short fiction. In J. Preece (Ed.), *The Cambridge companion to Kafka* (pp. 80–94). Cambridge: Cambridge University Press.
Gurvitch, G. (1932). *L'idée du droit social*. Paris: Recuil Sirey.
Hayward, J. (Ed.). (1986). *Out of slavery: Abolition and after*. New York: Frank Cass.
Heidsieck, A. (1994). *The intellectual contexts of Kafka's fiction: Philosophy, law, religion*. Columbia: Camden House.
Heidsieck, A. (2008). Fictional and non-fictional uses of administrative, civil, and criminal law by Kafka and his friends. SSRN: http://ssrn.com/abstract=1146587.
Kafka, F. (1973). *Letters to Felice*. New York: Schocken.
Kafka, F. (1977). *In the penal settlement* (Metamorphosis and other stories, pp. 167–200). London: Penguin.
Kafka, F. (1978). *The trial* (trans: Willa and Edwin Muir). London: Penguin.
Kafka, F. (1979). Description of a struggle and other stories (trans: Willa and Edwin Muir). London: Penguin.
Kafka, F. (1992). *The transformation ('Metamorphosis') and other stories*. London: Penguin.
Kafka, F. (1998). *The castle*. New York: Schocken Books (originally published in Germany as Das Schloß in Munich by Kurt Wolff Verlag, 1935).
Kafka, F. (2005a). *The castle* (trans: Willa and Edwin Muir's). London: Vintage Books.
Kafka, F. (2005b). The problem of our laws. *The complete short stories*. London: Vintage, pp. 437–438.
Kafka, F. (2007). *The trial* (trans: Stockes R). London: Modern Voices.
Kafka, F. (2008) Letters to my father (trans: Colyer H). North Carolina: Lulu (original publication 1919).
Kafka, F. (2009). Risk classification and accident prevention in wartime (1915). In S. Corngold et al. (Eds.), *Franz Kafka: The office writings* (pp. 194–212). Princeton: Princeton University Press.
Kelsen, H. (1934). *Reine Rechtslehre: Einleitung in die Rechtswissenschaftliche Prohlematik*. Leipzig, Vienna: Franz Deuticke.
Koelb, C. (1989). *Kafka's rhetoric: The passion of reading*. Ithaca: Cornell University Press.
Litowitz, D. E. (2002). Franz Kafka's outsider jurisprudence. *Law and Social Inquiry, 27*(1), 103–137.
Luhmann, N. (1986). The self-reproduction of law and its limits. In G. Teubner (Ed.), *The dilemma of law in the welfare states*. Berlin: Walter de Gruyter.
Minkkinen, P. (1994). The radiance of justice: On the minor jurisprudence of Franz Kafka. *Social and Legal Studies, 3*(3), 349–363.
Murray, N. (2004). *Kafka*. London: Abacus.
Norrie, A. (2005). *Law and the beautiful soul*. London: Glasshouse.
Posner, R. (1986). Law and literature: A relation reargued. *Virginia Law Review, 72*, 1351–1392.
Robertson, R. (2004). *Kafka: A very short introduction*. Oxford: Oxford University Press.
Robinson, M. S. (1982). The law of the state in Kafka's *The Trial*. *ALSA Forum, 6*, 127–147.
Sontag, S. (1966). *Against interpretation and other essays 8*. New York: Doubleday.
Tönnies, F. (1955). *Community and association (Gemeinschaft und Gesellschaft)*. London: Routledge and Kegan Paul.
Umphrey, M. M., & Sarat, A. (2007). The sacred in law: An introduction. In A. Sarat, L. Douglas, & M. Merrill (Eds.), *Law and the sacred* (pp. 1–27). Stanford, CA: Stanford University Press.
Wagenbach, K. (2003). *Kafka*. London: Haus.
Wagner, B. (2009). Kafka's office writings: Historical background and institutional setting. In S. Corngold et al. (Eds.), *Franz Kafka: The office writings* (pp. 19–50). Princeton: Princeton University Press.

Warner, M. (2007). Kafka, Weber and organisation theory. *Human Relations, 60*(7), 1019–1038.
Weber, M. (1922). *Wirschaft und Gesellschaft: Grundriss der verstehenden Soziologie*. Tübingen: J. C. B Mohr.
Weisberg, R. (1992). *Poethics and other strategies of law and literature*. New York: Colombia University Press.
West, R. (1985). Authority, autonomy, and choice: The role of consent in the moral and political visions of Franz Kafka and Richard Posner. *Harvard Law Review, 99*(2), 384–427.
Wood, M. (2008). Double thought. *London Review Books*. 20 November 2008. An e-copy is available at http://www.lrb.co.uk/v30/n22/wood01_.html.
Zeitlin, I. M. (2001). Max Weber's sociology of law. In P. Hamilton (Ed.), *Max Weber: Critical assessments (Part I)*. London: Taylor and Francis (Routledge).
Ziolkowski, T. (2003). *The Mirror of Justice: Literary reflections of legal crisis*. Princeton: Princeton University Press.

Chapter 7
The Politics of Legal Cultures

Abstract This chapter may be read as an attempt not only to further develop the critique of rationality, but also to elaborate on some of the theoretical and methodological concerns of the previous chapters regarding the tension between law and sociology. Sociology and the anthropology of law were developed from their inception partly to address empirically the complexity of the relationship between law and society. Many of their insights into how law is socially constructed through the interaction between cultural, religious, economic and political factors remain incompatible with the aims and concerns of mainstream legal scholarship. Most social-scientific approaches to the study of legal institutions and legal behaviour have revealed the plurality of forms of law, demonstrating that it can simultaneously manifest itself in different forms and at different levels of social reality. By contrast, various schools of legal positivism have conceptually separated law from morality, legality from justice and facts from norms, in order to create a normative basis for justifying the unity and autonomy of law. This chapter starts by exploring the tension between Western and Islamic legal cultures in relation to immigrant communities living in the West. It then goes on to argue that the use of such antinomies as facts and norms, or law and morality, which are employed by legal theory in order to organise itself conceptually, diverts our attention away from the fact that law, whether it is defined as the command of the sovereign or the inner order of associations, is not divided into two opposing or contradictory poles. Instead, it consists of countless fragments which are not necessarily related in a formal rational manner.

The concern with the limits of rationality, which we discussed in light of Kafka's writings in the previous chapter, constitutes the backdrop against which we shall explore the relationship between law and culture in contemporary society. By turning to the works of two contemporaries of Kafka, to Eugen Ehrlich's 'living law' and Hermann Hesse's *Steppenwolf*, this chapter will attempt to throw new light on the 'irrational' elements of modern law, legal thought and legal cultures. This also allows us to view the tension between sociology and legal studies, and the

This chapter is a revised version of 'The Politics of Legal Cultures'. In (2008) *Retfærd: The Nordic Journal of Law and Justice* 31(4): 37–60.

R. Banakar, *Normativity in Legal Sociology*, DOI 10.1007/978-3-319-09650-6_7

separation between facts and norms, from a different angle than the one we used in Chap. 2. Our immediate point of departure, however, is more mundane and concerned with how law and legality is debated in multicultural Britain. Can UK law recognise and accommodate aspects of Sharia, such as Islamic family law, which is widely employed by certain Muslim groups living in Britain? To explore this question, we need to form a general understanding of the relationship between law and culture generally and examine how various cultures, religions, systems of beliefs and groups interact in modern Britain. We also need to consider that the interaction between ethno-cultural and religious groups takes place within a societal context which is permeated by history and forms of power and domination.

A case is made that we cannot satisfactorily explore the interaction between Western legal cultures, which emphasise democratic values and principles of human rights, and those of certain Muslim immigrant communities, which are neither based on Western democratic principles nor are sensitive to Western standards of human rights, without considering the political processes through which such interactions are realised. In this chapter, the relationship between the Western and Islamic legal cultures of immigrant communities living in the West is conceptualised, not only in terms of the compatibility of their value systems, but also in terms of the imbalance of power and authority which shapes this relationship. Which factors influence the interface of legal cultures, where one legal system is operating within the jurisdiction of the other and thus is subject to its conception of legality and moral standards? To what extent is the acceptance or rejection of the legal culture of the 'other' the function of an assessment of the actual compatibility of the cultures in question, assessing whether they can or cannot coexist in the same social space, and to what extent is it the outcome of legal ideologies and transient socio-political interests?

This chapter is divided into four sections. Section 1 explores the interaction between legal cultures by reference to three case studies: (1) a study of how the Bolsheviks attempted to engineer the modernisation of Muslim parts of Soviet Central Asia during the 1920s, (2) a 25-year-old case of domestic violence from the lower court in Sandviken, Sweden (tingsrätten i Sandviken), where the court regarded the cultural background of a Kurdish immigrant as a mitigating circumstance in sentencing, and (3) the negative reactions to the Archbishop of Canterbury's proposal in 2008 to integrate parts of Sharia law into UK law, in order to address the needs of certain Muslim communities living in Britain. These case studies are used to conceptualise and examine the relationship between law, culture, religion and politics in the multicultural setting of late modern societies.

Section 2 defines 'legal culture' as a sub-category of the concept of culture, emphasising the importance of a shared language for the formation of a common cultural identity. This draws attention to the misleading presentation of Muslim communities in terms of a single mono-cultural or mono-ethnic identity.

Section 3 revisits Eugen Ehrlich's work and argues that his sociology of law, which was neither a contribution to legal pluralism nor to comparative studies of legal cultures, was nonetheless sensitised by the cultural diversity he experienced in the Bukowina, and that his theory of 'living law' remains a useful tool for studying law in multicultural settings. The incompatibility of Ehrlich's 'living law' with the formalist project of legal positivism of the time was captured in his debate with Hans Kelsen, who criticised him for confusing 'is' and 'ought'. This chapter argues that Kelsen could not acknowledge Ehrlich's sociology of law as a bona fide theory of law because 'living law' described how law manifested itself empirically and, at times, in a contradictory fashion. This allows a twofold reinterpretation of 'living law', either as an approach that recognises the irrational (or contradictory) elements of law or as a theory which introduces a different form of rationality (e.g. communicative rationality), thereby transcending the understanding of law as a system which coheres internally.

Section 4 concludes the discussions by referring briefly to Hermann Hesse's novel *Steppenwolf*. The story is about a middle-aged man who has become aware of his inner duality. Outwardly, he is a cultivated and moral man, while inwardly he is a 'wolf of the Steppes'. As the story unfolds, the man discovers that his belief that he was made of one or even two souls or personalities is illusionary, for every human being consists of ten, a hundred or a thousand souls or identities. This idea is used to return to the distinction between 'is' and 'ought' and to throw new light upon the three case studies in this chapter.

1 Three Case Studies on Law, Culture, Gender and Religion

1.1 The Bolsheviks' Modernisation

In a study published in 1968, Gregory Massell describes how the Bolsheviks, during the 1920s, attempted to engineer the modernisation of the Muslim areas of Soviet Central Asia, by legally strengthening the standing of women in these regions (cf. Kidder 1983, p. 39). The Bolsheviks decided that women, who hardly had any social or legal rights and were excluded from public life, could be used as 'a surrogate proletariat' and an instrument to remove 'backward' Islamic customary practices. Although women did not represent the working class, which in these agricultural regions was yet to emerge, they could nevertheless be empowered to gradually 'loosen and disintegrate traditional social relations' which hampered the progress of modernisation (Massell 1968, p. 184). The Bolsheviks assumed that Muslim women would readily welcome and embrace such a reform and that a fundamental improvement in their legal status would lead automatically to the gradual demise of traditional Islamic structures and institutions. This would in turn pave the way for the transformation of these communities into modern societies. Subsequently, Muslim women were granted civil rights, which were supported by a new judicial system staffed, in part, by women. These legal reforms ensured that women could publicise grievances against their husbands, file for divorce and take employment—and thus participate in public life. At the same time, traditional court structures, including religious and customary tribunals, were abolished and replaced by Soviet courts.

The changes that ensued took the Bolsheviks by surprise. Women took advantage of the new laws reluctantly, and the male population subjected those who did so to hostile treatment and acts of violence. Moscow-trained judges and officials, who were imported to administer the new system, had neither knowledge of the local language nor any understanding of the culture of the local people. Understandably, they soon felt lost in the maze of claims and counterclaims that flooded the courts. To make matters more complicated, women who dared to leave their husbands, in search of the promised emancipation, often found no employment and were either forced into prostitution or had to return to their husbands. Far from revolutionising or modernising Muslim societies, or improving the situation of women, Soviet social engineering through law reforms reinforced traditional attitudes, values and structures. The brand of modernity which the Bolsheviks—and other Western imperialist powers—brought to the underdeveloped areas of Asia and other continents aimed at establishing their colonial hegemony. This 'modernisation' was not mediated through enlightenment but *imposed* on natives through the barrel of the gun and without consideration for their cultural identity, religious beliefs, political autonomy or national sovereignty (for a discussion on 'colonial modernisation' see Dabashi 2007).

The Bolsheviks started transplanting their own set of political values, socio-cultural norms, brand of law and legal institutions into the body of communities which already had functioning cultural norms, formal and customary laws and legal institutions. In addition, they did not attach any importance to Central Asia's 'patchwork of religious and tribal tribunals, usages, and laws' (Massell 1968, p. 182). Far from being uniform, the natives' legal order consisted of two systems with local variations: official or semi-official Islamic courts, which implemented the rules of Sharia, and the local customary rules of *adat*. This meant that in these societies 'conflict resolution could be formal or highly informal, public or private, and the prevailing legal forms, norms and practices depended to a large extent on the particular region, communal organisation, and ethno-cultural milieu, as well as on the personal charisma of the particular judicial mediator' (Massell 1968, p. 182). The combination of formal Sharia laws and the local customary laws of *adat* were related intimately to the social structures and dominant forms of social life in these societies. While the Bolsheviks could restrict the practice of Sharia, which had to be conducted publicly, they could not curb *adat,* which was an extension of cultural traits and did not require publicly implemented procedures.

Similar examples to that of the Bolshevik experiment can be found in the studies of how British colonial rule disrupted the lives of the people of India, by reproducing its own legal system in the country, and how the natives reacted by 'perverting' the new legal system through, for example, flooding 'the courts with law suits against each other' (Kidder 1983, p. 41). In contrast to the Bolsheviks, the British did not try to transform the customary rules of the native Indians but instead tried to enforce Hindu and Muslim customs, using the procedural frameworks and traditional institutions of English law. This approach, which appears to be more sensible than the Bolshevik's method, was not without its problems. Hindu law 'assumed the hierarchical caste system, and the ancient codes prescribed different penalties for the same crime, varying with the caste of the offender', while Muslim law distinguished between the Muslims and the *Kafir* (infidel) (Smith 2005, pp. 160–161). In such a legal setting, where justice is realised through unequal treatment, the British introduced the principle of equality before law, but they gave too much regard to the homogeneity of Hindu and Muslim customary laws, which led them to ignore the differences between the practices of numerous Hindu sects and sub-sects, on the one hand, and Shia and Sunni Muslims, on the other. In addition, the British ignored the localised variations of Muslim laws and customs. In order to bring these customary rules within the framework of English law, they had to be recorded, which meant that the two laws had to be codified. This task was carried out by learned scholars using authoritative texts (Smith 2005). By codifying the customary law of Hindus and Muslims, the British deprived them of their dynamic property and their ability to register and respond to the changing conditions of the lives of the people who used them. As a result, the version of Hindu and Muslim customary laws, as described by the courts, soon came to be viewed as alien by the natives. According to Derrett (2005, p. 71), 'if Hindu law "stagnated" under the British, Islamic law died'.

1.2 The Sandviken Case

In October 1989, a 24-year-old Kurdish immigrant from Iraq was brought before the Sandviken Lower Court in Sweden charged with assaulting, coercing and threatening his pregnant ex-girlfriend, who had left him to live with another man (Case B 61/89, Sandvikens tingsrätt). Although the court found the defendant guilty as charged, it nevertheless released him on a suspended sentence and fined him 3,000 Swedish Kronor (ca $400). Convictions for this type of criminal offence against a person ordinarily carried six months' imprisonment, but in this case, when the court came to sentencing the accused, it argued that his 'cultural' background provided a mitigating circumstance'. According to the court's judgement, the fact that the accused had a different (non-Swedish) culture meant that his perception of his own actions, which were in Swedish law labelled 'assault', were different (Case B 61/89, Sandvikens tingsrätt, p. 7). Moreover, the court added that at the time when the assault took place, the accused felt that his integrity had been violated.[1] It should be noted that the judge and the lay judges who participated in making this decision were all Swedes and the court had not called for any independent expert opinion on Kurdish customs and traditions.

This ruling was met with protest from several quarters. Lawyers and the judiciary questioned the relevance of the assumed cultural background of the accused

[1] I previously discussed this case in Banakar (1994).

for sentencing, while various women's associations and interest groups highlighted that the ruling legalised violence against women. Immigrant associations, each in their own way, regarded the wording of the judgement as a threat to the precariously balanced ethno-cultural relations in the country. In an article in the editorial pages of one of the morning newspapers (*Svenska dagbladet*, 19 January 1990), Ingrid Fredriksson, the chairperson of the Conservative Women's Association in Malmö, asked if Swedish women married to foreigners, from that point onwards, were to be subjected to a different set of legal rules than those under Swedish law. Also, many Kurds challenged the court's interpretation, arguing that violence against women was not, as it was implied in the judgement, a part of their custom (during the 1980s, few people had heard of 'honour killing' among Kurdish immigrants). The prosecutor also criticised the ruling, pointing out that although an immigrant's cultural background might explain his actions, it could not provide an excuse for assault. Not surprisingly, the Sandviken ruling was appealed and the accused was sentenced to two months' imprisonment.

The significance of this case lies in the court's acknowledgement that Sweden was ethno-culturally diverse and that the recognition of the 'other' was unavoidable. What appeared as a progressive step failed disastrously because the ideological structures of Swedish law and legal policy were mono-culturally constructed and not conducive to recognising the 'other'. The court's attempt to acknowledge the ethno-cultural diversity of Swedish society thus revealed not only law's male-centric perceptions of gender relations, but also its ethnocentric images of other cultures.

A final issue concerning this 20-year-old case is that neither in the court's judgement nor in the public debate that followed the ruling can we find arguments that explain the defendant's behaviour in terms of his religious beliefs. This is in stark contrast to the way recent cases involving Kurds living in Sweden have been presented and discussed publicly. In these cases, the Kurdish culture is linked to, or defined in terms of, Islam. In a recent case of honour killing we read: 'The father who is suspected of the crime is a Muslim', suggesting a causal relationship between Islam and honour killing.[2] This demonstrates how religion, or more specifically Islam, has recently become an ethnic signifier in public debates. However, this religious marker of ethnicity can function meaningfully only as long as one works with a monolithic conception of Islam, in other words, as long as one regards Islam as a system of immutable principles which produce a uniform set of social practices across cultural, linguistic and national boundaries. It is noteworthy that a similar monolithic conception of Islam and Muslims also informed the Bolsheviks and the British colonialists' understanding of the religious and cultural practices of the natives. In addition, since 9/11, the public debate on Islam has been shaped by the paradigm of the 'clash of civilizations', according to

[2] See *Aftonbladet*, 8 January 2008. Islam's attitude towards women is one of the factors facilitating honour killing. However, the patriarchal traditions which in certain Muslim and non-Muslim societies perpetuate violence against women exist independently of Islam.

which Islam poses direct threats to Western civilizations and the spirit of democracy (cf. Huntington 1997).

1.3 Incorporating Aspects of Sharia into UK Law

In a lecture delivered to the Royal Courts of Justice in London on 8 February 2008, the Archbishop of Canterbury, Dr Rowan Williams, argued that the legal system in Britain needed to engage constructively with the religious concerns and motivations of members of the diverse communities which make up contemporary British society. There are some 1.6 million Muslims currently living in Britain (2.7 % of the total population), many of whom use Sharia law in matrimonial and private law-related matters to settle disputes. Yet, the decisions of Sharia courts are not recognised by UK law. In his lecture, the Archbishop argued that UK law should incorporate parts of Sharia into its corpus. He further pointed out that the accommodation of aspects of Sharia being placed into the law was ‘unavoidable’ and would, in his opinion, enhance community cohesion by making various religious minority communities part of the public process.

In an interview with BBC Radio 4, ahead of his lecture, Dr Williams explained that the recognition of certain aspects of internal laws of various religious communities by the British legal order could not be rejected casually as impossible, because there were already instances where UK law recognised the internal law of religious communities. Jewish courts, for example, already operated in Britain legally because there were ‘modes of dispute resolution and customary provisions which apply there in the light of Talmud’ (Williams 2008). The Archbishop made it clear, however, that he did not advocate the indiscriminate adoption of all aspects of Sharia, and neither did he condone the inhumane way in which it had been interpreted and enforced in certain Islamic states through extreme punishments and the oppressive treatment of women. UK law was in such a strong position in relation to Sharia to allow it to provide the right of appeal and the necessary safeguards against possible extreme and inhumane interpretation and the application of Sharia. The Archbishop added that Britain did well to avoid situations where the law challenged ‘religious consciences’ over issues such as abortion and treated them as a secular matter, saying ‘we have no room for conscientious objections’ (Williams 2008). Neither did Britain want a situation ‘where, because there’s no way of legally monitoring what communities do, making them part of public process, people do what they like in private in such a way that becomes a way of intensifying oppression within a community. . .’ (Williams 2008).

Despite these clarifications, most headlines run by both the broadsheet and the tabloid press suggested that the Archbishop was advocating the introduction of the whole of Sharia law to Britain. Even liberal newspapers such as the *Guardian* carried the headline: ‘Uproar as archbishop says Sharia law inevitable in UK’ (*Guardian* 8/2/2008). One of the free London papers (*thelondonpaper* 8/2/2008) wrote on its front page:

> Dr Rowan Williams said the adoption of elements of Islamic Sharia law – which includes all women wearing burkhas – in the UK seems unavoidable." He hopes a "constructive accommodation" in areas such as marriage which could allow Muslim women to avoid Western divorce proceedings.

The Archbishop was criticised by the British Government, his own church and the representatives of other religions, including the Muslim Council of Britain, Liberal Judaism and other organisations. The British prime minister's spokesman swiftly distanced the Government from the Archbishop's proposal by declaring that British law had to be based on British values and 'Sharia could not be used as a justification for committing breaches of English law, nor should principles of Sharia be included in a civil court for resolving contractual disputes (*Timesonline* 5/3/2008). Similarly, the Conservative Shadow Minister for Community Cohesion stressed that 'All British citizens must be subject to British laws developed through Parliament and the courts' (*Guardian* 7/2/2008). Britain's only Asian Bishop, the Bishop of Rochester, went further, by pointing out that it would be impossible to introduce Sharia into the corpus of UK law because 'English law is rooted in the Judaeo-Christian tradition' (*Timesonline* 5/3/2008). Dr Williams's predecessor, Lord Carey, who does not usually directly criticise the Archbishop, made an exception in this case, stating that '... there could be no exceptions to the laws of our land, which have been painfully honed by the struggle for democracy and human rights', adding, 'acceptance of some Muslim laws within British law would be disastrous for the nation' (*Independent* 11/2/2008). Finally, two members of the General Synod in London called for him to resign, whilst other senior figures agreed with the remark that 'Dr Williams's standing as the [Anglican] Church's worldwide leader had been diminished', thus making it difficult for him to resolve other disputes within his church (*Independent* 11/2/2008).

The Archbishop's lecture, published on his website, amounts to a 7,000-word long paper, in which he tries to '... tease out some of the broader issues around the rights of religious groups within a secular state, with a few thoughts about what might be entailed in crafting a just and constructive relationship between Islamic law and the statutory law of the United Kingdom' (Williams 2008). His overall approach is pluralistic. His message is based upon the assumption that we all possess overlapping identities and that the 'membership of one group' should not restrict our freedom as a member of other groups (Williams 2008). The sources which the Archbishop uses in his paper to argue his case consist of the works of reformist Muslim scholars who wish to bring about what amounts to the reformation of Islam. Sharia, admittedly, does depend on the Qur'an for its legitimacy, but as the Archbishop argues:

> [I]t is to some extent unfinished business so far as codified and precise provisions are concerned. To recognise *Sharia* is to recognise a *method* of jurisprudence governed by revealed texts rather than a single system... [A]n excessively narrow understanding of *Sharia* as simply codified rules can have the effect of actually undermining the universal claims of the Qur'an. (Williams 2008)

One interpretation of this notion is that the Archbishop is suggesting that by engaging with Sharia, which is currently operating within certain (but not all) Muslim communities in Britain, in a constructive fashion, and by recognising its already functioning courts, one could support the reformist movement in Islam. However, the angry reactions sparked by this suggestion revealed that the media and other interest groups and organisations in Britain were not concerned with having a 'constructive' dialogue with anyone related to or representing the Muslim faith. Instead of asking if such incorporation was feasible legally, if such a step would support the reformists to introduce a new interpretation and practices of Sharia, which were in line with the democratic underpinnings of English law, and if it would strengthen the community cohesion as suggested by the Archbishop, the general tendency was to reject the proposal as 'impossible' (*Telegraph*, 9/2/2008), denounce it as 'the pitiful contortions of a dying Church' (*Independent* 11/2/2008) or dismiss it as an idea which, if implemented, would lead to 'all women wearing burkhas' (*thelondonpaper* 8/2/2008). This is not to say that had the public debate on Sharia been informed by reason and a genuine attempt to explore the possibilities of incorporating it into UK law, various commentators and interest groups would have necessarily concluded that (1) the law in Britain was capable of accommodating Sharia and (2) it was desirable to engage with and recognise the cultural identity of various groups, Muslims in particular, because it enhanced community cohesion. Even the mere incorporation of Sharia family law, which discriminates against women, entails great challenges to a Western legal system.

Instead of denouncing the Archbishop's proposal out of hand, one could have asked concrete questions. For example, according to Sharia, a man may initiate divorce proceedings against his wife at will, while the wife is denied the right to appeal the outcome of such proceedings. However, if the wife wishes to initiate similar proceedings, she requires the consent of her husband. Sharia also allows polygamy, which means that the man has the right to leave his first wife, refuse to divorce her and re-marry. Was the Archbishop suggesting that UK law ought to recognise the decisions of Sharia courts, which are brought about through procedures pitched against women's rights simply because these courts are already operating? Or was he suggesting that by recognising these decisions as legally valid, UK law could give women the right to appeal and to initiate divorce proceedings? In the BBC interview quoted above, the Archbishop mentions the need to monitor legally what communities do, suggesting that when certain practices are forced into the private sphere, they can intensify 'oppression within a community' (*BBC* 11/2/2008). Is the Archbishop attempting to undermine the traditional conservative forces within Islamic communities living in Britain and pave the way for a reformist movement in Islam by giving Muslim women the right to appeal and to file for divorce? One cannot help noting the similarity between the latent (and perhaps even unintentional) consequences of the Archbishop's proposal and the Bolsheviks' experiment in Central Asia.

In the public debate, Sharia was presented as an undemocratic value system incompatible with UK law. Assumptions regarding the incompatibility of Islam and Western democracy are in line with the ideologically manufactured idea of the 'clash of civilizations', which, as mentioned above, sees insurmountable divisions between Islam and the West. The problem with this ideology of 'civilizational' conflicts, which was launched after the collapse of the Eastern bloc in the 1990s by people such as Samuel Huntington (a former White House aide), and gained currency in the aftermath of 9/11, is that it takes the moral superiority of the West for granted. Moreover, it applies a culturally monolithic and socio-politically coherent concept of civilization which disregards the plurality of worldviews and local practices within each so-called 'civilization'. Admittedly, it is true that the practices of Sharia have taken on inhumane and oppressive forms in some Islamic states, and much of this oppression is directed towards Muslim women. However, it does not mean that all Muslims, or all Islamic states for that matter, are in favour of such practices. Similarly, the fact that Britain is a parliamentary democracy does not mean that that UK law functions strictly in accordance with unalienable principles of human rights. English law, for example, has no insurmountable difficulty in incorporating provisions which allow the authorities to hold terrorist suspects without charge for 28 days, which clearly undermines the fundamental principles of civil liberty and the criminal law principle of the presumption of innocence.[3] Neither has English law any difficulty in incorporating provisions such as *Stop and Search Orders*, which indiscriminately target minority groups (Bowling and Phillips 2007). This means the reason for denouncing the Archbishop's proposal cannot be that Sharia is inherently undemocratic and subsequently will introduce contradictions into an otherwise democratically coherent system of English law, which actually already contains many such contradictions and appears equipped to cope with them accordingly.

The examples given above all relate to clashes of different systems of belief, mores and, ultimately, legal cultures. They also show that once cultural values and beliefs are brought face to face, political convictions and interests, rather than systematic investigation into the possibility of the co-existence of plural systems in the same social space, come to prevail. The political and ideological convictions of the Bolsheviks, together with their military dominance of Soviet Asia, made them oblivious to the significance of the natives' formal and informal laws. Similarly, in the Sandviken case, the question asking whether the decision of the court to recognise the 'otherness' of the defendant was justified, even though its sentencing decision might have been wanting, was overshadowed by the political interests of various groups and the mono-cultural policy of Swedish law. Finally, the Archbishop's proposal regarding Sharia was met with intense hostility and rejected not because UK law's internal modus operandi rendered it impracticable, but because it too was politically incorrect. No aspect of Islam, which in the

[3] The Home Secretary, Jacqui Smith, put forward a proposal to extend the period to hold 'terror suspects' without charge to 42 days in January 2008.

political climate after 9/11 is linked to terrorism and anti-Western sentiments, could find accommodation within the democratic structures of Western law and polity.[4]

The three cases which I used above suggest that the political discourse, against the backdrop of which the interaction between various legal cultures takes place, tends to stress the *differences* between rival systems. However, the political discourse can, and does, disregard differences, if focusing on the similarities between the rival cultures serves its ideological ends. The publication of Salman Rushdie's *Satanic Verses* in 1988, which provoked protests among some Sunni Muslim communities in towns such as Bradford, with large Pakistani and Bangladeshi immigrant populations, is a case in point. The protests were initially organised locally, but once the local organisers received financial support from sources outside Britain (allegedly with links to Saudi Arabia), the local protests spread beyond Britain's borders and transformed into an international movement. The Sunni organisers of the protest eventually took their grievance to Ayatollah Khomeini, the spiritual leader of Iran's Shia Muslims at the time, who declared the book as blasphemous and, on 14 February 1989, proclaimed a *fatwa* sentencing Rushdie to death. The point made here is that the politics surrounding the Rushdie affair required Sunni Muslims, who ordinarily do not recognise the legality and authority of Shia Islam, to set aside their legal-cultural differences and bring their case to a Shia court. They did so because the Shia court of the Ayatollah was the only place the Sunni protesters could obtain the type of verdict they wished to be imposed against Rushdie, i.e. a death sentence, but also a verdict which was more than a symbolic action (for a discussion *see* Banakar 1992). And surely enough, soon after the proclamation of the *fatwa* in 1989, the Hezbollah made an attempt to assassinate Rushdie in London.

2 Monolithic and Plural Conceptions of Legal Cultures

Legal culture, according to Nelken (2004, p. 1), refers to 'relatively stable patterns of legally-oriented social behaviour and attitudes', and as such it should be regarded as a sub-category of the concept of culture. Culture, in turn, is defined in terms of 'meaning' or the dynamic *processes* which make social life meaningful and help individuals and whole communities to develop their own particular worldviews (Nelken 2007). Expressed differently, culture refers to the process of reproducing beliefs and attitudes that people hold about the social world (Wuthnow 1987). These beliefs and attitudes help the individual to interpret, create and recreate the social reality within his/her own universe of meaning. At the same time, they form

[4] Since 9/11, the public perception of Islam as an extremist militant faith which condones, encourages and justifies political violence more often than other faiths has deepened in the West. See Ansari (2005).

cultural patterns by manifesting themselves as the intersubjectively shared *values* of a community. These cultural processes are either directly or indirectly dependent on the use of common language, which is, in fact, vital for the formation of cultural identities and, by extension, for the development of legal cultures. People who do not share a common language cannot form a cultural group or the same legal culture, so it is therefore misleading to suggest that Muslim communities belong to a single Islamic (legal) culture. Admittedly, it is important to recognise that Islam contains fundamental values in regard to how the private and public lives of Muslims are to be organised. In this sense, Islam can be used as an ideological beacon for mobilising groups of people who might otherwise have little in common, but such a mobilisation will be a political rather than a cultural project. Malaysians, Bangladeshis, Saudis, Iranians, Turks and Albanians are all Muslims, but they do not belong to the same cultural and linguistic spheres. The Islamic 'civilization' is thus unfolded through many socio-political processes and at many linguistic and cultural centres and geographic localities. A closer scrutiny of Islamic nations reveals that their cultural identity is not entirely a function of Islam but rather a product of social, political and historical processes, some of which have very little to do with Islam or other religions. More importantly, their interpretations of Islam and religious practices are shaped by their socio-historical backgrounds and experiences. To give an example, after the Mohammedans invaded Persia and converted Persians to Islam, the Persians revolted against the ruling Caliphate in order to reassert themselves and regain control of their country. Thus, Shia Islam was the resurrection of the Persian identity 'beneath a veil of religion' and a part of the political struggle against the Arab domination of Persia (Bausani 1971, p. 77).[5]

As we saw in relation to the case studies in the previous section, Islam and Muslim immigrant communities were depicted as homogenous entities in public political discourse. There was no recognition of cultural diversity among Muslims, whose language, history and customs are as diverse as Christians'. As Goodall points out, the word 'Muslim' is frequently used in Britain 'to mean someone who looks "Asian"'; more specifically, to indicate a person from Pakistan, India or Bangladesh, from where the majority of British Muslims have traditionally come (Goodall 2007, p. 98). In this way, the public discourse conflates Islam and race, or to put it differently, it 'racialises' Muslims—various cases of racial hatred brought before the courts show, for example, that the word 'Muslim' is used as a 'racist marker' (Goodall 2007, p. 96).[6] Notwithstanding the usage of 'Muslim' in public discourse, and despite the fact that both 'Jew' and 'Sikh' are recognised in law as racial groups and thus are protected against the offence of incitement to racial hatred, 'Muslim' is considered to be a religious category in English law. This is

---

[5] I should hasten to add that Shiʿism was first developed in Iraq and, thus, was originally an Arab, rather than a Persian, construction. Although it spread to Iran during the eighth century, it was first transformed into a political force in the sixteenth century when Persia was exposed to a 'systematic policy of Shiʿization' by the Safavid dynasty' (Halm 2007, pp. ix and 110).

[6] See for example *Norwood v DDP* [2003] EWHC 1564 (Admin); 2003 WL 21491815 (QBD (Admin Ct)).

correct in the sense that Islam is a world religion encompassing many ethnicities and cultures, but it is incorrect in the British context because its everyday usage has come to refer to South Asians as a racial category. Thus, the anti-Muslim hostility which has targeted Asians in Britain was not considered an offence of incitement to racial hatred and could not be successfully prosecuted until recently, when incitement to religious hatred was made unlawful by the new Racial and Religious Hatred Act 2006.

The everyday conception of 'Muslim' as a mono-racial or mono-cultural category also tainted the debate on the Archbishop's proposal, lacing it with negative sentiments. No attention was paid to the fact that there were different versions of Islam, and no notice was taken of the link between Sharia and local customs (a link which is often ignored by Western scholars). Arguably, the divine origin of Sharia is believed to render it immutable. However, Sharia also needs to be interpreted before it is put into practice, which opens it up to the possibility of change, a point which was underlined in the Archbishop's paper. According to Rosen (2006, p. 38), within every Muslim legal system we find 'some local variation of the proposition that custom must take precedence even over that which is sacred law; "[w]hatever is dictated by custom is as if dictated by law"'. Islamic law has a symbiotic relationship with the customs of communities which adopt it as a source of social order. This, in turn, means that there are as many versions of Sharia in operation in Britain as there are Muslim communities belonging to different ethno-cultural spheres. The public debate following the Archbishop's proposal ignored the plural character of Sharia, while depicting UK law as a fundamentally democratic and coherent unit whose internal cultural and moral integrity would be violated by the introduction of the undemocratic rules of Sharia.

It is not only the dominant political and cultural discourses in the West, but also militant and extremist Islamic groups that use the immutable dichotomy of the West and Muslims to describe the relationship between themselves and their host countries. These groups conceptualise the West as a mono-cultural entity and regard a rejection of the Western identity of their host countries as the first step towards the 'promotion of a single united *ummah*' (Akhtar 2005, p. 164). In countries such as Britain, second generation immigrants' return to Islam has increased since 9/11 and markedly intensified since the Iraq war. Why young Muslims turn to Islam is often explained by reference to their socio-economically marginalised place in British society. However, Akhtar argues that young Muslims' return to religion has a more complicated socio-cultural mechanism, 'one that offers individuals who feel in some way constrained by their circumstances an alternative ideology, a sense of belonging, solidarity and means of political mobilisation' (2005, p. 164). According to Akhtar, this also means that the young Muslims' return to religion is not a revival of Islam as such—it does not necessarily mean 'an increased adherence to the Islamic code', but 'instead refers more to individual empathy with a religious identity, an identity that provides group solidarity' (2005, p. 164). We are thus not dealing with a conventional cultural construction of Muslim communities but with the rise of a political movement among the young generation of Muslim immigrants, who make an instrumental use of Islam to unite a diverse group of people whose primary common denominator is not religious but socio-political. These children of immigrants feel that they are being victimised, marginalised and demonised—not for what they are or have done, but instead for how they are perceived by the majority culture.

The political discourse which shapes confrontations between Western and Islamic legal cultures is not uniform either. One important distinction can be made between concerns which are voiced from within the legal systems by the judiciary or other officials of the law, on the one hand, and concerns raised by those outside the legal system, i.e. by political actors, interest groups and citizens, on the other. The concerns and approaches of the judiciary are not always in agreement with those of the political system and the public in general, and in some cases they clash. For example, the judiciary in Britain has been, on the whole, opposed to the detention of terrorist suspects without charge and to the proposals to extend the period of detention from 28 to 42 days. Many members of the judiciary saw the proposal to extend the period of detention as being incompatible with several Articles of the European Convention on Human Rights and regard it as an unnecessary measure which further undermines the fundamental principles of law. In contrast, sections of the political establishment presented the proposal as a necessary and logical measure to ensure national 'security' and citizens' safety. Public opinion was also divided on this matter, but ordinary people's concern with 'security', and the fact that the majority of citizens would not be at the receiving end of such measures, tended to move public opinion in favour of the proposal. Such disparities could be explained by distinguishing between internal and external legal cultures, i.e. between legal meaning, which is generated by the judiciary and other functionaries of the legal system in relation to the internal operations of the law, as well as the attitude and perception of citizens towards law, legal institutions and legal regulation (Friedman 1977).

This distinction may, arguably, serve conceptual and analytical ends in certain circumstances—it helps, for example, to explain why there can never be one single legal culture in a modern society—but as with other dichotomies, it can draw our attention away from the dialectical interaction between various forms of legal meaning, for example between the attitudes of the officials of law and those of the citizens, which ultimately create our image of the law as a body of norms and practices (cf. Banakar 2003). Perhaps more importantly, it fails to reflect the diversity of views and attitudes which can exist both within and without a legal system. The judiciary is often divided on many important policy issues, such as how to treat terror suspects, while the public discourse on legal issues often consists of conflicting and contradictory viewpoints on the relationship between law, culture and religion. Yet, legal positivism, which remains the dominant perspective within legal studies, continues to propagate an understanding of law in terms of a single, coherent (i.e. free from internal contradictions) system of rules, doctrine and decisions which are largely, if not entirely, independent of moral, cultural and social forces. This perhaps explains why mainstream jurisprudence continues to debate the separation thesis, i.e. if and how law and morality are related, as if it were *the* fundamental problem of law (see Chaps. 2 and 4, where the separation thesis was discussed).

The remaining sections of this chapter hope to show how socio-cultural diversity of the type we have discussed above can be explained theoretically, while throwing some light on why both political and legal discourses tend to present the legal order as a single homogeneous unit.

3 Living Law and Cultural Diversity

3.1 Ehrlich's 'Living Law'

Concern with the complexity of the relationship between law and custom, in general, and law and cultural diversity, in particular, is hardly new in social-scientific studies of law. Eugen Ehrlich, one of the founders of the sociology of law, developed his notion of 'living law' partly as a response to cultural diversity found in Czernowitz in the Bukowina, where he worked and lived most of his life. There, Ehrlich could observe 'nine tribes: Armenians, Germans, Jews, Romanians, Russians (Lipowanians), Ruthenians, Slovaks (often taken for Poles), Hungarians, and Gypsies' living side-by-side (Ehrlich 1912; Ziegert 1979, p. 229). Being a jurist, he was also curious as to how this cultural plurality interacted with the legal order of the Austro-Hungarian Empire (even though, I must hasten to add, he did not express diversity either in terms of legal cultures or legal pluralism). He saw the attempts of politicians in Vienna to enforce their laws on the functioning normative orders of these culturally diverse, yet harmonious, ethno-cultural groups as socially detrimental. Also, being a Roman Catholic of Jewish descent with an interest in the Jewish question in eastern central Europe, Ehrlich had probably experienced at first hand the tensions involved in living at the intersection of cultures, religions and ethnic identities. In this sense, Ehrlich's sociology of law is a theory of legal pluralism sensitive to legal cultural diversity.

A similar approach to law also grew out of legal anthropology's preoccupation with social control and how the imposition of centralised colonial laws were received and experienced by the indigenous people of the colonised countries. Sociologists, such as Ehrlich, and social anthropologists, such as Malinowski (1961), were amongst the first scholars to develop pluralistic theories of law. Although the aims and the contexts of their research were different, they both defined law and legal order in broad terms that included not only traditional legal institutions, but also the 'non-legal forms of normative ordering' (Ziegert 1979, p. 229; also see Banakar 2002).

In *Fundamental Principles of the Sociology of Law,* Ehrlich distinguished between law created by the state and law produced by the organisational imperatives of non-state social associations. State law (*Staatsrecht*) was, in turn, differentiated into statutes (*Gesetze*) and juristic law, i.e. legal norms for decision-making (*Entscheidungsnormen*), which are developed by jurists through a process of universalisation and the 'reduction of unity' of legal norms (Ehrlich 2002,

p. 253). However, according to Ehrlich, it was not state law but 'living law' that dominated life itself. Living law did not need to be expressed in legal propositions, and it emerged independently of state law out of the inner order of associations. Ehrlich calls norms which emerge in this way 'facts of the law' (consisting of custom and usages, relations of domination and subjugation, property relations and declarations of will as in contracts and testaments) and argues that they have a considerably greater impact on the social structure and organisation of society than any law posited by the state.

Living law and theories of legal pluralism in general are often criticised for failing to distinguish between certain social and cultural norms, on the one hand, and legal norms, on the other. The requirement to differentiate sharply between legal and extra-legal norms is a normative standard belonging to legal positivism and state law. It is therefore not a benchmark for measuring the social-scientific validity of legal pluralism, which does not recognise the state as the primary source of law. The criteria for assessing the assumptions made by legal pluralism are in the first place *empirical*, i.e. whether or not ordinary men and women use certain rules and norms which are not posited by the state or other official institutions to resolve their disputes and organise their relationships (for a critique of this position see Tamanaha 1993). For both Ehrlich and Malinowski, the decisive factors in distinguishing between legal norms and social or cultural norms were to be found neither in relation to the legal *sources* of norms nor to their institutional *form*. That is to say, for a norm to be regarded as legal, it neither had to have been posited by the state, nor did it necessarily require some formal executive institutions, such as the courts or police, to ensure its enforcement. A norm gained legal status if it fulfilled other socially functional conditions, such as inducing social control and order. Ehrlich used the concept of *opinion necessitatis* to distinguish legal norms from other types of normative statements and behaviours (Ehrlich 2002, p. 165). He meant that a socio-cultural norm became legal when the group which had introduced it as a standard of conduct attached great importance to its application. This concept of law is fundamentally different from definitions found in Max Weber and Hans Kelsen's works, where the existence of sanctions, administered by special staff, against the violation of legal rules play a decisive role in identifying legal from extra-legal norms (Weber 1954; Kelsen 1967).

Clearly, there are significant overlaps between state law and living law. Among norms of decision, which are applied by courts, we find many that dominate social life and function as the inner order of certain associations. In fact, Ehrlich meant that living law, being the foundation of most forms of law, *ought* to be treated as the law proper and should be regarded as the foundation for legislation or legal decision-making. However, this amounted, according to Hans Kelsen, to confusing *Sein* ('is') and *Sollen* ('ought').

3.2 *Kelsen's Critique of Ehrlich*

Kelsen criticised Ehrlich on several points, arguing, for example, that the 'fact of the law' concept, defined by Ehrlich as 'usage, domination, possession, and dispassion (usually by contract or by testimony disposition)' (Ehrlich 1912, p. 118), was a contradiction in terms, because law is intrinsically normative (Kelsen 1915; Kelsen and Ehrlich 2003; for a discussion see: van Klink 2006). More importantly, Kelsen argued that it was one thing to argue that living law *is* the origin of all forms of law (a statement with which, incidentally, Kelsen did not agree) and quite another thing to argue, as Ehrlich did, that living law *ought* to be the basis of legislation and legal policy. Kelsen meant that sociology was an *empirical* science which could describe and explain law's operations, such as decisions made by courts, but such descriptions cannot lay the basis for assessing the normative soundness of these decisions.[7]

Although Ehrlich was offended by Kelsen's suggestion that he had confused *is* and *ought*, he nonetheless refused to defend himself against Kelsen's critique (Ehrlich 2003). Whatever the reason for his refusal to engage in direct debate with Kelsen, to accuse Ehrlich of confusing *is* and *ought* misses the main point of the theory of 'living law'. By *the main point*, I am not referring here to Ehrlich's systematic attempt to create a 'science' of law as a branch of social sciences which explores law as a social phenomenon, and neither am I referring to his novel argument that a body of rules does not necessarily require the threat of sanctions or the likelihood of being enforced by especially authorised staff, before it is recognised as law.[8] Moreover, I am not referring to his critique of the state-centred concept of law (Ehrlich 1996, p. 25),[9] upon which rests legal positivism, or his insight into the practical workings of law, which shows that the state is not the sole—or even the primary—source of law. Here, I am referring to living law's ability to bridge the gap between facts and norms, reason and belief, law and morality. Ehrlich's concept of law does not 'confuse' *is* and *ought*, but by observing law that, de facto, lives and operates in society, he reveals how the prescriptive and the descriptive properties of legal norms are *conflated* when people use law.

Law, as Ehrlich discovered it, refused to be conceptualised neatly in terms of *is* and *ought*, as two sharply defined opposites. This law could be *is* and *ought* at the same time, containing more than a grain of what probably appeared to Kelsen as 'irrationality'. Kelsen, arguably, was right in pointing out that Ehrlich's concept of

---

[7] This demonstrates that the sociology of law has from inception a normative, a descriptive and an analytical dimension. See van Klink (2006).

[8] Ehrlich explains that to 'a person... whose conception of law is that of a rule of conduct, compulsion by threat of penalty as well as compulsory execution becomes a secondary matter... [A]s a rule, the thought of compulsion by the courts does not even enter the minds of men' (Ehrlich 2002, p. 21).

[9] In *Die juristische Logik* (Aalenm Scientia Verlag, 1996, orig print 1925) he calls it 'die vulgäre staatliche Rechetsauffassung' (1996, p. 25).

law was contradictory, but his contradictions were paradoxes generated by social operations of law rather than by his analysis (for a discussion on legal paradoxes and contradictions see Perez and Teubner 2006). Unlike Kelsen, whose formal theory of law provided an account of how law ought to be identified and how a legal system ought to be constructed, Ehrlich was simply describing the social operations which generated forms of social control and organisation. Kelsen was unable to acknowledge Ehrlich's theory, because living law represents a type of rationality which was incompatible with Kelsen's understanding of a rationally constructed legal system. Living law is the foundation of social organisation. It captures how certain categories of norms which are generated within the 'lifeworld' (*Lebenswelt*) become intersubjective within a group of people and how these norms regulate the behaviour of the members of this group. Thus, its form of rationality is closer to what Habermas (1984) described as 'communicative rationality' than to Kelsen's formal rationality.

From a sociological standpoint, it follows that living law, which emerges out of the functional needs of social organisation and is related symbiotically to the mores, customs and social organisational reality of the people who have produced it, should provide a sound basis for law, legislation and legal decision-making. This does not, however, mean that living law is necessarily humane or democratic. The unofficial legal system of the Muslim communities of the Soviet Central Asia (*adat*), as well as the unofficial forms of dispute resolution used by immigrant Muslim communities living in Britain, are two cases in point. Both of these systems can be regarded, to different degrees, as living law, and both deny equal rights to women. As the colonial experiences demonstrate, the recognition of the social organisational significance of these forms of laws, undemocratic as they might be, is now, to use the Archbishop's word, 'unavoidable'. The Bolsheviks could have avoided the great harm they inflicted upon Central Asian societies in general, and women in particular, had they recognised the fundamental significance of forms of social control which were embedded in Asian people's customs and traditions. My argument here is that, even though this was most probably not Ehrlich's intention, the concept of living law, in addition to capturing the diversity of forms of law, also helps us to make sense of what might appear as the contradictory (or the 'irrational') elements which constitute law.

4 *Steppenwolf*

Steppenwolf, one of Hermann Hesse's novels (1965, first published 1927), is about a middle-aged man named Harry Haller who is, outwardly, a spiritually-refined intellectual and an artist, a cultivated man of high moral standing who seeks and enjoys the rational orderliness that a bourgeois life has to offer. Inwardly, however, Harry is a 'wolf of the Steppes', a wild animal of low moral standing, who cannot help challenging and violating the everyday conventions and what he regards to be the artificial limits of ordinary men and bourgeois life. Not only does Harry experience himself as consisting of two parts—part man and part animal—but he also feels torn apart by the ongoing struggle between the 'human' part, which is a creature of rational thoughts and habits and enjoys the middle-class order of things, and the 'wolf', which is a wild animal of irrational instincts and behaviour. This novel is the story of Harry's discovery that what he has experienced as his dual existence represents an oversimplification of the state of affairs. As the story unravels, Harry comes to realise that he does not consist of two souls, one human and one wolf, but of hundreds of souls. Even the wolf does not have one single soul and consists of fragments of identities.

Despite their fragmentation of souls, even the most intelligent of humans seem to have a deeply rooted inborn need that makes them see the world and themselves through 'delusive formulas and artless simplifications' which rest ultimately upon a false analogy (Hesse 1965, p. 70). No matter how often the illusion that every person is a single soul is shattered, it is somehow restored again:

> And if ever the suspicion of their manifold being dawns upon men of unusual powers and unusually delicate perceptions, so that, as all genius must, they break through the illusion of unity of the personality and perception that the self is made of a bundle of selves, they have only to say so and at once the majority puts them under lock and key, calls science to aid, establishes schizophrenia and protects humanity from the necessity of hearing the cry of truth from the lips of these unfortunate persons. Why then waste words, why utter a thing that every thinking man accepts as self-evident, when the mere utterance of it is a breach of taste? A man, therefore, who gets so far as making the supposed unity of the self two-fold is already almost a genius, in any case a most exceptional and interesting person. In reality, however, every ego, so far from being a unity, is in the highest degree a manifold world, a constellated heaven, a chaos of forms, of states and stages, of inheritances and potentialities. It appears to be a necessity as imperative as eating and breathing for everyone to be forced to regard this chaos as a unity and to speak of his ego as though it were one-fold and a clearly detached and fixed phenomenon. Even the best of us share the delusion. (Hesse 1965, pp. 70–72)

This novel concludes with Harry being led by a mysterious saxophonist to a 'magic theatre', where Harry's soul disintegrates and he takes part in several unbelievable events which end in him killing (or hallucinating killing) a young prostitute. It is, however, not the ending of Steppenwolf which provides us with the beginning of our account of law and legal discourse, but the struggle between the wolf and the ideal of rational order and, by extension, legal positivism's denial of the wolf and its imperative need to conceptualise its fragmentary and contradictory bundle of rules, decisions and practices as a coherent whole, to see and present the manifold as the onefold. Those who distinguish between the internal and external properties of law (such as Hart 1969) or internal and external legal cultures (such as Friedman 1977), or try to acknowledge the indivisibility of law and justice (such as Alexy 2002), only succeed in distinguishing the wolf *from* man or recognising the wolf *in* man. What they neglect is that both wolf and man are in turn made up of fragments of identities.

Steppenwolf, which is to some extent Hesse's autobiographical masterpiece, is influenced by Nietzsche, on the one hand, and Freud, on the other. It not only captures much of the tension in the European cultural tradition which started with the Enlightenment, but also it reflects the inner intellectual demons of a generation which includes Max Weber, Hans Kelsen, Eugen Ehrlich, Brasilow Malinowski, to mention a few, who set the scene for the debate on law and society. It is perhaps these men's concerns, their awareness of the limits of rationality as in the case of Weber's 'iron cage,' and the potential of the wolf in the case of Ehrlich's 'living law', or their systematic attempts to deny the role of the wolf in modernity, as in the case of Kelsen's 'pure theory of law', which are transferred to law. In short, I suggest here that the conceptual duality of law masks two important and interrelated characteristics thereof: (1) its 'irrational' qualities—'irrational' only in so far as they do not fit into the model adopted by legal positivism—and (2) its diversity—the acknowledgement that law is a collection of normative, factual, social, cultural, moral, regulatory, symbolic, educational and professional fragments. All of these characteristics are reflected in Ehrlich's 'living law'.

In the previous sections I argued that forms of law, culture and religion interact as part of an ongoing public discourse, the parameters of which are determined by the ideological concerns and political objectives of the time and the setting in which the discourse is realised. I also tried to demonstrate that both Western public opinion and Islamic extremist groups depict themselves and the culture of the 'other' as homogeneous entities. This is politically and psychologically functional, for by disregarding the plural characteristics of their own and other groups' cultural identities, they free themselves from the need to deal with the moral complexity of the social reality with which they find themselves confronted. This in turn allows them to act with conviction and the belief that they represent the good and the rational. Similarly, by regarding Western legal culture as democratically uniform, Western commentators and legal scholars can turn a blind eye to its otherwise contradictory and fragmented nature. This enables them to dismiss the 'wolf' as incompatible with the rational architecture of Western legal systems.

This chapter has tried to capture different discussions, expressed in different voices and from different times and places, on the relationship between law and culture. One way to summarise these discussions is by asking two new questions. Firstly, is it possible that the legal cultural identity of Muslim immigrant communities is part of the 'wolf of the Steppes' of Western legal cultures—a wolf which, as mentioned above, consists not of one single but of numerous identities? Secondly, is it realistic to expect Western legal cultures of the type we find in Britain or in Sweden to engage with the 'wolf' constructively, whilst they have not as yet discovered and acknowledged their own plurality of forms?

References

Akhtar, P. (2005). Return to religion and radical Islam. In A. Tahir (Ed.), *Muslim Britain* (pp. 164–176). London: Zed Books.

Alexy, R. (2002). *The arguments from injustice: A reply to legal positivism*. Oxford: Clarendon.

Ansari, H. (2005). Attitudes to Jihad, martyrdom and terrorism among British Muslims. In A. Tahir (Ed.), *Muslim Britain* (pp. 144–163). London: Zed Books.

Banakar, R. (1992). Salman Rushdie and the holy cow of liberalism (Swedish title: *Salman Rushdie och liberalismens heliga ko). Häften för kritiska studier (Swedish Critical Studies Review), 2*, 3–14.

Banakar, R. (1994). *The dilemma of law – Conflict management in a multicultural society* (Swedish title: Rättens Dilemma: Om konflikthantering i ett mångkulturellt samhälle). Lund: Bokbox Publishing.

Banakar, R. (2002). Sociological jurisprudence. In R. Banakar & M. Travers (Eds.), *An introduction to law and social theory*. Oxford: Hart.

Banakar, R. (2003). *Merging law and society: Beyond the dichotomies in socio-legal research*. Berlin: Galda + Wilch.

Bausani, A. (1971). *The Persians: From earliest days to the twentieth century*. London: Elek book.

Bowling, B., & Phillips, C. (2007). Disproportionate and discriminatory: Reviewing the evidence of stop and search. *Modern Law Review, 70*(6), 936–961.

Dabashi, H. (2007). *Iran: A people interrupted*. New York: The New Press.

Derrett, J. D. M. (2005). Administration of Hindu law by the British. In I. Deva (Ed.), *Sociology of law* (pp. 60–72). New Delhi: Oxford University Press.

Ehrlich, E. (1912). Das lebende Recht der Völker in der Bukowina (The living law of the peoples in Bukowina). *Recht und Wirtschaft*, 1, 273–279.

Ehrlich, E. (1996). *Die juristische Logik*. Aalen: Scientia Verlag (original publication 1925).

Ehrlich, E. (2002). *Fundamental principles of the sociology of law*. London: Transaction Publishers (original publication 1913).

Ehrlich, E. (2003). Entgegnung. In H. Kelsen & E. Ehrlich (Eds.), *Rechtssoziologie und Rechtswissenschaft: Eine Kontroverse (1915/1917)* (pp. 3–54). Baden-Baden: Nomos Verlagsgesellschaft.

Fredriksson, I. (1990). Rättens hänsyn drabbar kvinnor. *Svenska dagbladet*, 19 January 1990.

Friedman, L. M. (1977). *Law and society: An introduction*. Englewood Cliffs: Prentice-Hall.

Goodall, K. (2007). Incitement to religious hatred: All talk and no substance? *Modern Law Review, 70*(1), 89–113.

Habermas, J. (1984). *The theory of communicative action: Reason and the rationalization of society* (Vol. 1). Cambridge: Polity.

Halm, H. (2007). *The Shiites: A short history*. Princeton: Markus Wiener.

Hart, H. L. A. (1969). *The concept of law*. Oxford: Clarendon.

Hesse, H. (1965). *Steppenwolf*. London: Penguin (original publication 1927).

Huntington, S. P. (1997). *The clash of civilizations*. London: Simon and Schuster.

Kelsen, H. (1915). Eine Grundlegung der Rechtssoziologie. *Archiv für soziale Gesetzgebung und Statistik, 39*, 861.

Kelsen, H. (1967). *The pure theory of law*. Berkeley and Los Angeles: California University Press.

Kelsen, H., & Ehrlich, E. (2003). *Rechtssoziologie und Rechtswissenschaft. Eine Kontroverse (1915/1917)*. Baden-Baden: Nomos Verlagsgesellschaft.

Kidder, R. L. (1983). *Connecting law and society*. Engle-Wood Cliffs, NJ: Prentice-Hall.

Malinowski, B. (1961). Crime and custom in savage society. London: Routledge (original publication 1926).

Massell, G. (1968). Law as an instrument of revolutionary change in a traditional milieu: The case of Soviet Central Asia. *Law and Society Review, 2*(2), 179–240.

Nelken, D. (2004). Using the concept of legal culture. *Australian Journal of Legal Philosophy, 29* (1), 1–28.

Nelken, D. (2007). Defining and using the concept of legal culture. In E. Örücü & D. Nelken (Eds.), *Comparative law*. Oxford: Hart.

Perez, O., & Teubner, G. (Eds.). (2006). *Paradoxes and inconsistencies in the law*. Oxford: Hart.

Rosen, L. (2006). *Law as culture: An invitation*. Princeton: Princeton University Press.

Smith, D. (2005). Religion, law and secularism. In I. Deva (Ed.), *Sociology of law* (pp. 158–173). New Delhi: Oxford University Press.
Tamanaha, Z. (1993). The folly of the 'Social Scientific' concept of legal pluralism. *Journal of Law and Society, 20*(2), 192–217.
van Klink, B. (2006). *Facts and norms: The unfinished debate between Eugen Ehrlich and Hans Kelsen*. SSRN: http://ssrn.com/abstract=980957.
Weber, M. (1954). In M. Rheinstein (Ed.), *On law in economy and society*. New York: Simon and Schuster.
Williams, R. (2008). *UK law needs to find accommodation with religious law codes*. www.archbishopofcanterbury.org/1580. Posted on Thursday 07 February 2008.
Wuthnow, R. (1987). *Meaning and moral order: Explorations in cultural analysis*. Berkeley: University of California Press.
Ziegert, K. A. (1979). The sociology behind Eugen Ehrlich's sociology of law. *International Journal of Sociology of Law, 7*(3), 225–273.

Cases

Norwood v DDP [2003] EWHC 1564 (Admin); 2003 WL 21491815 (QBD (Admin Ct))
Case B 61/89, Sandvikens tingsrätt

Newspaper Items

Aftonbladet (8 Jan 2008) 'Skyll inte på islam'. Posted at 'www.aftonbladet.se/debatt/article1582947.ab. Accessed on 20 March 2008
BBC (11 Feb 2008) 'In Full: Rowan William's Interview' at http://news.bbc.co.uk/2/hi/uk_news/7232661.stm
Guardian (7 Feb 2008) 'Archbishop backs Sharia law for British Muslims' at http://www.theguardian.com/. Accessed on 25 Nov. 2013
Guardian (8 Feb 2008) 'Uproar as archbishop says Sharia law inevitable in UK' at http://www.theguardian.com/. Accessed on 25 Nov. 2013
Thelondonpaper (8 Feb 2008 'All Women Wearing Burkhas'. At http://thelondonepaper.newspaperdirect.com/. Accessed on 20 March 2008
Timesonline (8 Feb 2008) 'Archbishop of Canterbury argues for Islamic Law in Britain' posted at 'www.timesonline.co.uk. Accessed on 5 March 2008
Independent (11 Feb 2008) 'Rowan Williams has shown us one thing – why multiculturalism must be abandoned' at http://www.independent.co.uk/. Accessed on 25 November 2013
Telegraph (9 Feb 2008) 'Sharia Law May Result in "Apartheid"' at http://www.telegraph.co.uk/. Accessed 25 Nov. 2013
Svenska dagbladet (19 Jan 1990) 'Rättens hänsyn drabbar kvinnor'

Chapter 8
Comparative Law and Legal Cultures

Abstract This chapter continues to explore the relationship between law, culture and forms of power, but it will do so through the methodological lenses of comparative law and by developing the idea of contextualisation, which was discussed in Chap. 5. It will demonstrate that forms of contextualisation are also deployed widely within comparative law as part of the method of exploring similarities and differences between laws and legal systems in different jurisdictions.

Chapter 5 outlined various contextualising approaches which had been developed in response to the separation of law as a system of rules, with a degree of autonomy, and law as a set of institutional practices or processes embedded in the socio-cultural constitution of the society. The notion of contextualisation explores the implications of the 'gap', often demonstrating that law's operations remain dependent on socio-cultural processes. It also refers to efforts to minimise and where possible to eliminate the 'gap' between law as rules and law as social practices. The first contextualisation approach was a response to the insight that the implementation, interpretation and enforcement of legal rules were dependent on socio-cultural norms and extra-legal processes and institutional practices. The second approach was a critique of how modern law dislodged actions from their socio-cultural and historical contexts before examining them (this point was also discussed and developed in Chap. 4[1]). Finally, the third approach was a response to the need to restore the societal embeddedness of the legal system and as such was regarded as being linked to the second approach. These three contextualising approaches are interrelated and correspond with different conceptions of the 'gap' between law and society, which have informed a great deal of research and debate in legal sociology (see Chap. 3). As this chapter will demonstrate, forms of contextualisation are also deployed widely within comparative law as part of the method of exploring

This chapter is a revised version of 'Power, Culture and Method in Comparative Law'. In: (2009) *International Journal of Law in Context* 5(1): 69–85.

[1] We argued that law ignores and denies the relevance of its socio-historical roots and moral ties in order to enhance its operation as an autonomous system.

R. Banakar, *Normativity in Legal Sociology*, DOI 10.1007/978-3-319-09650-6_8

similarities and differences between laws and legal systems in different jurisdictions.

This chapter is divided in three sections. Section 1 discusses the recent developments within comparative law and touches on one of its central methodological issues by asking whether comparative studies should focus on similarities or differences between legal systems and traditions? It will do so partly by discussing various studies in Örücü and Nelken's (2007) edited handbook of comparative law, and partly in reference to the other recent comparative work. Section 2 starts by arguing that forms of contextualisation of law should be regarded as the indispensable methodological characteristic of all comparative studies of law that aspire to transcend the understanding of law as a body of rules and doctrine. The method of contextualisation situates legal action, behaviour, institution, tradition, text and discourse in specific time and socio-legal space, thus, revealing law's embeddedness in societal relations, structures, developments and processes. Section 3 presents the central concern of this chapter in relation to legal theory, socio-legal research and comparative law by proposing a combination of the top-down and bottom-up perspectives as a meta-methodological framework within which specific comparative techniques can be employed.

1 Studying Similarities or Differences?

Comparing laws is hardly a new exercise among philosophers and jurists, who have for centuries gained insights into how legal systems work by contrasting 'familiar' against 'foreign' ways of using law.[2] Lawmakers and businessmen have also engaged in comparing their own law-ways with foreign laws, but they have done so for purely practical reasons. Commercial transactions, for example, are very old and have always crossed national borders and geographic boundaries, compelling traders and rule makers alike 'to look beyond their own city, country, rules and laws' (Hopt 2008, p. 1162). In its modern form, comparative law is often 'dated back to the nineteenth century and to the promulgation of the great European codes' and to the efforts to locate and explore the universal core of all civilised legal systems (Donahue 2008, p. 3). This new search for the universal essence of all laws was conducted not so much in the speculative tradition of natural law but in the spirit of positivism, which located *the* source of law in empirically verifiable 'social facts' such as the command of the sovereign. As Cotterrell (2007, p. 134) explains, the epistemological roots of the search for a unifying foundation of law reveal unease with a concept of law and legal knowledge that 'is true (valid) in one town but invalid in another, a few miles away across the border'. After all, 'what kind of moral force can law have if here it says one thing about rights and wrongs, and there it says something else (perhaps the opposite)?' (Cotterrell 2007, p. 134). Thus, natural law philosophers' labours to improve man-made laws by identifying and

[2] Donahue (2008) traces the roots of comparative law back to Aristotle's *Politics*.

exploring the universal core of law in terms of nature or divine reason came to be replaced partly by comparatists' studies of foreign legal systems aimed at 'improving laws by harmonisation... or unification' (Cotterrell 2007, p. 134). Hence, the search for the harmonisation and unification of laws came to dominate the emergence of comparative law in the twentieth century.

As we currently stand, at the beginning of the twenty-first century, comparative law appears to be enjoying the wind in its sails. From being considered only a few decades ago as a topic 'for those who were of curious of mind', it has moved on to become one of the core subjects in the curricula of many European law faculties (Van Erp 2007, p. 399).[3] This change of fortune is documented by the number of new journals, research monographs and textbooks generated over the last few years to introduce and explore the various branches of comparative studies of law.[4] This increased interest is partly a result of 'the changing role and practical importance of knowledge of foreign legal systems' (Van Erp 2007, p. 399), partly due to the profound effects of globalisation processes 'on the practice and the organisation of law' (Flood and Sosa 2008, p. 1) and partly a result of the realisation that comparative law, after all, has practical applications and can be used by judges, lawyers and legislators in search of legal solutions, legal reform and the harmonisation of private law across borders. Within the European Union, we find a number of projects that aim at harmonising and unifying the various aspects of private law in order to eliminate 'differences across national private laws that are perceived [by the promoters of these projects] to be obstructing the optimal functioning of the European Market' and 'to redress incoherences caused by fragmentary EU directives' (Glanert 2008, p. 161). Along with the renewed interest in comparative legal studies comes also an enhanced awareness of the need to reconsider the assumptions, concepts, ideas and methodologies which have traditionally constituted these studies. For example, the idea of the harmonisation and unification of private law, which motivates much of the work carried out by comparatists, is being questioned

---

[3] Siems (2007) does not share this optimistic view, and instead he claims that comparative law is ignored by courts in the US and elsewhere, is academically on the decline and is either too complicated, esoteric and theoretical or too simplistic, thus rendering it useless for practitioners. The issues raised by Siems can be taken seriously only once we disregard the role of comparative law in law reform and apply a set of truth-values belonging to traditional legal scholarship to evaluate the usefulness and relevance of comparative law. Taking the traditional legal scholarship's notion of what is true, useful and relevant as the yardstick for assessing comparative law's diverse approaches is a misleading exercise, for comparative studies were developed partly to bring to law ideas and insights that traditional scholarship could not provide.

[4] Besides *Comparative Law: A Handbook*, edited by Örücü and Nelken, which is the focus of this chapter, we find two other impressive collections: *The Oxford Handbook of Comparative Law*, edited by Reimann and Zimmerman (2008), and *Elgar Encyclopaedia of Comparative Law*, edited by Smits (2006). Together with earlier work such as *Comparative Legal Studies: Traditions and Transitions* (2003), edited by Legrand and Munday, *Comparative Law in a Global Context*, by Menski (2000, second edition 2006), *Legal Traditions of the World*, by Glenn (2000), and *Comparative Law in a Changing World*, by De Cruz (2007, 1st ed. 1995), these new publications lay a solid foundation for comparative legal studies for many years to come.

by a number of scholars who doubt its practical feasibility and moral desirability (Smits 2007, pp. 227–229; Cotterrell 2007; Legrand 1996, 1997). Therefore, instead of *constructing* similarities intended to harmonise and unify legal systems across time and space, we need to recognise the differences distinguishing them from each other in time and space, for the *difference* is what endows two things, events or phenomena with their specific properties and sets them apart from each other (see Legrand 2003). The similarity/difference notion takes us back to the discussions on certainty/uncertainty in the Introduction. Those who either emphasise the existing parallels between legal systems or try to construct similarities where there are none, do so partly as an attempt to enhance certainty in an otherwise increasingly uncertain world. For them, recognising differences amounts to succumbing to uncertainty and discontinuity.

Comparative law is also questioned for its Euro-centric assumptions, namely the 'colonial hubris and the "white" supremacist presuppositions that went with it' (Menski 2007, p. 191). These are some of the issues and debates that are explored in a new handbook of comparative law, edited by Örücü and Nelken (2007), which will provide the point of departure for discussions in this chapter on socio-legal contextualisation and methodology.[5]

2 Contextualisation

2.1 Contextualising Laws

A simple but latently subversive methodological message unifies most of the chapters and debates in Örücü and Nelken's (2007) handbook on comparative law. Most chapters state implicitly or explicitly that the scope of comparative studies of law must transcend the notion of law as a body of rules, in order to include the dynamic institutional processes and practices which produce and reproduce the normative structures of legal systems. This overall methodology reveals the kinship between the handbook, on the one hand, and the sociology of law, legal anthropology and legal history, on the other, and it also explains the

[5] Örücü and Nelken's (2007, p. v) handbook aims at filling 'the gap in comparative law teaching and study', a gap brought on by the increased complexity and the changing role of law at national and transnational levels. In order to fill this gap, the handbook provides 'coverage not only of traditional private law topics but also public law matters including comparative constitutionalism and the increasingly important types of transnational legal processes such as criminal law and human rights law' (Nelken 2007a, p. 4). Besides being methodologically innovative, the handbook also seeks to look beyond the scope of traditional comparative law in order to bring into focus non-Western legal traditions and systems. The handbook consists of 19 chapters authored by a group of scholars with a vested interest in comparative law, legal cultures or globalisation, and it is divided into three sections devoted to the methodological, theoretical and substantive aspects of comparative studies of law.

consistent efforts made by its authors to *contextualise* comparative legal research by taking into account the social, cultural, historical, economic and political factors that are in constant interaction with law and legal institutions.[6] Different chapters engage with contextualisation in different ways and to different degrees, but they appear to follow the concerns of our first form of contextualisation (which we discussed above). John Bell, for example, who is more concerned with providing a descriptive account of administrative law in different jurisdictions than offering an in-depth contextualised discussion, nevertheless admits that certain aspects of law such as 'the use of bill of rights... raises issues of how far the enactment of a legal text has an impact on the way in which the legal system works and what is required to ensure that a culture of respect for fundamental values is embedded' (Bell 2007, p. 301). To answer these issues, Bell (2007, p. 301) informs us that we require 'legal sociology', yet to perform his immediate task he appears to be satisfied with the 'clues' he finds in the way the legal system 'has adapted to the new culture of rights'. In contrast, McCrudden gives a more thorough explanation of the gap between the rules and principles expressed in the text of law, on the one hand, and how these are unfolded in legal practice, on the other. In his chapter on human rights, McCrudden (2007, p. 372) distinguishes between 'theories supporting human rights – including the *general principles* of human rights – and their *application* in specific situations'. There is, admittedly, much agreement on the principles of human rights but little consensus on why, how and where these principles should be applied. As a result:

> All that is left is an empty shell of principle, and when principle comes to be applied, the appearance of commonality disappears, and human rights are exposed as culturally relative, deeply contingent on local politics and values. (McCrudden 2007, p. 372)

Paul Roberts also takes his discussions of international criminal justice research beyond mere legal rules and principles by highlighting the role of institutions and hybrid tribunals charged with developing and implementing the rules of international criminal justice. In his chapter, he explores 'international criminal justice through a series of seven "concentric" circles, starting with the core activities of international criminal tribunals and fanning out into the hinterlands of transnational legal cooperation, national trials of international criminality, and related... scholarly commentaries and research' (Roberts 2007, p. 364). Similarly, Harding and Leyland argue in their chapter that when comparing the role of constitutions in the political processes of more than one nation, we must remember that there is a 'gulf between the formal constitution and the manner in which government is actually conducted' (Harding and Leyland 2007, p. 323). We must therefore look beyond the written texts or designs of constitutions, to examine how constitutional rights and principles are implemented. Constitution is evidently a 'political' construct, so it is not difficult to argue that besides considering the text of the constitution, we also need to pay attention to the institutional arrangements and practices that are put in

[6] For a discussion on the relationship between comparative law and the sociology of law see Cotterrell (2006).

place to realise the rights, policy objectives and aspirations expressed therein. However, in this handbook, even comparative studies of areas such as commercial law, which have not been laden with specific political values or programmes, require gazing beyond the letter of the law. Commercial law has been traditionally presented and taught by commercial lawyers as a mere technical instrument for facilitating trade, which is in turn usually assumed to be 'an activity not affected by cultural values' (Foster 2007, p. 267). Nonetheless, Foster (2007) shows in his chapter that the application and development of commercial law is influenced by differences in cultural attitudes to commerce—differences which are determined historically. These ideas, arguably 'old hat' in socio-legal theory and law and society research (see, for example, Ehrlich 1936 and Pound 1943), are nonetheless expressed in the handbook with clarity of thought and intention by scholars, many of whom are versed in various substantive areas of law. They also appear to propagate the first contextualisation approach, which potentially generates data on how law as a system of rules operates in various societal conditions, or how it is mediated through various social institutions. It also aspires to close or minimise the disparity between legal rules and practices.

Some of the theoretical and methodological approaches we find in the handbook subvert the state-orientated positivistic methodology—what Michaels (2013) called 'the methodological nationalism'—of traditional legal scholarship. Most contributors agree that comparative studies must be informed historically, acknowledge the plurality of forms of law and recognise 'the various forms of non-state law, especially different kinds of religious and customary law that fall outside the "Westphalian duo"'[7] (Twining 2007, p. 76; also see Menski 2007 and Cotterrell 2007). Comparative law must accommodate not only top-down approaches to the study of law, which treat the state as the source of law and normative ordering par excellence, but also bottom-up analyses of the various processes of harmonisation and unification of laws, which take into account how various actors and institutions experience and cope with legal change. In addition, comparative law should not, as it is often the case, focus either on the macro (e.g. global legal networks, EU law and international law) or the micro level (e.g. local municipal law and private law doctrine). Instead, it needs to take into account the numerous intermediary layers of legal institutions such as the NGOs and international tribunals that play an important role in connecting the micro and macro realities of law (Twining 2007, pp. 70–73). In order to achieve these objectives, a comparative study of law has to become empirical, for the type of institutional knowledge it seeks cannot be obtained purely through the conceptual analysis of legal rules, doctrine and principles. Finally, it has to broaden its scope of investigation by refusing to limit its general approach to the methodological and theoretical constraints of one single discipline. Thus, comparative legal research must be conducted in an interdisciplinary and, perhaps, even multidisciplinary manner.

---

[7] 'Westphalian duo' refers to the assumption that law consists of the state law and public international law of sovereign states which, in turn, do not recognise any superior authority.

2.2 *Rethinking Comparative Law*

As mentioned above, comparative law has reached the stage in its development where it needs to reconsider some of its central ideas and assumptions, such as legal families, the harmonisation of laws and the relationship between law and the state. The notion of legal families was originally developed using ideal types of Western legal traditions in order to classify and make sense of the legal systems of the world. Legal families were defined in terms of 'law as rules', and they evaluated and classified with the help of criteria such as substance, style, method, ideology, structure and sources belonging to common law, civil law and socialist law. This approach, which has dominated much of comparative law, has been criticised for being too concerned with the study of private law relations at the expense of other areas such as family, public and criminal law and for promoting a Euro-centric approach. Following the third contextualisation approach we outlined above, Menski notes that once we consider legal traditions beyond Europe, we observe that the law is often culturally embedded, pluralistic and, in some cases, not geared to the state. In such a pluralistic context, harmonisation is neither meaningful nor necessary or desirable:

> Law is therefore not just about rules and their codified rule systems, but about a plurality of voices and values, and thus negotiations of difference and diversity at many different levels, and at all times. The book of law is never closed. Any form of law, even God-given Islamic law, is philosophically and practically perceived and applied as inherently dynamic and interactive (Menski 2007, p. 195)

Even within the EU, where regulations and directives hammer into member states the desirability to harmonise private law and to unify codes—a process aimed at creating a common European market and identity—we continue to find a great deal of diversity. Similarly, Smits (2007, p. 222) raises doubts on whether 'harmonisation of private law really promotes the internal common market' and if, as it is often claimed, it will substantially reduce the costs of trans-frontier contracts. He also believes that even the unified private law of the EU 'will continue to suffer an inevitable fragmentation' (Smits 2007, p. 227), for, ultimately, any unified private law has to be offered as an optional alternative to and remain organisationally dependent on existing national legal systems. At the micro level, differences in legal reasoning will persist, as civilian lawyers and common law lawyers will continue to think and reason differently. The only way one can promote convergence of the private laws of EU member states, and create a system which resembles the *ius commune* of the seventeenth and the eighteenth centuries, is by adopting a 'non-centralist method' (Smits 2007, p. 229), for example by devising a bottom-up perspective which starts with the Europeanisation of legal science and education. This means educating lawyers belonging to different jurisdictions to share a common legal training, speak the same language and think in European terms. This ideal is articulated through the European Commission's efforts to harmonise judicial training within the EU: 'Based on Mario Monti's report', writes Hammerslev (2013, p. 339) 'the Commission combines the development of union law with the effective implementation of EU law, which guarantees legal predictability, security and the uniform interpretation of law throughout European member states' (also see Monti 2010). Admittedly, this will be a slow and difficult process, and it will further reinforce the assumption that only 'lawyer's law' is worth treating as the law proper; however, it is perhaps the only realistic method of bringing about a genuine European legal culture.[8] The comparison with *ius commune* is an important one, for it reminds us of the importance of a common background and a shared language. In the discussions of harmonisation and legal cultures which are presented in Örücü and Nelken's handbook, there is a tendency not to highlight the role of language (with the exception of passing remarks in Van Erp's chapter on the process of law reform).[9]

Focusing on the possibility and desirability of the harmonisation and unification of private law in Europe, we easily lose sight of what lies beyond Europe. Besides common law and civil law, there are other 'ancestors' such as Chthonic, Talmudic, Islamic and Asian laws (Örücü 2007, p. 174; also see Glenn 2000), to mention just a few, which need to be taken into account when discussing legal families and traditions. More importantly, we need to acknowledge that there are no pure legal families and recognise that legal systems in certain geographic areas such as Europe, the Middle East or South America overlap, which therefore implies that all legal systems, to different degrees, are hybrids, i.e. cultural and legal mixtures consisting of various elements borrowed from different legal traditions and customs. It also means that legal systems and traditions are continuously changing and evolving through cross-fertilisation, fusion and borrowing from one another. Attempts to apply a fixed set of standards for evaluating legal families and legal systems of the world are bound to reify the otherwise dynamic social and cultural processes that produce and reproduce legal systems and traditions over time.

Menski and Smits distinguish themselves from comparatists who follow the first contextualisation approach. Instead, they follow the third type of contextualisation by broadening the scope of their analysis beyond the confines of the legal system. This enables them to ask new questions and ultimately to rethink comparative methodology. As we shall see in the next section, this approach is developed further by Patrick Glenn, Roger Cotterrell and Pierre Legrand, who also appear to emphasise the role of differences, rather than similarities, in comparative law.

---

[8] For a discussion on the concept of 'legal culture' see Chap. 7. In the following pages, legal culture refers to 'relatively stable patterns of legally-oriented social behaviour and attitudes,' and as such it is regarded as a subcategory of the concept of culture (Nelken 2004, p. 1). Legal culture is a relatively new concept which, according to David Nelken, can be traced to 'terms like *legal tradition* or *legal style*, which have a much longer history in comparative law or in early political science. It presupposes and invites us to explore the existence of systematic variations in patterns in 'law in the books' and 'law in action', and, above all, in the 'relation between them' (Nelken 2007b, pp. 369–370).

[9] David Nelken, however, has discussed the significance of language in the study of legal cultures elsewhere (see Nelken 2000).

2.3 *The Politics of Difference*

There is no single definition of comparative law and no consensus on its academic status, i.e. if it is a field of research, a discipline or just a method. On the one hand, we find black letter lawyers who use comparative law as a method for finding and juxtaposing two sets of legal rules and doctrines belonging to two different legal systems. On the other hand, we find scholars such as the contributors to Örücü and Nelken's handbook, most of whom compare laws in their socio-cultural and historical contexts. The main body of comparative research lies between these two positions, whereby some studies are more sensitive to the empirical aspects of law and less concerned with the normative analysis of rules, whilst others are more concerned with comparing legal rules and doctrine and less so with law's institutional makeup and cultural properties. There are therefore different ways of conducting comparative studies of law, and there are a number of different conceptions of what 'comparing' amounts to and aims to achieve.[10]

In his chapter, Glenn (2007, p. 92) argues that the Latin roots of 'com-paring' suggest 'bringing together and keeping together, of equals, which are presumed to endure, throughout and beyond the process of com-paring'. Thus, according to Glenn (2007, p. 92), the logic of comparing is not that of separation but 'living together in harmony and in a way respectful of difference...' in what amounts to 'an enduring *process* of peaceful coexistence'. Although Glenn makes no reference to Habermas, his argument that the process of comparison is intrinsically and unavoidably driven towards mutual coexistence, which in turn requires gaining greater understanding of the legal system of the 'other', is reminiscent of Habermas's communicative action, according to which the use of language is orientated towards mutual understanding, even when the participants in the communication are acting instrumentally (Habermas 1984). However, when Glenn refers to the legal history of colonialism and argues that 'the common laws [of the colonialists] yielded to local particularity, when local particularity so required', and that 'lawyers in the colonised world... engaged in an active process of reconciliation of law from the 15th century' (Glenn 2007, p. 102), unintentionally as it might be, he draws our attention away from the imbalance of power which defined the relationship between the colonialists and their lawyers, on the one hand, and the colonised natives, their cultures and laws, on the other. It is indeed true that

---

[10] In this respect, comparative law is similar to the sociology of law, as both are fields of research on the margins of mainstream legal scholarship, both contain diverse perspectives on law and legal research, some of which promote a concept of law different from that of legal positivism, and both see studies of law in interdisciplinary terms. Being theoretically and methodologically diverse, both appear as fragmented discourses lacking an all-encompassing theoretical framework which could assist them in confronting the ideology of legal positivism. However, in this very weakness lies their intellectual strength: since they do not restrict their studies theoretically or methodologically, they remain a dynamic field of study where new ideas (that do not comply with the concerns or assumptions of mainstream legal studies) are allowed, discussed and considered, and where innovative projects are given academic space to grow.

common law had to take notice of local variations and even accommodate 'alien' norms and practices in order to operate in colonised settings, but this did not imply the *recognition* of natives' laws or cultures as equal to those of the colonialists. It did not, in other words, amount to transcending one's own laws in order to engage discursively with and understand the laws of the 'other'.[11] As Cotterrell shows in his chapter, no mutual understanding or respect of the 'other' can be reached where one party uses its politically and/or culturally dominant position to control intercultural communications and dictate the terms and conditions of intercultural interactions.

In societies where the relationship between ethnic and cultural groups is defined by an imbalance of power in favour of one group, those who represent the politically dominant culture often demand that the politically less influential cultural groups assimilate themselves. This type of assimilation requires politically weaker cultures to submit to and internalise the values and worldviews of the politically dominant culture. In many cases, the internalisation of the prevailing culture's value system can amount to denouncing one's own cultural identity. Similarly, the politics of the differences in comparative law demands that politically less powerful legal systems harmonise their rules and institutions with those of the leading legal systems. The harmonisation and unification of laws brought about in this way is morally questionable, often blind to the socio-cultural mechanisms and historical context of law and its institutions, and it represents a form of domination. At the same time, many of the assumptions regarding the practicality and usefulness of harmonisation and unification remain unproven. One of these assumptions is that by making different legal systems similar, one automatically enhances communications between systems and moves them towards convergence and, at least in the European context, towards political and social unification. This reflects the efforts to harmonise laws and legal systems by a normative assumption: that law and politics must work hand in hand to enhance certitude and continuity in human affairs. This normative project is not based on the empirical reality of how late modern society is developing, and neither does it consider what the limits of law are under late modern conditions. As Legrand (1996, 1997) has argued, the harmonisation of legal rules does not necessarily lead to the emergence of a common legal understanding or the unification of legal practices, and it can actually take on different meanings in different legal systems. In Cotterrell's words:

> The same rule interpreted in two different national legal cultures will actually mean something different in each of them. So, legal harmonisation is illusory. There might be the standardisation of the letter of the rules but there will not be harmonisation of their meaning as law. (Cotterrell 2007, p. 141)

---

[11] Drawing on Norrie (2005), justice can be regarded as 'the ethical form of judgement that lies beyond the scope of positive law' (see Chap. 4). Thus, to step beyond one's own laws to understand the 'other' is a step taken towards justice. Interestingly enough, it can also amount to recognising the plurality of forms of law.

Similarly, the assumption that, by harmonising legal rules, one enhances law's system efficiency, thus significantly reducing cost factors, is based on 'anecdotal evidence' and remains in want of empirical confirmation (a similar point is also made by Smits 2007 in the context of the convergence of private law in Europe). Perhaps more importantly, we should not forget that communication between legal systems and cultures can and does take place whenever the willingness to do so, and mutual respect for others' autonomy and dignity, exist among the participants (a point also made by Glenn). Differences, admittedly, can be to one's disadvantage when they are used as a basis for negative discrimination and exclusion. Being different, Cotterrell argues, is not bad in itself, and it is definitely not a handicap when the differences are acknowledged with respect. Productive integration does not require assimilation but mutual understanding, acceptance and respect. Some comparatists thus argue that 'comparative law should shift its focus from seeking similarities (via harmonisation and unification) towards appreciating the virtues of legal diversity' (Cotterrell 2007, pp. 136–137).

2.4 Not Everything Is Culturally Determined

Most of the contributors to Örücü and Nelken's handbook pay special attention to the cultural context of law.[12] However, not all legal phenomena are necessarily cultural. This point is addressed by Nelken, who in reference to studies of the rate of litigation in the Netherlands, and how the Japanese use the court system, shows that what is often taken as cultural behaviour can also be due to institutional infrastructures of the legal system in different countries (Nelken 2007b, p. 113). For example, the Japanese 'make relatively little use of the courts', not necessarily because of their 'Confucian-shaped culture that emphasises harmonious and hierarchical relations' (Nelken 2007b, p. 113), but perhaps because 'the limited number of legal professionals and courts represents institutional barriers maintained by government bureaucracies and business elite' (Nelken 2007b, p. 113). Nelken is suggesting only in a tentative manner that an equally valid explanation may be applicable here. Yet, his example reveals that culture is one among many lenses we may employ to view, explore and interpret various social and legal phenomena. Taking this point further, I argue herein that it would be wrong to suggest that all aspects of law should be studied in terms of culture. Admittedly, all of its manifestations are—if not directly at least indirectly—connected with collective social psychological mechanisms and taken-for-granted patterns of thought and action. This does not provide a sufficient basis for treating all manifestations of law as culturally *embedded*, for we can use

[12] Patrick Glenn is the only one who does not subscribe to the notion of legal culture and continues to use 'legal traditions'; others, such as Menski, use the word 'culture' frequently, but they do not generally adopt the term 'legal culture' as the basis for their analysis.

the same type of reasoning to argue that all of its aspects are also historically, politically, linguistically and even perhaps economically embedded.

The standpoint that a cultural perspective does not necessarily offer a satisfactory understanding of all manifestations of law is demonstrated further by Ogus (2007), who draws attention to the link between the development of various legal systems and economic growth. Ogus shows that the willingness—or reluctance as the case might be—to open up one's jurisdiction to external influences, by borrowing legal rules, ideas and institutions from another jurisdiction and thus harmonising one's own laws with those of that jurisdiction, might be the outcome of cost-benefit calculations made by the legal profession which, belonging to one or both jurisdictions, might expect that the harmonisation of its laws results in an increase or decrease in demand for services. The fact that the reluctance of lawyers might be expressed by overstating, sometimes even constructing, the legal and cultural differences separating the two jurisdictions is another matter entirely, which has very little to do with the intrinsic cultural properties (i.e. properties that are reproduced through taken for granted values, attitudes and practices) of different legal systems and laws. In short, there are reasons to believe that the decision to refuse opening up one's legal system to external influences is not necessarily a cultural decision, a point which we shall miss once we regard all socio-legal action as culturally embedded.[13] Despite the insight that not everything legal is necessarily cultural, the significance of culture in comparative studies looms large in Örücü and Nelken's handbook, and not even Ogus, who might otherwise be seen as providing the antithesis to the emerging cultural approach in legal studies, seems able or prepared to avoid making use of the 'legal culture' concept.

[13] The idea of social action as culturally embedded can be traced back to the classical writings within sociology, but it was initially in the works of sociologists such as Williams (1982) and Bourdieu (1997) that it came to be treated as a specific perspective on the study of society. Bourdieu's notion of 'cultural capital' and 'habitus' is a good example of the culturalisation of social structures and human action. However, the 'cultural turn' should also be seen as a methodological measure deemed necessary by some sociologists to conceptualise the missing link between structure and agency (or the macro and micro levels of social analysis). The search for the missing link also implicitly informs some of the recent works in comparative legal cultures (see, for example, Hodgson 2000) and socio-legal research on globalisation (see, for example, Dezalay and Garth 1996), where the actions of individual actors such as prosecutors, judges or arbitrators are explored in relation to collective (structural or macro) cultural entities. For an overview of the 'cultural turn' in sociology see Sztompka (1999).

3 Towards a Meta-Methodological Framework

3.1 Culture

Undoubtedly, there are many ways of defining the notion of culture (see, for example, Rosen 2006; Cotterrell 2006), yet social scientists generally frame their definitions in terms of socially constructed and transmitted symbols, values, attitudes, perceptions, worldviews, conventions, customary practices and shared historical experiences (which are, at times, imaginary). Despite agreement among many socio-legal scholars on the cultural significance of law, it remains unclear *how* we are to introduce cultural understanding into a broader comparative law project that includes legal families and traditions. This uncertainty is due partly to the 'unbounded' and 'contested' character of the concept of culture, which is also geared to power relations (Merry 2003, quoted by Nelken 2007b, p. 114), and partly a result of the incompatibility of the cultural perspective with the definitions of a legal system which only recognises the 'positive law' of Western European legal traditions as the law proper and dismisses non-European systems and unofficial forms of law.

Culture is a multidimensional and interpretive notion which is hard to operationalise in concrete and unambiguous terms. Sociologists and social anthropologists often define it in terms of 'meaning', or the dynamic *processes* that make social life meaningful and help individuals and whole communities to develop their own particular worldviews. Expressed differently, culture refers to the process of reproducing beliefs and attitudes that people hold about the world surrounding them (Wuthnow 1987). These beliefs and attitudes help the individual to interpret, create and recreate social reality within his/her own universe of meaning, while forming patterns of behaviour which embody the intersubjectively shared *values* of a community. Thus, the notion of meaning gains cultural significance when it becomes intersubjective. It is also at this stage when intersubjectively shared values contribute to the social integration of groups, communities and whole societies. Culture is not, however, an entirely subjective phenomenon, for its various value formations possess observable 'objective' properties (it can also refer to artefacts, a notion which for lack of space has to be omitted from this discussion). Although these formations are products of human consciousness, they are by no means confined to the individual actor's subjective inner life. Values are externalised through symbolic and non-symbolic social interactions and given an objective status which, in turn, helps to create and maintain patterns of behaviour. Language, which is one of the most basic expressions of any culture, provides the best example of how the subjective and objective aspects of a cultural process are linked. Language is created subjectively by sharing and reproducing symbols, rules and conventions, and it is objectively manifested in writing and speech, making it independent of any individual actor's personal usage. Expressed differently, language does not determine what is communicated (the content of the communication is decided by the individual actor's interest and the context of the interaction), but because of its objective characteristics it determines *how* the communication takes place. This also suggests that the objective features of a culture are to be observed by focusing on the *mode* of symbolic communication rather than on the content of such communication.[14]

In short, culture refers to both the subjective/interpretive qualities of social life (and in legal studies to the underbelly of law and legal practice), which are produced and reproduced through the taken-for-granted norms, values and attitudes in face-to-face interactions, and to the objective/'factual' properties of society (and in legal research to law's institutional properties). The concept of culture is therefore sensitive to different levels of social action (lifeworld/system, agency/structure or micro/macro levels), compatible with the combination of top-down and bottom-up methods of inquiry and thus can lend itself to the contextualisation of various types of social behaviour and institutional practices, hence the attraction of employing cultural perspectives in comparative studies that aim to go beyond legal rules and highlight the connection between law and its context. Having said that, we must remember, as we saw above, that the cultural perspective is not a necessary prerequisite for undertaking comparative studies of law contextually, and there are certain aspects of law and legal behaviour which can be discussed in non-cultural terms. Anything *of* or *about* law can be interpreted in cultural terms, but it is perhaps our interpretation and not necessarily the law and its various expressions that is culturally formed. The cultural approach to the study of law, i.e. when we describe and analyse it as a cultural expression, becomes problematic if it leads us to treat culture as both the cause and the effect of an event at the same time. The use of a culture as a method also becomes potentially misleading in cases where law is used as a site of cultural struggle in order to promote group-specific, non-cultural (i.e. political or economic) goals, e.g. when references to cultural differences are used instrumentally by lawyers who do not wish for the harmonisation of their private law for fear of losing their clients. The concept of culture is useful in comparative studies, but it needs to be applied with great discrimination, especially when it is employed as an explanatory tool to conceptualise what is already defined and interpreted in cultural terms by the participants in law's processes (Nelken 2007b, p. 115).

Nelken does not dismiss criticism directed at the concept of legal culture, but he does relate the conceptual and empirical shortcomings of legal culture to 'the complexities of what needs to be explained' (Nelken 2007b, p. 117). On balance, the final test of the validity and applicability of the notion of legal culture lies in the possibility of its operationalisation, i.e. if it can be broken down into a set of concrete, observable entities which can serve empirical investigations. Here too

[14] I have elsewhere (see Banakar 1994) drawn on Van Dijk's study of discourse analysis (1992) to explore the *mode* of symbolic communication. In this study Van Dijk shows how racist ideas can be disseminated by a form of public debate which avoids using overt racist language but nevertheless retains the mode of racist discourse.

there are no straightforward answers, for Nelken readily admits that there are many reasons to be wary about where and how we use the term 'culture'.

The other reason for the uncertainty surrounding the application of a culturally contextualised concept of law is in relation to the continuing prevalence of the ideology of legal positivism.[15] Legally positivistic descriptions are part of law's *self-descriptions*, i.e. its communications about itself, of how legal systems *ought* to be constructed and how law ought to operate. Law's self-descriptions exert a powerful normative influence over how it is perceived and conceptualised by all those who participate in legal processes (e.g. judges, lawyers, juries and defendants) and those who describe it (e.g. academics and journalists). These descriptions uphold an ideal of law as an autonomous system (independent of political, economic, cultural, religious, racial or gender interests) capable of operating as an instrument of regulation and as an impartial arbiter of disputes. Legal positivism is an ideologically powerful instrument for a range of other reasons, for example being born out of the processes of rationalisation that define modernity (see Chap. 4). In addition, as we discussed in Chap. 2, by distinguishing sharply between law, morality and other culturally determined value systems, legal positivism serves the disciplinary aims of doctrinal scholars who treat law as a normatively sealed system which, according to them, should be studied and analysed on its own terms alone. That is why the legal systems of Africa and Asia, which accommodate many voices and are sensitive to cultural practices and customs, have often been ignored in comparative law. That is also why the idea of 'living law' has been dismissed by legal positivists from the outset, even though it is being 'discovered' by branches of legal theory engaged in the study of transnational law (see Hellum et al. 2011, pp. 4–13).[16] In short, the approach to the study of law, which is shaped by different schools of legal positivism, is incompatible with the social-scientifically defined notion of laws as culturally embedded forms of social organisations that do not *necessarily* have the state as their source.

Much confusion is caused by applying criteria belonging to legal positivism—criteria such as the sovereign (treating the state as one of the primary sources of law), autonomy (emphasising law's separation from other normative spheres such as politics and religion), coherence (constructing a rational architecture for law) and objectivity (passing judgement based on law alone)—to evaluate the validity of the social-scientifically constructed pluralistic theories of law which do not define it in terms of the state or as an autonomous sphere of action. Those who try to employ cultural insights within the traditional framework of legal positivism often 'reify' culture, for only an immutable concept of culture devoid of its dynamic processual properties can be reconciled with the traditional assumptions of legal positivism,

[15] Legal positivism is not a homogeneous approach and contains different schools which emphasise the autonomy of law in different degrees and discuss the separation between positive law and morality in different terms. For a discussion see Chaps. 2 and 3.

[16] We discussed the clash between Hans Kelsen and Eugen Ehrlich in Chap. 7. See Van Klink (2006).

which conceptually divorces law from extra-legal norms and practices. They also disregard the bottom-up perspective, which shows how law also emerges out of the needs of social organisations, or how it is used and experienced by ordinary citizens and officials, at the expense of a top-down, state-oriented view of its sources.

3.2 Limits of the Top-Down Approach

The importance of combining top-down and bottom-up perspectives is revealed by Masha Antokolskaia's paper on comparative family law, in which she tries to show that a degree of harmonisation has been achieved in the field of family law through the doctrinal and interpretive techniques of the European Court of Human Rights (ECtHR), i.e. by applying a top-down method. Antokolskaia recognises that European societies have radically transformed their attitudes to marriage, family formation and sexual relationships since the 1960s. Although much of this transformation can be attributed to recognising the plurality of family and marital values at the socio-cultural level, on the one hand, and the success of the women's rights movement in overcoming 'the centuries-long dominance of the man within the family', on the other, she nonetheless regards the ECtHR as *the* driving force behind the transformation of family law (Antokolskaia 2007, pp. 241–242). Furthermore, she recognises that attitudes toward many aspects of family formation, marriage, divorce, cohabitation and, to a lesser extent, transsexual marriage became *first* socially relaxed and then normalised, before being legally recognised. Yet, she somehow sees law and social development as two separate but parallel processes, suggesting that the process containing social conditions is mysteriously 'reflected' in the legal process (Antokolskaia 2007, p. 243). Antokolskaia thus appears to be suggesting that the ECtHR decided on its own accord (i.e. without any input from social movements that mobilise public opinion and exert pressure on European governments) to 'reflect' social conditions by applying 'the so-called "dynamic interpretation of the Convention"', to 'involve factors external to the Convention' and to use the doctrine of the 'margin of appreciation' to develop and extend the scope of the protection of family rights (Antokolskaia 2007, p. 242). It is true that law, being inherently conservative, often lags behind social and technological developments, therefore 'reflecting' rather than leading them, but this does not happen automatically or passively, and law does not 'mirror' every socio-cultural development in the same way or to the same extent. The 'mirroring' effect therefore has a social mechanism that needs to be addressed here—a mechanism that interconnects the top-down and bottom-up processes.[17]

[17] The idea of law 'mirroring' or 'reflecting' social developments is, at best, based on a problematic metaphor, for it fails to capture the dialectical nature of the relationship between law and society. 'Mirroring' always suggests passivity and emphasises the separateness of law and society rather than their ongoing *interaction*.

The type of analysis we find in Antokolskaia's paper is admittedly not devoid of merit, for it describes the inner workings of the ECtHR and shows that legal instruments can become a *vehicle* for consolidating progressive ideas. Nevertheless, at least in the field of family law, progressive ideas emerge first in the society at large and are recognised and incorporated into law as a result of the pressure exerted by various social movements or for purely pragmatic reasons (for example, for resolving income tax or inheritance problems). The missing link in Antokolskaia's analysis is the role played by grassroots participation in this process, i.e. by women's and gay and lesbian movements in different countries across Europe, in mobilising public and political opinion in support of an extension of family rights.[18] A study of grassroots and social movements cannot be carried out by focusing on the ECtHR's methods of interpretation or doctrinal innovation but by applying a bottom-up perspective which brings into focus the formation of demands for the extension of family protection rights at the socio-cultural level.

3.3 Combining the Top-Down and Bottom-Up Perspectives

The comparative studies and debates we referred to above demonstrate that each aspect or area of law has its own specific context and, subsequently, interacts with society in its own unambiguous way. Constitutional law, for example, has a more pronounced political dimension than, say, commercial law, which consequently is linked more intimately to the economic makeup of society than, for instance, family law. However, most studies in Örücü and Nelken's handbook either place an emphasis on culture, i.e. irrespective of the substantive area, they tend to subscribe to the standpoint of 'law as culture', or make use of the word (legal) 'culture'. This could mislead us into regarding the cultural approach as a reliable general method of contextualising law. The cultural perspective, despite its conceptual fuzziness, has, as mentioned above, a number of important reflexive properties that can facilitate contextualisation. When used dynamically to study ongoing societal processes, culture becomes sensitive to historical developments, power relationships and various levels of legal reality. In comparative studies, culture helps us to describe and explain the hybrid character of legal families and to explore how legal

[18] In a study of anti-discrimination laws in Sweden, I have argued that rights that are introduced from above, such as those expressed in the Swedish Act Against Ethnic Discrimination, and work their way top-down by introducing new non-discriminatory values which are not already embedded in the majority culture, are at best only partially effective. Their partial effectiveness depends on the extent to which these values are already shared by employers and decision-makers. In contrast, rights that are generated at the grass root level first, such as those expressed in the Swedish Equal Opportunity Act, which aims at protecting and promoting the position of women in employment and the labour market, are relatively effective. The values underpinning women's rights emerged through women's movements and thus enjoyed widespread political support among sections of society long before they become a basis for legislation. See Banakar (2004).

transplants grow and change in their new socio-legal environments. We also see that not all forms of law and legal behaviour are determined culturally and/or should be studied in cultural terms. Although the focus on the cultural constitution of law, which incidentally can mean many different things (see Nelken 2007a), will continue to offer a powerful general method of contextualising law and legal instruments, it does not provide a universally valid guideline for contextual study. A general guideline might instead be found in a combination of the top-down and bottom-up approaches which situate law at the macro level of legal systems, at the intermediary level of legal implementation and enforcement and at the micro level of citizenry, where law is used to underpin expectations and organise everyday collaborative activities and relationships.

One way to integrate these three levels is by starting with legal rules at the macro level, thus working our way down the legal system through the layers of formal and informal institutional practices of the law, to the level of social interaction. Starting at the level of legal systems, we analyse how legal rules are employed to bring about an interaction between the normative structures of law and society. Rules in general, whether social or legal, are standards that guide action in a specific way and against which action can be assessed and judged (Galligan 2006, p. 50; for a discussion see Chap. 5). Since they are expressed in language, they have an open texture, which allows outside factors to affect their interpretation and application. Thus, even clear and precise rules are contextual and contingent upon the surrounding considerations. The recognition that all rules need to be interpreted before they make an impact on social life is of little value if it fails to consider the full extent and significance of the contextual contingencies of rules. Social and legal rules often signal that 'a certain kind of deliberative process has to be gone through, a process of which the rule is a vital but not conclusive part' (Galligan 2006, p. 57). Deliberations are required to determine if a specific rule is applicable in a particular situation, and if it is, what it means. For example, 'it may require consideration of related rules, the weighing of presumptions, and the consideration of factors to take into account' (Galligan 2006, p. 57). To repeat the point made in Chap. 5, rules are the starting point of deliberations and, as such, they neither dictate fully what action should be taken 'nor exhaust the range of actions that may be properly taken' (Galligan 2006, p. 57).

What happens to legal rules, whether they are adopted, enforced, alternatively modified or marginalised, depends to a great extent on the institutional settings in which they are used. Institutions consist not only of rules but also of values, standards, dispositions etc., which are created spontaneously once people join together over time collaboratively (Galligan 2006, p. 106).[19] To quote Galligan again, 'where an activity is itself created by legal rules, as in the case of administrative agencies, say, informal rules often emerge in order to interpret the legal rules, or even to modify or marginalise them' (Galligan 2006, p. 108). This insight

[19] See Selznick (1949). This type of reasoning is rooted deeply in the sociology of law and can be traced back easily to Roscoe Pound and Eugen Ehrlich.

corresponds with what we described above (see the introduction) as the gap between 'law as rules' and 'law and social practices'. Understanding these informal rules, and describing how they interact with formal rules, requires the application of the bottom-up perspective using qualitative methods of social enquiry sensitive to the social-psychological mechanism of face-to-face interaction. The unit of such analyses cannot be rules, whether legal or social, but the communicative mechanisms through which rules are generated and mediated within the lifeworld. The focus of micro analysis will differ depending on the object of our study—in one study it will be the conception, perceptions and usages of businessmen, in another study those of the lawyers or officials of law and in yet another study those of ordinary citizens. The point is to confront and merge the micro usages and perceptions of law with the macro applications of the law at the level of legal systems or international law. Such a combination, in many situations, will lead to recognising the diversity of sources and forms of law within the same social space (legal pluralism) or within the same legal system (legal polycentricity).

In the approach outlined above, we started our analysis at the level of legal systems and used legal rules to capture the interaction between law and society at the macro level. Such a starting point has certain methodological ramifications—unwillingly, as it might be, we endorse some of the assumptions of legal positivism, e.g. treating the state (or the 'rules of recognition' as practiced by judges and other officials of law)[20] as the primary source of law. It also corresponds with our first contextualisation approach and the most widespread understanding of the gap, which addresses the disparity between the claims of the law, or lawmakers' objectives (to bring about, for example, social reform through new legislation), and its real impact on social conditions. It is used frequently to criticise forms of 'legal instrumentalism', i.e. the view that the law may be employed as a universal device by policymakers to bring about social change and reform (Banakar 1997, p. 113). Alternatively, it may refer to the gap between 'law in the books' and 'law in action' (Pound 1910). Studies which concern the gap often criticise the misconception that the law is an independent variable which can act upon social behaviour and institutions. However, many of these studies, albeit unwittingly, continue to suggest the possibility of closing or minimising the gap. This misconception is maintained partly because the 'instrumentalist paradigm', to borrow from Griffiths (1995, pp. 205–206), continues to appeal to policymakers who seek effective modes of regulation which may be implemented to bring about social reform, but without modifying power structures in society.

Alternatively we can start our analysis at the micro level, i.e. establish how law is used to organise relationships in everyday life, before working our way up the legal system, thus contrasting the formation of law and experience of legality at the level of social interaction with the manifestation of laws at the level of nation state or international law. This method highlights the differences between laws introduced and enforced by the state and rules which are followed *de facto* by ordinary

[20] On Herbert Hart's 'rule of recognition' see Chap. 5.

people in the course of their everyday life (cf. Sumner 1906; Pound 1910; Ehrlich 1936; Nelken 1981; Tamanaha 1997, pp. 101–103 and 117–118). Within the classical sociology of law, the application and experience of law at the level of everyday life have been treated as sociologically more fundamental than occasional laws and regulations. In an almost polemical debate against legal positivism, state law has been degraded occasionally as normatively superficial (cf. Gurvitch 1947). Massell's study of how the Bolsheviks tried to modernise the Muslim areas of Soviet Central Asia, which we discussed in the previous chapter, exemplifies this conception of the gap, which emphasises the power of 'folkways' over 'law-ways' (Sumner 1906) and argues that for law to be effective it needs to be embedded in the culture of those who are subjected to its regulatory force.[21] Therefore, it corresponds with our third approach to contextualisation, which makes the point that a law which is not embedded in the culture of those whom it governs will constitute neither a legitimate order nor an effective medium of governance.[22] The point made here is that the choice of starting point (whether we start our analysis at the level of the state and work our way down, or start at the level of social organisation and work our way up) will conceptualise the gap between 'the legal' and 'the social' differently, and as a result it will have an impact on the outcome of our studies. Nevertheless, irrespective of the starting point, we need to consider the three levels of social action in order to contextualise laws and legal systems.

A combination of top-down and bottom-up perspectives might not find a positive reception within law reform projects funded by international agencies interested in spreading Western models of trade, politics and democracy in different parts of the world. Leaving aside the moral issues discussed above in connection with the harmonisation of private law, those who carry out such projects need much more than knowledge of the legal institution that is to be 'transplanted'. They need knowledge not only of the recipient legal system, but also how law operates in relation to various social institutions in the receiving country. Thus, it is not enough to draft a new constitution, or even set up a new court system and train a new

[21] The debate within comparative law reveals that this point is often articulated in a somewhat simplistic way in mainstream studies of law in society. For example, the comparatist Watson (1977) has used his studies of legal transplants, i.e. legal institutions and ideas borrowed from one jurisdiction and transplanted in another, to refute the dependency of law on its socio-cultural context (for an overview of the debate, see Nelken 2001). Admittedly, legal institutions will undergo socio-cultural transformation once they are transplanted into a new legal environment, but the fact remains that they can 'travel' (Nelken 2001) across national borders and cultural boundaries.

[22] It is noteworthy that our second contextualisation approach does not correspond with any of the gaps described herein. One possible reason is that the understanding of how modern law de-contextualises social events before judging them comprises a critique of modernity and the modern legal system, and by implication it argues that the attempts of policymakers to close or decrease the gap by increasing the rationality of the law and legal processes are misplaced. Once viewed from this angle, the gap becomes, as we argued in the introduction, part of the definition of modern law as an autonomous social system, and ultimately it reflects social conflicts and contradictions incorporated in the project of modernity.

judiciary, in order to democratise countries such as Iraq or Afghanistan. Any attempt to reform the legal systems of such countries by importing legal ideas and institutions from outside needs to recognise their political history and incorporate in the new institutions the sense of law and justice which is embedded in the existing social and economic structures of their societies—a sense of justice which, incidentally, might be at variance with the Western notion of democracy. Legal transplants undergo meaning transformation once they are implanted into a new legal system.[23] Despite the relative autonomy of law and the legal profession (which might prefer transplants to constructing legal institutions from scratch), transplants are reconstructed by the internal culture of their 'host' and transformed by the new context of the legal system as they determine and define their functions in a new social environment (see Tuebner 1998).

To sum up, in order to capture the complexity of these transformations and reconstructions, one needs to study law at different levels and from different perspectives simultaneously. Thus, top-down and bottom-up approaches need to be integrated into one single methodological framework that contextualises legal instruments, legal ideas or legal institutions at three levels of analysis: (1) at the macro level of the legal system, asking how law, as a body of rules, interacts with society, (2) at the level of intermediary legal institutions, asking how legal rules are interpreted by officials and implemented and enforced by courts, tribunals and other agencies, and (3) at the level of social action, asking how law is identified, employed and experienced by ordinary citizens as part of their attempt to organise social relationships. To address these three points in research, we have to step out of law's domain of authority and into social theory, in order to explore reflexively law's taken-for-granted values and assumptions. This is where studies of law have to merge with studies of social institutions and behaviour, i.e. with the forms of knowledge generated by sociology, social anthropology, history, psychology, political science, economics and so on. This means that contextualisation cannot be confined to paying lip service to social theory by recognising in passing the social forces that interact with law and its institutions. It must instead apply an empirically informed conceptual framework that helps us to explore these social factors as an integral part of the way law manifests itself. Thus, the focus of our study is neither the law nor the social forces underpinning it, but rather the ongoing *interaction* between the two fields. The central unit of our analysis can be neither legal rules nor social norms of organisation, but instead they must be the communicative actions which make the production and reproduction of norms and rules, whether social, cultural or legal, possible.[24]

---

[23] Legal transplant is another misleading metaphor. It suggests the possibility of transplanting a legal institution belonging to one legal system into the body of another legal system, without it (i.e. the transplanted institution) undergoing fundamental functional and legal identity change.

[24] For an earlier comparative work where law is considered as a communicative phenomenon see Allott (1980).

References

Allott, A. (1980). *The limits of law*. London: Butterworths.
Antokolskaia, M. (2007). Comparing family law. In E. Örücü & D. Nelken (Eds.), *Comparative law: A handbook* (pp. 241–262). Oxford: Hart.
Banakar, R. (1994). *Rättens dilemma – Om konflikthantering i ett mångkulturellt samhälle (Conflict management in a multicultural society)*. Lund: Bokbox.
Banakar, R. (1997). *Doorkeepers of the law*. Aldershot: Ashgate.
Banakar, R. (2004). When do rights matter? In S. Halliday & P. Schmitt (Eds.), *Human rights brought home* (pp. 165–184). Oxford: Hart.
Bell, J. (2007). Administrative law in a comparative perspective. In E. Örücü & D. Nelken (Eds.), *Comparative law: A handbook* (pp. 287–312). Oxford: Hart.
Bourdieu, P. (1997). *Outline of a theory of practice*. Cambridge: Cambridge University Press.
Cotterrell, R. (2006). *Law, culture and society*. Aldershot: Ashgate.
Cotterrell, R. (2007). Is it so bad to be different? Comparative law and the appreciation of diversity. In E. Örücü & D. Nelken (Eds.), *Comparative law: A handbook* (pp. 133–154). Oxford: Hart.
De Cruz, P. (2007). *Comparative law in a changing world*. London: Routledge-Cavendish.
Dezalay, Y., & Garth, B. G. (1996). *Dealing in virtue*. Chicago: University of Chicago.
Donahue, C. (2008). Comparative law before the code Napoleon. In M. Reimann & R. Zimmermann (Eds.), *The Oxford handbook of comparative law* (pp. 3–32). Oxford: Oxford University Press.
Ehrlich, E. (1936). *Fundamental principles of the sociology of law*. Cambridge, MA: Harvard University Press (original publication 1912).
Flood, J., & Sosa, F. P. (2008). Lawyers, law firms and the stabilisation of transnational business. *Northwestern Journal of International Law and Business*. An e-copy available at: http://ssrn.com/abstract=1078820.
Foster, N. H. D. (2007). Comparing commercial law. In E. Örücü & D. Nelken (Eds.), *Comparative law: A handbook* (pp. 263–286). Oxford: Hart.
Galligan, D. (2006). *Law in modern society*. Oxford: Clarendon.
Glanert, S. (2008). Speaking language to law: The case of Europe. *Legal Studies, 28*(2), 161–171.
Glenn, H. P. (2000). *Legal traditions of the world by and comparative law in a changing world*. Oxford: Oxford University Press.
Glenn, H. P. (2007). Comparing. In E. Örücü & D. Nelken (Eds.), *Comparative law: A handbook* (pp. 91–108). Oxford: Hart.
Griffiths, J. (1995). Legal pluralism and the theory of legislation: With special reference to the regulation of Euthanasia. In H. Petersen & H. Zahle (Eds.), *Legal polycentricity: Consequences of pluralism in law* (pp. 201–234). Aldershot: Dartmouth.
Gurvitch, G. (1947). *Sociology of law*. New Brunswick, NJ: Transaction Publishers (original publication 1942).
Habermas, J. (1984). *The theory of communicative action* (Vol. I). Boston: Beacon.
Hammerslev, O. (2013). Studies of the legal profession. In R. Banakar & M. Travers (Eds.), *Law and social theory* (pp. 325–340). Oxford: Hart.
Harding, A., & Leyland, P. (2007). Comparative law in constitutional context. In E. Örücü & D. Nelken (Eds.), *Comparative law: A handbook* (pp. 313–338). Oxford: Hart.
Hellum, A., et al. (Eds.). (2011). *From transnational relations to transnational laws: Northern European laws at the crossroads*. Farnham: Ashgate.
Hodgson, J. (2000). Comparing legal cultures: The comparativist as participant observer. In D. Nelken (Ed.), *Contrasting criminal justice: Getting from here to there*. Aldershot: Ashgate.
Hopt, K. J. (2008). Comparative company law. In M. Reimann & R. Zimmermann (Eds.), *The Oxford handbook of comparative law* (pp. 1161–1192). Oxford: Oxford University Press.
Legrand, P. (1996). European legal systems are not converging. *International and Comparative Law Quarterly, 45*(1), 52–81.

Legrand, P. (1997). Against a European civil code. *Modern Law Review, 60*(1), 44–63.
Legrand, P. (2003). The same and the different. In P. Legrand & R. Munday (Eds.), *Comparative legal studies: Traditions and transitions* (pp. 240–311). Cambridge: Cambridge University Press.
Legrand, P., & Munday, R. (Eds.). (2003). *Comparative legal studies: Traditions and transitions.* Cambridge: Cambridge University Press.
McCrudden, C. (2007). Judicial comparativism and human rights. In E. Örücü & D. Nelken (Eds.), *Comparative law: A handbook* (pp. 371–398). Oxford: Hart.
Menski, W. (2006). *Comparative law in a global context.* Cambridge: Cambridge University Press.
Menski, W. (2007). Beyond Europe. In E. Örücü & D. Nelken (Eds.), *Comparative law: A handbook* (pp. 189–216). Oxford: Hart.
Merry, S. E. (2003). Human rights law and the demonization of culture (and anthropology along the way). *PolaR: Political and Legal Anthropology Review, 26*(1), 55–76.
Michaels, R. (2013). Globalisation and law. In R. Banakar & M. Travers (Eds.), *Law and social theory* (pp. 287–304). Oxford: Hart.
Monti, M. (2010). *A new strategy for the single market: At the service of Europe's economy and society.* Report to the President of the European Commission.
Nelken, D. (1981). The gap problem in the sociology of law: A theoretical review. *Windsor Yearbook of Access to Justice, 1*, 35–61.
Nelken, D. (Ed.). (2000). *Contrasting criminal justice: Getting from here to there.* Aldershot: Ashgate/Dartmouth.
Nelken, D. (2001). Towards a sociology of legal adaptation. In J. Feest & D. Nelken (Eds.), *Adapting legal cultures* (pp. 7–54). Oxford: Hart.
Nelken, D. (2004). Using the concept of legal culture. *Australian Journal of Legal Philosophy, 29* (1), 1–28.
Nelken, D. (2007a). Comparing law and comparative legal studies. In E. Örücü & D. Nelken (Eds.), *Comparative law: A handbook* (pp. 3–42). Oxford: Hart.
Nelken, D. (2007b). Culture, legal. In D. S. Clark (Ed.), *Encyclopedia of law and society: American and global perspectives* (pp. 369–374). London: Sage.
Norrie, A. (2005). *Law and the beautiful soul.* London: GlassHouse.
Ogus, A. (2007). The economic approach: Competitions between legal systems. In E. Örücü & D. Nelken (Eds.), *Comparative law: A handbook* (pp. 155–168). Oxford: Hart.
Örücü, E. (2007). A general view of "Legal Families" and "Mixing Systems". In E. Örücü & D. Nelken (Eds.), *Comparative law: A handbook* (pp. 169–188). Oxford: Hart.
Örücü, E., & Nelken, D. (Eds.). (2007). *Comparative law: A handbook.* Oxford: Hart.
Pound, R. (1910). Law in books and law in action. *American Law Review, 44*, 12–36.
Pound, R. (1943). Sociology of law and sociological jurisprudence. *The University of Toronto Law Journal, 5*(1), 1–20.
Reimann, M., & Zimmerman, R. (Eds.). (2008). *The Oxford handbook of comparative law.* Oxford: Oxford University Press.
Roberts, P. (2007). Comparative law for international criminal justice. In E. Örücü & D. Nelken (Eds.), *Comparative law: A handbook* (pp. 339–370). Oxford: Hart.
Rosen, L. (2006). *Law as culture: An invitation.* Princeton: Princeton University Press.
Selznick, P. (1949). *TVA and the Grass Roots.* Berkeley: University of California Press.
Siems, M. M. (2007). The end of comparative law. *The Journal of Comparative Law, 2*(2), 133–150.
Smits, J. M. (Ed.). (2006). *Elgar encyclopedia of comparative law.* Cheltenham: Edward Elgar.
Smits, J. M. (2007). Convergence of private law in Europe. In E. Örücü & D. Nelken (Eds.), *Comparative law: A handbook* (pp. 219–240). Oxford: Hart.
Sumner, W. G. (1906). *Folkways: A study of the sociological importance of usages, manners, customs, mores, and morals.* Boston: Ginn and Co.
Sztompka, P. (1999). *Trust: A sociological theory.* Cambridge: Cambridge University Press.

Tamanaha, B. Z. (1997). *Realistic socio-legal theory: Pragmatism and a social theory of law*. Oxford: Clarendon.
Tuebner, G. (1998). Legal Irritants: Good faith in British law or how unifying law ends up in new divergences. *Modern Law Review, 61*(1), 11–32.
Twining, W. (2007). Globalisation and comparative law. In E. Örücü & D. Nelken (Eds.), *Comparative law: A handbook* (pp. 69–90). Oxford: Hart.
Van Dijk, T. A. (1992). Discourse and the denial of racism. *Discourse and Society, 3*(1), 87–118.
Van Erp, S. (2007). Comparative private law in practice: The process of law reform. In E. Örücü & D. Nelken (Eds.), *Comparative law: A handbook* (pp. 399–410). Oxford: Hart.
Van Klink, B. (2006). *Facts and norms: The unfinished debate between Eugen Ehrlich and Hans Kelsen*. An e-copy is available at SSRN: http://ssrn.com/abstract=980957.
Watson, A. (1977). *Society and legal change*. Edinburgh: Scottish Academic.
Williams, R. (1982). *The sociology of culture*. New York: Schocken.
Wuthnow, R. (1987). *Meaning and moral order: Explorations in cultural analysis*. Berkeley: University of California Press.

Chapter 9
A Case-Study of Non-Western Legal Systems and Cultures

Abstract This chapter originally grew out of reflections on the applicability of socio-legal theory to the study of non-Western societies and jurisdictions. Are theories and assumptions which were initially developed as part of studies of law in Western societies applicable to the study of non-Western law and legality in non-Western legal cultures? Legal sociology was developed in Western Europe and North America, and only more recently has it spread to other countries in the South and Central Americas. We find no established tradition of socio-legal research in most Middle Eastern and African countries. Understandably we need to question if legal sociology's conceptualisation of the relationship between law and society does not harbour great limitations when it comes to the study of law in non-Western societies. This concern is hardly new and has been among the methodological considerations which have preoccupied social and cultural anthropologists (most of whom initially were Westerners studying non-Western cultures). In the context of the methodological discussions of this book, this chapter shows that theories developed on the basis of studying Western legal systems have both limitations and possibilities. The relationship between Iranian law, state and culture is, for example, rooted in the country's long and turbulent history and differs radically from that of Western European nations. However, Iran has the oldest democratic constitution in the Middle East, a constitution which was originally inspired by legal developments in Western Europe, and part of the architecture of its legal system is based on French civil law.

1 Prologue: One Word

In *A Treatise on One Word*, an essay on constitutional government written in 1871, Yusef Khan Mustashar od-Dawleh argued that all Iran needed, in order to transform itself into a modern nation, could be summed up in one word.[1] This magical word

This chapter is based on 'Driving Dangerously: Law, Culture and Driving habits in Iran'. In (2012) *British Journal of Middle Eastern Studies* 39(2): 241–257. It was originally co-authored with Shahrad Nasrolahi Fard who conducted the interviews in Tehran.

[1] The Persian title of this book is: *Resaleh Mosumeh be Yek Kaleme*. Yusef Khan Mustashar od-Dawleh (d. 1898) was an Azarbaijani scholar, a political reformist and Iran's *chargé d'affaires* in Paris (see Seyed-Gohrab and McGlinn 2007; Kia 1994; Atabaki 1993, p. 20).

R. Banakar, *Normativity in Legal Sociology*, DOI 10.1007/978-3-319-09650-6_9

was *qānon* (from the Greek *kanon*), which he went on to describe as a French-style body of written legal codes uniformly applicable to all. Mustashar od-Dawleh was not alone in wondering why Iran had stagnated economically and was in a state of social disarray while European countries were prospering through technological progress. He was, however, amongst the first few who identified the main cause of Iran's economic backwardness and social malaise as its failure to develop a modern constitutional government.

The publication of *One Word* in 1873 is part of the germination of a historically unique political movement for the establishment of the rule of law, which grew into the Iranian Constitutional Revolution between 1905 and 1911. The political momentum of this movement, which was supported by members of the clergy, merchants and royals, eventually forced the Qajar monarch, Mozaffar al-Din Shāh, to concede the election of a Parliament on 12 January 1906 and sign the first Iranian Constitution, which was drafted later the same year. By injecting the idea of democracy and the rule of law into the political life of the nation, the Constitutional Revolution permanently transformed Iranian politics and yet failed to create an executive branch which de facto operated and was accountable under the law. The establishment of a constitutional government was resisted by courtiers, state officials and the monarch, whose arbitrary powers it aimed to curtail. It was also opposed by the colonial powers, whose plans for the region were undermined by the rise of a revolutionary and democratic Iran.[2] However, a more important reason for the failure of the Constitutional Revolution to achieve its ultimate goals can be found in its lack of grassroots support. The underpinning ideology of the movement had not grown organically in Iran but was rather imported from Europe by the first generation of Iranian intellectuals during the nineteenth century and did not gain currency among their ordinary countrymen. Moreover, establishing the rule of law requires continuity in lawmaking and democratic processes, not to mention a public space which facilitates political debates and disagreements. Such continuity and space have not been characteristics of the historical processes which have defined Iran's social and political development over the centuries.[3]

The institutionalisation of the Iranian Constitution was interrupted by external and internal political events, and plans to replace the arbitrary rule of the state (or *estebdād*) with the rule of law were brought to a premature end when Reza Khān (later Reza Shāh), an officer in the Persian Cossack Brigade, overthrew Ahmad Shāh Qajar and established the Pahlavi dynasty in 1925. With the reign of the Pahlavis began Iran's modern era of *estebdād*. The Pahlavis carried out an extensive programme of construction and modernisation, setting up inter alia a modern judiciary, but their modernity was not introduced through a process of democratisation. Instead, it took the form of sham Westernisation imposed on the

---

[2] The Russians and the British divided up Iran into two spheres of influence in 1907. The British were to control the south and the Russians the north of the country.

[3] The new monarch, Muhammad Ali Shāh, who wished to abolish the Constitution, ordered the bombardment of the Parliament building in 1908.

people of Iran, largely through the barrel of the gun.[4] The Pahlavi family ruled Iran through 54 years of political turmoil and social instability until it too was swept aside by the tide of a revolutionary movement.

2 Reckless Driving and Legal Culture

> Aside from the overwhelmingly friendly and welcoming people, any first-time visitor to Iran will be stunned by the country's driving habits. Seatbelts and mirrors are for sissies... Lanes are ignored in an all-out free-for-all. Traffic merges at 90 degrees and just pushes through. People drive backwards for blocks on one-way streets. U-turns in the middle of crowded thoroughfares are common. For some reason there seem to be very few wrecks (or even dings on cars) and nobody takes it personally. McLean (2007)

> I don't know why everyone is driving so fast... All they do when they get to their destination is drink tea.[5] De Bellaigue (2004, p. 13)

This chapter may be read as an attempt to explore the driving habits of Iranians in light of Homa Katouzian's historical thesis, which posits that Iranian society was not founded on written or unwritten 'canons' of law (*qānon*) and therefore has not acquired a strong tradition of rule by law (see Katouzian 1997, 2009). Although this study concludes by providing empirical support for Katouzian's thesis, it originally started as a socio-legal inquiry into how Iranians perceive, conceptualise and experience their driving habits. During my recent visits to Iran, I was struck by the deterioration of the traffic situation and could not help wondering if it mirrored some structural dysfunctions embedded in Iranian society and culture. Otherwise, how could a group of people, who pride themselves, as one of the interviewees in this study put it, on being 'courteous', behave so recklessly towards the rights and safety of each other when driving their cars?

Iran has the highest rate of road traffic accidents (RTAs) worldwide—five times the world average. According to UNICEF (2007), 'in 2006 nearly 28,000 people died in traffic accidents in Iran, compared with roughly 17,000 in 2000',[6] constituting the second most frequent single cause of mortality in the country (Amani and Kazemnejad 2010; Abbasi-Shavazi 2004).[7] It is estimated that as many as 70 % of RTAs may be due to reckless and dangerous driving, with illegal overtaking and

[4] For a discussion on 'colonial modernisation', see Dabashi (2007).

[5] A female taxi passenger in Isfahan; quoted in De Bellaigue (2004).

[6] UNICEF (2007) *Iran Representative: early safety training for children best way to reduce high rate of injuries and accidents*. http://www.unicef.org/iran/media_3810.html. Also see UNICEF, *Road Traffic Injuries in Iran and their Prevention, A Worrying Picture*. http://www.unicef.org/iran/media_4783.html. Accessed on 10 December 2010.

[7] The primary cause of mortality in 2007 was coronary heart disease, which claimed 25 % of all those who died in Iran that year. It was followed by road traffic accidents, which claimed 12.5 % during the same period. See Amani and Kazemnejad (2010).

high-speed driving the main causes (See *Iran Car Accidents* 2011). In 2010, the population of Iran was about 74 million, the majority (65 %) of which lived in urban areas. According to the Statistical Center of Iran, more than 50 % of the population is under the age of 25 years, which means that the country has one of the youngest—and thus car accident-prone—populations in the world (cf. Abbasi-Shavazi 2004, p. 2; Ghajarieh et al. 2010, p. 342). The Iranian government has been concerned about the exceptionally high rate of RTAs for some time, and officials believe that current traffic regulations, which were introduced in the 1970s, are no longer fit for purpose (see *Tehran Times*, 8 November 2008). Consequently, the authorities have been seeking ways to improve driving habits by introducing severer penalties (*Financial Times*, 10 June 2008), and a new Bill entitled 'Traffic Penalty' has been submitted to Parliament, which introduces tough penalties for dangerous and reckless driving. It is, however, doubtful if tougher penalties will result in improved driver behaviour. Traffic researchers recognise the importance of law in regulating traffic and driving behaviour, but they point out that laws designed specifically to change driving habits are ultimately dependent on the legal culture of those responsible for enforcing the law, as well as on the legal culture of those who are expected to obey it accordingly (see McCartt and Geary 2004; Mashaw and Harfst 1990).[8] The cultural dimensions of driving, and the fact that it is mediated through the technology of the automobile, which in itself affects behaviour in particular ways, turn it into a highly complex activity. As a result of its socio-cultural complexity, driving does not lend itself easily to formal methods of regulation.

There is a growing body of Iranian research, conducted with very few exceptions by various groups of medical doctors based at university hospitals, which describes and analyses the rising levels of RTAs as a new social problem 'caused by the rapid modernisation of society' (Salamati et al. 2009, p. 6). These studies often highlight growing car ownership (or the rapid increase in output of Iran's car manufacturing industry), the constitution of the population in Iran (as mentioned above, Iran has a youthful population) and the changed lifestyles of Iranians (see Zamani-Alavijeh et al. 2010; Vafaee-Najar et al. 2010; Vafaee et al. 2009; Ardalan et al. 2009; Naghavi et al. 2009; Nevadeh et al. 2008; Karkhaneh et al. 2008; Karbakhsh and Zargar 2006; Muntazeri 2004; Ayati 2004; Rousari 2004). Moreover, they discuss RTAs in terms of morbidity, pathology, epidemiology, injury and trauma, and—unwittingly as the case might be—they 'medicalise' RTAs. What is otherwise a societal problem requiring public policy debate is thus presented from a medical or epidemiological angle—a 'neglected epidemic', as Muntazeri (2004, p. 110) calls

[8] Legal culture refers to 'relatively stable patterns of legally-oriented social behaviour and attitudes' (Nelken 2004, p. 1) and as such should be regarded as a sub-category of the concept of culture (Banakar 2008). Culture, in turn, is defined in terms of 'meaning', or the dynamic *processes* which make social life meaningful and help individuals and whole communities to develop their own particular worldviews. Expressed differently, culture refers to the process of reproducing the beliefs and attitudes people hold about the social world (Wuthnow 1987).

it.[9] With one exception (see Zamani-Alavijeh et al. 2010), these studies are based on hard data collected by hospitals and traffic authorities. They conceptualise driving primarily as a set of skills or a form of performance and, as a result, disregard the possible significance of perceptions, attitudes, culture, law, history or forms of regulation for driving habits.[10] In addition, they disregard the body of social-scientific research that examines the complex relationship between the automobile, which is a form of technology mediated socio-culturally, and driving, as a socio-cultural behaviour mediated through said technology (Urry et al. 2005; Urry 2007; Miller 2001; Evans 1991; Neal 1985; Lewis 1980; Dettelbach 1976). One objective of this study is to bring some balance to the debate on RTAs in Iran by highlighting driving habits as a complex behaviour informed by cultural as well as legal and technological processes. Through the historical interconnectivity of both law and culture, this chapter will also pay attention to the historical context of Iranian legal culture.

In the following pages, sections 3.1 and 3.3 describe 20 open and 15 semi-structured interviews conducted to explore how Iranians perceive and describe their driving habits and how they experience the traffic problems in their country. Sections 3.2 and 3.4 places the results of the interviews in a socio-cultural and historical context, examining the impact of the arbitrary exercise of power by successive Iranian states on the formation of a type of individuality and sense of community which is hostile to the state (and to state law and regulation) and oblivious to the needs of the larger society. Above, I have made references to Iranians and Iranian culture in sweeping terms. Iran is an ethno-culturally and linguistically diverse country, consisting of a large number of ethno-cultural groups including Persians (who constitute the majority at about 60 % of the population), Azerbaijanis, Kurds, Lurs, Arabs, Baluchis, Turkmen, Turkic tribal groups such as the Qashqai, Armenians, Assyrians, Iranian Jews, Georgians and other small ethnic groups. In order to minimise issues arising from the internal diversity of Iran, this study will limit its scope to Farsi-speaking urban regions—to the cities of Tehran and Shiraz. It will also focus on traffic accidents in urban areas rather than on highways between cities.

---

[9] There are other similar tendencies in Iran to use the secular language of medicine to transform socio-political issues. For example, homosexuality is considered a cardinal sin and prohibited in law, but the authorities allow transsexuals to be 'treated' medically, i.e. to undergo sex change operations. Through the secular methodology of medicine, transsexuality is defined as a 'gender identity disorder' (Javaheri 2010, p. 369) brought under control by restricting it to the individual's body and treating it through medical intervention.

[10] To give an example, Naghavi et al. (2009, p. 293) conclude their study by arguing that in order to bring RTAs under control the country needs to '... keep reinforcing traffic safety regulations, build more public health infrastructure, and increase people's access to health services and control the growth of motorized vehicles'. Most importantly, Iran should build fewer and safer cars and motorcycles.

3 Iranians' Perceptions of Driving

This section presents two sets of interviews conducted in Farsi (Persian). The first set is based on 20 in-depth interviews conducted by the author, each about one hour long, and held in Shiraz, Iran's sixth largest city (population 1,227,000) in June 2010. The second set consists of 15 semi-structured interviews (each about 45 min) conducted by Mr Shahrad Nasrolahi Fard specifically for this study in Tehran in December 2010 and January 2011. The interviews were recorded and the following is based on the analysis of the recordings.

3.1 Interviews in Shiraz

Shiraz has a severe traffic problem, and the driving habits of the people there are believed to be worse than in, for example, Tehran. Twenty in-depth interviews were conducted to explore how people living in Shiraz perceived RTAs and how they conceptualised and expressed their experience of driving habits and the traffic situation. Although no claim is made here that the interviewees represent the population of the city, attempts were nonetheless made to ensure the spread of interviews across sociological categories such as class, age and gender. The interviewees include professionals, such as doctors, teachers, lawyers and civil servants, as well as students, taxi drivers, shopkeepers and shop assistants. The interviews began by asking why Iran had a disproportionately high rate of RTAs and what the interviewees thought of Iranians' driving habits—no question was asked regarding law or the legal system. The interviewees were encouraged to account for their personal experience of RTAs and driving, and then to explain in their own words what driving a car meant to them.

Each interviewee saw the problem from his or her own point of view, emphasising various aspects of driving and traffic; some saw it mainly from the point of view of the driver, while others who did not drive saw it instead from the point of view of pedestrians. Some emphasised its social and cultural dimensions, while others focused on its technological aspects. A taxi driver blamed women drivers for their incompetent driving, while a female driver blamed taxi drivers for their aggressive driving. Various interviewees also touched in passing on a large number of disparate issues which according to them were among the causes of RTA. These ranged from the general stress associated with living in large cities, to the refusal of many drivers to wear seatbelts and to the impact of increased migration from rural to urban areas. Despite all these differences, the overwhelming majority of these interviews overlapped to varying degrees, suggesting certain commonality in attitudes towards driving and the experiences of RTAs and traffic regulation. This commonality took two forms: using exactly the same words, such as 'lawlessness' or 'individuality', or various terms such as the 'lack of the culture of driving'. In this section, I will identify and describe these common points, hereon referring to them as the *recurrent themes* of the interviews. These were raised or emphasised by at least 17 of the 20 interviewees. Three of the interviewees diverged from the mainstream by not talking about disorder, one explanation for which is that they identified themselves with the political order in Iran, as speaking of disorder would have implied a critique of the law enforcement agencies. Once they were pressed to explain the causes of the high levels of RTAs, they blamed the public's disregard of traffic rules.

Law enforcement, or the lack thereof, is the first theme which recurs in 17 interviews. On the one hand, the interviewees blamed the police for their ineffective enforcement of the traffic rules, while, on the other, they criticised both drivers and pedestrians for not respecting or obeying the law. One other recurrent point raised by most interviewees concerned the culture of driving. The majority implicitly or explicitly said that the Iranians did not have a 'culture of driving'. The lack of driving culture, in turn, was linked to another recurrent issue regarding the excessive individuality of Iranians, namely that they drive for themselves, oblivious to other drivers or pedestrians. Similarly, those who saw the problem from a driver's point of view pointed out that pedestrians follow no rules—they cross roads wherever they like, causing chaos and accidents. When they were asked about their experience of being a pedestrian, they simply repeated that there were no rules—one of the problems was that no traffic rules applied to pedestrians or protected their rights. Finally, more than half of those interviewed made passing remarks on the role of the car as a status symbol—referring to the 'new rich with their expensive cars', who think that they own the roads. The following excerpts from the interviews illustrate the recurrent themes and the main concerns of the interviewees.

Theme One: The unreliability of laws and the inconsistency of law enforcement:

1. A 60-year-old (male) civil servant: 'The police often don't enforce the traffic rules, but when they do enforce them they discriminate in favour of certain groups... Iranians will obey the driving regulations, but only if they know that they will be caught and penalised if they break them... Police don't enforce the law and people don't respect it'.
2. A 20-year-old (female) student: 'The traffic rules aren't taken seriously... Driving to Iranians means pressing the gas pedal. It isn't about knowing the traffic rules or following the signs... Anyway, the traffic rules aren't enforced effectively and we know that there is one law for ordinary people and one law for those who are connected...'.
3. A 25-year-old (male) taxi driver: 'These people need to be educated and taught how to drive. The authorities... should take away their driving licences and force them to relearn the driving rules and retake the driving tests. But then, of course, you also must make sure that the laws are obeyed. There is no point in having traffic rules if they are neither followed nor enforced...'.

Theme Two: The excessive individuality of Iranians

1. A 51-year-old (female) nurse from Shiraz: 'The problem with us Iranians is that we all want to get ahead of each other, no matter what. That is why we don't show any consideration when driving and cannot give way or show patience…'.
2. A 20-year-old (male) shop assistant: 'When I am driving, I have to get through the traffic the best as I can. I'd never get where I'm going if I start giving way to others… You cannot follow the traffic rules when everyone else sets them aside…'.

Theme Three: Culture and Technology

1. A 35-year-old (female) teacher: 'We Iranians pride ourselves on being courteous, but turn into the most inconsiderate and selfish people as soon as we get behind the driving wheel… Something happens to us which makes us blind to other people, whether drivers or pedestrians…'
2. A middle-aged (male) medical doctor: The car was imported more than a hundred years ago… but the culture of driving couldn't be imported with it. You might think a hundred years is long enough to develop the culture… But we haven't developed a culture of driving yet. There are traffic rules but they are set aside by everyone and enforced selectively and ineffectively by police…'.

Comparing these excerpts, we notice that they are not exclusive. The way these themes are expressed shows how interconnected the issues of law enforcement, driving culture, individuality and technology are within this context.

3.2 Preliminary Reflections

Driving habits are shaped by a variety of social norms and cultural values learnt in childhood, including our attitude to the larger society, to rules and to other people's rights (cf. Durkin and Tolmie 2010), as well as by peer groups, personal experience and psychological factors such as personality and temperament (Lupton 2002). All of the interviewees regarded Iranian driving habits as a social problem, and they also discussed directly or indirectly the importance of a 'culture of driving'. Here are two typical examples:

A 50-year-old (male) shopkeeper: 'The way we drive is based on a bad habit we have picked up over many years. Now it is so entrenched that we can't change it. Perhaps by educating our children from an early age to respect the traffic rules, and by using the mass media to inform people about the correct driving culture, we could change our ways'.

A 35-year-old (female) teacher: 'I don't say everyone, but most people I know understand that the way they drive is not right. They know we shouldn't behave towards each other in this way, but they still do it'.

The first interviewee contrasts actual driving habits against a set of standards of driving (a culture of driving) to make a value judgement, which suggests that there are behavioural expectations (prescriptive social norms) at the level of society regarding a 'culture of driving' or orderly driving behaviour. The second interviewee suggests that there are general prescriptive norms which should ideally be applicable to driving. These norms, which belong to the category of *injunctive norms*, are defined by Kallgren et al. (2000) as what should be done or what is commonly approved and disapproved of, while Elek et al. (2006) describes them as people's perceptions about what ought to be done. Injunctive norms regularise and bring to bear the normative force of discrete social values existing at the level of society on social action at the level of the individual. The decision to obey or defy them involves making a conscious or unconscious value judgement in regard to social goods. These 'ought norms' concern prescribed patterns of behaviour, reciprocity (expectations), a sense of responsibility and obligations. Moreover, they generate shared expectation and mutual trust among the members of a social group by indicating the desirable form of conduct. At the same time, they influence the actor's conduct accordingly and promise 'rewards or punishment externally imposed by others, such as the society at large, parents or peers' (Venkatesan 1966). These injunctive or ought norms should be contrasted with 'descriptive norms', which indicate 'what is commonly done' (Kallgren et al. 2000), or standard de facto behaviour (Elek et al. 2006). Descriptive norms capture a social group's standard ways of doing things, in contrast to what the social group might think it should be doing. Furthermore, they can mediate practical knowledge, social habits, usages and experience gathered through generations on how to perform a particular task effectively or make a decision in a specific situation.

There is normally a gap between injunctive norms and their corresponding descriptive norms. In instances where the gap causes social dysfunctions, the legislature introduces laws backed by sanctions to add to the normative weight of the injunctive norms and reduce the gap between what people ought to be doing and what they actually do in reality. As we discussed in the previous chapters, laws which are introduced to bring greater conformity to injunctive norms often fail or only partially succeed (cf. Griffiths 2003). One reason for this partial efficacy of laws is that the law as a body of rules, decisions and principles is dependent on institutions which implement and enforce them, as well as officials who interpret and apply them to individual cases. This means that the law itself can be divided into 'ought' (prescriptive legal norms) and 'is' (what the courts and law's officials actually do)—what Pound (1910) distinguished as the difference between 'law in books' and 'law in action'. It also implies that law itself suffers from the gap between injunctive and descriptive norms.

When the interviewees in this study complain that Iranians do not have a 'culture of driving', they indicate that there are certain standards of driving, i.e. injunctive or ought norms, shared by the majority of Iranians, which, to judge from the way Iranians drive, are disregarded by individual drivers. These injunctive norms are defined vaguely in terms of the standards of conduct. When the interviewees were asked to elaborate on what they meant by 'a culture of driving', only a few translated it into tangible traffic rules; others instead referred to the need to show consideration for others' safety and, above all, recognise pedestrians and drivers as individuals. We find similar discrepancies between injunctive and descriptive norms of driving in Western countries, but what distinguishes the Iranian situation is the almost total break between injunctive and descriptive norms, i.e. between what is prescribed at the level of society as orderly driving and how drivers commonly drive their cars and behave in traffic.

The interviewees also suggested that the rampant individuality of Iranians interfered with and undermined the development of a 'culture of driving'. When considering the importance of the tension between individualism, collective behaviour and state regulation, we should also remember that we are dealing with a form of behaviour that is mediated through the automobile, with its own specific form of domination and discipline (Urry 2007). Various studies that have been conducted in Western countries indicate that the car brings out a sense of individualism in people, generates certain cultural values, transforms our experience of time and space and stimulates the driver's longing for freedom (Redshaw 2008). These are partly products of systematic advertising and partly because automobiles generate a sense of control over our physical environment (see Urry et al. 2005; Miller 2001; Neal 1985; Lewis 1980; Dettelbach 1976). Moreover, driving is experienced as an inalienable right, even though it is, arguably, a privilege granted by the state through its issuance of driving licences. The important point is that the car is much more than a means of travel or transportation, and driving is much more than a set of skills or driver performance (Evans 1991). The car is also a powerful cultural artefact representing modern men and women's desire for autonomy, freedom, power, control, status and identity. This sense of freedom and power, admittedly, is largely superficial and, at least in Western countries, constrained by injunctive norms which are upheld with the help of formal rules of driving and legal rules of traffic.

The rising levels of RTAs in Iran, and concerns about Iranians' sense of individualism and (lack of) driving culture, as voiced by the interviewees, suggest that driving clearly fuels the individualistic side of the Iranian identity. That is, however, not a problem unique to Iranians. What is unique to the Iranian situation is the inefficacy of the injunctive norms of driving, which in most other countries exert the minimum degree of constraint on driving habits, thus maintaining a relatively orderly and safe driving environment. One question begs to be asked: why do injunctive norms, which ultimately concern social goods that benefit everyone, fail to exert any perceptible regulatory impact on the rampant sense of individualism of Iranian drivers?

3.3 Interviews in Tehran

Partly to explore this question, and partly to broaden the empirical scope of this study, 15 further in-depth interviews were carried out by Mr Shahrdad Nasrollah Fard in Tehran between December 2010 and January 2011. These interviews had more of a structure in the sense that they consisted of a number of themes related to law. Each interview consisted of two main parts, the first of which aligned with the interviews previously conducted in Shiraz and explored: (1) how the interviewees experience the traffic situation, (2) in what terms they conceptualise it, (3) their perception of the causes of the collective disregard for traffic laws, for human life and for the rights of other people—such as the collective disregard of drivers for the rights of pedestrians, (4) attitudes to traffic rules and conventions, (5) if and how they thought driving was related to law and social order and (6) what they thought of the enforcement of traffic regulations. The second part examined the interviewees' perceptions, attitudes and conceptions of law and social order. A number of broadly formulated questions were raised to allow for probing into legal issues voiced during the interviews in Shiraz.[11] The interviewees were asked to explain (1) what images the word 'law' conjured up in their mind, (2) who they regarded as the primary source of legal authority, (3) to whom they would turn if they needed legal advice and protection or sought to resolve disputes (4) whether they felt that laws made by the government and Parliament addressed their needs (5) how these laws were enforced (6) whether they trusted the courts and other legal authorities and (7) their conception of justice.

The first part of the interviews, which focused on driving habits, matched those conducted in Shiraz. Besides finding identical keywords such as 'arbitrary enforcement' we also found broadly identical forms of expression by both cohorts in Tehran and Shiraz. For example, a 30-year-old (male) taxi driver from Tehran complained about those who used their car as a symbol of status ('... just because they are driving an expensive car, they think they own the road and everyone should give way') and went on to cover almost all the main issues raised by the interviewees in Shiraz. He touched on the issue of individuality, saying that:

> All they [the drivers] care about is driving their cars. They pay no attention to traffic signs. We should not need the police to watch over us all the time to obey the rules... You cannot respect the traffic rules when nobody else does.

He saw 'the absence of law and legal regulation' as the main cause of the traffic problem, and he distinguished between the law and its enforcement, arguing that not only was the law lacking in strength (saying several times that 'our law is weak'), but also its enforcement was inadequate and arbitrary. Effective enforcement of the law was crucial because, as he put it:

[11] The questions used in the second part of the interviews draw on a comparative study of legal cultures conducted by Kurkchiyan (2011).

> We will not follow the law if there is no force and threat behind it… Everyone has his/her own set of rules… Authorities plan a lot of improvements but don't carry them through – like the rule to wear a seatbelt, which isn't enforced… Laws are enforced, but they are not the same for everyone. The law does not view or treat everyone the same.

For him, 'law' conjured up the image of courts and police, and he regarded Parliament as the primary source of law. However, when he was asked about his attitude to the law he said 'law means trouble'. He explained that he had firsthand experience of legal processes and would 'avoid the law and the courts' as far as he possibly could do so. If he had a legal problem, he would instead first turn to the community elders to resolve it, for 'law and courts have no effect'.

Another interviewee (a 35-year-old male interpreter) also expressed misgivings regarding the law and the courts. He stressed that 'people are not equal before the law', and 'when ordinary people are brought before the court, they are treated as guilty till proven innocent' (a similar point was also made by most interviewees, including a female defence lawyer). Thus, insofar as people were able, they would avoid the courts and resolve their disputes either by negotiating themselves or with the help of elders. However, when there were issues which could not be settled in this way, they had no alternative but to turn to the courts.

A (second) female lawyer, on the other hand, indicated that the law itself was up to scratch and satisfied all international standards of draftsmanship. However, referring to how her own car was once towed away, despite the fact that she had parked it legally in a permitted zone, she admitted that the law was not enforced correctly, uniformly or effectively by the police. Moreover, it was not obeyed by the people. She was one of the few interviewees who linked the way law was enforced with the way it was obeyed: 'The arbitrariness of the law turns ordinary people away from the law'. She also drew attention to inconsistencies in the implementation and enforcement of legal rules and principles which, according to her, undermine ordinary people's belief and trust in the legal system:

> They [the legislature] tell us that we must obey the law because it is based on principles enshrined in Islam. But they are inconsistent in implementing the rules of Islam. Where the rules of Islam do not serve their ends…, they circumvent them by arguing that they don't fit today's society. But when it suits them, for example, when they want to dismiss the rights of women, then they insist that certain rules must gain the force of law because they are part of the principles of Islam.

She also stated that Iranians did not have a culture of driving and added that 'we are individualists, and as long as we get our way we don't care about other people's rights'.

It is of interest that all the interviewees saw law in terms of positive law and regarded Parliament as the primary source thereof. The lawyer quoted above referred to Islamic law but regarded law and its sources in terms of Parliament, legislative organs and the executive. As the quote suggests, she is sceptical of the way Islam is used to justify (man-made) laws. Three other interviewees connected the sources of law to *Shari'a* and Islam. A female medical doctor mentioned in passing that the source of law was partly religious and partly parliamentary (she did not, however, refer to the Quran or *Shari'a* as a source, and used the word 'religious'). An advertising agent also recognised the religious aspect of Iranian law, but he referred to 'customs and traditions' as equally important legal sources. Finally, a 50-year-old shopkeeper, whose answers deviated on many points from the other interviewees, said that the law of the land was rooted in *Shiah* Islam. When asked what constituted justice, all the interviewees defined it in terms of equal treatment before the law. None described justice in religious terms or defined it in phrases which implied any awareness of what justice means in *Shari'a*. This could, arguably, suggest a deep-rooted secular understanding of law, or equally imply that Iranians regard *Shari'a* as being embedded in their legal order (cf. Arjomand 2008, p. 37).[12]

To sum up, although some of the interviewees suggested that driving habits had deteriorated over the last few decades, none of them stated or suggested that RTAs constituted a recent problem. The interviewees in Tehran, who were asked directly about the increase in the number of vehicles over the last few years, did not regard it as the main cause of the problem. However, although some suggested that many people used their cars excessively, causing unnecessary congestion, they were concerned primarily with the poor and arbitrary enforcement of traffic rules, the public's disregard of these rules and the lack of what they called a 'culture of driving'. All of the interviewees either touched on or discussed at some length what we could broadly term 'excessive individualism' as a problem, suggesting Iranians' inability to follow rules and respect other people's rights. Finally, most of the interviewees expressed misgivings about the legal system and courts of law. Some felt the laws were fine, whereas a 35-year-old shopkeeper wondered 'what is the point of having good laws when the lawmakers don't follow the laws they have made?' The main point emerging out of the second set of interviews is that injunctive norms fail to curtail the rampant sense of individualism of Iranian drivers for two reasons: firstly the enforcement of traffic rules is experienced as arbitrary and the legal system as hostile and, secondly, because the disregard for norms and rules of traffic is a widespread behaviour.

3.4 Driving Habits and Legal Culture

Differences between road traffic safety in different countries are often analysed using a combination of factors such as the quality of infrastructure, driving conditions, the culture of driving or the efficacy of how traffic rules are enforced (McAndrews 2010). Only a handful of the interviewees mentioned the poor quality of roads and the conditions of cars as one of the causes of RTAs. Most of those

[12] Krämer (2007, p. 25) points out that in *Shari'a*, justice could refer to a wide range of ideas 'from straightness and evenness, to fairness, equity and impartiality... Justice could also be inextricably linked to God's will, but it is not necessarily or exclusively so'. In other words, the fact that the interviewees did not refer to the 'will of God', or Islamic values, when asked to define justice does not mean that they necessarily have a secular conception of justice.

interviewed, including one interviewee who mentioned 'dilapidated vehicles', emphasised the role of the culture of driving and (the lack of) enforcement of traffic rules as the main reasons for the high levels of RTAs. The remaining part of this chapter will therefore concentrate on the cultural and legal dimensions of driving that are reflective of how people interact with each other at the micro level and with society at large to create a form of social order. As mentioned above, this interaction is mediated through mobility technology, which in some respects constrains and forms behaviour—one important aspect discussed above regarding cars is that they stimulate the sense of individuality of drivers and their yearning for freedom and control. In the case of Iranian drivers, these effects on behaviour take disproportionate dimensions because injunctive norms fail to exert the minimum degree of constraint on their behaviour. This point is linked intricately with the external legal cultures of Iranians, who, as the interviews suggest, perceive the law and the legal system in a negative light, and with the internal culture of the police force, which does not enforce traffic laws uniformly and effectively.[13] To understand the Iranian legal culture, we must analyse the views and sentiments expressed by the interviewees in the historical context of Iranian society. I shall therefore draw on the historical thesis elaborated by Katouzian (1997, 2009) regarding the relationship between the Iranian state and society.

4 Iranian State, Law and Society from a Historical Perspective

4.1 State and Society in Iran

Iranian states and dynasties have existed without popular legitimacy, and their forms of governments and laws have never lasted more than a few hundred years at a time. A law similar to what developed in ancient Greece (cf. Salehi-Esfahani 2008), or resembling Roman law, which has existed throughout the history of Europe, has not existed in Iran. Systems of laws devised during various periods proved as ephemeral as the states which introduced them originally. In the post-Islamic era, *Shari'a* came close to providing a more permanent legal basis; however, even the enforcement of its rules was restricted, in that they 'could be applied only in so far as they did not conflict with the wishes of the state' (Katouzian 2009, p. 6). The state would find ways of legitimatising its rule in the short term, but the long-term rejection of state rule by the people left a mark on the formation of

[13] Lawrence Friedman has distinguished between internal and external legal cultures; the former referring to the legally-oriented values, attitudes and practices of the judiciary and other functionaries of the law and the latter to how the citizenry views and experiences the law and the pressures that various social groups exert on the legal system in order to promote their interests (cf. Friedman 1994).

Iranian society and affected, for example, how rights and responsibilities were developed and employed: '*Since the people had no independent or intrinsic rights, they did not accept any independent and intrinsic responsibility*' (Katouzian 2009, p. 7 [my emphasis]). This can potentially explain Iranian drivers' disregard for the rights of pedestrians and other drivers, and throw light on the disjuncture between the injunctive and descriptive norms of driving.

Katouzian (2009) stresses the point that *estebdād* should not be confused with absolutism or totalitarianism in the European sense. He writes (2009, p. 208), for example, that it would be misleading to compare Reza Shāh (who ruled Iran from 1925 to 1941) with Ataturk or Mussolini, for he wielded arbitrary (personal) power over his subjects' lives and property, while Ataturk or Mussolini were dictators who worked within certain impersonal political/ideological and even legal frameworks.[14] One way to distinguish Iranian arbitrary state rule from other types of dictatorship is by defining it in terms of short-term states and society, which do not allow for the development of social, political and legal structures into long-term institutionalised practices. Arbitrary rule creates an arbitrary state and a form of government not constrained by legal frameworks existing independently of the state or outside its sphere of power. This, in turn, creates an arbitrary society which tends towards social disorder and political chaos whenever the state loses its control of society. Lastly, an arbitrary state and short-term society give rise to a particular form of individualism which privileges clan and family. Being concerned with the good of society, or acting in such a way as to address the normative needs of the larger abstract society, becomes an irrational behaviour where society is seen as a short-term, unstable and unreliable project.

4.2 Iranian Individualism

Iranians pride themselves on being cordial, courteous and hospitable. Some of these cultural traits—like *t'aarof*—have roots in the nation's long history and are probably thousands of years old. These ancient customs are also ill at ease with modernity, and they show the contradictory nature of contemporary Iranian culture. As one of the interviewees explained:

> Three Iranians can spend several minutes standing at a door imploring each other to be the first to step out... But as soon as the same three people step out of the door and into the driving seats of their cars, they change. Once behind the wheel of their cars, the last thing crossing their mind would be to give way to other cars or, God forbid, break at a zebra crossing to allow a pedestrian to cross the road.

[14] Others also have noted that regarding Iran as a totalitarian state is misleading. Contemporary Iran 'is not a totalitarian state like those of the Soviet bloc during the Cold War', writes Axworthy (2007, p. 291); instead, it 'is a complex polity, with different power centres and shades of opinion among those in power'.

One explanation is that when these three Iranians are 'imploring each other to be the first to step out of the door…' they meet and perceive each other as individuals. Later, when they are driving, they perceive each other as strangers—as abstract entities towards which they have no responsibility. The first situation involves concrete face-to-face interaction, while the second situation is mediated through the use of the automobile. The car as a modern technological innovation has what appears to be an alienating effect on drivers—this applies as much to Iranians as to North Americans, Africans or Western Europeans. The major difference is that neither the injunctive norms of driving, nor the traffic rules introduced to close the gap between the injunctive and descriptive norms, have any perceptible effect on Iranians' driving behaviour. That is also why they do not recognise the strangers driving the other cars, walking on the pavements or trying to cross the roads as right holders. The question that has to be asked is thus: why do Iranians feel no sense of responsibility towards these strangers, while drivers in other countries do?

Political and legal short-termism combined with *estebdād*, which have characterised Iran's history and its legal culture from antiquity to modern times, have produced a particular form of individualism. Katouzian calls it 'personalism', indicating that it is an old historical phenomenon that 'has been part of Iranian social psychology and attitudes for centuries and affects modern and traditional Iranians alike' (Katouzian 2009, p. 16). Personalism lays the basis for a particular sense of community and legal culture, the significance of which becomes apparent once it is explored in the context of Iran's political history. Katouzian (2009, pp. 16–17) explains that personalism manifests itself in two ways:

> First, Iranians who are not related by family bond or friendship are unusually detached from one another: the sense of social cohesion and regard for *unknown individuals* among Iranians at large is not very strong. That is why collective activity, such as party politics, voluntary social institutions and so forth, does not have strong roots in the country… This side of Iranian personalism is most readily and clearly observed in Iranians' driving habits, where everyone behind the wheel is anonymous and virtually every driver cares little about traffic regulations and the rights of other drivers. Nor does any driver apparently care about the rights of pedestrians, even at designated pedestrian crossings… The second characteristic of personalism runs in the opposite direction and results in an unusual care for and attachment to others. Iranians are unusually attached to members of their own family, extended family, clan and close friends, and will help, defend and even make sacrifices for them when they are in need.

Katouzian's thesis can be challenged in many ways. For example, Iranians, as he readily admits, do act collectively and with regard for 'unknown others' under certain conditions. The Islamic Revolution in 1979 was an example of such collective action, as were the demonstrations in June 2009, when mainly middle-class urban Iranians took to the streets collectively to challenge the outcome of the presidential election (see Dabashi 2010). Moreover, traits similar to personalism occur in other societies, including Western ones, and Iranians are hardly the only people with reckless driving habits or a lack of consideration for people outside their immediate circle of family and friends. The socio-cultural specificity of Iranian personalism therefore appears too thin, too subtle and too tenuous to be taken seriously as a keystone of Iranian identity. Yet, returning to the interviews, we see that every interviewee raised the issue of Iranian individualism as one of the main causes of RTAs. The same individualists do not turn to the courts when they have a legal problem but to community elders. They do not identify themselves with the courts and state law—as one interviewee quoted above put it, 'law means trouble', and as a female defence lawyer said, 'the court officials humiliate you'—while they regard their community as a source of dignity, security and support. Analysing the data collected through the interviews in the context of the political history of Iran as described by Katouzian, we can find support for the hypothesis that the failure of injunctive norms to regulate the driving behaviour of Iranians is largely an outcome of a form of individualism which is disconnected from the larger society. The excessive individualism of Iranians, which is enhanced through the technology of the automobile, is part and parcel of the arbitrary state and legal culture of *estebdād*.

5 Epilogue: Towards a Culture of *Qānon*

One Word was reprinted several times during the nineteenth and the twentieth centuries and was read, debated, praised and criticised by several generations of Iranian political activists, reformists and constitutional revolutionaries. Yusof Khan Mustashar od-Dawleh, who wrote this influential work, was not a revolutionary but a liberal-minded reformist and an experienced senior diplomat with firsthand knowledge of European technological progress.[15] He was painfully aware of the socio-economic decline of his country and knew that Iran's loss of political and military standing in the world placed it at the mercy of the colonial powers. Although he was captivated by the economic and military potential of modern technology, he nonetheless identified the law (*qānon*), rather than technology, as Iran's gateway to socio-economic modernisation and prosperity.[16] He believed that for Iran to prosper it had to embrace modernity, but he also knew that modernity could be a threat to both traditionalists, for whom it undermined the Perso-Islamic culture, and to state officials, who would lose their arbitrary power. He thus called for justice (*adālat*), which when translated as the rule of law and legality was as central to modernity as it was to Islam. Seyed-Gohrab and McGlinn (2007, p. xi) write:

> Mustashar od-Dawleh sees *adālat* as an old Perso-Islamic concept, but claims it can also be found in the French term *égalité*. His chief aim... is to replace the arbitrary power of tribal,

[15] Mustashar od-Dawleh's status as an insider, however, did not protect him against slander. Following the publication of *One Word*, he was seized, birched, shackled, imprisoned and heavily fined at the order of Naser ad-din Shāh Qajar (Seyed-Gohrab and McGlinn 2007, p. vi).

[16] Mustashar od-Dawleh was, of course, not alone in this respect. When Malkam Khan Nazem al-Dawleh, Iran's envoy to Britain, turned against the Iranian government of the day and started a newspaper to propagate a new vision for the country, he called his newspaper *Qānon* (Law) (Shahidi 2008, p. 740).

urban, royal, and clerical establishments with an independent, democratically endorsed code of law, in which Muslims and non-Muslims, men and women of all social classes would be treated equally.

Mustashar od-Dawleh's attempts to reconcile Islam with a Western-style constitutional government were unconvincing, and his belief that the force of the rational argument could persuade the monarch to employ his arbitrary power to abolish the culture of *estebdād* was naïve. His understanding of codified law was uncritical, while his understanding of the legal system was wanting in respect to the central role of legal institutions and the judiciary, who were to interpret, implement and enforce the codes. Nevertheless, he correctly identified the law as a mechanism with the social potential to unite an Iran divided along the lines of class, ethnicity and religion. His unsuccessful attempt to build a bridge between Perso-Islamic culture and modernity, naïve and contradictory as it might appear, was also correct, for although Iran had to adapt itself to modernity, modern thoughts and approaches could be employed effectively only once they were adopted on Iran's own cultural terms.

Echoing Mustashar od-Dawleh, we can only repeat that all Iran needs today to develop into a modern democracy is still summed up in one word: *qānon*. We also know that this law is much more than a set of legal codes and principles cohering logically in a larger legal system based on some abstract notion of Western democracy or Perso-Islamic justice. To realise the law that Mustashar od-Dawleh had in mind, we also need a form of institutionalised culture and practice adhering to values and principles enshrined in the Constitution. Such fidelity to the values of law and legality requires rule by law (if not the rule of law) and will remain incompatible with the rule of *estebdād*. In the years to come, the driving behaviour of Iranians and the rate of RTAs will be measures of the extent to which Iranian society has come to terms with its internal contradictions and moved from the ancient culture of *estebdād* towards a culture of *qānon*.

References

Abbasi-Shavazi, M. J. (2004). *Preliminary notes on trends and emerging issues of mortality in Iran*. Department of Demography, Faculty of Social Sciences, University of Tehran. http://www.unescap.org/esid/psis/meetings/health_mortality_sep_2004/H_M_Iran.pdf. Accessed 20 Dec 2010.

Amani, F., & Kazemnejad, A. (2010). Changing pattern of mortality trends in Iran, South, South-West Asia and World, 1970–2010. *Iranian Journal of Public Health, 39*(3), 20–26.

Ardalan, A., et al. (2009). Road traffic injuries: A challenge for Iran's health system. *Iranian Journal Public Health, 38*(1), 98–101.

Arjomand, S. A. (2008). Islam and constitutionalism since nineteenth century: The significance and peculiarities of Iran. In S. A. Arjomand (Ed.), *Constitutional politics in the middle east* (pp. 33–62). Oxford: Hart.

Atabaki, T. (1993). *Azerbaijan: Ethnicity and the struggle for power in Iran*. London: I.B.Tauris.

Axworthy, M. (2007). *Iran: Empire of the mind*. London: Penguin.

Ayati, E. (2004). *Drowsiness and fatigue, the most frequent causes of sever accidents among heavy vehicle drivers in Iran.* A paper submitted to the 3rd International Conference on Traffic and Transport Psychology (ICTTP 2004). http://www.psychology.nottingham.ac.uk/IAAPdiv13/ICTTP2004papers2/Impairment/Ayati.pdf.

Banakar, R. (2008). The politics of legal cultures. *Retfærd: The Nordic Journal of Law and Justice*. SSRN: http://ssrn.com/abstract=1540606.

Dabashi, H. (2007). *Iran: A people interrupted.* New York: Caravan.

Dabashi, H. (2010). *Iran, the green movement and the US: The fox and the paradox.* London: Zed Books.

De Bellaigue, C. (2004). *In the rose garden of the martyrs: A memoir of Iran.* London: HarperCollins.

Dettelbach, C. (1976). *In the driver's seat. The automobile in American literature and popular culture.* Westport and London: Greenwood.

Durkin, K., & Tolmie, A. (2010). *The development of children's and young people's attitudes to driving: A critical review of the literature* (Road Safety Web Publication No. 18). London: Department for Transport.

Elek, E., et al. (2006). Influences of personal, injunctive, and descriptive norms on early adolescent substance use. *Journal of Drug Issues, 36*, 147–172.

Evans, L. (1991). *Traffic safety and the driver.* New York: Van Nostrand Reinhold.

Friedman, M. L. (1994). Is there a modern legal culture? *Ratio Juris, 7*(2), 117–131.

Ghajarieh, S., et al. (2010). Reducing the burden of chronic diseases: A neglected agenda in Iranian health care system, requiring a plan for action. *Archives of Iranian Medicine, 13*(4), 340–350.

Griffiths, J. (2003). The social working of legal rules. *Journal of Legal Pluralism and Unofficial Law, 48*, 1–85.

Iran Car Accidents. (2011). http://www.car-accidents.com/country-car-accidents/iran-car-accidents.html. Accessed 1 Mar 2011.

Javaheri, F. (2010). A study of transsexuality in Iran. *Iranian Studies, 43*(3), 365–377.

Kallgren, C. A., et al. (2000). A focus theory of normative conduct: When norms do and do not matter. *Personality and Social Psychology Bulletin, 26*(8), 2002–2012.

Karbakhsh, M., & Zargar, M. (2006). Road traffic accidents in Iran: Results of National Trauma Project in Sina Trauma Research Center. http://www.ccsofts.com/Articles/ITAC1st/30.pdf.

Karkhaneh, M., et al. (2008). Epidemiology of bicycle injuries in 13 health divisions, Islamic Republic of Iran 2003. *Accident Analysis & Prevention, 40*(1), 192–199.

Katouzian, H. (1997). Arbitrary rule: A comparative theory of state, politics and society in Iran. *British Journal of Middle Eastern Studies, 24*(1), 49–73.

Katouzian, H. (2009). *The Persians: Ancient, Mediaeval and Modern Iran.* New Haven: Yale University.

Kia, M. (1994). Constitutionalism, economic modernization and Islam in the writings of Mirza Yusef Khan Mostashar od-Dowle. *Middle Eastern Studies, 30*(4), 751–777.

Krämer, G. (2007). Justice in modern Islamic thought. In A. Amanat & F. Griffel (Eds.), *Shari'a Islamic law in contemporary context* (pp. 20–38). Stanford, CA: Stanford University Press.

Kurkchiyan, M. (2011). Perceptions of law and national order: A cross-national comparison of collective legal consciousness. *Wisconsin International Law Journal, 29*(2), 366–392.

Lewis, D. (Ed.). (1980). *The automobile in American culture.* Ann Arbor: University of Michigan.

Lupton, D. (2002). Road rage: Drivers' understandings and experience. *Journal of Sociology, 38* (3), 275–290.

Mashaw, J. L., & Harfst, D. L. (1990). *The struggle for auto safety.* Cambridge, MA: Harvard University Press.

McAndrews, C. A. (2010). *Road safety in the context of urban development in Sweden and California* (Doctoral thesis). University of California, Berkeley.

McCartt, A. T., & Geary, L. L. (2004). Longer term effects of New York State's law on handheld cell phone use. *Injury Prevention, 10*(1), 11–15.

McLean, A. (2007). *Friends in high places: Ski maintaining in Iran*. http://www.pawprince.com/trips/Iran_07/index.htm.

Miller, D. (Ed.). (2001). *Car cultures*. London: Bloomsbury.

Muntazeri, A. (2004). Road-traffic-related mortality in Iran: A descriptive study. *Public Health, 118*(2), 110–113.

Mustashar od-Dawleh, Y. K. (1898). *One word – Yak Kalame*. Leiden: Leiden University Press (Iranian Series, original publication 1870).

Naghavi, M., et al. (2009). Adverse health outcomes of road traffic accidents in Iran after rapid motorization. *Arch Iranian Med, 12*(3), 284–294.

Neal, A. G. (1985). Animism and totemism in popular culture. *The Journal of Popular Culture, 19* (2), 15–24.

Nelken, D. (2004). Using the concept of legal culture. *Australian Journal of Legal Philosophy, 29*, 1–28.

Nevadeh, S., et al. (2008). Driving environment in Iran increases blood pressure even in healthy taxi drivers. *Journal of Research in Medical Sciences, 13*(6), 287–293.

Pound, R. (1910). Law in books and law in action. *American Law Review, 44*, 12–36.

Redshaw, S. (2008). *In the company of cars: Driving as a social and cultural practice*. Aldershot: Ashgate.

Rousari, B. S. (2004). Sex and age distribution in transport-related injuries in Tehran. *Accident Analysis and Prevention, 36*(3), 391–398.

Salamati, P., et al. (2009). Health status in Iran. *The Maghreb Review, 34*(1), 5–17.

Salehi-Esfahani, H. (2008). Rule of law: A comparison between Ancient Persia and Ancient Greece. *Iranian Studies, 41*(5), 629–644.

Seyed-Gohrab, A. A., & McGlinn, S. (2007). *The essence of modernity: Mirza Yusof Khan Mustashar ad-Dowla Tabrizi's treatise on codified law (Yak Kaleme)*. Amsterdam: Utrecht.

Shahidi, H. (2008). Iranian journalism and the law in twentieth century. *Iranian Studies, 41*(5), 739–754.

Urry, J. (2007). *Mobilities*. Oxford: Polity.

Urry, J., et al. (Eds.). (2005). *Automobilities*. London: Sage.

Vafaee, A., et al. (2009). Epidemologic study of motor vehicle accidents resulting in injury and death in Mashhad, Iran (2006–2007). *Journal of Applied Science, 9*(13), 2445–2450.

Vafaee-Najar, A., et al. (2010). Motorcycle fatal accidents in Khorasan Razavi Province, Iran. *Iranian Journal of Public Health, 39*(2), 95–101.

Venkatesan, M. (1966). Study of consumer behavior, conformity and independence. *Journal of Marketing Research, 3*(November), 384–387.

Wuthnow, R. (1987). *Meaning and moral order: Explorations in cultural analysis*. Berkeley: University of California Press.

Zamani-Alavijeh, F., et al. (2010). Risk-taking behaviors among motorcyclists in Middle East countries: A case of Islamic Republic of Iran. *Traffic Injury Prevention, 11*(1), 25–34.

Chapter 10
The Shift to Risk Management

Abstract This chapter demonstrates a shift from traditional forms of social control and regulation, which aim at ensuring security, to risk management strategies of late modernity, which aim at pre-empting threats and insecurities. To exemplify this move, the chapter will explore the effects of the UK's anti-terrorism policy and legislation on the socio-political status of Muslim migrants living in Britain. HMA vs. Mohammed Atif Siddique and R vs. Malik are used as points of entry to the legal discourse on counter-terrorism. These two decisions provide starting points for examining how certain basic rights, such as the presumption of innocence, are reconsidered in light of the threat of terrorism. They also show how legal and policing measures employed to combat the threat of terrorism interact with ethno-cultural relationships in contemporary Britain. In addition, they allow us to view the UK's anti-terrorism policy and legislation in relation to what David Garland termed a 'culture of control', which marks the move from a criminal policy based on 'penal welfarism' to a governance of crime based on 'the management of risks'. Finally, they throw light on the tension between the UK government and the judiciary.

This chapter explores the development of anti-terrorism laws, which are constructed to *pre-empt* the threat of terrorism. The UK's anti-terrorism legislation is used here as an example of the gradual move from a form of traditional regulation (TR) to a risk management strategy (RMS). TR operates through 'control and command', issued by the state and implemented through laws backed by sanctions, which are often punitive (see Black 2002). It also requires durable structural relationships and long-term processes which create an enduring social milieu where new norms and values may be imbedded and given time to take effect.[1] By contrast, RMS does not necessarily require top-down governmental interventions

This chapter is an extensively revised and expanded version of 'Poetic Injustice'. In: (2008) *Retfærd: The Nordic Journal of Law and Justice* for volume 31(3): 69–90.

[1] TR attempts to shape the conduct of individuals, groups and the general public as well as private organisations by inserting values and norms into social structures and institutions (Black 2002; Orbach 2012). New norms and values may be introduced through governmental intervention using educational measures, economic incentives and punitive sanctions. Alternatively, TR may be introduced to safeguard current social patterns and organisational arrangements by strengthening some norms, or relationships, which already exist, in order to ensure certain expectations or

R. Banakar, *Normativity in Legal Sociology*, DOI 10.1007/978-3-319-09650-6_10

(even though in the case of anti-terrorism policy, which we shall discuss below, the state plays a central role). Instead, it is employed to *govern* organisations and relationships by protecting them against unforeseen threats and dysfunctional developments.

RMS uses rational calculations and instrumental measures to *manage* risks, and it is therefore not concerned with reforming society or resolving social problems. In the context of UK anti-terrorism law and policy, it amounts to arresting and convicting persons who pose a terrorist risk to national security, before they have committed a terrorist act. 'Risk' is not a legal concept, but as we shall see below it is used in making legal decisions (cf. the Rt Hon Lord Carloway's statement on 23 October 2007). In everyday language, risk refers to a variety of forms and activities, but it always suggests the need to 'colonise and control the future' (see Garland 2003, p. 49). In the context of this chapter, it is defined as a source of uncertainty and insecurity, or 'the potential for [the] realisation of unwanted, negative consequences of an event' (Rowe 1977, p. 24). The notion of 'security' is in turn understood in terms of certainty and 'safety', or freedom from risk and danger, and it is therefore employed in public political discourse as an unqualified good. However, as Zedner (2003) has pointed out, there are reasons to question whether pursuing security through policies backed by law is such an unqualified good, considering that it presumes the continuance of crime and increases anxiety and social exclusion while eroding civil liberties.

The growing application of RMS reflects public and private agencies' awareness of the intractable difficulties associated with employing TR to control certain social processes and activities generally, but those processes and networks which exist at the global level in particular. For example, new terrorist or criminal organisations which have grown horizontally (often using cyberspace) are diffuse transitory transnational networks without a command centre, and as such they are difficult to regulate through traditional forms of crime control. The move away from TR may also indicate the growing realisation that knowledge is fragmented and information is a social construct dependent on its source and the medium through which it is transmitted (cf. Black 2002). Both of these insights fuel uncertainty and a sense of insecurity. In contemporary society, to borrow from Black (2002, p. 4), 'no single actor has the knowledge required to solve complex, diverse and dynamic problems, and no single actor has the overview necessary to employ all the instruments needed to make regulation effective'.[2] RMS, which does not require a deep understanding of the complexity of social conditions, can thus become an attractive option to TR under conditions characterised by the fragmentation of knowledge, uncertainty and insecurity. On the other hand, RMS isolates risks from their socio-political and organisational contexts, draws our attention away from the causes of social problems and generates new risks. To give an example,

---

favourable outcomes. This is also the essence of social engineering, i.e. the belief that we can contrive social change and bring about reform by formal rational planning.

[2] Fragmentation of knowledge goes hand in hand with the fragmentation of power.

police surveillance aimed at pre-empting various threats posed by organised crime or terrorist groups generates new threats to privacy.

In the context of this book, this development exemplifies the move from a modern understanding of law as an instrument of social control and reform, capable of generating certainty and security, to a late modern concept of law as a tool for managing risks, insecurities and uncertainties. TR has not become redundant in late modernity and continues to be deployed alongside new forms of regulation which are not centred on the state (cf. Black 2002.). However, as enduring social institutions and relationships give way to forms of social organisation based on short-term associations and transient networks, and as the state reduces its regulatory interventions by allowing the partial or total privatisation of public services, the traditional institutions of law and politics lose their normative drive and become less relevant to social organisation. We shall discuss the transformation of the state in Chaps. 12 and 13, but in what follows we shall focus on how the realisation that the state cannot control certain social developments normatively (i.e. through the application of legal rules and by strengthening social norms and introducing punitive measures) gradually translates into devising a new concept of law and regulation. The introduction of indefinite detention measures for people who are considered a danger to national security (which amounts to abandoning one of the fundamental doctrines of criminal law, namely the presumption of innocence), the globalised mass surveillance of entire populations across national borders and the growing number of CCTV cameras which constantly record activities mark the rise of a new form of social control which is interested in pre-empting threats by removing the sources of risk and insecurity. As the normative pendulum of law swings from TR towards RMS, new hybrid regulatory forms such as the UK's anti-terrorism legislation, which conflates the symbolic force of law with risk management, are born.

This chapter consists of four sections. Section 1 briefly describes three cases of anti-terrorism involving British-born Muslims, before examining them in relation to the development of anti-terrorism legislation in the UK. It will argue that the symbolic/ideological dimension of this body of legislation is realised within a neo-liberal paradigm of managerialism which has come to dominate the criminal justice system. Thus, this chapter will explore the anti-terrorism policy of the British government in light of what David Garland termed the 'culture of control', which marks the move from a criminal policy based on 'penal welfarism' to a governance of crime based on 'the management of risks' (Garland 2001, p. 18; also see Lazarus and Goold 2007, pp. 4–5). Section 2 discusses the identity politics of the 'War on Terror' by examining the selective enforcement of anti-terrorism laws. Section 3 asks if modern liberal law can be a medium for dispensing justice in the 'War on Terror' and safeguarding the rights of those who are affected by this 'war'. The chapter concludes in Sect. 4 by arguing that managerially-inspired counterterrorist measures aggravate the social conditions that give rise to terrorism and generate new threats.

1 Three Cases of Anti-Terrorism

1.1 The Terrorist from Alva

Mohammed Atif Siddique, a 21-year-old British-born Muslim student from Alva, a small town in Clackmannanshire, Scotland, was detained at Glasgow International Airport on 5 April 2006 as he was boarding a flight to Pakistan. He was released on the same day, pending an examination of his laptop,[3] which later revealed to contain what the prosecution described as 'terrorist propaganda, partly emanating from al-Qaeda, glorifying terrorism…' (Lord Carloway's Statement, 23 Oct 2007). This material was purportedly to be used in the 'recruitment of English speakers, notably British nationals' (Lord Carloway 23 Oct 2007). A week later, Siddique's family home was raided at dawn by the police and security services, who arrested and charged him under the Terrorism Acts 2000 and 2006. More than a year later, and after a trial lasting 19 days, he was found guilty of four terrorism-related offences[4] and, on 23 October 2007, sentenced to 8 years' imprisonment (*HMA v Mohammed Atif Siddique*). When sentencing Siddique, the Rt Hon Lord Carloway explained that:

> The Terrorist Acts are designed by Parliament to stop, or at least reduce the risk of, terrorist outrages before that imminent stage is reached by creating a number of specific crimes, some of which you have been convicted of. These crimes enable a potential terrorist to be arrested, tried and ultimately convicted before actually committing whatever outrage he had in contemplation. (Lord Carloway 23 Oct 2007)

On the day the jury delivered its verdict, Aamer Anwar, Siddique's lawyer, read a statement to journalists outside the courthouse criticising the Scottish judiciary, the jury and the media reporting of the case. On this occasion, Anwar failed to explain if the statement he was reading represented either his client's response to the court's decision or his personal opinion on the outcome of the trial. He started by claiming that his client had been 'found guilty of doing what millions of young people do every day—looking for answers on the Internet', and went on to add that the verdict was a tragedy for justice and freedom of speech:

> It is farcical that part of the evidence against Atif was that he grew a beard, had documents in Arabic which he could not even read and downloaded material from a legitimate Israeli website… The sensational and biased reporting of this case breached the most important principle of justice – that people are innocent until proven guilty… Atif Siddique states that

[3] His laptop was seized by police officers who switched it on and opened the files—against police protocol. *Stv.Tv News* August 28, 2007.

[4] Siddique was found guilty of the following four offences: (1) possession of articles which gave rise to a reasonable suspicion that they could be used 'for a purpose connected with the commission, preparation or instigation of an act of terrorism', (2) breach of peace—he had shown images of suicide bombers and of the murder and beheading of persons by terrorists to various students, (3) provided 'instruction or training in the making or use of firearms and explosives' by means of the Internet and (4) distributing or circulating 'terrorist publications by means of websites'. See the Rt Hon Lord Carloway (6 Nov 2007) 'High Court of Justiciary: Note'.

> "he is not a terrorist and is innocent of the charges, that it is not a crime to be a young Muslim angry at global injustice". The prosecution was driven by the state, with no limit to the money and resources used to secure a conviction in this case, carried out in an atmosphere of hostility after the Glasgow Airport attack and ending on the anniversary of 9/11. In the end, Atif Siddique did not receive a fair trial and we will be considering an appeal.[5]

Lord Carloway described Anwar's statement as 'untrue or misleading' and referred it for contempt of court (*Scotsman* 30 April 2008). Thus, Anwar became the first lawyer in UK legal history to be charged with contempt of court over a statement made after a trial and outside the courthouse. After considering all the relevant material in detail, a panel of three judges at the High Court of Justiciary in Edinburgh cleared Anwar of contempt of court, but they did criticise his conduct, reminding him that 'any solicitor practicing in the High Court of Justiciary owes a duty to the court', which 'implies certain obligations upon such a solicitor' to ensure that his public utterances are accurate and not misleading (see *Aamer Anwar Case – Judgement Summary*, 1 July 2008).

Although the cases of Siddique and Anwar raise separate legal questions concerning terrorism offences and contempt of court, they are nonetheless parts of the same discursive process aimed at managing the risk of terrorism. As Lord Carloway, the trial judge, explained above, Siddique had been convicted of a crime before he could actually commit it; the law is then used to remove a potential 'risk' to national security. Inaccurate as Anwar's statement might have been from a legal standpoint, it constituted an attempt to *contextualise* Siddique's actions and intentions, the trial process leading up to his conviction and the 8-year sentence he was handed by the court, in the broader political setting of what it means to be a young Muslim living in post-9/11 and post-7/7 Britain. This broader *social context* can only be understood by taking into consideration the problematic relationship between mainstream British culture and politics, on the one hand, and British Muslims, on the other. A study conducted by Voas and Ling (2010), on behalf of *the British Social Attitudes Survey*, shows, for example, that more than half of the British population are suspicious towards Muslims and perceive them as a threat to their national identity and security (also see *Telegraph* 9 January 2010).[6] The experience of living in a society where more than half of the population considers one as a threat to its national security and cultural identity is an important part of the social context which is excluded from the judicial gaze. As argued in Chap. 4, modern liberal law dislodges from their social contexts the actions and intentions of individuals brought before the law, before examining them legally. However, in anti-terrorism cases where the law is employed to 'stop, or at least reduce the risk, of terrorist outrage' (to borrow from Lord Carloway 23 Oct 2007), the modern legal system's tendency to decontextualise actions is enhanced. It could even be argued that the sociocultural context becomes completely irrelevant to any legal

[5] The complete text of the statement can found in The Rt Hon Lord Carloway, 'High Court of Justiciary: Note' (6 Nov 2007).

[6] This point is examined further in Sect. 2, where Islamophobia is discussed.

considerations based on RMS. Moreover, since societal risks are constructed socially, law must 'construct' terrorist events, which have not yet occurred, before it can eliminate them entirely. This does not suggest that law's 'construction' is not based on realistic scenarios and predictions of unforeseen future terrorist attacks; however, it does raise questions about the facticity of threats, which are constructed internally by the law, as a basis for prosecuting teenagers and young Muslims for what may, arguably, be described as "thought crimes." As we shall see in the coming sections, anti-terrorism laws are based on the presumption that there will be a constant threat to national security, which also means that the law must continually *construct* threats, if it is to be effective. As Zedner (2003, p. 155) will explain below, it amounts to reversing the logic of crime control: 'instead of crime requiring crime control…, crime control requires that there will be crime'. These points will be unfolded gradually in the next sections, wherein Samina Malik and Hammad Munshi's cases are discussed and placed in the context of the development of anti-terrorism legislation.

Malik and Siddique's cases are similar insofar as they both concern young British-born Muslims convicted of possessing material downloaded from the Internet. However, the symbolic aspects of the UK's counterterrorism policy, i.e. its potential to discipline young Muslims while pre-empting the risk they might pose to national security, are pronounced more clearly in the case of Malik.

1.2 *The Lyrical Terrorist*

Samina Malik, a 23-year-old British-born Muslim who worked as a shop assistant at Heathrow Airport, became the first woman convicted under the Terrorism Act 2000. The police arrested Malik at home, where she lived with her parents and siblings, in October 2006 after searching her room and finding her in possession of records likely to be used for terrorism purposes. This material, which included *The Al-Qaeda Manual*, *The Mujahidin Poison Handbook*, *Encyclopaedia Jihad* and *How to Make Bombs*, all downloaded from the Internet, became the basis for the prosecution's prima facie evidence. Some of these documents had been downloaded, opened, then deleted' (*R v Malik* [2008] All ER (D) 201 (Jun)). On the basis of this evidence, Malik was charged with two counts of offences contrary to Sections 57 and 58 of the Terrorism Act 2000:

> Count one alleged that the defendant had "in her possession an article, namely, a computer hard drive with a collection of documents on it, in circumstances which gave rise to a reasonable suspicion that her possession of it was for a purpose connected with the commission, preparation or instigation of an act of terrorism," contrary to s 57 of the Act. Count two alleged that she had had "in her possession a record, namely, a computer hard drive with a collection of documents on it, which contained information that was likely to be useful to a person committing or preparing an act of terrorism," contrary to s 58 of the Act. (*R v Malik* [2008])

At the Old Bailey, the court heard that Malik had posted poems on extremist websites under the screen name 'Lyrical Terrorist', 'praising Bin Laden, supporting martyrdom and discussing beheading' (*BBC News* 8 November 2007). In addition, she had written on the back of a WHSmith receipt, 'The desire within me increases every day to go for martyrdom' (*Sun* 8 November 2007). She told the court that her poems were 'meaningless' and she had used the nickname 'Lyrical Terrorist' because she thought that it sounded 'cool' (*Independent* 11 November 07). According to the Court of Appeal:

> Following her arrest, the defendant wrote several pages of notes in which she gave an account of how, two or three years earlier, she had been influenced by radical Islamic preachers and, as a result, had downloaded articles, books, talks and videos from the Internet and had started to write poetry about killings and beheadings. That was something she had come to regret and, for around two years, had had no further dealings with extremist material. (*R v Malik* [2008])

In response, the prosecution argued that the records Malik had in her possession strongly indicated that she was 'deeply involved with terrorist-related groups' (*BBC News* 8 November 2007). The prosecution also argued that she was 'an "unlikely" yet "committed" Islamic extremist, with a library of material which she had collected for terrorist purposes' (*Guardian* 9 November 2007). The head of the Metropolitan Police Counterterrorism Command supported the prosecution by pointing out that:

> Malik held violent extremist views which she shared with other like-minded people over the Internet. She also tried to donate money to a terrorist group… She had the ideology, ability and determination to access and download material, which could have been useful to terrorists. Merely possessing this material is a serious criminal offence. (*BBC News* 8 November 2007)

The jury deliberated for 19 h before reaching its verdict. Malik was found not guilty of an offence under Section 57 of the Terrorism Act 2000, which criminalises the possession of an article for terrorist purposes, but guilty under Section 58, according to which an offence is committed if a person (a) collects or makes a record of information of a kind likely to be useful to a person committing or preparing an act of terrorism or (b) possesses a document or record containing information of that kind. The maximum sentence at Crown Court is 10 years.

The judge bailed Malik on 'house arrest' and ordered reports into her family background ahead of sentencing on 6 December 2007. He told Malik that her 'crime was on the "margins" of the offence of which she was found guilty' and admitted that she was 'of "good character" and from a "supportive and law-abiding family who are appalled by the trouble that you are in"' (*Guardian* 6 November 2006). The judge also admitted that Malik was in many ways 'a complete enigma' to him. Malik, who had already spent 5 months in custody, was sentenced to 9 months' imprisonment, suspended for 18 months, under Section 58 of the Terrorism Act 2000.

However, on 17 June 2008 the Court of Appeal quashed her conviction after the Crown conceded that it was unsafe. In his judgement, Lord Phillips explained:

> There had been a case to answer, based on the seven documents identified by the prosecution; however, the problem was that the case had been left to the jury on the basis that the other documents were also capable of forming the basis of the conviction. In relation to the issue of "practical assistance" to a person committing or preparing an act of terrorism, the jury had not received a direction as to the issue of practical utility. There was not a great deal of difference in directing the jury that the document or record had to be likely to be useful, and directing them that it was likely to be of practical utility. In the right context, that direction might be unexceptionable. However, the primary problem in the instant case was that the jury had considered not merely documents which were capable of practical utility but also a large number which were not. There was scope in the instant case for the jury to have become confused. In all the circumstances, the conviction was unsafe. (*R v Malik* [2008])

The 'other documents' which were presented to the jury as 'capable of forming a conviction' included Malik's poetry and other personal records.

Sue Hemming, Head of the Crown Prosecution Service's Counterterrorism Division, responded by explaining that Malik had not been prosecuted for her poetry but for possessing documents that could provide practical assistance to terrorists. In addition, while working at Heathrow Airport, she had supplied information about airport security procedures to Sohail Qureshi, who later pleaded guilty to a terrorist offence and, subsequently, was jailed for four-and-a-half years for 'planning to travel to Afghanistan on a mission of "revenge" against British troops' (*Telegraph* 17 June 08). Hemming also added that since Malik's conviction, the meaning of Section 58 of the Terrorism Act 2000 had been clarified in a Court of Appeal decision.[7]

This case raises several interrelated questions. Firstly, it remains unclear whether Malik is a danger to national security. The Court of Appeal has clarified the law, but the prosecution and the Police Counterterrorism Command remain adamant that it was right to prosecute Malik on terrorism charges. Why were Malik's terrorist connections not emphasised when she was prosecuted at the Old Bailey in 2006? And why did Hemming not explain the nature of Malik's involvement and the type of security information she passed on to the 29-year-old Qureshi, who had been prosecuted for planning to travel to Afghanistan to fight the British troops? Furthermore, did the CPS drop Malik's case because there was no 'public interest' in pursuing a conviction? I use the term 'public interest' in two senses here: (1) in the sense of public safety and (2) in a broader sense of attracting the attention of the general public and the media. Secondly, there is more than a hint, in particular in the media, that Malik's poetry was sufficient grounds alone for her conviction. Notwithstanding Hemming's clarifications that Malik was not prosecuted for her poetry, her posting of poems on extremist websites was used by the prosecution to prove that she was 'deeply involved with terrorist-related groups'

[7] According to the Crown Prosecution Service (CPS), in *R v K* in February 2008, the Court of Appeal 'ruled that an offence would be committed only if the document or record concerned was of a kind that was likely to provide practical assistance to a person committing or preparing an act of terrorism. A document that simply encouraged the commission of acts of terrorism was not sufficient'. See the *CPS response to Samina Malik appeal.*

(*BBC News* 8 November 2007). This shows that in anti-terrorism cases of this type, the rights of terrorism suspects can be obscured by a public discourse which combines official anti-terrorist rhetoric—anxious to talk and act tough—and Islamophobic sentiments. This was one of the controversial points in the statement made by Siddique's solicitor and the reason why he was charged with contempt of court after the trial and outside the court. Thirdly, why was Malik 'an enigma' to the judge? Had the court not been told that she was '20 years old when she "first started to consider Islam" and was "like most teenagers, somewhat rebellious"'? (*Guardian* 6 November 2006). Finally, what do this case and other similar cases such as Munshi (discussed below in the next section) and Siddique's say about the relationship between law, justice and politics in today's Britain and in the wake of 9/11 and the 7 July bombings in London? Should we understand the actions of Malik and Siddique in terms of how British society views its Muslim communities, or should we instead attribute them to the influence of anti-Western terrorist networks external to Britain?

1.3 The Youngest British-Born Terrorist

Our third case concerns the teenager Hammad Munshi, the youngest British-born Muslim to be convicted of offences under the Terrorism Act 2000. Munshi was convicted on 18 August 2008 of offences under Sec 57 (1) and 58 (1) of the Terrorism Act 2000 for possession of an article which gave reasonable suspicion that it was for a purpose connected with the commission, preparation or instigation of an act of terrorism. Sec 57 (1)—possessing an article for a purpose connected with terrorism—carries a maximum sentence of 10 years. Section 58 (1)—making a record of information likely to be useful in terrorism—also carries a maximum sentence of 10 years.[8]

Munshi, who was 16 when he was arrested, had, according to the British media, 'led a double life' for over a year, attending lessons by day at the local comprehensive and 'surfing jihadist sites' by night, 'distributing material to others' as part of 'a "worldwide conspiracy" to wipe out non-Muslims' (*Telegraph* 18 August 2008 and *Daily Telegraph* 18 August 2008). The schoolboy had been recruited and radicalised when he was 15 by Aabid Khan, a 23-year-old British-born Muslim, who was also found guilty of four counts of offences under Sec 57(1) of the Terrorism Act 2000. Khan wanted to arrange Munshi's passage to Pakistan to 'fight jihad' (*Timesonline* 18 August 2008). The prosecution told the court that the schoolboy was in fact a dangerous individual 'dedicated to the cause of al-Qaeda' (*AFP* 20 August 2008). Khan was sentenced to 12 years and Munshi to 2 years in a young offenders institution. While sentencing Munshi, the judge told him that he had brought 'great shame' on himself, his family and religion. The

[8] Central Criminal Court (Old Bailey), 19-09-2008, Case Number: U20080716/TS2008/0050.

judge admitted that Munshi, being naïve and vulnerable, had been misled by Aabid Khan's 'malign influence', but there was no doubt that Munshi was 'aware of the nature of the record of information' on deadly chemical weapons that he had collected and sent to Aabid Khan (*Daily Mail* 20 September 2008). In such a case, the judge added, 'a custodial sentence is inevitable and unavoidable' (*Daily Mail* 20 September 2008).

1.4 The Urge to Transgress Boundaries

Notwithstanding the rising number of cases such as Malik and Munshi's, we find no public political debate on the possibility that perhaps British society might bear some responsibility in respect to British-born Muslims who are drawn to terrorism. Instead, authorities draw the public's attention to factors external to British society and culture. For example, an Islamic think-tank, set up by the government, asserted in its report (published a few months after Munshi had been sentenced) that 'young Muslims are pushed towards extremism because their mosques are run by elderly and out of touch cliques' (*Daily Mail* 24 February 2009). Reports which locate the root of Islamic extremism among British-born Muslims outside the UK's national, political and cultural borders do surface on regular intervals in the British media. However, those arrested for terrorist activities are often more likely to be independent individuals with a mind of their own, more likely to have been radicalised at school, university or in cyberspace than in a mosque run by Urdu-speaking, elderly mullahs from the rural backwaters of Pakistan.

By blaming the mosques and their elderly Pakistani mullahs, British society denies young Muslims' agency while absolving itself from any responsibility towards them. Moreover, it avoids the moral issues pertaining to their marginalisation, which is in turn caused by what they, rightly or wrongly, perceive as the demonisation of Islam and Muslims after 9/11. After the July 7 bombings in London, UK authorities responded to the threat posed by young British-born Muslims by increasing political pressure on the so-called 'Muslim communities', which were to take responsibility for the actions of their youngsters (see *Telegraph* 6 April 2007). On the one hand, the authorities ignore the fact that these communities are socio-culturally fragmented entities which exist partly as a reaction to outside pressure. Their self-appointed leaders, who lack political clout and legitimacy, are incapable of exercising authority over the younger generations. On the other hand, the authorities disregard the agency of the young British-born Muslims, many of whom belong to a new generation of hyper-individualists. Among them we find many who evade the structural constraints of the traditional communities to which their parents belonged (for a discussion see Banakar and Lort Phillips 2014). Malik, Munshi and Saddique came from law-abiding families with no sympathies towards radical Islam, a fact which was underlined by the judges who passed sentence. During his trial, Saddique was described by his headmaster as a model pupil who was always very polite and respectful towards the staff (*BBC News*

22 August 2007). While Munshi was 'misled' by an older person, Malik chose the path of extremism herself. This hyper-individuality, which we shall discuss in Chaps. 12 and 13 in more detail, must be understood in terms of increased reflexivity which accompanies the move from industrialisation to a late modern network society. These young Muslims' actions are imbued with agency and the desire to resist and transgress the social order of their community as well as the larger society. By transgressing the boundaries of what is acceptable, by breaking taboos, 'outsiders' such as Malik defy their marginalisation (cf. O'Neill and Seal 2012). Defying the social order and confronting the hegemonic images which define them as 'outsiders' can have a liberating effect at the individual level, but as these cases demonstrate, it can easily come at a surprisingly high price.

The very application of the labels 'radical', 'extremist' and 'jihadist', intended to explain the threat of terrorism posed by British-born Muslims, hides more than it reveals. The labels conceal the uncertainty, confusion and alienation which underpin their radicalisation, as well as the feeling of social exclusion felt by many young British Muslims whose voices, concerns and the first-hand experiences of social justice both at home and overseas are marginalised in public political discourse in Britain, or instead are misplaced in the context of an increased threat of terrorist attacks. Furthermore, it hides existing power relationships and modes of cultural domination in Britain, which essentialises the discourse on Islam, portrays it as a threat to democracy, stigmatises Muslims in public opinion and dismisses the concerns and experiences of the likes of Munshi and Malik.[9] Finally, it hides the fact that the involvement of many young British-born Muslims in terrorist activities—destructive, misguided and deluded as these individuals and their involvements might be—is part of their resistance to what they perceive and experience as a form of domination pitched against their ethno-cultural identity.

Before taking this point further, we need to consider how the UK's anti-terrorism policy and legislation have grown since 1974 and how anti-terror laws' symbolic effects have become intertwined with a new form of managerial strategies of crime control.

1.5 The Anti-Terrorism Legislation

The first Prevention of Terrorism (Temporary Provisions) Act (PTA 1974) was introduced in 1974 as a response to Irish terrorism soon after the Birmingham pub bombings in which 21 people died and over 180 were injured.[10] This legislation,

[9] For a discussion on the relations of power and domination in relation to Western Muslims see Cesari (2006).

[10] Police arrested and charged six Irish Catholic men with 21 counts of murder for the Birmingham pub bombings. However, it transpired that the police had beaten out the confessions which led to their conviction. They subsequently spent 16 years in jail before the Court of Appeal freed them in 1991. See *Legislation Against Terrorism: A consultation paper*, December 1998.

which was originally intended as a strictly 'temporary provision', was extended in 1984 to meet the rising incidents of international terrorism in the UK. Parliament enacted the Terrorism Act 2000 (TA 2000) following a review of terrorism legislation by Lord Lloyd. The British government agreed with Lord Lloyd that 'there will be a continuing need for counterterrorist legislation for the foreseeable future', and that there were sound reasons for replacing the temporary provisions of the PTA 1974 with a permanent form of legislation (Bailey 2001, p. 567). The TA 2000 introduced, for the first time, the main body of the anti-terrorism legislation in one code. It was further expanded a year later when, in a response to the 9/11 attacks, the government rushed through emergency legislation to increase powers to deal with individuals suspected of planning or assisting terrorist attacks in the UK. The 9/11 attacks became a watershed for how the UK dealt with the issue of terrorism, and they shaped its counterterrorist response accordingly (Fenwick 2007, p. 1329). The UK's new approach to terrorism is reflected in the controversial provisions of Part 4 of the Anti-Terrorism, Crime and Security Act 2001 (TCSA 2001), according to which:

> Firstly, the Act allows for indefinite detention without trial of certain suspected international terrorists. Secondly, it excludes the courts' customary powers of judicial review. Thirdly, in order to be compatible with the UK's international obligations under the European Convention of Human Rights (ECHR), the Government derogated from Article 5 which provides for an individual's right to liberty and security.[11]

The TCSA 2001 marked the UK's shift from a traditional, reactive counterterrorism policy to 'intelligence-based proactive methods [with] the primary aim of preventing terrorist attacks' (Whitty et al. 2001, p. 143). The new provisions enabled the authorities to 'target and control the activities of suspected terrorists' and more effectively manage the risk of terrorism and protect public safety by intervening earlier (Fenwick 2007, p. 1332). However, in *A and Others v Secretary of State for the Home Dept*, the House of Lords declared the key provisions of Part 4, which allowed detention without trial, as incompatible with Articles 5 and 14 of the European Convention of Human Rights (ECHR).[12] To remedy this incompatibility, the government introduced the Prevention of Terrorism Act 2005 (PTA 2005), in which Parliament repealed the key provisions of Part 4 and, instead, gave the Home Secretary powers to impose so-called 'control orders', restricting the freedom of terrorist suspects. The orders, issued in 2005, often amounted to house arrests, and 'several were subsequently struck down by the courts as incompatible with Article 5 of the ECHR' (Walker 2007, p. 183). The Terrorism Act 2006 (TA 2006) did not introduce further proactive measures, but it did give the police the powers to detain terrorist suspects for up to 28 days without charge.

---

[11] *Detention of Suspected International Terrorists: Part 4 of the Anti-Terrorism, Crime and Security Act 2001*. Research paper 02/52 (16 Sep 2002).

[12] *A and Others v Secretary of State for the Home Department* [2004] UKHL 56; [2005] 2 AC 68; [2005] 2 WLR 87; [2005] 3 ALL ER 169.

1.6 *Symbolic Effects of Anti-Terrorism Legislation*

Fenwick points out that 'one of the most striking aspects of these provisions is their under-use' (Fenwick 2007, p. 1333). Although they apply to a wide variety of groups and individuals, from 'freedom fighters' to terrorists and to ordinary people who might unknowingly come into contact with terrorists, the executive applies these measures with discrimination, which is due partly to difficulties that security services face in relation to producing evidence that can endanger, for example, their informants. However, Fenwick means that there are other reasons for the 'under-use' of these counterterrorism sanctions:

> The counterterrorism provisions... appear to be intended to have an effect that, to an extent, is more symbolic than actual. They are viewed by the government as playing an important role in signalling this society's rejection of the message of certain groups – to isolate and marginalise them, to deny them some legitimacy on the basis that they have refused to use democratic methods, restoring instead to an anti-democratic course of creating terror by using violence targeted at civilians. (Fenwick 2007, p. 1333)

Fenwick's insight can be supported by numerous cases where British Muslims have been arrested and charged for terrorist offences, with maximum publicity and under the media's watchful eye, but eventually found innocent. However, their acquittal as a rule fails to attract much media attention.[13] Fenwick's hypothesis also throws light on some of the unusual circumstances of the Malik case and provides tentative answers to some of the questions we raised earlier in the previous section. It explains, for example, why the Crown Prosecution Service (CPS) was not willing to pursue the case further; the CPS had succeeded in what it set out to do, namely to make an example of Malik. It also explains why there was so much emphasis on Malik's poetry by the prosecutor and the press; they represented the type of ideas and thoughts that 'this society' does not tolerate. In this sense, Malik, but also others such as the teenager Munshi and Siddique, were, arguably, prosecuted for 'thought crimes'. I should hasten to add that there is no conspiracy between the government, the courts, law-enforcing agencies or the press to depict Muslim communities in a negative light, in order to stigmatise them as terrorists, because, as we shall see in the next section, there is no need for such conspiracy, as a large section of public opinion already regards Muslims as a continuing threat to security and as being implicated in terrorism.

Zedner (2003, p. 155), to whom we referred briefly above, has related this sense of continuing threat to the conflation of three meanings of the word 'security', as a

[13] The so-called 'Ricin case' is a case in point. Police raided a flat in North London with maximum publicity and arrested several people. On 6 January 2003, Scotland Yard issued a press release that ricin had been found. The *Daily Mail* carried the headline: **POISON GANG ON LOOSE: huge hunt for terrorists armed with deadly Ricin**. Three years later, on 8 April 2005, the jury found those accused of the ricin plot innocent. Their acquittal, however, failed to make the headlines. In the meantime, Moulmoud Sihali, one of those arrested on suspicion of being involved in planning a ricin attack, spent 2 years and 7 months in a high security prison. See Atkins et al. (2007, pp. 120–130).

'condition of being without threat', a 'neutralisation of threats' and a 'form of avoidance of non-exposure to danger'. The conflation of these three senses of security leads to a:

> ... curious inversion of the usual logic of crime control. Instead of crime requiring crime control, we might say that crime control requires that there will be crime. The presumption of a continuing threat is an important factor in keeping crime high on a political agenda that has invested so much capital in its control. (Zedner 2003, p. 155)

Muslims in general, and individuals such as Malik, Munshi and Siddique, are used in public political discourse to sustain and enhance this 'presumption of continuing threat'. How the symbolic effects of anti-terrorism legislation translate into the normative ordering of social relations, and influence other areas of law and law enforcement, can be seen, for example, in the discretionary enforcement of Stop and Search Powers under the TA 2000, which we discussed in Chap. 4.

1.7 Stop and Search Powers

The power to stop and search terror suspects, under Section 44 of the TA 2000, provides a senior police officer with the power to authorise blanket stop and search powers in a designated area, if he or she considers it expedient for the prevention of acts of terrorism.[14] The 'law enforcement authorities enjoy extremely wide discretion in deciding how—and in particular against whom—to use these far-reaching powers' (Moeckli 2007, p. 660). Stop and Search can also be authorised under the Police and Criminal Evidence Act 1984 (PACE). However, it is also an important part of the TA 2000—important in the sense that it demonstrates how discretionary powers, which allow officers to stop and search persons or vehicles 'on reasonable grounds',[15] affect the individuals and communities which happen to find themselves at the receiving end of such policies. As we pointed out in Chap. 4, the official statistics collected by the police and the Home Office showed that the uses of these powers had been disproportionately targeted at young black and British Asians (*Guardian* 31 January 2008). We also argued that, in practice, Stop and Search powers had come to rely on racial profiling and targeted primarily blacks and other ethnic minorities of colour in deprived areas of large cities. As Bowling and Phillips (2007, pp. 936–937) pointed out, 'the concept of "reasonable suspicion" was frequently absent in many instances of the use of police stop/search powers', and instead were often based 'on generalisations and stereotypes, particularly where levels of discretion are highest'.

---

[14] The power conferred under the TA 2000 allows an officer to search for articles of a kind which could be used in connection with terrorism, whether or not there are grounds for suspecting the presence of such articles [sections 45(1) and (2)]. See *Home Office, Circular HPAN-628GM4*.

[15] Moeckli (2007, p. 669) argues that a stop and search under TA 2000 does not meet the proportionality requirement of Article 14 of the ECHR. Also see Bowling and Phillips (2007).

1.8 The Culture of Control

Not only the application of stop and search powers but also the enforcement of counterterrorism legislation in general, as in Malik's conviction at the Old Bailey, should be studied against the backdrop of the recent development of crime control strategies and the debate on the rise of punitiveness in contemporary Britain and other Western nations.[16] In the face of rising criminality and the failures of criminal policies of the 1960s and 1970s, which were based on rehabilitation and reform, penal-welfarism, according to Garland, has been replaced with a new form of repressive and managerial crime control strategy:

> The penal-welfare approach proceeded as if the interest of society and the interest of the offender could be made to coincide. Rehabilitating offenders, reforming prisons, dealing with the roots of crime—these were in the interest of everyone... today the interests of convicted offenders in so far as they are considered at all, are viewed as fundamentally opposed to those of the public. If the choice is between subjecting offenders to greater restrictions or else exposing the public to increased risk, today's common sense recommends the safe choice every time. In consequence, and without much discussion, the interests of the offender, and even his or her rights, are routinely disregarded. (Garland 2001, p. 180)

The basic assumption of this new strategy is that significantly high levels of criminality should be regarded as permanent features of social life (similarly, the introduction of the TA 2000 was justified by arguing that 'there will be a continuing need for counterterrorism legislation'). The question is no longer how the levels of criminality can be brought down, for all such attempts have failed, but how to manage the risks that criminality poses to the public (similarly, we are told that we must live with the continuing threat of terrorism). The general approach to criminality, whether it is traditional forms of crime against person and property or the more recent forms of terrorism, is to minimise its risk of happening. Judging from the evidence, this can also mean detaining those who, for whatever reason, have come under suspicion without charge. Admittedly, the detention of all those who fit the terrorist profile and/or draw the suspicion of authorities might reduce the short-term risk of terrorism, and it also sustains and enhances what Zedner meant by the 'presumption of continuing threat' (Zedner 2003, p. 155). Nevertheless, the problem with such a policy is that it concentrates on the symptoms rather than the causes of the problem, and it is nonchalant towards the rights of those who happen to fit the authorities' profile of a terrorist. In addition, as the incidents that led to Jean Charles de Menezes, a Brazilian immigrant living in South London, being gunned down

[16] Nicola Lacey uses the idea of 'penal populism' to denote the same development within contemporary democracies. She writes: 'A substantial scaling down of levels of punishment and criminalisation is regarded as politically impossible, the optimism of welfarism a thing, decisively, of the past. The rehabilitative ideas... seem distant echoes of a lost world...' (Lacey 2008, pp. xv–xvi).

mistakenly by anti-terrorist police officers showed,[17] the police's profiling method is essentially based on ethnic categories (De Schutter and Ringelheim 2008). Counterterrorism policies, which fail to ensure that the state's response to terrorism is 'limited, well-defined and controlled', will pose 'a greater threat to the political and civil traditions that are central to the liberal democratic way of life' (Chalk 1988, p. 373).

The text quoted above, from Garland's *Culture of Control*, would give us a description of the UK's anti-terrorism policy, if we replaced the word 'offender' with 'terrorist suspect'. There is, however, a significant difference between an 'offender' and a 'terrorist suspect': the latter has neither been charged, nor tried, nor convicted of any crime; yet, his/her rights are disregarded in the same way—a fact that has caused several clashes between the judiciary and the UK government. The fact that the most draconian anti-terrorism measures, such as Control Orders[18] and Stop and Search powers, are imposed on ethnic minorities, and Muslims in particular, racialises the legislation as a whole.

The judicial system is often criticised for being oblivious to the racial aspects of law's internal operations (see, for example, Tuitt 2004). This said, and in respect to issues arising out of the UK government's anti-terrorism policy and legislation, the judiciary generally regards itself bound by the principles of human rights and the doctrine of the rule of law. The government of the time, on the other hand, publicly portrayed the judiciary's emphasis on the rights of the suspects as an obstacle in the way toward ensuring the safety of the public.

1.9 The Human Rights Act

Over the last few years, the Human Rights Act 1998 (HRA), which has enabled UK courts to adjudicate directly on the basis of the ECHR, has been a source of increased tension between Parliament and the judiciary. At the same time, it has given rise to a growing public perception that the HRA 1998 'protects only the undeserving, such as criminals and terrorists, at the expense of the law abiding citizens' (*Joint Committee On Human Rights*, Thirty-Second Report of Session 2005–06). Subsequently, because of the HRA, which is also said to prevent the

[17] This event took place 2 weeks after the London bombings of 7 July 2005. Armed police shot Jean Charles de Menezes seven times in the head at the Stockwell Tube station after officers identified him by mistake as a terrorist. De Menezes just happened to live in an area under police surveillance and, being of dark complexion, he fitted the police's terrorist 'profile', i.e. he looked Middle Eastern.

[18] The Secretary of State needs only reasonable grounds to impose a Control Order, such as house arrest, on anyone who is suspected of, or has been involved in, terrorism-related activity. Control Orders were created by PTA 2005 as a response to the House of Lords ruling against the detention powers in Part IV of the TCSA 2001. See *Explanatory Memorandum to the Prevention of Terrorism Act 2005) Continuance in Force of Section 1 to 9) Order 2008 No. 559.*

democratically elected government of the UK 'from responding effectively to serious challenges that threaten the country', there have been recommendations that the government withdraws the UK from the ECHR (*Joint Committee*, Session 2005–06).[19] Public misgivings about the effects of the HRA in turn threaten the independence of the judiciary, who are blamed for the failure to deal effectively with problems related to organised crime and the threat of terrorism.

In 2006, a cross-party group of senior MPs and peers criticised Tony Blair and his senior ministers for using the HRA to conceal their own administrative failings (*Joint Committee*, Session 2005–06). According to this joint human rights committee, 'every senior minister' fuelled widespread public misunderstandings and myths about the HRA, which will persist as long as they fail to retract their 'unfortunate comments' and continue to use it to cover up administrative failings in their departments (*Guardian* 14 November 2006). The committee looked into three high-profile cases during 2006, which had triggered calls for the HRA to be repealed or amended, and found that:

> In each case, senior ministers, from the Prime Minister down, made assertions that the Human Rights Act, or judges or officials interpreting it, were responsible for certain unpopular events, when in each case those assertions were unfounded. Moreover, when those assertions were demonstrated, there was no acknowledgement of the error, or withdrawal of the comment or any other attempt to inform the public of the mistake. (*Joint Committee on Human Rights Act: the DCA and Home Office Review* 2005–06)

The government, indeed, does make a point of clashing with the judiciary at every opportunity, in order to demonstrate that it is constantly struggling to protect the public against the risk of crime and terrorism. To give two examples, the government rushed through Parliament a new law allowing for the anonymity of witnesses in criminal cases, following a House of Lords ruling against anonymous evidence which led to a murder trial collapsing. According to Jack Straw, the Justice Secretary, the government had to act quickly to fill the gap that was created by their Lordships' judgements: 'anonymous evidence is... fundamental to the successful prosecution of a significant number of cases, some of which involve murder, blackmail, violent disorder and terrorism' (*Metro* 27 June 2008). The second development concerns the government's proposal to extend the period of the pre-charge detention of terrorist suspects from 28 to 42 days, despite the lack of any evidence supporting that (1) the law enforcement agencies require such an extension and (2) that such an extension will allow a more effective approach to combatting the threat of terrorism. In addition, as the *Joint Committee on Human Rights Counterterrorism Policy and Human Rights (Eighth Report)* pointed out:

> [The] proposals are in breach of the right of a detained person to be informed "promptly" of any charge against him; are an unnecessary and disproportionate means of achieving the aim of protecting the public; and fail to provide sufficient guarantees against arbitrariness.

---

[19] All references to 'the government' made in this section refer to the Labour government, which was in office during 2008.

As such, they are incompatible with Articles 5(1), 5(2), 5(3) and 5(4) ECHR (paragraphs 10–21).

A new Counterterrorism Bill that allowed terrorist suspects to be held up to 42 days scraped through the House of Commons by the small majority of nine votes (see *Guardian* 11 June 2008). This again paved the way for a renewed clash with the judiciary, in which the government would portray itself as the defender of public safety. In contrast, the judiciary was depicted as disconnected from reality and unconcerned with the safety of ordinary, law-abiding citizens.

2 Islamophobia

2.1 A Growing Culture of Hostility

'The post-9/11 climate', McGhee writes, 'is both a culture of fear and a culture of indignation in which established and asylum seeker migrant communities are viewed with suspicion' (McGhee 2005, p. 100). In this climate, complex historical and global conflicts are described in simplistic terms which fit into the ideological scheme of 'the clash of civilisations' (Huntington 1997), in that terrorists belonging to the Islamic culture are on the one side and law-abiding citizens of Western democracies reside on the other. It is thus hardly surprising if we read in a report by the Muslim Council of Britain that 'Muslims in the United Kingdom feel particularly vulnerable, insecure, alienated, intimidated, marginalised, discriminated against and vilified since the 11 September tragedy' (*House of Lords Select Committee on Religious Offences in England and Wales* 2003: para 1.4.). Since 9/11, '... attacks on Muslims, Sikhs and other Arab and Asian communities in the UK have increased four-fold in some areas' (McGhee 2005, p. 102). Shahid Malik, Britain's first Muslim minister, states that there is a growing culture of hostility against Muslims in the United Kingdom which allows them to be targeted in the media and political discourse in a way that would be unacceptable for any other minority. As a result, 'many British Muslims now feel like aliens in their own country' (*Independent* 4 July 2008). A poll accompanying a documentary in a Channel 4 Dispatches programme, made to coincide with the third anniversary of the London bombings of 7 July, highlights:

> ... the growing polarisation of opinion among Britain's 1.6 million Muslims, who say they have suffered a marked increase in hostility since the London bombings. The ICM survey found that 51 per cent of Britons blame Islam to some degree for the 2005 attacks, while more than a quarter of Muslims now believe Islamic values are not compatible with British values. While 90 per cent of Muslims said they felt attached to Britain, eight out of 10 said they felt there was more religious prejudice against their faith since the July bombings. (*Independent* 4 July 2008)

The word 'Islamophobia', which has been coined to capture the new social reality that confronts Muslim communities in Britain and elsewhere in the West, consists of eight attributes:

1. Islam is seen as a monolithic block; static and unresponsive to change.
2. Islam is seen as separate and 'other'. It does not have values in common with other cultures, is not affected by them and does not influence them.
3. Islam is seen as inferior to Western Christianity. It is seen as barbaric, irrational, primitive and sexist.
4. Islam is seen as violent, aggressive, threatening, supportive of terrorism and engaged in a clash of civilisations.
5. Islam is seen as a political ideology, used for political or military advantage.
6. Criticisms made of 'the West' by Islam are rejected out of hand.
7. Hostility towards Islam is used to justify discriminatory practices towards Muslims and the exclusion of Muslims from mainstream society.
8. Anti-Muslim hostility is seen as natural and normal.[20]

The post-9/11 approach adopted by Britain, in order to meet the threat of terrorism, strengthened existing ethno-cultural prejudice and legitimised racist violence against Britain's ethno-cultural groups. For many immigrants who are seen as Muslims (including Sikhs wearing turbans), Islamophobia is translated into daily violence, including murder, assaults, arson attacks and racist emails. Islamophobic violence, admittedly, is not new in Britain, but it has been on the rise since 9/11 and shows a significant increase after specific events, such as the 7 July bombing in London.[21] To quote Shahid Malik again:

> Somehow, there's a message out there that it's OK to target people as long as it's Muslims. And you don't have to worry about the facts, and people will turn a blind eye. (*Independent* 4 July 2008).

The social, and by implication also the legal, status of diverse groups of people, who in the eye of the majority culture in Britain are seen, classified and treated as Muslims, adds a social-psychological dimension to the 'War on Terror'. British society is organised in part by using hierarchical racial categories (and the term 'Muslim', as mentioned before, is used in everyday discourse as a racial marker). These racial categories, in turn, are an essential part of the unarticulated, self-evident, commonplace assumptions and values that ultimately determine our conception of the social world and shape the relations of power.[22] In other words, we are dealing with those basic socio-cultural assumptions regarding the nature of

---

[20] Quoted from *Muslims in the European Union: Discrimination and Islamophobia*. European Monitoring Centre on Racism and Xenophobia (EUMC) 2006: 61.

[21] A few weeks after the London bombings of 7/7, *Timesonline* (3 August 2005) reported that religious hate crimes had 'soared by 600 per cent in London as people attacked mosques and insulted Muslims'. All large police forces in Britain reported significant increases in racial violence.

[22] Bourdieu (1977) introduces the concept of 'doxa' to explain this point.

social relations that are taken for granted and treated as patently true. As Bourdieu explains, 'the subjective and self-evidence of the commonplace world are validated by the objective consensus on the sense of the world, what is essential *goes without saying because it comes without saying*' (Bourdieu 1977, p. 167). This method of objectifying assumptions renders legitimate the exercise of power through the force of law (Bourdieu 1987, p. 814). In the same way, culturally-embedded assumptions, regarding Muslims as a racial category, justify Islamophobic sentiments, rationalise targeting them as a national security threat and legitimise the harsh treatment of Muslims suspected of acts of terrorism.

2.2 Alarming Rhetoric

To clarify this point, we could compare the Malik case (but also the Siddique and Munshi trials, which attracted a great deal of media attention) with the case of Martyn Gilleard, a 31-year-old Nazi, whose flat was raided by the police in search of child pornography. Besides some 39,000 indecent images of children, the officers found four homemade nail bombs, 'along with machetes, swords, bullets, gunpowder, balaclavas and racist literature' (*Metro* 25 June 2008). The bombs were intended to be used to attack Jewish and Asian targets. The Gilleard case is of interest for several reasons. Firstly, this case failed to attract the media's attention or cause public debate. *The Times* did not even carry a report of this case in its hard copy on 25 June, which was the day after Gilleard was convicted.[23] Secondly, and more significantly, Gilleard was not under police surveillance for his terrorist activities but was instead caught accidentally when the police searched his flat for reasons unrelated to terrorism. Gilleard, a paid-up member of extreme right organisations such as the National Front and the White Nationalist Party, who had openly and publicly expressed violent racist views and his 'desire to act on them' (*Metro* 25 June 2008), did not draw the authorities' suspicion upon himself and was not considered a threat to national security or public safety.

In another case, police discovered 12 firearms, 54 improvised explosive devices, including nail bombs, and a large collection of bomb-making manuals, books and magazines about guns and the military hidden at the Yorkshire home of Terrence Gavan, a bus driver and former soldier. Although Gavan was a member of the BNP and had expressed 'strong hostility' towards immigrants, according to the *Yorkshire Post*, 'counterterrorism experts could find no clear ideological purpose to his campaign and were surprised by the sheer volume of weapons that were hidden in [his] bedroom' (*Yorkshire Post* 15 January 2010). Passing sentence at the Old Bailey, Mr Justice Calvert described Gavan as 'a lone operator with what amounts to almost an obsession with guns and explosives' (*BBC News* 15 January 2010).

[23] *Timesonline* (17 June 2008), however, did carry a four-line notice a few days earlier announcing the trial of Gilleard.

This case also failed to attract much attention, but what makes it of particular interest in this connection is the language used by police and the court in regard to Gavan's intentions to commit acts of terrorism. Despite his right-wing connections and membership of the BNP, and the fact that he had 'planned to target an address... he believed was linked to the 7 July bomb attacks in London' (*Guardian.co.uk* 15 January 2010), police regarded him as "non-ideological." The judge, for his part, pointed out that although he had '"the potential to cause serious injury if activated"... there was no suggestion Gavan had tried to use them to injure people or passed on or sold them' (*Timesonline* 15 January 2010). Here we find nothing of the alarming rhetoric employed by the court in, for example, Siddique's case concerning the need 'to stop, or at least reduce the risk of, terrorist outrages before that imminent stage is reached' (the Rt Hon Lord Carloway 23 Oct 2007). The language used by police and the court to describe Gavan is sober, recognising him as a dangerous man, but strikingly free from the *fear* of the imminent terrorist outrage which we find in the cases of British-born Muslims discussed above.

Cases such as Gilleard and Gavan's give further support to the thesis regarding the symbolic effects of the UK's anti-terrorism policy and legislation discussed above, but they also suggest that anti-terrorism laws operate in a racially selective fashion.

3 Constructing an 'Enigma'

The social-psychological aspect of the anti-terrorism cases discussed in this chapter—that those suspected of terrorism may be disadvantaged in their defence due to what Siddique's solicitor called 'an atmosphere of hostility'—is enhanced by the way modern liberal law reconstructs the relationship between the individual and society (see Chap. 4). Malik's actions were abstracted from the socio-historical context of her life as a British-born Muslim. Her poetry, which arguably expressed her social and psychological need to 'transgress' the social order that marginalised her, was treated as proof of her commitment to a form of Islamic extremism. Furthermore, it was not considered as the fruit of her alienation in a society where she lived—a society that treated her as a terrorist by association. Similarly, Siddique's possession of material which could be used for terrorist purposes cannot be understood without considering what his solicitor called being 'angry at global injustice', an anger which is embedded in the specific situation of Siddique's life as a British-born Muslim. Liberal law abstracts Malik and Siddique from the context of the social conflict that generated their actions and excludes 'that context from the judicial gaze' (Norrie 2005, p. 30). In addition, it distorts their image in such a manner as to allow and justify a decontextualised legal and moral assessment of their transgressions. Malik, as the judge admitted, became an 'enigma' because the court had excluded from its considerations her social and historical relations which had created her as a social agent. This in turn excluded the causes of Malik's actions from the judicial gaze. The fact that liberal law is not the arena in which to counterbalance the effects of Islamophobia gives free rein to the managerial approach which has come to permeate the UK's counterterrorism policy. While liberal law operates by abstracting actions from their socio-historical contexts, managerialism focuses on coping with risk in a cost-effective way. This, in turn, often requires disregarding the rights of the accused terrorists and omitting from the calculation the causes of problems.

4 Managerialism

The 'war on law' started long before the atrocities of 9/11, writes Philippe Sands, but 9/11 'added the spur with the argument that international rules were somehow not up to the new challenge which the world now faced' (Sands 2005, p. xii). The events of 9/11 constituted a decisive turning point, not only in international politics, but also in international and national law. To borrow a phrase from John Strawson, 9/11 'turned law to Ground Zero', revealing 'international law as feeble [and] constitutional law as insecure' while transforming human rights law into something negotiable (Strawson 2004, p. xi). The conviction of Malik at the Old Bailey, and the 8-year sentence meted out to Siddique, as well as incidents such as the execution of Jean Charles de Menezes (see above, Footnote 17) in the underground, exemplify what it means for national law to turn to Ground Zero. They show how the fundamental rights underpinning the rule of law may be set aside in dealing with terrorist suspects, how the burden of proof is reversed and how the presumption of innocence gives way to the presumption of guilt. This is one aspect of the new reality of law, mediated through RMS and motivated by an incessant search for security. The other aspect is the emergence of the 'culture of control', which at the expense of disregarding the rights of offenders or those suspected of terrorism 'manages' the risk of terrorism in what appears to be a cost-effective manner (Garland 2001, p. 18). National and international forms of terrorism are thus viewed as examples of individual or organised criminality existing independently of social, historical, political, cultural and economic developments, or the interests of the UK and the US governments.

To sum up, the UK's anti-terrorism legislation operates in a highly selective manner, targeting members of minority groups whose religion, ethnicity and culture exclude them from mainstream culture and politics. The new paradigm of managerialism, which informs to a great extent the UK's late modern penal policy, also shapes its anti-terrorism legislation. This new form of 'penality' disregards the rights of the offenders (and subsequently also the rights of terrorist suspects) and focuses instead on minimising the risks of crime at the expense of engaging with the causes of criminality. The judiciary, not known for its radical political views in times of emergency, clashes repeatedly with the government on human rights issues, yet it fails to counterbalance the negative side effects of the rise of punitiveness in contemporary Britain. This failure is also associated with the way modern liberal law operates by abstracting the individual from his/her socio-historical context, before considering his/her actions and intentions. This new managerial criminal policy, together with the modus operandi of liberal law, perpetuates the Islamophobic sentiments shaping the UK's anti-terrorism policy and legislation. As a result, the UK's anti-terrorism legislation contains not only some of the most draconian provisions enacted over the last few decades, but also operates in a highly racialised fashion. Furthermore, it allows and legitimises the overt over-policing of Muslim communities while legalising efforts to target and victimise Muslims.

These managerially-inspired counterterrorism measures are not part of the solution but part of the problem. They cannot ensure long-term national security or citizens' safety, because they systematically aggravate the social conditions that give rise to terrorism. This will probably sound like a tune out of the 'discredited' criminal policies of the 1960s, but we shall succeed neither in managing nor in resolving the threat of domestic terrorism as long as we have not acknowledged and addressed the link between marginalisation, racialisation and victimisation of British-born Muslims and their turn to Islamic extremism and anti-democratic methods. However, this is easier said than done.

References

Atkins, C., et al. (2007). *Taking liberties*. London: Revolver Books.

Bailey, H. J. (2001). *Civil liberties cases and material*. London: Butterworths/Lexis Nexis.

Banakar, R., & Lort Phillips, A. (2014). Law and community in the 2011 London riots. In R. Nobles & D. Schiff (Eds.), *Law, society and community: Socio-legal essays in honour of Roger Cotterrell*. Farnham: Ashgate.

Black, J. (2002). *Critical reflections on regulation* (CARR Discussion Papers, DP 4). Centre for Analysis of Risk and Regulation, London School of Economics and Political Science, London, UK.

Bourdieu, P. (1977). *Outline of a theory of practice*. Cambridge: Cambridge University Press.

Bourdieu, P. (1987). The force of law: Towards a sociology of the judicial field. *Hasting Law Journal, 38*(5), 805–853.

Bowling, B., & Phillips, C. (2007). Disproportionate and discriminatory: Reviewing the evidence on police stop and search. *Modern Law Review, 70*(6), 936–961.

Cesari, J. (2006). *When Islam and democracy meet: Muslims in Europe and the United States*. New York: Palgrave Macmillan.

Chalk, P. (1988). The response to terrorism as a threat to liberal democracy. *The Australian Journal of Politics and History, 44*(3), 373–388.

De Schutter, O., & Ringelheim, J. (2008). Ethnic profiling: A rising challenge for European human rights law. *The Modern Law Review, 71*(3), 358–384.

Fenwick, H. (2007). *Civil liberties and human rights*. London: Routledge/Cavendish.

Garland, D. (2001). *The culture of control*. Oxford: Oxford University Press.

Garland, D. (2003). The rise of risk. In R. V. Ericson & A. Doyle (Eds.), *Risk and morality* (pp. 48–83). Toronto: Toronto University Press.

Huntington, S. P. (1997). *The clash of civilisations*. London: Simon and Schuster.

Lacey, N. (2008). *The prisoner's dilemma: Political economy and punishment in contemporary democracies*. Cambridge: Cambridge University Press.

Lazarus, L., & Goold, B. J. (2007). Introduction: Security and human rights: The search for a language of reconciliation. In B. J. Goold & L. Lazarus (Eds.), *Security and human rights* (pp. 1–24). Oxford: Hart.
McGhee, D. (2005). *Intolerant Britain: hate, citizenship and difference*. Maidenhead: Open University Press.
Moeckli, D. (2007). Stop and search under Terrorism Act 2000: A comment on R (Gillan) v Commissioner of Police for the metropolis. *Modern Law Review, 70*(4), 659–679.
Norrie, A. (2005). *Law and the beautiful soul*. London: Glasshouse.
O'Neill, M., & Seal, L. (2012). *Transgressive imaginations: Crime, deviance and culture*. London: Palgrave Macmillan.
Orbach, B. (2012). What is regulation. *Yale Journal on Regulation, 30*(1), 1–10.
Rowe, W. D. (1977). *An anatomy of risk*. New York: Wiley-Interscience.
Sands, P. (2005). *Lawless world: America and the making and breaking of global rules*. London: Allen Lane.
Strawson, J. (Ed.). (2004). *Law after ground zero*. London: GlassHouse.
Tuitt, P. (2004). *Race, law, resistance*. London: GlassHouse.
Voas, D., & Ling, R. (2010). Religion in Britain and the United States. In A. Park et al. (Eds.), *British social attitudes: The 26th report* (pp. 65–86). London: Sage.
Walker, C. (2007). The United Kingdom's anti-terrorism laws: Lessons for Australia. In A. Lynch et al. (Eds.), *Law and liberty in the war on terror* (pp. 181–195). Sydney: The Federation Press.
Whitty, N., et al. (2001). *Civil liberties in human rights era, 2001*. London: Butterworths.
Zedner, L. (2003). The concept of security: An agenda for comparative analysis. *Legal Studies, 23* (1), 153–176.

Cases and Related Material on Sentencing Etc.

Aamer Anwar Case – Judgement Summary, 1 July 2008, posted at www.sacc.org.uk
A and Others v Secretary of State for the Home Department [2004] UKHL 56; [2005] 2 AC 68; [2005] 2 WLR 87; [2005] 3 ALL ER 169
HMA v Mohammed Atif Siddique, High Court of Justiciary, Glasgow, 14th September 2007. http://news.bbc.co.uk/1/shared/bsp/hi/pdfs/23_10_07_siddique.pdf
Lord Carloway (23 October 2007) 'Statement on Sentencing Mohammed Atif Siddique' at http://www.sacc.org.uk/press/2007/sentencing-mohammed-atif-siddique
Lord Carloway (6 Nov 2007), 'High Court of Justiciary: Note' at http://www.scotcourts.gov.uk/opinions/CAR2510.html. Accessed on 15 August 2008
Norwood v DPP [2003] EWHC 1 564 (Admin)
Norwood v United Kingdom (dec), (2004) 40 EHRR SE 11.1
R v Malik [2008] All ER (D) 201 (Jun), Court of Appeal, Criminal Division, Lord Phillips of Worth Matravers CJ, Goldring and Plender JJ, 17 June, 2008 http://cyberlaw.org.uk/2008/06/18/r-v-malik-2008-all-er-d-201-jun/

Official Reports

Detention of Suspected International Terrorists: Part 4 of The Anti-Terrorism, Crime and Security Act 2001. Research paper 02/52 (16 Sep 2002) at http://www.parliament.uk/commons/lib/research/rp2002/rp02-052.pdf.
CPS response to Samina Malik appeal at http://www.cps.gov.uk/news/pressreleases/143_08.html

Explanatory Memorandum to the Prevention of Terrorism Act 2005) Continuance in Force of Section 1 to 9) Order 2008 No. 559 at http://www.opsi.gov.uk/si/si2008/em/uksiem_20080559_en.pdf

Home Office, Circular HPAN-628GM4 at http://www.knowledgenetwork.gov.uk/HO/circular.nsf, accessed on 28 January 2008.

The House of Lords -Select Committee on Religious Offences in England and Wales, 2003: para 1.4. at http://www.publications.parliament.uk/pa/ld/ldrelof.htm.

Joint Committee On Human Rights, Thirty-Second Report at http://www.publications.parliament.uk/pa/jt200506/jtselect/jtrights/278/27811.htm

Joint Committee on Human Rights Act: the DCA and Hone Office Review, Thirty-second Report of Session 2005–06 at http://www.publications.parliament.uk/pa/jt200506/jtselect/jtrights/278/278.pdf

Joint Committee on Human Rights Counter-Terrorism Policy and Human Rights (Eighth Report): Counter-Terrorism Bill, Ninth Report of Session 2007–08, at http://www.publications.parliament.uk/pa/jt200708/jtselect/jtrights/50/50.pdf

Legislation Against Terrorism: A consultation paper (December 1998) at http://www.archive.official-documents.co.uk/.

Muslims in the European Union: Discrimination and Islamophobia (2006) European Monitoring Centre on Racism and Xenophobia (EUMC)

News Items

AFP (20 August 2008) '"Youngest terrorist" jailed' at http://www.thefreelibrary.com/'Youngest+terrorist'+jailed-a01611621597 accessed on 22 April 2014

BBC News (8 November 2007) '"Lyrical Terrorist" Found Guilty' at http://news.bbc.co.uk/2/hi/uk_news/7084801.stm accessed on 22 April 2014

BBC News (15 January 2010) 'Bomb cache bus driver Gavan "obsessed with weapons"' at http://news.bbc.co.uk/1/hi/uk/8462205.stm. accessed on 22 April 2014

BBC News (22 August 2007) 'Terror accuse was "model pupil"' at http://news.bbc.co.uk/2/hi/uk_news/scotland/tayside_and_central/6959182.stm accessed on 22 April 2014

Daily Mail (6 January 2003) 'Poison Gang on Loose' At http://www.dailymail.co.uk/home/index.html. Accessed on 15 May 2010

Daily Mail (20 September 2008) 'Schoolboy Terrorist Locked Up, The 16-Year-Old who Joined Islamic Fanatics Targeting the Royal Family' at http://www.dailymail.co.uk/news/article-1058227/Schoolboy-terrorist-locked-The-16-year-old-joined-Islamic-fanatics-targeting-Royal-Family.html accessed on 22 April 2014

Daily Mail (24 February 2009) 'Islamic Group Slams out of Touch Imams for Causing Drifts Towards Extremism' at http://www.dailymail.co.uk/news/article-1153544/Islamic-group-slams-touch-imams-causing-drift-extremism.html accessed on 22 April 2014

Gurdian (15 January 2010) 'BNP member given 11 years for making bombs and guns', posted at http://www.guardian.co.uk/uk/2010/jan/15/bnp-member-jailed-guns-bombs accessed on 22 April 2014

Guardian (6 November 2006) 'Lyrical Terrorist Sentenced over Extremist Poetry' at http://www.guardian.co.uk/uk/2007/dec/06/terrorism.books accessed on 22 April 2014

Guardian (14 November 2006) 'Ministers Accused of Fuelling Myths on Human Rights' at http://www.theguardian.com/politics/2006/nov/14/humanrights.immigrationpolicy accessed on 22 April 2014

Guardian (31 January 2008) 'Stop and search' at http://www.theguardian.com/politics/2008/jan/31/uk.conservatives1 accessed on 22 April 2014

Guardian (9 November 2007) '"Lyrical Terrorist" convicted over hate records' at http://www.guardian.co.uk accessed on 22 April 2014
Guardian (11 June 2008) 'Brown wins dramatic victory on 42-day detention' at http://www.theguardian.com/politics/2008/jun/11/terrorism.uksecurity
Independent (4 July 2008) 'Muslims Feel Like Jews in Europe' at http://www.independent.co.uk/news/uk/home-news/muslims-feel-like-jews-of-europe-859978.html. Accessed on 22 April 2014
Independent (11 November 07) 'UK Woman Found Guilty of Terror Offences' at http://news.independent.co.uk accessed on 22 April 2014
Law Gazette (7 June 2007) 'Silencing Hatred' at http://www.lawgazette.co.uk/print/2183 accessed on 22 April 2014
Metro (27 June 2008) 'Anonymity Law to be Rushed Through' https://metro.co.uk/. Accessed on 15 May 2010
Metro (25 June 2008) 'Nazi Sympathiser is Guilty of Terrorism' https://metro.co.uk/
Scotsman (30 April 2008) 'Lawyer Faces Jail for Contempt' at WWW.News.scotsman.com. Accessed on 15 May 2010
Stv.Tv News (August 28, 2007) 'Terror trial told procedures were not followed' at http://video.stv.tv/bc/news-Terror_trial_told_procedures_were_not_fo-20070828-terror-trial-told-procedures-were-not-followed/?redirect=no
Sun, 'Woman Convicted over Terror' at http://www.thesun.co.uk 8 November 2007
Telegraph (6 April 2007) 'Muslims must take responsibility' at http://www.telegraph.co.uk/news/uknews/1547805/Muslims-must-take-responsibility.html, accessed on 20 December 2013
Telegraph (17 June 08) '"Lyrical Terrorist" Samina Malik Cleared on Appeal' at www.telegraph.co.uk, accessed on 20 December 2013
Telegraph (18 August 2008) 'Britain's "youngest terrorist" jailed'. Posted at http://www.telegraph.co.uk/news/uknews/2579566/Britains-youngest-terrorist-jailed.html. Accessed on 15 May 2010
Telegraph (9 January 2010), 'Britons are suspicious towards Muslims, study finds' posted at http://www.telegraph.co.uk/news/newstopics/religion/6958571/Britons-are-suspicious-towards-Muslims-study-finds.html, accessed on 20 December 2013
Timesonline (15 January 2010) BNP member Terrance Gavan kept gun and bomb cache at home at http://www.timesonline.co.uk/tol/news/uk/crime/article6989752.ece accessed on 15 May 2010
Timesonline (3 August 2005) 'Religious Hatred Crimes Shoot Up' at http://www.timesonline.co.uk/tol/news/uk/article550961.ece
Timesonline (17 June 2008) 'In Court Today' at http://business.timesonline.co.uk/tol/business/law/article4152235.ece 17 June 2008
Timesonline (August 18 2008) 'Britain's youngest terrorist, Hammad Munshi, faces jail after guilty verdict' at http://www.timesonline.com/news/
Yorkshire Post (15 January 2010) 'Secret arsenal of the bus driver who harboured arms obsession' at http://www.yorkshirepost.co.uk/news/The-BNP-man-who-hid.5986794.jp

Chapter 11
Norms and Normativity in Socio-Legal Research

Abstract The aim of this chapter is twofold. First, it examines the relationship between norms and normativity arguing that normativity is generated by the system as well as the lifeworld, and it is not necessarily reducible to the effects or functions of individual norms. Second, it challenges the assumption that legal sociology should apply itself to the external or factual properties of the law and leave the internal and normative aspects of legal phenomena to doctrinal scholars and moral philosophers. It argues further that legal sociology explores the normative contexts of the law and other social systems, but being restricted by its 'scientific' mode of expression it describes and analyses them in sociological rather than in moral terms. Legal sociology is, and should be seen as, a different language game to moral and legal philosophy, and its treatment of normativity should be understood on its own terms.

1 Normativity

1.1 Internal and External Aspects of Norms

Looking at the works of the founders of legal sociology, such as Eugen Ehrlich (2002) and Emile Durkheim, we note that norms have played an important role in socio-legal theorising and research. Norms have been used to address the materiality of the law (i.e. its institutional facts and practices) as well as its ideal dimensions (i.e. its values, autonomy, legitimacy and authority). Legal theory too has had a deep-seated interest in the study of norms (see, for example, Kelsen 1967, 2002), albeit an interest which is more concerned with the *ought* dimension of norms than with their observable behavioural manifestations. These two aspects of norms—'ought' versus 'behavioural regularities'—are interrelated and are discussed by Hart (1998) as the internal and external perspectives on social *rules*. I shall use Hart's internal/external distinction liberally to discuss different manifestations of 'social norms', which may be regarded as a category broader than 'social rules'. The discussion

---

This chapter is an extensively revised version of 'Can Legal Sociology Account for the Normativity of Law'. In: Baier M (ed) (2013) *Social and Legal Norms*. Farnham: Ashgate, pp. 15–38.

R. Banakar, *Normativity in Legal Sociology*, DOI 10.1007/978-3-319-09650-6_11

which follows is otherwise more in line with the distinction made between descriptive and injunctive norms by Kallgren et al. (2000: 2002; also see Elek et al. 2006) in Chap. 9.

The external or descriptive aspect of a norm is revealed through tangible and observable behaviour and can be studied by employing empirical methods. There are also certain norms which are primarily descriptive, i.e. people follow them more or less unreflectively, or habitually, doing what is commonly done. Their habitual actions constitute a significant part of the lifeworld, i.e. the part that brings a perceptible sense of continuity and solidity to our everyday experiences and lays the foundation for institutionalising certain activities (cf. Berger and Luckmann 1987, pp. 70–73). By contrast, the internal aspect of norms can require the social actor's reflexivity. The fact that the subject has an understanding of the internal view point of a norm does not imply that he/she will necessary follow it. Nevertheless, his/her refusal, as well as acceptance, involves reflexivity. There are also certain norms which are primarily evaluative—we called them 'injunctive norms' in Chap. 9—underscoring what 'ought' to be done rather than highlighting what 'is' done. The subject's reflective commitment to the norm's underpinning reason or value, to what should be done and to what is commonly approved, varies significantly depending on the social setting where decisions are made and actions are taken. In traditional settings, customs and rituals—which are often based on *one* religion, *one* collective memory and *one* set of cultural codes—dominate all social activities by exerting a binding force on behaviour. Rituals eliminate alternative courses of action and their authoritative force constrains the subject's reflexivity by not leaving much space to employ values to make judgements or to choose between various courses of action. Under traditional conditions, the moral content of most norms are not necessarily spelt out, even though, as Giddens (1994, p. 65) points out, 'they are interpreted within the activities or directives of guardians'. Otherwise these norms are followed habitually.

By turning to the past in order to create the present and the future, tradition brings a measure of continuity and ontological security to human affairs and the everyday experience of reality. In traditional settings, we often find one primary way of defining institutions, relationships and identities. Using the institution of family as an example, we can say that in a traditional society, there is one primary way of building a family, which is dictated by a relatively fixed authority structure and a division of labour along the gender line. In contrast, modern settings bring an end to traditional forms of organisation by allowing alternative modes of action and by heightening the social actors' awareness of different ways of defining the same relationships. Using the same example, a *modern* family unit does not necessarily consist of a married heterosexual couple, who are committed to a lifelong relationship and who define their union in terms of procreation. There are also continuities in how family has developed over time. In both traditional and modern settings, family remains an important site for primary socialisation and for economic and emotional security. Under *late modernity*, actors are continuously faced with a plurality of choices and possibilities of acting differently. Same-sex marriages, single-parent families and family units which no longer define their function in terms of procreation provide alternative ways of forming a family. Late modern families neither reproduce the authority structures of traditional families, nor foster lifelong associations.[1] Whereas under traditional conditions, we were confronted with one primary way of building a family, under late modernity, we are confronted with an open-ended situation where we need to exercise our values to make conscious choices. The normative openness, which creates behavioural unpredictability and ontological uncertainty, is not limited to the sphere of family and can be extended to describe recent developments in other areas, ranging from the labour market to public administration, education, religion and the legal system. One of the problems raised in this book concerns the way late modern conditions, which are characterised by cultural hybridity and pluralism, influence the actor's commitment to the internal aspect of norms. In short, how and why would a social actor subscribe to a particular social norm and way of doing things when he/she is constantly confronted with equally viable alternative courses of action? What is the role of law in this context? Is the law part of the shifting landscape of late modernity or is it independent of 'the river of flux' and capable of reshaping the flow of the constantly changing social life? And if so, where does law's normativity come from?

The internal dimension of norms is intangible and as such does not have a directly observable expression that may be studied using empirical methods of investigation. It does, however, possess a cognitive element that requires thought processes and confrontation with 'facts' which are external to the subject's cognition. One can form a general idea about the evaluative aspect of norms by studying the perceptions (attitudes, opinions and beliefs) of various groups, but social scientists are aware of the limitations of this method, as attitudes and perceptions do not necessarily translate into action.[2] The internal aspects of norms lose their force rapidly as the intersubjective values and the relationships, structures and institutions which produce and reproduce them over time are undermined by the socio-cultural consequences of globalisation and the actor's enhanced reflexivity. Globalised spheres of action (the cyberspace being one of the more important ones) consist of multiplicity of cultural codes, overlapping transitory social networks and temporary social contexts, where knowledge is fragmented, action is ahistorical and power is decentred. In cyberspace, we find no single source of authority capable of generating intersubjectivity or enforcing socio-cultural rules and regulation in the traditional sense of the word.

We shall discuss the methodological limitations of social sciences in respect to the study of normativity, law and justice in Sect. 3, but before that we need to take a

[1] According of the Office for National Statistics (2014), '34% of marriages [in England and Wales] are expected to end in divorce by the 20th wedding anniversary'.

[2] As I have argued elsewhere, it 'is now a social psychological commonplace notion that a discrepancy between attitudes and behaviour can exist. The fact that a person expresses a belief does not necessarily mean that that person will act in accordance with that belief. See Banakar (2003, p. 201).

closer look at law's normativity and consider the extent to which it is linked to norms which constitute the context of social action.

1.2 Normativity Beyond Social Norms?

'Normativity' is used when exploring why, under certain circumstances, we feel *obliged* to act in specific ways (for a recent contribution to the debate on normativity see Raz 2011; Turner 2010; Wedgewood 2007; Delacroix 2006). In non-traditional contexts where there are several alternative ways of doing things, the notion of an 'obligation to act in a particular way' requires conscious commitment to a norm and is thus linked to the internal (non-empirical) aspect of the norm. The normative efficacy of a norm can be explained in turn by reference to the authority of the source of the norm (*who* said that we should act in a particular way) and/or the social functions thereof (we might follow a rule because it fulfils certain social functions or upholds certain values such as justice, equality or fairness). In other words, norms in general, but the internal aspects of norms in particular, provide *reasons* to act in particular ways.[3] The *reason* itself (that I, for example, support a local charity foundation because I would like to make a contribution to the community where I live, or I follow certain traffic rules because I care about other people's safety) is articulated consciously, while its underpinning values (why I should care about my community or the safety of other people) can be intersubjective, taken for granted and rooted in the culture or customs of a group of people. Under late modern conditions, aspects of the underpinning values that generate a commitment to the internal aspects of norms can be weakened by the experience of belonging to several communities, which might propagate conflicting values at the same time, by the realisation that one does not belong to a community as such, or that one's community no longer exerts a cohesive moral force. Late modern communities are thus temporary networks of interests and activities, which do not require ethical commitments from their members (cf. Bauman 2001, p. 71: Banakar and Lort Phillips 2014). I must hasten to add that not all communities lose their moral force under late modernity. In fact some communities, those which congregate around religious beliefs and traditions, tend to show remarkable resilience in the face of globalisation.

Limiting our discussion to the normativity of law and its implications for legal sociology, we are led to ask one of legal philosophy's classical questions: Why does law provide the majority of the people with a reason for action? Moreover, why do some people comply with the letter of the law, even when there is no threat of sanction against their non-compliance and even though they know that following

[3] As Raz (1999, p. 113) points out, *reason* (or rationality) in itself can have a normative dimension, therefore suggesting that normativity is not restricted to social norms.

the law is not in their self-interest and will cost them in material and other terms?[4] The answer to this question takes us to the heart of law's normativity. For natural lawyers, such as Cicero, the normative force of law resided in some form of 'higher law', while for legal positivists, such as Austin (1995), it was to be found in the intimate relationship between legal norms and coercion. Subsequent legal positivists, such as H.L.A. Hart,[5] Kelsen (2002) and Raz (1979), have questioned the centrality of coercion in upholding the normative force of law and maintained that coercion was neither an essential part of what constituted all the aspects of the law nor an indispensable requirement for what it did. Some laws are brought about to empower and facilitate social action, rather than coercing people into acting in particular ways.

From a sociological standpoint, people comply with the law for a number of empirically ascertainable *reasons* not necessarily related to the threat of violence or whether the law is morally justifiable. Following Max Weber's forms of action (1978), we can say that one might follow a legal norm as a force of habit or a custom (i.e. Weber's 'traditional action', which we described above as descriptive norms). Alternatively, one might abide by the law for emotive reasons (i.e. Weber's 'affective action'). Then again, one might believe that the law represents foundational values, such as rights and justice (this would correspond with Weber's value rational action), or follow the law because of the way it was enacted, i.e. because of its authoritative source. Finally, one's fidelity to law might be motivated by purposive rationality, the belief that it accomplishes certain tasks which are required for an efficient governance of society. These *ideal types* of reason for action suggest that normativity can emerge out of system imperatives (purposive or instrumental rationality) as well as the lifeworld (value rationality). Moreover, normativity can be the source, rather than the effect, of norms. Thus, system imperatives exert a normative force by urging and guiding action at the societal (macro) and institutional levels. Norms then become labels we use to refer to the normativity generated by system imperatives, which in turn can provide *reasons* for action but not a sense of obligation. The sense of obligation, i.e. the feeling that one is morally obliged to act in particular ways, emerges instead out of the lifeworld, i.e. the sphere of spontaneously generated values and worldviews which are taken for granted by social actors and out of which the 'system' is born (cf. Habermas 1984). In that sense, lifeworld (and not system) provides values which underpin the internal aspect of norms. This means that normativity not only can have other sources beyond social norms, but also that per se it can be a source of norms. In other words, system imperatives on the one hand and the lifeworld on the other guide conduct, giving rise to repeated patterns of behaviour which are identified as

[4] This is not to suggest that law (or the threat of violence) necessarily deters people from committing a crime. Although the legal system does deter crime generally, the relationship between individual criminal action and the law (or the threat of sanctions) remains contingent on a host of factors. See Robinson and Darley (2004).

[5] Hart (1998) criticises Austin's predictive model, i.e. that the subject follows rules because he/she predicts sanction, and instead he argues that the normativity of legal rules resides in their ability to provide reasons or justifications for action.

social norms. These norms are not the cause of normativity, but equally they are not mere labels either, for they feed back into the system and lifeworld, thus strengthening systematic imperatives and community values, respectively. We should bear in mind that normativity generated by social systems is based on a different type of rationality than normativity emanating from the lifeworld. These two types of normativity, following Habermas (1975, 1984), correspond with two types of integration, namely system and socio-cultural integration (also see Banakar 2003, pp. 291–292).

Descriptive norms emanating from habitual conduct, as well as injunctive norms expressing behavioural regularities motivated by value rationality and ethical commitment, will continue to define certain walks of life, which have retained their solidity even under late modernity and explain why certain people continue to obey the law in situations where there is contextual continuity. Habits and value rational action will increasingly lose their grip over other areas, which are exposed to rapid social changes and cultural hybridity brought on by the consequences of globalisation and the spread information technology. What distinguishes late modern era from early modernity in this context is that the constantly shifting normative landscape generated by what Archer (2012, pp. 5–6) has conceptualised as 'morphogenetic' social mechanisms, i.e. processes that 'tend to elaborate or change system's given form, structure or state,' gradually predominate over solid, or 'morphostatic' mechanisms that ensure a degree of contextual continuity and normative certitude.[6] According to Archer, the emerging morphogenesis slowly undermines habitual action and subverts the normative force of habitus, while at the same time enhancing the actor's reflexivity. Viewed in a negative light, the actor is forced to determine how he/she must behave in a growing number of situations where habitual action was previously a reliable guideline. Seen positively, the actor is given the opportunity to define the situation one finds himself/herself in.

1.3 What Is Unique About the Law?

One of the functions of modern law may be described in terms of its ability to mediate between the two types of normativities generated by the system and lifeworld. However, law being a social system or institution, is not an empty vessel which may be employed at will to mediate between spheres of action and their respective forms of normativity. Law generates and exerts its own normativity which is moulded by the socio-historical context of its institutions. The uniqueness of the legal system's purported normativity is not captured by Weber's ideal types of action sketched above. Moreover, legal theory and legal sociology deal with

[6] 'Morphostatis' refers to the properties of social systems which generate inflexible, but also stable, internal structures, while 'morphogenesis' refers to those system characteristics which allow and facilitate structural flexibility (see Archer 2012, p. 5).

law's normativity by using epistemically incompatible terms (see Chap. 2). What mainstream legal scholarship regards as the principal values of the legal system, such as law's autonomy, objectivity and commitment to the rule of law, become the primary focus of critical inquiry within legal sociology.

Whereas Weber sought an explanation for the normativity of law in reason, calculations and motivations that the social actor employs to justify his/her actions (in this case following the law), others have tried to find it in the law itself, in its specific form of reasoning or discourse, and thus implicitly attribute it to the law rather than to the subject's use of the law or to the actor's cognition or thought processes. We argued that the actor's role in this respect has become increasingly unstable as, on the one hand, his/her habitus starts losing its normativity while, on the other hand, he/she gains reflexivity vis-à-vis social structures. Now let us take a closer look at the normativity of law as a phenomenon which is generated by the law itself and ask if it can provide solidity and certitude under late modernity.

Robert Alexy's theory of legal discourse (1998), discussed in Chap. 4, provides us with a suitable starting point. According to Alexy, besides a factual side law also comprises 'a critical or ideal dimension', which is defined *internally* by a 'claim to correctness' (Alexy 2000; see also Bulygin 2000), a claim which when made by law also entails making a claim to justice. Alexy means that 'there are moral elements active in law', that adjudication (at least in hard cases) requires making moral judgements and that 'legislation claims to be morally justifiable even in the case of political compromise' (Alexy 2000, p. 143). Law is occasionally unjust, yet it remains and is recognised as law as long as it aims to serve justice. Galligan (2006), whose take on law and society is fundamentally different from Alexy's, also suggests that there is something unique about the law as a social formation. Paraphrasing Galligan, had law not been a social formation distinct from the other social phenomena with which it interacts, had it not possessed its own very specific social properties and mechanisms, it would have long collapsed into polity, economy, religion, morality or culture (Galligan 2006; for a discussion see Chap. 5). Galligan (2006, p. 244) lists several aspects of the law which, by creating legal frameworks for security and stability, 'direct society in order to achieve social goods'. Galligan, who follows Hart's concept of law, does refer to the role of officials and citizens in determining what constitutes the law, but in the final analysis it is the law which empowers officials and the citizenry to play an active role in realising socially desirable values. The institutional facts of the law are in a sense being transformed into values, thus suggesting 'a projective movement of sorts from the "is" to the "ought"' (Minkkimmen 1999, p. 39).

From Mauro Zamboni's positivistic vantage point, the normative movement is in the opposite direction, from values to facts. Zamboni (2007, pp. 172–185) identifies the specific property of the law in its ability to transform values entrenched in political decisions into legally relevant concepts and categories. While Zamboni describes how values and moral rights and concerns are transformed into (some would say *reified* as) legal codes and rules, Radbruch (1990) contends that for legal concepts to *become* law, they need to be translated back into the language of values. Although Zamboni conceptually separates law from values, one cannot but wonder if a part of the normative force of legal rules does not retain the link to their underpinning values or social sources (or the normativity which emanates from system and lifeworld). It is reasonable to assume that laws which are generated by transforming political decisions based on existing community values or system imperatives continue to bear the legitimising seal of the community or the administrative system which initially generated them and can more easily be translated back into a language that can be used by the system or lifeworld to realise 'social goods'. In contrast, laws which are not rooted in community or system imperatives and are brought about to modify common usages, and mores have to fight an uphill battle.

Zamboni, the ardent advocate of legal positivism, and Alexy, 'the apologist or polemicist in defence of the law' (see Goodrich 2008, p. 105), conceptualise law and normativity in different ways, and yet their approaches belong to the discourse of legal theory, i.e. they take certain values and ideas belonging to legal theory for granted. To tease out their disciplinary distinctiveness, we can contrast their take on law's normativity with Pierre Bourdieu's sociological exposition of the binding force of law. Bourdieu (1987, pp. 843–844) maintains that law's 'symbolic power' extends itself beyond the circle of 'believers', i.e. jurists, law's officials, law professors and others, who have internalised the values of the legal system, such as its objectivity and autonomy, not to mention its ability to deliver 'social goods':

> The specific property of the symbolic power is that it can be exercised through the complicity of those who are dominated by it. The complicity is all the more certain because it is unconscious on the part of those who undergo its effects—or perhaps we should say it is more subtly extorted from them... [One] of the functions of the specifically juridical labor of formalizing and systematizing ethical representations and practices is to contribute to binding lay people to the fundamental principle of the jurists' professional ideology—belief in the neutrality and autonomy of the law and of jurists themselves. (Bourdieu 1987, p. 844)

What was described above by Alexy as the 'claim to correctness', by Galligan as 'social goods' and by Zamboni as the 'transformative capacity of positive law, which turns values into legal rules', is reduced by Bourdieu to (and *demystified* as) the power of the jurist's professional ideology. This reveals the epistemic gap between Bourdieu's legal sociology and mainstream legal theory.[7] Perhaps understandably, from the standpoint of legal philosophers, such sociological explanations miss the target by miles and at best trivialise law's *sui generis* normative property. More importantly, Bourdieu appears to be treating the legal profession as a culturally and ideologically homogeneous group, which has internalised the same values, occupy the same field of legal practice and share the same habitus. Admittedly, legal education and legal training socialise lawyers and create the 'juridical gaze'. Yet, it is important to recognise that the legal profession consists of a diverse group

[7] Bourdieu's point that the force of law requires 'the complicity of those who are dominated by it' reminds us of Michel Foucault's discussions of power, knowledge and discipline (for a discussion see Gustafsson 2011).

of lawyers with different tasks, objectives, aspirations and career trajectories within the law.

Although arguing for a *sui generis* normative legal content for law is reminiscent of natural law theories, those who evoke 'normativity' in this way often do not appeal to the metaphysics of natural law tradition. Instead, according to Turner (2010, p. 5), they maintain that this binding quality is neither natural nor mystical or empirical, and yet it is necessarily inherent in law and moral norms. 'Normativists', as Turner calls them, do not deny 'the empirical sociological phenomenon of normativity' but insist that sociological explanations, such as the one produced above by Bourdieu, are 'not enough to explain what needs to be explained' (Turner 2010, p. 5). The sociologist can explain that law rhetorically engenders its binding (symbolic, ideological or normative) power, on the one hand, by claiming to be an objective or an impartial arbiter of disputes, while conflating legality and justice, on the other. In the English language, for example, the word 'justice' is frequently employed as a synonym to law. We refer to lay magistrates in English courts as 'Justices of the Peace' and to Supreme Court judges as 'Justices of the Supreme Court'. Similarly, we talk about 'access to justice' when we mean access to courts and legal services, 'the criminal justice system' when we mean the penal system, 'bringing offenders to justice' when we mean prosecuting suspects or sentencing offenders and 'delivering justice' when we mean deciding cases. Although following Bourdieu one could say that these are examples of how law exercises its symbolic power, the 'normativists' would still demand an explanation as to why *justice* remains such a compelling force in public political discourse, not to mention in the minds of individual citizens, despite legal positivism's attempts to distinguish it sharply from legality. This is true under early and late modernity. What distinguishes contemporary social movements—which range from animal rights to environmental and anti-globalisation and Arab Spring movements—from the earlier social movements is their global reach and concern with issues which transcend local politics.

We should also note that law's normativity as it was defined by Alexy and Galligan cannot be extended to explain how law's based on risk management strategies (RMSs), which we discussed in the previous chapter, exert their normativity. RMSs are neither driven by the urge to make a 'claim to correctness' nor by achieving 'social goods'. We shall develop this point in the next section.

2 Justice as Law's Primary Source of Normativity

2.1 Defining Justice

Justice has been defined as a virtue or a moral value of the highest order. Its sources range from divine command to the practices of the wise ruler, and from the law of nature to the living law of the community. For our immediate purposes here, we will depart from the understanding of justice formulated as a general norm in Justinian *Institutes* as 'the constant and enduring will to render to each what is due' (Barden and Murphy 2011, p. 5)—a will which involves an unconditional, and arguably asymmetrical, responsibility to recognise and respond to the singularity of the Other (Derrida 1992; also see McVeigh 2002). 'Rendering to each what is due', most people would concede, should be one of the key considerations when determining how society is organised and how the activities of individuals and social groups are regulated. Some would even argue that it is one of the defining characteristics of a functioning human community and harmonious society. Nonetheless, few would agree on what 'rendering to each what is due' amounts to and how it *ought* to inform human affairs in practice. This renders debates and discussions on what constitutes justice inevitable, even though, as pointed out by MacIntyre (1981, p. 6), we know that 'they apparently can find no terminus' and, as argued by Derrida (1992), they require making an infinite, incalculable and ultimately impossible judgement. Nevertheless, law is required to be just, and unjust law is never recognised or accepted as a legitimate exercise in political and legal authority. This does not imply that it is expected to deliver justice in every case, but it should be committed to the principle of justice and not produce 'grossly unjust' outcomes, to borrow again from Alexy (this point is made in reference to Alexy's appropriation of Gustav Radbruch's legal theory; see Alexy 2002). Expressed differently by Simmonds (2007, p. 197), '[...] while justice and legality are distinct and can compete with each other, legality can only fully be achieved where justice is achieved also'. By extension, any society not governed in accordance with the principle of justice is prone to social conflict and political upheaval; in such a case, the society will be no more than a precarious social order maintained over time purely through coercion, oppression and the threat of violence.[8] On this basis, justice becomes the source of law's normativity *par excellence*. This view, however, is not shared by legal positivists, who argue that there is no necessarily *specific* connection between law and morality, and then move on to locate justice (which involves making an ethical judgement) beyond the legal system, in that it becomes not an integral part *of* the law's operations but a moral judgement *about* the law. For them, justice is not an intrinsic attribute of legal decision-making but a normative benchmark which exists independently of the law and legal institutions. This allows legal positivism to construct a rule-based theory of law independently of morality,[9]

[8] Admittedly, lawyers, lawmakers, policymakers and ordinary people employ the law as a tool to protect and promote their own interests, if necessary at the expense of others and without consideration for the principles of justice or the rule of law. Nonetheless, Tamanaha (2006) maintains that the instrumental attitude to the application of the law reduces it to a tool without any intrinsic value of its own, or moral properties capable of promoting the common good. The fact that law is an instrument for achieving particular ends is not a problem in itself—it becomes a problem and a threat to a democratic and just society once the institution of law is divorced from considerations of the public good.

[9] Tracing the development of legal positivism back to the critique of natural law in the sixteenth century, the separation between law and morality was initially a method for circumventing the

while at the same time drawing a disciplinary borderline between themselves and others, such as natural lawyers and legal pluralists, who conflate *is* and *ought* (for the debate between Kelsen and Ehrlich see Van Klink 2006, discussed also in Chap. 7).

Luhmann (2004) is one of the few scholars to have elaborated on the essence of legal positivism's separation thesis into a sociological theory, according to which morals belong not to the systems, such as polity or law, but 'to the environment of all subsystems of the society' (Dallmann 1998, p. 89). It is important to note that Luhmann's unit of analysis is not norms but communication—his social systems are communication systems which continuously objectify 'meaning'. The normativity of a legal system is generated internally by law recursively referring to its own previous communications or operations. In this way, the system excludes the diversity of its environment while reducing its own complexity (Luhmann 1986, 1990). The normativity which is generated internally within the legal system has no *direct* impact on how other systems operate, or on social action, but it does produce 'juridical justice', which is a watered down version of justice, as discussed above.

2.2 *Justice as Law's Contingency Formula*

Luhmann's systems theory conceptualises justice as the contingency formula of the legal system (Luhmann 2004, pp. 213–215). The law, according to Luhmann, does not 'recognise' but *reacts* to normative demands and other 'irritations' in its environment. Justice is neither internal nor external to law but is instead generated within the internal constraints of the legal system as 'a programme of all programmes on the level of the programmes of the system' (Luhmann 2004, p. 213),[10] which guides the operations of the law from the outside. According to Teubner's reading of Luhmann, this means that:

> Within the boundaries of law, justice cannot be weighed against anything. In this respect juridical justice differs from its counterparts in morality, politics and economics. For them justice is one normative programme among many – legitimacy, welfare, efficiency – while within the law, justice is invoked as the central non-contestable orientation formula. (Teubner 2009, p. 9)

Although Teubner acknowledges the importance of justice within the legal system, by describing it as law's 'central non-contestable orientation formula',

---

contingency of law-making practices. As Delacroix (2006, p. x) explains, 'Montaigne invited us to proceed *as if* any inquiry into the context of social interaction giving rise to law were irrelevant to accounting for its normative dimension'.

[10] For Luhmann (2004, p. 213), the normative closure of the legal system excludes morality as a valid criterion for decision-making within the legal system, although this exclusion is compensated by law internally constructing 'programmes' (such as justice, legitimacy, welfare and efficiency) which, per definition, cannot recognise, accommodate or address all moral issues and points of view (Luhmann 2004, p. 214).

his 'juridical justice' remains nevertheless limited in its practical scope and normative claims. The strengths and weaknesses of Luhmannian justice lie in its simplicity, which, firstly, reduces justice to 'an individualisation process that looks for the (in)equality of new cases with old cases' (Teubner 2009, p. 7) and secondly, refuses to provide any substantive criteria for evaluating the justness of law's internal operations. Whether or not binary distinctions made inside the law succeed in realising justice constitutes an effect observable only from the outside. This notion of 'juridical justice' can be criticised for being an abstract version of formal or procedural justice, essentially confirming the trivial claim that, inside the law, justice is reducible to the equality of cases before the law ensured by due process. It also fails to generate a specific legal value associated with justice and does not produce a set of substantive standards which can be employed to evaluate the correctness of individual decisions. Teubner recognises the critique directed at 'juridical justice' but dismisses it for ignoring Luhmann's point regarding 'adequate complexity' (Teubner 2009, p. 9), i.e. according to Luhmann (2004, p. 219), justice requires 'adequate complexity of consistent decision-making'. This suggests that the full realisation of 'juridical justice' requires a broader normative context produced by the legal system's 'adequate complexity of consistent decision-making'. It is also noteworthy that although Luhmann departs from a positive concept of law (law in terms of state law), he nevertheless constructs a theory of justice fundamentally different from that of mainstream legal studies. Luhmann's application of a specific set of concepts and ideas belonging to systems theory demarcates a disciplinary border not only between his sociological approach and mainstream legal studies and natural lawyers, but also between systems theory and other socio-legal theories of law, such as legal pluralism or Bourdieusian legal sociology.

2.3 The Inter-Connectedness of Law and Justice

For Barden and Murphy, justice is explained neither by reference to 'irritations' external to the juridical system nor by the ethical properties of legal discourse. Instead, they find it in the emergence of the human community and the functional necessity of maintaining social order over time. The relationship between law and justice evolved historically, Barden and Murphy (2011, p. 3) maintain, through what they call 'the living law', i.e. 'a set of communally accepted norms that express how in certain types of situation members of the community are obliged to act'. They argue that the living law 'constitutes the commonly accepted rules of the community' and, conversely, that 'the communal moral law is the evolving principle of those who live together' (Barden and Murphy 2011, pp. 4–5). Barden and Murphy do not refer to the role of the lifeworld and system in generating communal moral law, but their analysis corresponds with the discussion above (see Sect. 1.2), in that the lifeworld can be a source of normativity and generate a sense of obligation (or moral law) underpinned by intersubjectively shared values. In short, law and justice have emerged historically as an integral part of the cohesive moral force which holds the human community together. Through their interplay, they foster social integration, which is the prerequisite of an orderly modern society and gives rise to a normative context. MacCormick (2007, pp. 16–17) calls this 'a normative order' and writes:

> There is a shared or common sense of the "right thing to do", but this does not at all depend on there being one single officially formulated rule that each person can recite or learn by rote. For indeed the practice is an interpretative one, in which each party "reads" the situation as s/he thinks others are reading it and forms an opinion with regard to the opinion he/she thinks others hold, though this is not necessarily any kind of reflective deliberation about others' opinions.

This normative context (or normative order) is rich in history and culture, provides reasons for action (reasons for obeying norms and rules), possesses 'adequate complexity', to use Luhmann's terminology, and as such is not reducible to specific norms or the collection thereof. It is, to borrow from MacCormick again, about a shared and unreflective *sense* of 'the right thing to do', and as such it is a form of *sensibility* embedded in the lifeworld. Once this taken-for-granted sensibility becomes intersubjective, i.e. commonly shared among a group of people, it generates the foundation for a social institution—it creates a rational basis for repeated patterns of behaviour, while at the same time it is reproduced over time by the institutional practices it supports.[11] However, MacCormick's 'normative order' describes the ideal conditions of early modernity and not the conditions brought on by late modernity where social spaces are culturally hybridised, knowledge is fragmented and the sense of 'the right thing to do' is constantly undermined by the equally feasible alternative ways of doing things. As we argued in the previous chapter, under late modernity, the traditional forms of law and regulation give way to risk management strategies.

2.4 Risk Management Strategy's Normativity

In the context of the concerns of this book we cannot avoid asking how RMSs generate their normativity in a late modern context. The previous chapter argued that the pendulum of social control was gradually swinging away from the traditional forms of regulation (TRs), which control social action through the application of norms, towards RMSs aimed at coping with the unpredicted dysfunctional consequences of social developments. The gradual shift to RMSs is brought on by the awareness that in a growing number of areas—where social interactions, relations and institutions are either becoming transitory or moving outside the

[11] Social institutions are more than aggregates of repeated patterns of interaction. They permit and entail the concentrated reflexive monitoring of social relations across indefinite time/space distances, thus constituting highly dynamic expert systems of social control (Giddens 1991, p. 16).

regulatory reach of governments and state law—social control is no longer realised by inserting norms and values in social structures. This change of attitude towards TRs corresponds with a shift in social policy from welfare capitalism to market capitalism, which we shall discuss in the next chapter. It also resonates with one of the central debates of social theory on the decentring of the subject. On the one hand, 'the self' has become unstable and fragmented while, on the other hand, it has gained in reflexivity in respect to social structures. Viewed from a different vantage point, the social structures which previously crystallised and mediated norms and values, or provided a stable habitus, dissolve placing much greater burden on the actor to create his/her own social reality. As we argued in the Introduction, this does not amount to the melting away of all solid social structures, institutions, communities and relationships, but describes a trend towards increased liquefaction of society.

RMSs are more effective methods of responding to the consequences of globalisation and the growth of network society partly because they are not driven by the need to control and steer the social sphere (which would require interplay with social and cultural values), or to engender social goods, social change and reform. Instead, they 'seek to govern without governing society' (Rose 1996, p. 328), thus, allowing both public (state-centred) and private (non-governmental) orderings to grow. This, however, mean a disengagement with justice and lack of concern with social injustice. However, although RMSs are weak on justice, they are strong on upholding the status quo by ensuring some form of continuity in social and economic activities. In this sense, their normativity emanates from system imperatives and is based on instrumental rationality. RMSs are not rooted in the lifeworld and do not mediate between system and lifeworld as social welfare laws did. They are neither concerned with creating 'social goods' in the sense that Galligan proposed, nor claiming correctness in the sense that Alexy was arguing. Instead they appear to aim at maintaining system imperatives and system integrity in the face of an increasingly volatile social environment. However, as we also pointed out, RMSs generate new uncertainties and thus at the same time undermine the stability of systems. Following Ulrich Beck, one can argue that many of 'the "manufactured uncertainties," created by human industry in the economy, science and via the institutionalization of society...,' such as 'environmental pollution, crime and terrorism, are global, unpredictable and defy institutional regulation' (Walklate and Mythen 2010, p. 48).

In the previous chapter, we also argued that the growing application of RMS has not made the traditional forms of regulation (TRs), which interact with norms and values in the environment of legal system, obsolete. TR is instead used alongside other forms of social control giving rise to hybrid forms of regulation. As a result, many walks of life are exposed to more than one form of regulatory regime and normativity.

3 Dealing with the Normativity of Justice

The discussions so far should demonstrate that all sociological studies of law, which deal with issues of institutionalised order and social or system integration, are inquiries into forms of normativity. Nevertheless, some legal sociologists (see Black 1972) and legal theorists (see Kelsen 2002; Tuori 2006; Zamboni 2006) have treated legal sociology as an empirical science, which should engage with the external aspect of laws, legal rules and principles, which generate observable regularities, and leave their internal aspects which deal with their 'ought' dimension and the sense of obligation, to legal theorists and moral philosophers. In the final part of this chapter, we return to the initial interest of this book on methodology in an attempt to throw light on the methodological limitation of the sociology of law.

3.1 Facts and Values in Social and Legal Research

In *A Treaties of Human Nature*, published in 1739, David Hume pointed out that norms and values could not be derived from 'facts' (see Hume 1896). Empirical methods of research do reflect this insight and sharply distinguish between *is* and *ought*, a distinction which also acts as one of the defining criteria of legal positivism (cf. Black 1972, p. 1092). Perhaps understandably, most socio-legal researchers who rely on empirical methods—with a few exceptions, such as the works of Petrazycki (1956) and Selznick (1992)—have avoided probing the normative core of rights and justice, leaving it to moral and legal philosophers to deal with the normativity of law conceptually and analytically (also see Nonet and Selznick 2007). However, Emile Durkheim's identification of 'social facts' as the primary domain of sociological inquiry has undoubtedly played a more decisive role than Hume's facts/norms distinction in determining the methodological scope of legal sociology. As Morris (2006, p. 1) points out, Durkheim's 'insistence on the analysis of social facts as things ruled out a consideration of normative concerns'. Although Morris's (2006) view of sociology's treatment of rights is shared by many scholars, there are other notable readings of classical sociology which strongly suggest a more complex picture of the relationship between the normative and the empirical. One such interpretation is found in the work of Cotterrell (2010), which we shall discuss below. It suffices to point out here that Durkheim was drawn to the study of law precisely because he sought a sociological method of grasping the normative phenomenon.[12] For Durkheim morality constituted the normative core of law.

---

[12] In reference to the sociology of human rights, Somers and Roberts also question the belief that sociology is incapable of studying normativity. They maintain that the sociology of human rights must transcend, negotiate or deconstruct the methodological barriers within social sciences which hold back sociology's engagement with the normativity of rights. See Somers and Roberts (2008).

Max Weber, to mention another founder of the sociology of law, distinguished between three ways of thinking about the law informed by: (1) the method of dogmatic jurisprudence, (2) a sociological/empirical approach and (3) the moral attitude towards the law which sharply differentiates between legal and moral standards, applying itself to the study of the latter (for an overview see Kronman 1983, p. 7). However, Weber also explained that these were *ideal types*, i.e. 'exaggerated or one-sided descriptions that emphasised particular aspects of what is a richer and more complicated reality' (Kronman: 1983, p. 7). The 'unreality' of this distinction, Kronman explains, was supposed to assist us in 'disentangling the different elements that existing practices and institutions invariably involve' (Kronman 1983, p. 7). Otherwise, Weber never intended to reduce the complexity of the operations of the legal system in respect to other social systems or spheres of action to simple distinctions between the internal and external operations of the law, for such sharply drawn distinctions abstract and differentiate law into parts which are then interconnected and should be understood in terms of ongoing processes.

Notwithstanding what Weber intended, a threefold division of labour is largely in force within contemporary legal studies, according to which: (1) legal scholars will study positive law's internal processes, (2) legal sociologists will investigate the empirical manifestations of the law, such as its efficacy in regulating behaviour and its impact on social relationships and vice versa, and (3) legal philosophers will investigate the moral foundations of the law, which include justice.[13] As suggested above, this division of labour is maintained over time through the internal disciplinary discourses of various fields of legal research and as part of these fields' attempt to reproduce specific epistemic identities. As we argued in Chap. 2, these discourses compete simultaneously for 'scientific stakes' (see Bourdieu 1975) such as academic prestige and scarce resources. While various branches of legal studies, such as doctrinal research and legal philosophy, compete externally with each other and with legal sociology, they are at the same time constituted internally by their own competing discourses, i.e. by the internal debates between their various schools of thought. In this scheme of things, socio-legal studies and legal positivism focus on positive law, writes Constable (2005, p. 9), while employing a broadly conceived empirical approach, thus converging around a cluster of characteristics:

> Most texts of and about law take law to be a social phenomenon [...]. Even scholars interested in what they call the "normative" aspect of law situate law in an empirical social world. That "society" is real, that "reality" is social and empirical, holds such sway that one wonders what else law could be.

Subsequently, according to Constable, we run the risk of forgetting that the empirical understanding of law is a relatively new insight generated to describe the operations of modern legal systems. Otherwise, law has not always been positivist,

[13] Legal theorists and philosophers will also clarify the general framework of legal ideas and formulate general and abstract descriptions of legal systems. For a discussion see Galligan (2006, pp. 7–12).

empirical or sociological, even though viewing it as a positive phenomenon has become the norm—the only reasonable way of comprehending and describing what actually constitutes law. It should therefore not come as a surprise if the dominance of positivism within legal scholarship and socio-legal research comes at a price, namely the relegation of 'connections between law and justice, if any, to the empirically contingent social realities' (Constable 2005, p. 10). Modern law and its socio-legal partner are thus both silent about justice, argues Constable. This does not mean that justice is absent in the discourses of legal positivists and socio-legal researchers, however, as it can be sought in places where they are silent.

It is worth noting that *injustice*, rather than *justice*, prompts—not least of all amongst law-and-society researchers—most debates and research on the impact of law on society. While the debate on justice is always shrouded in conceptual ambiguity and uncertainty, its opposite, *injustice*, is deliberated with some degree of conviction. The debate on justice is often marked by fundamental disagreements because it concerns itself with how things *ought* to be and with how to bring about and ensure basic rights, fairness and equal treatment, whereas debates on injustice, generally, and miscarriages of justice, in particular, are often concerned with actual cases pertaining to the abuse of power, existing unfair practices and the experience of wrongs and harm being perpetrated against oneself or others. We tend to respond to injustice more readily perhaps because, as Douzinas and Geary (2005, p. 28) point out, it has the power to stir us emotionally. In the context of socio-legal research, the emphasis placed on injustice is not only emotive, or as Tamanaha (1997) has suggested part of a political commitment,[14] but also partly due to its 'facticity', i.e. that it offers an empirically tangible starting point for the study of the interaction between law and various social forces. Among these social forces, power looms large, for injustice is often about the abuse of power through law and other formal means of social control which is exercised top down. However, unlike justice, power is treated as an empirical phenomenon.

Justice is therefore left to the legal philosophers, who are generally concerned with clarifying the general framework of legal ideas and formulating general and abstract descriptions of legal systems (for a discussion see Galligan 2006, pp. 7–12). As a result they tend to discuss the law at a level of generality and analyse its operations in terms of either its *sui generis* normative properties (see discussions under Sect. 1.3) or judge-made law and court judgements, i.e. justice becomes dependent on the judge's virtue and on the social interactions between the judge and other actors (for an overview of such an approach see Andersen 2011). In contrast, a sociological approach to how justice is delivered often departs from a much broader understanding of law, treating legal phenomena in view of their institutional properties, for example as empirically observable clusters of social practices or

[14] The Law and Society scholarship has been criticised for focusing on the interests of marginalised groups and subsequently on injustice in society. Brian Tamanaha, for example, regards this tendency as proof of the politicisation of Law and Society research (cf. Chapter 1 in Tamanaha 1997). For a discussion see Chap. 3.

repeated patterns of behaviour which produce a sense of legality. One empirical aspect of the law, which affects the delivery of justice and yet stands out by its absence in most traditional moral philosophical treatments of law, concerns the impact the socio-cultural identity of officers of the law (identity in terms of gender, class, ethnicity, religion, etc.) has on their practices. Traditional legal theory often works with an idealised concept of the judge, existing apparently beyond the constraints of sociological factors such as gender or class and independently of problems arising out of the polycontexturality of late modern societies. The issue at hand can therefore be summarised in the following way. Legal sociology neglects the normativity of justice (or is 'blind' to the normative possibilities[15] and constraints of law) and traditional legal philosophy overlooks the empirical dimensions of the legal system and practices (or processes) which reproduce law and its institutions, while doctrinal studies reduce them to rule-based reasoning. This makes traditional legal philosophy and doctrinal studies blind to the possibilities of and constraints imposed by the institutional settings within which the search for justice unfolds.

3.2 Scientific Methodology

The presumed inability of social sciences in general, but sociology in particular, to address the normative cores of rights and justice is caused by their 'scientific' methodology, which makes them resistant to normativity on two different levels. It makes them suspicious of foundationalist and universalist claims inherent in (human) rights and justice (see Somers and Roberts 2008; Deflem and Chicoine 2011) and urges them to remain 'objective' in respect to the aims of their study, describing and analysing how things *are*, rather than speculating on how they *ought* to be. This means that they refuse to take at face value the normative claims made by social actors (including institutions of law and polity) while abstaining from making value judgments themselves. This is linked closely to another characteristic of sociology, which requires researchers to stay empirically grounded—seeking and exploring empirically tangible phenomena. In his essay *Science as Vocation*, Max Weber states that 'historical and social sciences teach an understanding of social and political phenomena, but give no answer to the question as to how to judge activity in these realms' (Morris 2006, p. 4). Similarly, Black (1972, p. 1092), echoing Hume, maintains that 'value judgements cannot be discovered in the empirical world' and are therefore irrelevant to the sociology of law. Instead of speculating on the nature of a good life, social sciences should describe how people use values in their practices, how they employ moral arguments and how they experience justice and deal with injustice by using the law or other means available

[15] Following Norrie (2005, p. ix), I argue that 'law plays a central role in structuring, shaping and limiting the ethical possibilities in Western liberal societies'.

to them at the time. In this sense, social sciences do study normativity, but they do so by using a non-normative language, in order to comply with the methodological standards of (social) sciences. In short, legal sociology's inability to deal satisfactorily with the normativity of justice must be placed in the context of social-scientific debate on the relationship between facts and values—or the is/ought problem—and the basic observation that 'ought' cannot be logically inferred from 'is'.[16]

This conclusion—that sociology as a primarily empirical science can describe and analyse what there *is*, but not what *ought* to be—is accurate yet deceptively simplistic, if not erroneous, once it is extended to legal sociology's ability to account for normativity. Firstly, not all sociologists endorse or apply a positivistic methodology, and legal sociology is arguably influenced more by interpretive (qualitative) than by positivistic (quantitative) methods of inquiry. In debates where non-sociologists criticise the limits of socio-legal theory (see, for example, Constable 2005; Tuori 2006, p. 28), the works of positivists such as Donald Black or Niklas Luhmann[17] are somewhat misleadingly taken to represent mainstream socio-legal research on law (Luhmann's work is often also misrepresented).[18] Subsequently, the theoretical diversity of the field, and sociological debates on rights and justice, are neglected (see, for example, Cotterrell 2010; Travers 2010; for a classical example, see Gurvitch 1947).

More importantly, most sociologists would readily admit that a combination of personal and professional values determines the angle from which they view social problems. Expressed differently, the way sociologists 'problematise' a particular issue is often determined by their values, some of which are rooted in their personal experience of social life and the position they occupy in society. Closely related is the argument that sociology's empirical data do not qualify as 'facts', if by 'facts'

[16] Some legal sociologists such as Black, who have written on justice, limit their analysis to the *administration* of justice, to the empirically observable and measurable aspects of what is done in the name thereof (Black 1998; for a discussion see Banakar 2003, pp. 55–57). Black's theory of justice is constructed sociologically and supported empirically by data gathered from the outcomes of legal cases. Although his conceptualisation of the social structure of legal cases is socio-legally useful, it nonetheless avoids evaluating justice as a normative or emotional experience inseparable from the internal operations of the law and the legal system. In essence, it does not tell us if the right decision was made and justice done. As a result, in Black's final analysis, justice is reduced to the exercise of power and authority through the medium of law and legality in the sense criticised by Constable.

[17] Luhmann is a positivist, but only in the narrow sense of identifying law with state law. Otherwise, as we saw in connection with his discussion on justice, he distinguishes himself from mainstream legal positivists.

[18] Black is a double positivist. He is a positivist in the social-scientific sense of searching for aspects of social life which lend themselves to measurement, but he is also a positivist in the legal sense of restricting law to legal rules issued by the state or generated through the operations of the legal system. This cannot be said in Luhmann's case. Although his concept of law is positivistic, his methodological approach draws on a number of traditions that defy a simple classification as positivist. Also, Luhmann does not adhere to legal positivism's sharp distinction between law and morality; instead, he proposes a sociologically sophisticated description of law's autonomy.

we are referring to entities existing independently of the observer. Alternatively, sociology's empirical data are located theoretically and are thus dependent on and a function of sociologists' basic theoretical (or rather epistemological) assumptions. Even when a study is conducted inductively in search of viable working hypotheses, the sociologist cannot avoid employing certain preconceptions about valid knowledge and how to locate and collect data (this point draws our attention to conceptual, empirical and analytical limits of sociology as a vantage point of social reality). It also means that the choice of perspective in social research, i.e. deciding from whose standpoint a particular study is to be conducted, qualifies as a value judgement. I should hasten to add that the dependency of researchers' perspectives on values is not limited to sociology and applies to all social research, including doctrinal research, which is driven by the concerns and taken-for-granted values of the researcher or those who have commissioned the research, such as policymakers.[19] Expressed differently, deciding which perspective provides the correct point of departure for studying a social or legal problem entails making a value judgement, which in turn impacts upon the outcome of our research. This choice of perspective largely determines our method of inquiry.[20] In a study of hate speech, to give an example, we can produce very different results depending on whether we approach the problem from the standpoint of those who become the target of racist violence or from the vantage point of those who consider themselves the custodians of free speech and argue that legitimate public debates must be protected at all costs, even when this debate concerns issues which are deemed politically incorrect or offensive.

There is yet another way of considering facts and values, or the relationship between empirical research and normative evaluation—one which can be traced back to the founders of American Legal Realism. An understanding of what law *could* do in actual fact would assist us when negotiating and determining what law *should* do (see Llewellyn 1931). Expressed differently, law can benefit from the social scientific studies of the world it tries to govern by employing empirical knowledge to improve its normative judgements (see Nonet 1980, p. 58). Although values cannot be generated out of facts alone, accurate accounts of the relationship between law and society can lay the basis for addressing normative issues arising out of law's operations in society. This point has been elaborated on recently in Cotterrell's reading of Durkheim:

> [S]ociology cannot reveal *universal moral truths* [...]. Any criteria governing what is morally appropriate will relate to the sociological character of the particular type of society

[19] Sociology tries to cast light on the taken-for-granted values and concerns of sociological research. In this sense, it possesses a form of reflexivity which we do not find, for example, in doctrinal studies. For a discussion on doctrinal methods see Chaps. 2 and 5.

[20] If we depart from the authorities' conception of a problem, we are likely to use a top-down approach, while departing from the ordinary people's understanding of the same problem will most probably lead us to employ a bottom-up approach. Whether we use a top-down or a bottom-up approach can, in turn, have implications for the particular techniques we need to gather data. See Chaps. 3 and 5.

> concerned. Durkheim claims that sociology can study social life objectively as a matter of "social facts". In doing so it can identify moral principles and practices compatible with (or even necessary to) stable social relations in particular kinds of societies. To this extent sociology can provide guidance on moral issues. It is not limited to describing what people think in moral terms and what moral choices they actually make. To some extent it can also provide criteria to evaluate and criticize those choices. Thus, sociology can sometimes advise on what law should prescribe or permit. When sociology reveals the fundamental importance of certain moral principles, in particular social conditions, the question of whether these should be expressed and defended through law will need to be faced. (Cotterrell 2010, p. 5)

Last but not the least, sociology studies not only social norms, moral principles and legal rules, but also the normative contexts which give *reasons* for following norms, rules and principles and bestow *meaning* upon the sense of obligations and responsibilities towards others. The main point of this chapter, a notion which was developed in Sect. 2, is that some of the central concerns of sociology with, for example, social integration are ultimately concerns with justice and normativity. Legal sociology's ability to capture normativity in general and the normativity of law in particular has not been recognised for two reasons. Firstly, normativity is often understood in the narrow, rule-based sense of making a moral judgement (a process which may be decontextualised and reduced to the application of norms and values to the facts of a case), thus ignoring the possibility that normativity may emerge from socio-historical contexts of law and other institutions. In this latter sense, norms become labels which we use to describe already existing regularities and normativities and not the cause of regularities or the source of normativity. Secondly, sociology, being a different 'language game' than moral philosophy, studies normativity by using social-scientific terms rather than concepts employed by moral philosophy. Bourdieu's study of the symbolic power of law, and Luhmann's theory of justice, were used above to exemplify how sociological analysis distinguishes itself from mainstream legal theory by using different concepts to discuss normativity. Closely linked to this point is the need for various fields of legal study to produce and reproduce an academic identity. Thus, legal sociology, legal philosophy and doctrinal studies identify themselves discursively by reference to specific ideas and interests. Legal sociology consists of a host of various theoretical perspectives and epistemologies, but a broadly conceived commitment to the study of the empirical aspects of the law and legality, which often leads to an understanding of law in terms of institutional practices and social processes rather than a system of rules, principles, judgements and doctrines, brings these together under the same discursive/disciplinary order and distinguishes them from legal philosophy and doctrinal studies. As part of the attempt to define the boundaries of legal research fields, many legal sociologists as well as legal scholars, from Kelsen (2002, pp. 13–14) to Tuori (2006) and Zamboni (2006), have used the distinction between normative and empirical research as a marker for disciplinary inclusion and exclusion and a building block upon which part of their disciplinary identities may rest (for a discussion on the disciplinary boundaries of legal studies see Gustafsson 2011).

3.3 Concluding Remarks

Sociology in general and legal sociology in particular are concerned with and study the normative contexts of social action. Many of the studies of law conducted from a social-scientific point of view, for example, are driven by a concern with (in) justice but focus on the institutional relationships and practices through which (in) justice materialises, rather than evaluating the normativity of legal decisions. However, since socio-legal engagement with normativity is couched in the empirical language of social sciences, rather than the normative language of moral philosophy, it appears incapable of addressing the normativity of law. The methodological requirement of socio-legal research to remain empirically grounded admittedly restricts its mode of expression and the way it deals with the normativity of law—some studies tend to reduce law to the exercise of power, thus overlooking what distinguishes it from other forms of social regulation—but it does not exclude normativity from socio-legal analysis. Hence, the second argument of this chapter is that any analysis of law, which goes beyond the mere study of the technical aspects of positive law and tries to throw light on how it operates as an integral aspect of the social order, necessarily involves the study of justice, which as we argued above is the primary source of law's normativity and an integral element of social integration. There might not be a conceptually necessary link between the factual and the moral dimensions of the law, as legal positivists claim, but justice and law emerged together historically as inseparable parts of the common moral force which integrated the human community.

Constrained by its scientific conceptual lenses, sociological analysis cannot unearth the inner reality of law's normativity, but it can analyse and explain how the various expressions of its 'being' are generated discursively and produced and reproduced over time. Moreover, by studying law's normativity from specific angles—for example by emphasising people's experience of injustice, or alternatively emphasising norms at the expense of social conflicts—it does, indirectly as it might be, take a stance on the nature of a good society.

References

Alexy, R. (1998). *Theorie der juridischen Argumentation. Die Theorie des rationalen Diskurses als Theorie der juridiscen Begründung* (1983) translated by Neil MacCormick as *A Theory of Legal Argumentation: The Theory of Rational Discourse as Theory of Legal Justification*. Oxford: Clarendon.

Alexy, R. (2000). On the thesis of a necessary connection between law and morality: Bulygin's critique. *Ratio Juris, 13*(2), 138–147.

Alexy, R. (2002). *The argument from injustice*. Oxford: Clarendon.

Andersen, S. S. (2011). Justice and other judicial virtues. *Retfærd: The Nordic Journal of Law and Justice, 134*(3), 58–98.

Archer, M. (2012). *The reflexive imperative in late modernity*. Cambridge: Cambridge University Press.

Austin, J. (1995). *The province of jurisprudence determined*. Cambridge: Cambridge University Press (original publication 1832).
Banakar, R. (2003). *Merging law and sociology: Beyond the dichotomies of socio-legal research*. Berlin: Galda + Wilch.
Banakar, R., & Lort Phillips, A. (2014). Law and community in the 2011 London riots. In R. Nobles & D. Schiff (Eds.), *Law, society and community: Socio-legal essays in honour of Roger Cotterrell*. Farnham: Ashgate.
Barden, G., & Murphy, T. (2011). *Law and justice in community*. Oxford: Oxford University Press.
Bauman, Z. (2001). *Community: Seeking safety in an insecure world*. Cambridge: Polity.
Berger, P., & Luckmann, T. (1987). *The social construction of reality*. London: Pelican.
Black, D. (1972). The boundaries of legal sociology. *Yale Law Journal, 81*(May), 1086–1100.
Black, D. (1998). *Sociological justice*. Oxford: Oxford University Press.
Bourdieu, P. (1975). The specificity of the scientific field and the social conditions of the progress of reason. *Social Science Information, 14*(6), 19–47.
Bourdieu, P. (1987). The force of law: Toward a sociology of the juridical field. *Hastings Law Journal, 38*(5), 814–853.
Bulygin, E. (2000). Alexy's thesis of the necessary connection between law and morality. *Ratio Juris, 13*(2), 133–137.
Constable, M. (2005). *Just silences: The limits and possibilities of the modern law*. Princeton: Princeton University Press.
Cotterrell, R. (2010). Justice, dignity, torture, headscarves: Can Durkheim's sociology clarity legal values? *Social and Legal Studies, 20*(1), 3–20.
Dallmann, H.-U. (1998). Niklas Luhmann's systems theory as a challenge for ethics. *Ethical Theory and Moral Practice, 1*(1), 85–102.
Deflem, M., & Chicoine, S. (2011). The sociological discourse on human rights: Lessons from the sociology of law. *Development and Society, 40*(1), 101–115.
Delacroix, S. (2006). *Legal norms and normativity: An essay in Genealogy*. Oxford: Hart.
Derrida, J. (1992). Force of law: The "Mythical Conditions of Authority". In D. Cornell et al. (Eds.), *Reconstruction and the possibility of justice* (pp. 3–67). London: Routledge.
Douzinas, C., & Geary, A. (2005). *Critical jurisprudence: The political philosophy of justice*. Oxford: Hart.
Ehrlich, E. (2002). *Fundamental principles of sociology of law*. New Brunswick: Transaction Publications (original publication 1913).
Elek, E., et al. (2006). Influences of personal, injunctive, and descriptive norms on early adolescent substance use. *Journal of Drug Issues, 36*(1), 147–172.
Galligan, D. (2006). *Law in society*. Oxford: Clarendon.
Giddens, A. (1991). *Modernity and self-identity: Self and society in the late modern age*. Cambridge: Polity.
Giddens, A. (1994). Living in a post-traditional society. In U. Beck et al. (Eds.), *Reflexive modernisation: Politics, traditions and aesthetics in the modern social order* (pp. 56–109). Cambridge: Polity.
Goodrich, P. (2008). Alexy ad Iustitum. *Social and Legal Studies, 17*(1), 105–108.
Gurvitch, G. (1947). *Sociology of law*. London: Kegan Paul.
Gustafsson, H. (2011) *Dissens: Om det rättsliga medvetandet*. Göteborg: Juridiska institutionens skriftserie, Skrift 9.
Habermas, J. (1975). *Legitimation crisis*. Boston: Heinemann Education.
Habermas, J. (1984). *The theory of communicative action* (Vol. I). Boston: Beacon.
Hart, H. L. A. (1998). *The concept of law*. Oxford: Clarendon.
Hume, D. (1896). *A treatise of human nature* (pp. 1739–1740). Oxford: Clarendon (original publication 1739–1740).
Kallgren, C. A., et al. (2000). A focus theory of normative conduct: When norms do and do not matter. *Personality and Social Psychology Bulletin, 26*(8), 2002–2012.
Kelsen, H. (1967). *Pure theory of law*. Berkeley: University of California Press.

Kelsen, H. (2002). *Introduction to the problems of legal theory*. Oxford: Oxford University Press (original publication 1934).
Kronman, A. T. (1983). *Max Weber*. Stanford, CA: Stanford University Press.
Llewellyn, K. N. (1931). Some realism about realism. *Harvard Law Review, 44*(8), 1222–1264.
Luhmann, N. (1986). The self-reproduction of law and its limits. In G. Teubner (Ed.), *The dilemma of law in the welfare states* (pp. 111–127). Berlin: Walter de Gruyter.
Luhmann, N. (1990). Meaning as sociology's basic concept. In N. Luhmann (Ed.), *Essays on self-reference* (pp. 21–79). New York, NY: Columbia University Press.
Luhmann, N. (2004). *Law as a social system*. Oxford: Oxford University Press.
MacCormick, N. (2007). *Institutions of law*. Oxford: Oxford University Press.
MacIntyre, A. (1981). *After virtue: A study of moral theory*. Notre Dame: University of Notre Dame Press.
McVeigh, S. (2002). Postmodernism and common law. In R. Banakar & M. Travers (Eds.), *Introduction to law and social theory* (pp. 268–283). Oxford: Hart.
Minkkimmen, P. (1999). *Thinking without desire: A first philosophy of law*. Oxford: Hart.
Morris, L. (2006). Sociology and rights: An emerging field. In L. Morris (Ed.), *Rights: Sociological perspectives* (pp. 1–16). London: Routledge.
Nonet, P. (1980). For jurisprudential sociology. In W. M. Evan (Ed.), *The sociology of law: A social-structural perspective* (pp. 46–59). New York: Free Press.
Nonet, P., & Selznick, P. (2007). *Law and society in transition: Toward responsive law*. New Brunswick: Transaction Publishers (original publication 1978).
Norrie, A. (2005). *Law and the beautiful soul*. London: GlassHouse.
Office for National Statistics. (2014). *Divorce in England and Wales in 2012*. http://www.ons.gov.uk/. Accessed 2 Jan 2014.
Petrazycki, L. (1956). *Law and morality*. Harvard: Harvard University Press.
Radbruch, G. (1990). In A. Kaufman (Ed.), *Rechtsphilosophie III*. Vol 3 of the Gustav Radbruch Gesamtaugsgabe. Heidelberg: CF Mueller.
Raz, J. (1979). *The authority of law*. Oxford: Clarendon.
Raz, J. (1999). Explaining normativity: Reason and the will. In J. Raz (Ed.), *Engaging reasons: On the theory of value and action* (pp. 90–117). Oxford: Oxford University Press.
Raz, J. (2011). *From normativity to responsibility*. Oxford: Oxford University Press.
Robinson, P. H., & Darley, J. M. (2004). Does criminal law deter? A behavioural science investigation. *Oxford Journal of Legal Studies, 24*(2), 173–205.
Rose, N. (1996). The death of the social? Re-figuring the territory of the government. *Economy and Society, 25*(3), 327–356.
Selznick, P. (1992). *The moral common wealth*. Berkley and Los Angeles: University of California Press.
Simmonds, N. E. (2007). *Law as a moral idea*. Oxford: Oxford University Press.
Somers, M. R., & Roberts, C. N. J. (2008). Toward a new sociology of rights. *Annual Review of Law and Social Sciences, 4*, 384–425.
Tamanaha, B. (1997). *Realistic socio-legal theory: Pragmatic and social theory of law*. Oxford: Clarendon.
Tamanaha, B. Z. (2006). *Law as a means to an end: Threat to the rule of law*. Oxford: Oxford University Press.
Teubner, G. (2009). Self-subversive justice: Contingency or transcendence formula of law? *Modern Law Review, 72*(1), 1–23.
Travers, M. (2010). A sociological critique of rights. In R. Banakar (Ed.), *Rights in context: Law and justice in late modern society* (pp. 41–54). Aldershot: Ashgate.
Tuori, K. (2006). Self-description and external description of the law. *Foundations: Journal of Extreme Legal Positivism, 2*, 27–43.
Turner, S. P. (2010). *Explaining the normative*. Cambridge: Polity.
Van Klink, B. (2006). *Facts and norms: The unfinished debate between Eugen Ehrlich and Hans Kelsen*. SSRN: http://ssrn.com/abstract=980957.

Walklate, S., & Mythen, G. (2010). Agency, reflexivity and risk. *British Journal of Sociology, 61* (1), 45–62.
Weber, M. (1978). *Economy and society* (2 vols.). Berkeley: University of California Press.
Wedgewood, R. (2007). *The nature of normativity*. Oxford: Clarendon.
Zamboni, M. (2006). A reply to Reza Banakar's review of "The Policy of Law". *Retfærd: The Nordic Journal of Law and Justice, 29*(2), 81–85.
Zamboni, M. (2007). *A policy of law: A legal theoretical framework*. Oxford: Hart.

Chapter 12
The Changing Horizons of Law and Regulation: From an Industrial to a Post-Industrial, Digital Society

Abstract This chapter sketches two parallel, albeit sociologically interrelated, historical transformations. First, it briefly describes the move from industrialisation, when economies were nationally-based and dependent on manufacturing, to post-industrialisation, in which economies are shaped by the production and consumption of services and information. Second, it depicts the move from "welfare capitalism," which sought social integration through public policies administered by the state, to "market capitalism," whereby market forces are given free rein to shape society. As national markets expand and become part of global marketplaces, they also become increasingly volatile and risk-prone, thereby impacting on how society is regulated and organised. This chapter will argue that these two transformations give rise to new forms of law and regulation which require a new understanding of law in society. Although we have moved from a form of society dominated by industrial relations and manufacturing to a post-industrial information society shaped by digital networks and immaterial labour, a large part of socio-legal research remains geared toward a concept of society and social action that was developed during the heyday of industrialisation. The aim of this chapter is to highlight the necessity of developing a concept of law and an understanding of regulation which meet the challenges of the digital age.

Many of the sociology of law's original premises, concepts and ideas regarding the relationship between law and legal behaviour, on the one hand, and legal change and social reform, on the other, were formulated initially by studying conditions specific to Western industrial societies. The socio-cultural consequences of globalisation over the last three decades, however, have enhanced the "radicalisation of modernity," thus accelerating the process which melts the apparently solid contours of the industrial society and consequently paving the way for the emergence of a radical (or "reflexive"[1]) form of modernity (Beck et al. 1994). The transformative

This chapter has borrowed material from 'Sociology of Law'. In (2011) *Online Journal of International Sociological Association: Sociopedia.ISA* 1–14.

[1] According to Ulrich Beck, reflexivity refers to modernity's "self-confrontation," i.e. the bases of modernity are confronted with the unforeseen and undesired consequences of modernisation—consequences with which modern social systems can neither cope nor assimilate (cf. Beck et al. 1994, p. 6). For Giddens, too, reflexivity refers to a form of self-confrontation, but whereas

R. Banakar, *Normativity in Legal Sociology*, DOI 10.1007/978-3-319-09650-6_12

process engendered by globalisation has not only influenced the relationship between the individual and the community, but also redefined the relationship between the state, law and society (Twining 2000; Cotterrell 2006; Gessner and Nelken 2007). Moreover, it has blurred sharply drawn distinctions between the West and the rest of the world (Menski 2007) and transformed the socio-cultural setting within which legal regulation is devised and social reform planned. These aspects of globalisation were discussed briefly in the previous chapters (see Chaps. 2 and 3 in particular), but in this chapter we draw attention to the role of information technology in accelerating the spread of globalisation. As globalising processes become ever more intertwined with the expansion of the information society, communication technology which fuels the development of the so-called global electric markets penetrates deeper into our lives, creating 'new forms of action and interaction in the social world, new kinds of social relationships and new ways of relating to others and to oneself' (Thompson 1995, p. 4).

This chapter will explore the extent to which the sociology of law (henceforth "legal sociology") has reconsidered its sociological premises regarding the relationship between law, the state and society, in order to grasp the new social, cultural and technological forms of organisation specific to global network societies of the twenty-first century. Are concepts and ideas introduced during the early 1900s (which we shall call the period of telegraphy) by, for example, Emile Durkheim and Max Weber continuing to provide adequate tools for describing and analysing social interaction in cyberspace and social organisation in a digital society? Answers to these questions are sought in three sections. Section 1 discusses the development of legal sociology in the first half of the twentieth century—before World War II—as a response to the regulatory problems of industrialisation. It then describes how the growth of the welfare state in West European countries helped to establish legal sociology as a field of research. Section 2 brings into focus the move from the industrial to the post-industrial information society, and it argues that each type of communication technology, such as telegraphy, telephony and digital communication systems that introduce a specific form of communication, produces its own brand of social organisation, which in turn promotes the technology in question. Each new technology also necessitates its own form of social control and regulation. Section 3 concludes the chapter by arguing that the socio-cultural consequences of globalisation, enhanced by the spread of digital communication technology, erode the traditional boundaries of law and legal systems, hybridise legal cultures and create new conditions for legal regulation. The move from telephony and telegraphy to digital media signals a shift in social organisation which requires new conceptual approaches when studying the regulatory mechanisms in our contemporary network society.

Beck defined it in terms of the (in)ability of social systems to deal with the unforeseen and dysfunctional consequences of modernity, Giddens defines it in terms of social practices. He writes: 'The reflexivity of modern social life consists in the fact that social practices are constantly examined and reformed in the light of incoming information about those very practices, thus constitutively altering their character' (Giddens 1999, p. 38).

1 Law and Social Engineering in Industrial Society

1.1 Classical Socio-Legal Theory

The intellectual pedigree of legal sociology can be traced back to the works of two groups of scholars. The founders of sociology included scholars such as Herbert Spencer (1820–1903), William Graham Sumner (1840–1910), Emile Durkheim (1858–1917) and Max Weber (1864–1920), while jurists interested in employing social scientific methods in the study of law included Eugen Ehrlich (1862–1922), Leon Petrażycki (1867–1931) and Roscoe Pound (1870–1964) (see also Sect. 1.3 in Chap. 3, where sociological jurisprudence is presented). The first group, which was driven by sociological concerns, explored the development and application of law as part of an overall effort to describe and analyse the salient features of modern society. At the risk of oversimplification, Weber employed law as a vantage point from which to study forms of rationality and authority (cf. Weber 1978; Hunt 1978), whereas Durkheim explored it as a means of describing the transformation of society from a form of social organisation based on mechanical solidarity to one based on organic solidarity (cf. Durkheim 1984). As Durkheim's elaboration of the concept of "social fact" reveals, he was concerned with the totality of society, which for him had an objective reality external to, and coercive of, the social actor. While Durkheim studied the structural functional characteristic of society, Weber developed ideal types of social action. This is reflected in both his methodological statements (for example, his concept of *verstehen*) and his analysis of forms of rationality and authority. However, his substantive sociology shows that his main interest was nevertheless in the study of 'the large-scale structures and institutions of society' (Ritzer 1992, p. 156). The reason for emphasising the basic focus of Durkheim and Weber's sociologies (and this point may be extended to sociological theories inspired by Marxism), which have informed and continue to inform socio-legal theorising,[2] is that they employed a concept of the "social" and advanced an understanding of the "totality of society" as a unified, coherent and fundamentally rational entity, which has since been contested. As we explained in the introduction to Chap. 10, the move to risk management strategies was motivated partly by the insight that to grasp the *totality* of a contemporary society is a highly problematic undertaking. Late modern society, to reiterate, generates many (often conflicting) sets of knowledge, values and truths as well as socio-cultural contexts which foster different meanings, expectations and experiences. Already we are confronted with a difficult question: to what extent do Durkheim and Weber's sociologies, not to mention Marx's theory of modernity, provide a point of departure for the sociological analysis of law in contemporary society? Any answer to this question has to consider how successive generations of social scientists and social philosophers have deliberated upon and debated classical sociology. The re-examination of

[2] For a recent application of Weber's social action theory to the study of community, see Cotterrell (2006).

classical sociology, some of which has taken the form of ideological confrontations between various sociological perspectives, has brought into question two central assumptions of sociology regarding social order and social action. At the same time, the postmodern assault upon the foundations of totalising knowledge and truth has forced many sociologists to reconsider the feasibility of constructing universal theories.

In the wake of the postmodern critique of truth and knowledge, the development of classical sociology may be described in terms of the clash of two contrasting understandings of social order and social integration in contemporary society. These two paradigms regroup sociological schools in a way which goes beyond the simple distinction between the conflict and consensus approaches we discussed in the introduction. The first, which we can call the modernist paradigm, departs from the assumption that society is 'a structured, systematically integrated and ordered realm subject to laws that are both real and accessible to human reason' (Bendle 1996, p. 70)—a concept of social order which was central to the social theories of Kant, Hegel, Marx, Durkheim and Parsons. The other standpoint, which we can refer to as postmodernist, regards the social world as 'an ultimately unsystematic and undetermined realm where any appearance of structure, integration or order is imposed and all so-called laws are constructions, frequently reflecting relations of power and domination within society' (Bendle 1996, p. 70). This latter approach was latent in Kafka's conception of modernity, which we discussed in Chap. 6, and has been inspired by Schopenhauer, Nietzsche and Foucault. The spread of globalisation, which has accelerated the rate of change and created conditions characterised by fluidity, diffusion, fragmentation, indeterminacy, plurality and localism, has provided empirical support for the postmodern and poststructuralist critiques of knowledge and totalising theories of society

Classical sociology has also been influenced by the structure/agency and micro/macro debate. Works of Jürgen Habermas, Pierre Bourdieu, Anthony Giddens and Niklas Luhmann exemplify how social theories of Marx, Durkheim, Weber and Parsons were dissected and how their concepts and ideas were re-evaluated and reconstructed from the 1960s onwards (for an overview see Banakar and Travers 2013). Both Habermas (1984) and Luhmann (2004), for example, avoid simplistic descriptions of the relationship between social structures and social action, which by implication would treat one as the cause of the other. Neither Habermas nor Luhmann employs the notion of a conscious agent as a basis for constructing a concept of society; instead, they depart from the notion of communication, which they incidentally conceptualise in different terms, as their point of departure for describing social developments. This does not mean that either the concept of the social actor or the idea of structural relations has become sociologically obsolete. Instead, it reflects the awareness that the Cartesian "I" in 'I think, therefore I am' does not provide an epistemological platform from which one may launch social theories. As Giddens (1987, p. 88) explains, 'The "I" is not immediately available to itself, deriving its identity as it does from its involvement in a system of signification'. This amounts to a 'decentring of the subject', which has had a profound impact on the way classical sociological theories have been revised and reconstructed, and it also exemplifies how social theory has been reassessing its classical assumptions. The disqualification of the Cartesian "I" draws attention to the significance of reflexivity—the ability of all social actors to assess and reassess their social position as both subjects and objects, as well as the awareness that they are the observer and the observed at the same time—in understanding the relationship between actor and structure. According to Archer (2010, p. 5):

> [I]t is the process through which reasons become causes of the courses of action adopted by social subjects. Their subjective internal deliberations – internal conversations – are responsible for mediating the conditional influence of objective structural and cultural factors upon social action.

Although reflexivity has always been a mental property of human sociality, it has nevertheless taken various forms under different historical periods. First, under modernity, reflexivity becomes the link between self and society (or agency and structure), thereby enabling people to react to their social situation in ways which are no longer governed by tradition. Under a contemporary globalised society (late modernity), people are increasingly confronted with new and unfamiliar circumstances in which habitual patterns of behaviour (descriptive norms) do not provide a reliable normative guide for action. Under these circumstances, agency's reflexivity is enhanced, thus forcefully undermining social structures and subverting the normative force of traditional institutions, which during early modernity provided a stable "habitus" and guidelines for action.

In short, sociological efforts to address the postmodern critique of totalising knowledge, but also the attempts to meet changing social conditions caused by the consequences of globalisation, have resulted in a number of social theories which to various degrees have ushered in a new notion of society and its corresponding concept of social action. Some theories, such as those developed by Habermas and Luhmann, retain a totalising and universal ambition (they deal with, and include, all that is social) and continue to promote the project of modernity as a rational construct. In the wake of globalisation, however, the need to break into new theoretical territories which are free from the constraints of universalism has become palpable. Theories of risk society, reflexive modernity and late modernity, which we shall discuss below, represent attempts to revise the classical ideas of society and modernity in view of social developments which characterise the contemporary global society. The limited space herein does not allow for a presentation of the way these two main debates have branched into various research approaches within legal sociology and how they have given rise to studies of law-in-society from feminist, Focauldian, Bourdusian and system theoretical perspectives, to mention just a few (for an overview see Samuels 2013; Dezalay and Garth 1996; Wickham 2013; King 2013).

The second group of socio-legal scholars, who have had an impact on the development of legal sociology, including Ehrlich, Pound and Petrażycki, were, as mentioned in Chap. 3, "jurists" whose primary commitment was to law. In other words, they were concerned with ensuring law's "well-being" and integrity as a tool for realising social justice (we also explained that the notion of a "jurist" was to be understood as an "ideal type"; see Cotterrell 2013). Although jurists' commitment to the law may be expressed in philosophical as well as sociological terms which go beyond the practical conception of the law deployed by practicing lawyers and judges, their work nevertheless remains closely linked to problems associated with the operations of the law and the limits of legislation. Therefore, they are often not interested in developing sociological theories, and alternatively they steer their studies away from theorising. Instead, they employ sociology (or philosophy as the case might be) as a tool to better understand the law and its operations in a social context, in order to improve the science of law and legal education and to develop law as a more effective instrument of social engineering (cf. Nelken 2009, pp. 1–2; Banakar 2003, pp. 189–222). Thus, our second group of scholars influenced the development of legal sociology, not by developing sociological theories of law but by criticising analytical jurisprudence for its conceptual formalism and for neglecting the role played by social forces in creating the legal order and shaping legal behaviour. They also argued that legal research, legal education and juridicial decision-making should adopt the methods and insights of the social sciences, in order to counterbalance this shortcoming. As we pointed out in Chap. 3, Ehrlich and Petrażycki refuted natural law theories which sought a permanent and universally valid basis for law in nature and/or divine reason and contested the claims of legal positivism that a norm became a legal rule only if it was posited by the state (new versions of legal positivism, however, do not treat the state or the sovereign as the primary source of law; see Gardner 2001).

They too worked with a concept of society which belonged to early modernity and to the era of industrialisation, yet it continues to be used frequently in socio-legal research which studies the discrepancies between the claims of law and the reality of legal practices. Ehrlich's concept of "living law," however, has demonstrated great resilience in the wake of globalisation, and it has been employed more recently to throw light on the forms of law and regulation which are generated outside the nation state and at the transnational level (see Hellum et al. 2011, pp. 4–5) as well as studying socio-legal mechanisms in non-Westerns settings (see Urinboyev and Svensson 2013). The continued relevance of Ehrlich can be explained in at least three ways: (1) in line with the argument promoted in Chap. 11, we can maintain that Ehrlich's identification of the norms of social organisation, and how people organise themselves spontaneously as the essence of law and legality, is based on a historical understanding of the relationship between law, morality, community and justice which continues to have empirical relevance for understanding the role of law in contemporary society; (2) Ehrlich's theory of "living law" was a critique of legal positivism (see the discussions on "methodological nationalism" in Chap. 2). As the empirical reality of globalisation undermines the ideology of legal positivism, Ehrlich's 'living law' is deployed to construct an alternative understanding of law's development, for example in relation to the growth of transnational law, and (3) Ehrlich's theory was a product of the pluralistic environment in which he lived, and although he did not intend to create a culturally pluralistic theory of law, as argued in Chap. 7, his "living law" is nevertheless sensitised to socio-cultural diversity, and it can therefore be used to study the social and cultural implications of globalisation in relation to the law.

1.2 The Rise and Fall of the Welfare State

Initial interest in the sociological studies of law, which was reflected in the works of Durkheim, Weber, Ehrlich and Pound and others, somewhat abated during the period between the two World Wars (cf. Black and Mileski 1973, p. 2),[3] but it received new impetus in the decades following World War II as the social landscape underwent dramatic changes. Renato Treves and Glastra van Loon describe the revival of legal sociology in terms of industrialisation and urbanisation:

> The general development of industrialisation and urbanisation, the increase in social mobility, and the great economic and sociological transformations which have taken place since the end of the Second World War... have drawn attention, with increasing emphasis, to a number of pressing needs: The need to study the relations between static and often antiquated legal systems and the continually changing social structure; the need to appreciate how law and the various practitioners of law operate within society; the need to examine public attitudes towards the current legal situation and to calculate and forecast the consequences of possible legislative reforms. (Treves and Glastra van Loon 1968, p. 1)

Thus, legal sociology emerged as a distinct field of research after World War II and consolidated itself in Western European and North American universities from the mid-1960s onwards.[4] As Treves and Glastra van Loon explain, legal sociology developed partly to explain and analyse the interaction between static legal structures and the forces of industrialisation, which were speeding up the rate of social change, and partly to seek ways of reforming society, i.e. carrying out social

---

[3] During this so-called half a century of sociological 'neglect' of the law (Black and Mileski 1973, p. 2), some significant contributions were nonetheless made by social anthropologists such as Malinowski (1926) and American lawyers such as Llewellyn and Hoebel (1941). We could even include the sociology of law of Gurvitch (1932) in the list of significant contributions made during this time.

[4] In Western Europe, as well as in North America, the establishment of professional bodies, such as the *Research Committee on Sociology of Law* (RCSL), the *Law and Society Association* (LSA) and the *Socio-Legal Studies Association* (SLSA), and research institutes, such as the *Centre for the Study of Law and Society*, Berkeley, *Centre for Socio-Legal Studies*, Oxford and the *Institute for the Sociology of Law*, Lund, *Zentrum für Europäische Rechtspolitik* (ZERP), Bremen, played a significant role in consolidating the growth of the subject within academia from the 1970s onward (see Cotterrell 1997; Hawkins 1997). This move would not have been possible without the financial support of various funding agencies such as the Ford Foundation, Russell Sage in the US and Social Scientific Research Council (SSRC) in the UK and Deutsche Forschungsgemeinschaft (DFG) and the Volkswagen Foundation in Germany, which promoted research into welfare and social justice. The creation of the *International Institute for the Sociology of Law* (IISL) in Oñati, which operated as a joint venture between the RCSL and the government of the autonomous Basque region of Spain in 1989, marked the coming of age for legal sociology (Guibentif 2000).

engineering. Legal sociology and other branches of sociology, such as social/public policy research and criminology, were promoted as specific research areas once they attracted the attention of policymakers and subsequently were allocated research funding. Their attractiveness was partly due to their focus on law, policy and regulation, but also because they employed empirical rather than normative methodologies.

Building on the legacy of legal realism (the works of scholars such as Oliver Wendell Holmes and Roscoe Pound), the law and society movement in the US promoted social-scientific studies of law in response to the need to introduce moderate social reform through public policy in areas such as 'the civil rights movement, the War on Poverty, and the rights expansion of the Warren Court' (Trubek 1990, p. 9). The founders of law and society, according to Trubek (1990, p. 9), were mainly liberal-minded "legalists" who were committed to social justice but also 'believed that most of the "flaws" in American society could and would be corrected through legal means'. In Western Europe, legal sociology also developed in response to the need to bring about social reform through law, but this need was linked more directly to the rise of the welfare state. The modern welfare state, which started its growth gradually in the late nineteenth century, expanded rapidly in Western countries through governmental intervention in various walks of life from the 1950s onward. Industrialisation furnished society with stable employment opportunities for large groups, including the working classes, and thus laid the ground for society's long-term socio-economic expansion. The welfare state may be seen as a society-wide policy for addressing disparities in income distribution, political power, opportunities and burdens which were brought to the surface as a result of industrialisation. These policies, however, were motivated and driven by an inclusive ideology that sought to integrate a diverse population, by introducing social policy measures aimed at protecting all citizens (see Young 1999). Viewed from a different standpoint, we could argue that welfare strategies were also devised to *neutralise* the social conflicts generated as a result of industrialisation's economic expansion. These strategies redistributed some of the wealth, rewards, opportunities and burdens throughout society, but they also reformed social conditions in order to engineer a "better" society—"better" not only in terms of being more efficient and productive, but also in terms of social justice. The welfare state has also been described as 'socially controlled welfare capitalism', in which 'state intervention serves to curtail the free workings of the market in order to moderate or cancel out its more adverse effects on labour' (Lane 1989, p. 586). During this period we also notice a proliferation of 'protective legislation and collective agreements' in Western countries, such as the UK, to strengthen the employment rights of workers (Lane 1989, p. 587). Inadvertently, these welfare measures contributed to the emergence of the consumer society.

The notion of 'social policy' is not, as Marshall (1965, p. 7) noted, 'a technical term with an exact meaning', but refers commonly 'to the policy of governments with regard to action having a direct impact on the welfare of the citizens, by providing them with services or income'. Social policies therefore consist of action- and problem-oriented measures, devised by the state (or the government) and expressed and authorised in law.[5] They are generally *rationalistic* instruments incorporating the belief in the likelihood of reforming society through the applications of socio-economic programmes. Moreover, they are top-down governmental interventions in the lives of citizens and their everyday activities and relationships, which are introduced through legislation or administrative ordinance and implemented by various authorities. Therefore, they represent a fusion of rationalism, a belief in social and moral progress, confidence in the normative force of law and a concern for social justice and equality. Hence the question: how should we employ the law to support social policy formations which are designed to govern or to change the behaviour of individuals and groups in an effective manner?

A host of social policy measures were introduced through legislation or legal frameworks, implemented and enforced by lawyers working within traditional institutions of the law as well as by non-lawyers such as social workers and civil servants, thus resulting in increased juridification of the social sphere (Habermas 1984; Teubner 1987). Law was often employed by the welfare state as a regulatory device to bring about not only social integration and social justice, but also conformity and social change. Moreover, it was assumed that the law had universal applications and could be treated as superior to, and independent of, other norm-generating social fields. By contrast, socio-legal research demonstrated that law was mediated through, and its implementation and enforcement were contingent upon, social and legal institutions with their own socio-cultural mechanisms and imperatives (for an early but influential post-war study, see Selznick 1949). Law's dependency on these institutional mechanisms caused divergence between the intentions of the legislature and policymakers, on the one hand, and the outcome of policies that were executed by law, on the other. The insight that law was not an effective vehicle for social engineering is shared commonly by various approaches within legal sociology, and some have argued that it is not only an ineffective exercise (cf. Griffiths 1995),[6] but it also endangers the very autonomy of the legal

---

[5] Earlier experiments with social engineering, which were backed by law but not supported by social scientific knowledge, heaped destructive consequences upon those subjected to it. Eugenics was first legally implemented in the US state of Indiana in 1907 (see Indiana Supreme Court Legal History Lecture Series, 'Three Generations of Imbeciles are Enough: Reflections on 100 Years of Eugenics in Indiana') and adopted later in countries such as Sweden and Nazi Germany. Eugenics was driven by assumptions regarding the ability of the modern man to shape society through science. This assumption was initially underpinned by a racist ideology which aimed at racial purification of the population, but in countries such as Sweden it developed into what could be called 'welfare eugenics'—'a welfare community for "the fittest"' (Spektorowski and Mizrachi 2004). The last time a person was subjected to compulsory serialisation in Sweden was in 1975 (also see Jonsson 1986; Broberg and Tydén 1991).

[6] Griffiths (1995) calls this approach 'legal instrumentalism' and contends that it is based on three erroneous assumptions concerning the relationship between law, society and the social actor: (1) that society consists of atomistic individuals bound together by state organisation only, (2) that it is possible to have perfect communication between the legislator and individual actors and (3) that the state has a normative monopoly so effective that it can surpass all other sources of normativity. Underpinning these three erroneous assumptions is the supposition that 'the social

system (for a debate, see Paterson 2006). As we argued in the introduction, the discrepancy between "law in books" and "law in action" must be analysed in terms of the autonomy of modern law; the "gap" cannot be closed without undermining law's system autonomy.

Many policymakers continue to entertain a conception of society which privileges security, stability and certitude in social relations. For them, social relations possess durability in time and space, which in turn allows for devising public policies aimed at shaping and reshaping individual and collective conduct in such a way as to control and direct social developments. Nevertheless, the spread of globalisation and the advancement of new technologies impact on social organisation and the developments of law and regulation. As the consequences of globalisation gradually permeate various walks of life, traditional forms of regulation give way to risk management strategies (RMSs) and forms of 'soft law' designed for promoting forms of governance in contrast to regulation. This marks the move from the era of the welfare state, when the state sought to stabilise society through social integration, to the era of globalisation, when stability was sought through market integration—Lane (1989) calls it the move from 'welfare capitalism' to 'market capitalism'. It also corresponds with the move from industrialisation, during which time economies were dependent on manufacturing and wage labour, to post-industrialisation, in which economies are globalised and shaped by the production and consumption of services and information.

1.3 From Social Integration to Market Integration

The spread of globalisation has taken place in concert with the growth of neo-liberal ideology and other politically conservative approaches, which since the 1980s have sought the dismantling of the welfare state (Lane 1989; Centeno and Cohen 2010). As national and local economies expanded and turned into global market places, businesses started to demand the liberalisation of trade regulations and the introduction of more flexible labour and employment laws which would potentially reconstruct the relationship between employers and employees in such a way as to allow the former to compete in an increasingly volatile global market (see Chap. 13). Multinational corporations moved outside the regulatory reach of nation states—while national governments became increasingly unwilling to regulate them—thus becoming accountable mainly to their shareholders scattered across the globe. At the same time, the welfare state came under critical scrutiny and was criticised for failing to resolve social problems (from unemployment and housing to criminality), for its economic inefficacy and for creating "welfare dependency" among certain social groups. 'For neo-liberals,' Williams explains (2000, p. 249),

space between the legislator and the individual is conceived of as a *normative vacuum*, empty of norms and structures other than those of the state itself' (Griffiths 1995, pp. 205–206).

'the welfare state is a threat to freedom, is ineffective and inefficient and is economically, politically and socially damaging'. Public policies providing social insurance and employment rights and introducing redistributive taxation were defined as incompatible with the far more efficient operations of the markets. By deregulating the economy and cutting back on public expenditure, one could lower corporation and income taxes, which in turn would stimulate competition, promote investment and increase productivity and economic growth. In a report on globalisation and the welfare state, Scharpf (2000) expresses the underpinning logic of a neo-liberal economy from the standpoint of the European Union and shows how the ideology of neo-liberalism merges symbiotically with the empirical reality of globalisation to construct a realpolitik fit for the global era:

> Nation states are no longer able to use a wide range of policy instruments that had depended on control over their own economic boundaries. These constraints are particularly tight for member states of the European Union and of the European Monetary Union. Countries must now defend or regain the competitiveness of their exposed sectors in highly contested international product markets; they must maintain or restore the attractiveness of national locations for profit-seeking investments; and they must cope with the impact of high capital mobility on their revenue bases. As a consequence, all welfare states are operating under tighter fiscal constraints, and all have to cope with stagnant or declining rates of employment in the exposed sectors of their economies. (Scharpf 2000, p. 18)

Conditions specific to the globalisation era give rise to several overlapping legal developments which challenge the modernist understanding of the law in terms of one single source of normativity and legal authority. Legal pluralism, i.e. the situation whereby more than one legal system or tradition coexists in the same socio-cultural sphere, becomes almost unavoidable in a global society where diverse groups of people meet and live side by side. Globalisation also promotes the proliferation of transnational law, i.e. forms of law, legal regulation and ordering, which exists alongside traditional domestic and international law but also extends beyond the traditional boundaries of nation states (Cotterrell 2012). It also furthers the production of 'soft law', which produces quasi-legal instruments such as codes of conduct not legally binding (Abbot 2012) and provides flexible alternatives to traditional formal legislation. Finally, globalisation brings about laws aimed at managing risks. Focusing here on the symbiosis of neo-liberal ideology and the economic reality of global markets, we find their form of law in measures which are designed to manage risk—in stark contrast to welfare state laws and policies which were aimed at social reform and social integration. Risk management strategies (RMSs) backed by or exercised through law become globalisation's natural regulatory partner, and within those areas where RMSs are employed as the primary forms of governance, socio-legal concept and ideas which were produced during early industrialisation and the welfare state lose their empirical relevance and analytical force. This point begs further clarification. Part of this argument was elaborated in Chap. 10, by arguing that RMSs were not concerned with social reform (which was at the heart of many welfare state policies) but only with managing the unforeseen dysfunctional consequences of social developments.

Nor did RMSs presuppose or require a universal knowledge of society which many social and legal theories of industrialisation tried to provide.

The shift from an industrial to a post-industrial society must also be understood in terms of the technological developments that made this shift possible. It will be argued that neo-liberalism's ideological belief on individualism, i.e. making the individual rather that society responsible for one's social welfare, appears to have found a natural ally in new information technology, which promotes individualism by enhancing reflexive processes in modernity that dislodge social relations from the constraints of time and space (cf. Baker 2011).

2 Ideology, Law and Technology

2.1 From Telegraphy to Digital Communication

Using telecommunication as a point of reference, the move from an industrial to a post-industrial society may also be described as the transition from the era of telegraphy and telephony to the era of computer networks and digital media. Each form of communication engenders, and is engendered by, its own distinct social formations, power constellations, sense of togetherness and specific types of community, administration, political economy, regulatory practices and law.[7] According to Eriksson (2011, p. 14), electric telegraphy was used, for example, in the United States to promote national unity and to 'foster the community as a political entity at a time when disintegration was a heavy threat to the early republic'. Not only did telegraphy unify the otherwise fragmented nation, but it also laid the foundations for 'the networks of conditions and possibilities necessary for big-business organizations' (Eriksson 2011, p. 15). By contrast, one of the primary characteristics of the Internet lies in its ability to transcend national boundaries. Legally, cyberspace is a multi-jurisdictional place, and thus it cannot be associated with any nation state, while culturally it reflects an unlimited number of values and norms. Furthermore, the multi-jurisdictional character of the Internet obfuscates a range of legal activities, from the very idea of crime control to the limits of legal work and legal practice. For instance, with relative ease, a person can commit a criminal act such as online fraud in several jurisdictions but without having a physical presence in any of them and without having to reveal his/her physical location. In addition, lawyers can provide online legal services in jurisdictions where they are not authorised to practice law. Communication networks such as the Internet open up new opportunities for human intervention and

[7] Communication and technology relate to each other in a symbiotic and socially complex manner. For example, the Internet produces its own type of community (so-called "virtual communities") and its own form of communication. However, as argued by Slevin (2000), only under conditions specific to late modernity can the Internet and digital media generally reach their full potential.

innovation, while at the same time they create new challenges, risks and uncertainties. As Slevin (2000, p. 2) points out, they make us aware of how risky and unpredictable the world is. Whereas telegraphy and telephony solidified national political entities, the Internet creates 'virtual communities', i.e. 'a community of people who have never met, who may be hiding behind false identities and who may meet in spaces that don't exist in substance' (Mided 2000, p. 70). The Internet offers new opportunities for interaction between people, the mobilisation of individuals with similar interests and ideals, forms of expression and the dissemination of knowledge. It also generates new types of criminality such as online fraud and takes other types of criminality, such as hate crime, child pornography and terrorism, to another level where they cannot be counteracted by employing traditional forms of regulation. That is why in many of these areas we can observe a clear move away from traditional forms of regulation and toward risk management strategies (anti-terrorism legislation serves as the prime example).

The advancement of information technology transforms various areas of law, legal services and legal enforcement differently. Let me give two instances of such a transformation. First is the shift from crime control, which tries to induce behavioural conformity through physical coercion, rehabilitation, the threat of punishment and actual bodily punishment, through to widespread forms of surveillance. Surveillance techniques employed by public authorities as well as private security companies, ranging from the widespread use of CCTVs to the monitoring of emails, web traffic and instant messaging, have proliferated over the last two decades and transformed policing. The second example is the introduction of different types of online advice systems, auctions for procuring legal services, virtual case rooms and electronic case management systems which deploy new technology, which are not only transforming what we understand by legal services, but are also transforming the legal profession (Susskind 2010, 2013, p. 21). Another striking way in which information and computing technology has reorganised and at the same time globalised legal work is found in outsourcing and/or offshoring legal services to places such as India and the Philippines.

Earlier forms of communication technology, such as telegraphy and telephony, objectified the positions and relationships of the communicating parties, thus 'solidifying' communities and constituting institutions (Eriksson 2011). By contrast, digital technology appears to fuel individualism and as we shall argue below enhance reflexivity, thus allowing people to experiment with community and identity, and unwittingly as it might be, subverting attempts to totalise the world through the World Wide Web. New technologies do not necessarily dissolve communities and institutions, but they do create new forms thereof which are based on temporary networks of people and interests. These transitory late modern networks distinguish themselves from the traditional forms of community by not requiring mutual interpersonal trust or long-term stable interaction between the members of the network. As a result they do not generate a web of ethical responsibility, which was the foundation of traditional community, as discussed in Chap. 11 (also see Banakar and Lort Phillips 2014).

2.2 Reducing the Social World to a Binary Baseline

Digitalisation is associated with a large number of developments and subsequently is described in different terms, ranging from three-dimensional visualisations and the development of websites to digital communications and smartphones, all of which entail complex sets of social and cultural implications. For our purposes here, *digital* refers to all forms of technology, electronically-mediated communication systems and networks which are based on binary logic. Defining digital in binary terms, Horst and Miller (2012) argue, enables us to compare it with another historical development associated with the industrial era:

> If the digital is defined as our ability to reduce so much of the world to the communality of a binary, a sort of baseline 2, then we can also reflect upon humanity's ability to previously reduce much of the world to baseline 10, the decimal foundation of the systems of modern money... Just like the digital, money represented a new phase in human abstraction, where, for the first time, practically everything could be reduced to the same common element. This reduction of quality to quantity was in turn the foundation for an explosion of differentiated things, especially the huge expansion of commoditization linked to industrialization. In both cases the more we reduce to the same, the more we can thereby create difference. (Horst and Miller 2012, p. 5)

Money abstracts human relations, thereby allowing exchanges to be conducted at distance and without need for face-to-face interaction in time and place. It has existed throughout the ages, but it was first under industrialisation and with the rise of the world markets that it became the measure of all goods and services; it was even used to define human relations and gradually gained a level of abstraction that defied common logic. As Hart (2007, p. 5) explains, the form of money which came to dominate modernity was not the coins and the banknotes in circulation and which were issued by the government, but the money which was (and is) created at the 'stroke of a pen' by the banks whenever they approved a loan. This type of money is closely linked to credit and debt, for banks lend money which they do not have in the first place. It was incidentally the abuse of this power to "create" money that caused the near collapse of the global financial system in 2007–2008 (this point will be discussed in more detail in the final chapter). It is however noteworthy that the global financial crisis could not have happened without the digital network of computers which cut across national borders and continents. Whereas money is a medium of exchange for goods and services, i.e. the economic system's imperative, digital technology is a medium of communication which scythes through all spheres of action and systems. The combination of these two modes of exchange provides a potent amalgamation whereby money, which abstracts social relations to baseline 10, is further abstracted to baseline 2 by the digital technology that mediates it across national economies.

Additionally, digitalisation enhances the potential of money to abstract human relations and thereby exacerbates commodification's alienating effects. At the same time, it opens up new emancipatory possibilities. Digital technology facilitates communication at very little cost, allows the sharing of software and offers its users a degree of freedom from social control. It also stimulates agency's reflexivity (for a definition of reflexivity see footnote 1) and gives rise to such a proliferation of forms of culture that, as Horst and Miller point out (2012, p. 6), 'we cannot manage and engage with it', thus rendering us 'superficial, shallow or alienated'.

By reducing social communications to a binary baseline, digital technology creates a new social milieu which structures and recreates human interaction and relations in ways that are different from face-to-face interaction. In this sense digital technology represents a specific form of social organisation which requires its own corresponding form of regulation. The kernel of this idea was developed by Lawrence Lessig in his influential work entitled *Code: And Other Laws of Cyberspace*, published in 1999. In this book, Lessig argued that the basic code, or the architecture, of the Internet employs a set of "protocols" which allow the exchange of data within networks of computers, but without the networks detecting the content of the data which is communicated or identifying the person who transmitted it in "actual life." As a result, cyberspace provides a social environment which is new in several ways, in that it expands and extends the communicative reach of its users and affords them 'relative anonymity' (Lessig 2006, p. 19). Furthermore, the code makes it difficult to regulate the content of what is exchanged or how any particular data is deployed, while at the same time, the combination of software and hardware that creates cyberspace exerts a regularising effect on the behaviour of users. The code, maintains Lessig, defines the terms according to which interaction in cyberspace takes place; it is therefore the technological law of cyberspace. This also means that the Internet and other forms of digital communication require a new understanding of regulation, which for him consists of the complex interplay between four normative spheres of social action, or modes of regulation: laws, markets, norms and architecture/code.

2.3 *Social Media and Reflexivity*

The "virtual reality" generated by digital technology however, is dependent on "actual life" processes in the sense that it cannot exist without people in actual time and space who employ the technology and thus give rise to its virtual manifestations. At the same time, it is a collective construct that exists parallel to the "actual life" experiences of its creators, thus interacting with the physical reality of everyday life and influencing the ways in which people act and organise themselves in unexpected ways. The impact of computer-generated reality on "actual life" also requires a reconsideration of our notions of social control and regulation. This point was ably demonstrated by the unfolding of the London riots in 2011. On 6 August 2011, a group of people marched to the police station in Tottenham demanding answers over the fatal shooting of a local black man, 29-year-old Mark Duggan, by the police 2 days earlier. The protest, which had been initially peaceful, spiralled out of control when the police restrained a 16-year-old girl who had allegedly thrown a missile at them. This triggered public disturbances in Tottenham, which in turn generated waves of violent unrest that spread first across many parts of London and then to other cities such as Birmingham, Bristol and Manchester. The violence, looting and arson which followed were reminiscent of the Brixton and Toxteth riots of 1981, which were also triggered by confrontations between the police and ethnic minorities. However, the 2011 riots distinguished themselves from the previous disturbances on several points—social media 'speeded up the exchange of information' (Morrell et al. 2011, p. 3) and allowed the rioters to organise themselves once they were out on the street (Baker 2011) and, according to the tabloid press, to prolong the looting (*Sun*, 8 August 2011). Moreover, there was a break in the unfolding of the events whereby a peaceful political protest was transformed into widespread looting. Admittedly, the previous London riots also had been used as a catalyst for looting, but whereas the Brixton and Toxteth riots of 1981 retained their political character throughout the unrest, the 2011 riots quickly lost any form of political dimension.

Admittedly, the 2011 London riots were not *caused* by Blackberry handsets, but once it was started in real time and space, trouble spread rapidly across the country with the help of social media and smartphones and turned into what appeared at least on the surface as apolitical unrest. Was there a connection between the depoliticisation of the riots and the mobile digital technologies (smartphones, broadband Internet access and digital cameras) through which news of the riots was disseminated and many rioters communicated? As Baker (2011, p. 2) points out, 'new mobile technologies... enable instant modes of mediated exchange', which broadens and transforms 'the spatial and the temporal configuration of contemporary public life'. Baker (2011, p. 2) adds that the 'ubiquitous online communication' characteristic of new social media can, under certain circumstances, give rise to what she calls the '"mediated crowd" mobilised through instant and mobile social networking in the virtual sphere'. This "mediated crowd" concept captures a form of social action and organisation which is not limited to physical congregation in physical space; rather, it takes place in the virtual and geographic arena as a *temporary* association which does not require the type of commitment to a political cause which initiated the riots on 6 August 2011. The speed at which the "mediated crowd" spreads in virtual and actual spaces does not allow targeted political recruitment, though this does not mean that actual political networks in physical space cannot play an important role in organising protests and social movements. For example, the 'Occupy' movement and the Arab Spring protests were organised by politically-motivated actors, who in the physical space made the optimal use of social media. The point is that the "mediated crowd" is a transient construction in time and space which does not require of its participants any form of political commitment. As we shall argue in the next chapter, it represents a late modern network, which unlike traditional forms of community does not generate a web of ethical commitment. This may in turn be explained, to borrow from Baker again, by social media's ability to enhance agency's reflexivity:

> The "mediated crowed" is formed through reflexive communication in the virtual public space... While reflexivity is a pervasive feature of modern social life... developments in media technologies have intensified reflexive processes in modernity through the expansion of "disembedding mechanisms" which... increasingly dislocate social relations from the

confines of time and space. Media communication technologies have accentuated this process of reflexivity. (Baker 2011, pp. 3–4)

How could a person who has been dislodged from the constraints of time and space be subjected to behavioural regulation? The mass media and authorities' reactions to the rioters suggested they were not thinking in terms of traditional forms of regulation, which guide action by implanting values and norms in social structures and institutional settings. Instead, they were thinking in terms of the surveillance of individuals' mobile phones.

2.4 The Neo-Liberal Ideology

Neo-liberalism individualises social issues, thus passing on the responsibility for social problems to individual citizens or to local communities which often have little control over developments. [It is worth noting that a similar individualisation was also described in Chap. 4 in respect to the way criminal law operates by decontextualizing social conduct (see Norrie 2005)]. Therefore, instead of discussing the social causes of the riots, many journalists and politicians appeared to blame social media and mobile Internet for provoking the riots, suggesting that they could be controlled by the surveillance of mobile phones and social media (for a discussion, see Fuchs 2012). The Prime Minister, David Cameron, expressed this point by stating:

> And when people are using social media for violence we need to stop them. So we are working with the police, the intelligence services and industry to look at whether it could be right to stop people communicating via the websites and services when we know they are plotting violence, disorder and criminality. (*Guardian* 2011)

Cameron does not consider the social causes of the riots, but thinks automatically in risk management terms as if it was the most natural reaction to the riots. In doing so, he disregards the specific social conditions, such as excessive degrees of income inequality and lack of opportunities, which define deprived urban areas in contemporary Britain and which played a part in the riots. Instead, he blames the technology behind social media for the unrest and suggests 'banning suspected rioters from social media' (*Guardian* 2011), which in effect provides an individualised solution to a collective societal problem. However, the riots did not have technological causes and were not provoked by social media or smartphones. As Christian Fuchs argues (2012, p. 387), the interaction between social media and technology, on the one hand, and society, on the other, is multidimensional and complex, and their interplay cannot be reduced to a simple one-dimensional cause-and-effect relationship. What we can state with some degree of certainty, however, is that the riots could not have spread as they did via previous modes of communication, e.g. by telegraph or the landline telephone in this manner. Also, the 'break' in the unfolding of the riots was related to how they were reconstructed in a virtual environment and transferred into a different protest, which was much broader in scope but also fragmented in respect to its socio-cultural meanings and objectives.

In short, the London riots were depoliticised by at least two factors. First, by the way they were spread via social media and subsequently diversified in respect to their aims and meaning. As noted above it remains to be seen if the structure of the technology might have had an impact on the way the riots spread. However, there is evidence that social media enhances agency's reflexivity. Second, by the unwillingness of the media and politicians to debate social issues behind what appeared as random acts of criminality, or to grasp the new dynamics of protest movements, parts of which take shape in cyberspace. Both these factors, which are not exclusive, are indicative of the move from industrialisation and the welfare state to late modernity.

3 Law and Regulation in a Global Society

3.1 New Public Spaces and Forms of Community

The consolidation of legal sociology as an academic field of research after World War II was described above in terms of the development of industrialisation, increased mobility and urbanisation and the rise of the welfare state, all of which changed the social landscape of many countries in the West. The spread of globalisation has brought about a transformation of the state, the dismantling of welfare systems, the rise of transnational forces and the increased socio-cultural diversification of contemporary societies. At the same time, it has made us aware of the necessity to consider the law beyond Europe in its own right (Menski 2007). The law beyond Europe, however, can no longer be limited to international relations or kept at arm's length within international human rights, refugee law or relationships between states. In contemporary society, the more important aspects of this interface are realised *internally* at the level of municipal state law. To borrow from Twining (2009, p. 43), a gradual 'diffusion of law' is taking place through the interface 'especially of religious and customary practices' of migrant communities with municipal state law in northern countries. Our analysis can no longer be limited to, say, the interaction between Islamic law and English or German law at the level of international relations or within traditional legal areas such as conflict between laws (for a study of the application of religious arbitration by British Pakistani Muslim women, see Bano 2007; for a general discussion on recent debates on the role of Sharia in the UK, see Chap. 7). These global developments bring about a gradual erosion of the boundaries between legal systems by hybridising legal cultures.

Sociologists have been debating these same developments since the 1990s in terms of reflexive modernity (Giddens 1999, 1994), the risk society (Beck 1992) and late modernity (Bauman 2000). Modernity replaced the claims of tradition with reason and conferred a "solid" appearance upon social institutions by transforming their authority from one based on traditional relationships to one based on legal-bureaucracy, which facilitated the centralisation of institutional power (Lee 2005, p. 63). According to Giddens (1999, p. 39):

> [W]hen claims of reason replaced those of tradition, they appeared to offer a sense of certitude greater than that provided by the pre-existing dogma, which traditional authority could not provide. But this idea only appears persuasive so long as we do not see that the reflexivity of modernity actually subverts reason, at any rate where reason is understood as the gaining of certain knowledge.

The combined power of modern institutions made the expansion of modernity unavoidable, yet this power, which reached its peak under industrialisation, could not totally dominate social developments. As Lee points out, 'charisma and reflexivity' were the solvents that could 'dissolve the existing institutional arrangements' (Lee 2005, p. 63). The social consequences of globalisation are enhanced through the widespread use of digital technology which, as we argued above, increases agency's reflexivity, thereby accelerating the rate change and discontinuity in human affairs. This in turn causes the "liquefaction" of the ostensibly "solid" structures and relations of early modernity. For Bauman, contemporary society is best described in terms of "liquid modernity," in other words:

> [A] society in which the conditions under which its members act change faster than it takes the ways of acting to consolidate into habits and routines. Liquidity of life and that of society feed and reinvigorate each other. Liquid life, just like liquid modern society, cannot keep its shape, or stay on course for long. (Bauman 2005, p. 1)

Under these conditions, the individual social actor becomes increasingly independent of social structures which previously exerted a regulating effect on its behaviour, while systems such as polity and law become less capable of responding to socio-cultural complexity and moral diversity in their environment through further functional differentiation (Beck 1992, p. 2).[8] Social forces, which could be harnessed to reshape society and mould social behavioural patterns under the first stage of modernity, have now either lost their efficacy or become redundant. The spread of various forms of cybercrime, ranging from child pornography to money laundering, identity theft, terrorism and illegal file-sharing, exemplifies the point made herein. As Grabosky and Smith suggested, a large part of growing 'computer-related illegality lies beyond the capacity of contemporary law enforcement and agencies' (2000, p. 29). This is not only because cyberspace does not recognise social, cultural or national boundaries, because it is a multi-jurisdictional space or because internet service providers (ISPs) 'have a rather fluid status' (Wall 2000, p. 173), but also because, as we argued above, the digital environment shapes social interaction and behaviour in ways which are different from everyday face-to-

[8] A similar concern is raised by Gunther Teubner, who describes contemporary society as 'a plurality of mutually exclusive perspectives which are constituted by binary distinctions. They are not compatible with one another and can be overcome only by rejection of values which in their turn lead to nothing but to different binary distinctions' (Teubner 2009, p. 5).

face interactions. This point gains significance as communication, trade, commerce, entertainment and education become increasingly more dependent on the Internet. The digital network which creates the Internet is different in noteworthy ways from the early institutions of modernity, which were organised along other communication systems (such as telephony), did not have the spontaneous reach of digital technology and communicated through a decimal rather than a binary baseline.

At the level of social interaction, we find the increased significance of agency vis-à-vis structures (Beck 1992). Following Denscombe (2001, p. 160), this 'does not imply that "structural" factors cease to exert any influence at all. But it does mean that there is a tendency for them to exert less influence than in the past and for greater significance to attach to individual choices in terms of the creation of self-identities'. The increased significance of agency in relation to structures could have long-term implications for our understanding of regulation, as these modern structural relationships, which could be manipulated through legal and economic policy measures to regulate patterns of behaviour at the level of the social actor, exert less influence over individual behaviour. An example of this notion can be found in the widespread infringement of copyrights through file-sharing (Strahilevitz 2003a, b). The traditional methods of regulating social behaviour have proved inadequate in compelling loosely-knit networks of people in cyberspace to respect the copyrights of record- and movie-producing companies. The perplexing aspect of this development does not lie in why millions of people choose to download files containing sound recordings illegally instead of paying for them, but why they allow their fellow anonymous users to upload for free, for, as Strahilevitz (2003a, p. 3) points out, 'downloading content from a peer-to-peer network depends entirely on another user's willingness to upload such content'. Strahilevitz explains the puzzle in the following way:

> File-swappers share their content with anonymous strangers mainly because charismatic technologies make the community of file-swappers appear to its users far more cooperative than it really is. In so doing, the networks tap into deeply held social norms of reciprocity that people develop offline and bring with them to cyberspace. (Strahilevitz 2003b, p. 509)

Whatever the social-psychological mechanisms of the file-sharing phenomenon, the fact remains that the loosely-knit community behind the practice cannot be regulated using traditional forms of legal regulation.

At the level of social organisation, we observe the coming into being of public spaces which exist beyond the reach of formal (official) and informal (unofficial) regulatory mechanisms of early modernity. These formal mechanisms—nationally generated policy and legal measures, backed by the threat of sanctions against non-compliance and enforced by the nation state—prove to be ineffective when applied to transnational relations and the mobile elite (cf. Banakar 2010).[9] Informal

[9] One example of the infectivity of such measures can be found in the attempt by the UK government to regulate the bonuses of investment bankers in the City of London. To avoid the collapse of the UK's banking sector, the government had to intervene and bail out many banks. This cost the country the staggering amount of £850 billion—equivalent to £40,000 for every

(unofficial) mechanisms such as social norms, moral rules and cultural values regarding fair play, social responsibility and trust also prove ineffective, because late modern societies no longer aspire to one set of apparently solid moral and cultural values. These spaces provide a fertile ground for the development of neo-modern communities—new forms of community which appear to require some degree of objectivity but 'are not necessarily fixed or limited and may be fluid and transient' (Cotterrell 2006, p. 65).[10]

The advancement of digital technology has created a burgeoning virtual environment where new forms of social interaction and relations can grow. The introduction of 'Web 2.0' revealed the potential of the World Wide Web by enabling users to generate their own content and to interact through social media, thereby changing the way people interact online. Today, millions of people develop their own content on the Internet and exchange it online 'via blogging, tagging, wikis, and media sharing, and [. . .] network socially in novel ways via the proliferation social networks sites, such as Facebook, YouTube and Twitter' (Baker 2011, p. 1). This environment creates a virtual reality of its own, while at the same time it impacts upon how people act in face-to-face situations and organise themselves in physical space in an unprecedented fashion. The London riots of 2011 exemplified some of the consequences of digital technology's advancement in the way the riots took shape. These are all phenomena which did not exist at the turn of the previous century and during the early stages of industrialisation and which require a new conception of regulation. Perhaps concepts such as "social control", "regulation" and "governance" have too much classical sociological baggage belonging to the industrial and welfare state eras to allow innovative reflection on the challenges posed by the advent of the digital age. Regulation is a concept which suggests 'being in control', which in turn requires long-term solid relations and institutions. As our previous discussions on the rise of risk management strategies indicated, there is a growing realisation even among policymakers that either we cannot control social developments or the knowledge we require for bringing about effective regulation is too complex and fragmented to provide a basis for new regulatory regimes. These ideas will be developed further by reference to recent developments, such as the financial crisis, in the next chapter.

---

family in the country. However, many of these failed state-backed banks continued to use taxpayers' money to pay out substantial bonuses to their elite investment bankers. To curb the bonus culture of the City, the Labour government proposed a super-tax on bonuses, causing a very strong reaction from the City. Boris Johnson, the Mayor of London, claimed that up to 9,000 bankers would leave London to escape paying the taxes (*Evening Standard*, 1 January 2010). The chief executive of one of the state-backed banks warned a few months later that a large number of investment bankers were quitting the UK, causing a 'rapid exodus' as a result of the 'bonus fiasco' (*Evening Standard*, 4 March 2010).

[10] The circle of investment bankers who brought about the near collapse of the global financial system is a case in point. As we shall discuss in the next chapter, this group of young traders was able to generate its own rules independently of the structural (financial) constraints of early modern society.

References

Abbot, C. (2012). Bridging the gap – Non-state actors and the challenges of regulating new technology. *Journal of Law and Society, 39*(3), 329–358.
Archer, M. (2010). Reflexivity. *Sociopedia.isa.*
Baker, S. A. (2011). The mediated crowd: New social media and new forms of rioting. *Sociological Research Online, 16*(4), 1–5.
Banakar, R. (2003). *Merging law and sociology: Against the dichotomies in socio-legal research.* Berlin: Galda + Wilch.
Banakar, R. (2010). Studying the rights discourse: A tentative theoretical framework. In K. Bettina (Ed.), *Nordisk retssociologi (The Nordic sociology of law)* (pp. 109–129). Copenhagen: DJØF Forlag.
Banakar, R., & Lort Phillips, A. (2014). Law and community in the 2011 London riots. In R. Nobles & D. Schiff (Eds.), *Law, society and community: Socio-legal essays in honour of Roger Cotterrell.* Farnham: Ashgate.
Banakar, R., & Travers, M. (Eds.). (2013). *Law and social theory.* Oxford: Hart.
Bano, S. (2007). Muslim family justice and human rights: The experience of British Muslim Women. *Journal of Comparative Law, 1*(4), 1–29.
Bauman, Z. (2000). *Liquid modernity.* Cambridge: Polity.
Bauman, Z. (2005). *Liquid life.* Cambridge: Polity.
Beck, U. (1992). *Risk society: Towards a new modernity.* London: Sage.
Beck, U., et al. (1994). *Reflexive modernisation: Politics, traditions and aesthetics in the modern social order.* Cambridge: Polity.
Bendle, M. F. (1996). Logics of integration and disintegration in contemporary social theory. *Journal of Sociology, 32*(3), 70–84.
Black, D. (1972). The boundaries of legal sociology. *Yale Law Journal, 81*, 1086–1100.
Black, D., & Mileski, M. (1973). *The social organisation of law.* New York: Seminar Press.
Broberg, G., & Tydén, M. (1991). *Oonskade i folkhemmet: Rashygien och sterilisering i Sverige.* Stockholm: Gidlunds.
Centeno, M. A., & Cohen, J. N. (2010). *Global capitalism: A sociological perspective.* Cambridge: Polity.
Cotterrell, R. (1997). Establishing sociology of law in Sweden. *Socio-Legal Studies Newsletter* 23 (Autumn Issue).
Cotterrell, R. (2006). *Law, culture and society: Legal ideas in the mirror of social theory.* Aldershot: Ashgate.
Cotterrell, R. (2012). What is transnational law. *Law and Social Inquiry, 37*(2), 500–524.
Cotterrell, R. (2013). The role of the jurist: Reflections around Radbruch. *Ratio Juris, 26*(4), 519–522.
Denscombe, M. (2001). Uncertain identities and health-risking behaviour: The case of young people and smoking in late modernity. *British Journal of Sociology, 52*(1), 157–177.
Dezalay, Y., & Garth, B. G. (1996). *Dealing in virtue.* Chicago: University of Chicago.
Durkheim, É. (1984). *The division of labor in society.* New York: The Free Press.
Eriksson, K. (2011). *Communication in modern social ordering.* New York: Bloomsbury.
Fuchs, C. (2012). Social media, riots, and revolutions. *Capital and Class, 36*(3), 383–391.
Gardner, J. (2001). Legal positivism: 5 ½ myths. *American Journal of Jurisprudence, 46*(1), 199–227.
Gessner, V., & Nelken, D. (Eds.). (2007). *European ways of law: Towards a European sociology of law.* Oxford: Hart.
Giddens, A. (1987). *Social theory and modern sociology.* Cambridge: Polity.
Giddens, A. (1994). *Reflexive modernization.* Cambridge: Polity.
Giddens, A. (1999). *The consequences of modernity.* Cambridge: Polity.
Grabosky, P., & Smith, R. (2000). Telecommunication fraud in the digital age. In D. Wall (Ed.), *Crime and the Internet* (pp. 18–28). London: Routledge.

Griffiths, J. (1995). Legal pluralism and the theory of legislation: With special reference to the regulation of Euthanasia. In H. Petersen & H. Zahle (Eds.), *Legal polycentricity: Consequences of pluralism in law* (pp. 201–234). Dartmouth: Aldershot.

Guardian. (2011). David Cameron considers banning suspected rioters from social media. www.guardian.co.uk. 11 August.

Guibentif, P. (Ed.). (2000). *Oñati IISL-IISJ. 1989–2000: Introduction to the institute and report about its activities*. Oñati: IISL.

Gurvitch, G. (1932). *L'idée du droit social: Notion et système du droit social*. Paris: Librairie de Recueil Sirey.

Habermas, J. (1984). *The theory of communicative action, volume 1: Reason and the rationalization of society*. Boston, MA: Beacon.

Hart, K. (2007). Money is always personal and impersonal. *Anthropology Today, 23*(5), 12–16.

Hawkins, K. (1997). *Donald Harris and the early years of the Oxford Centre* (The human face of law: Essays in honour of Donald Harris, pp. 1–18). Oxford: Clarendon.

Hellum, A., et al. (Eds.). (2011). *From transnational relations to transnational laws*. Farnham: Ashgate.

Horst, H., & Miller, D. (Eds.). (2012). *Digital anthropology*. Oxford: Berg.

Hunt, A. (1978). *The sociological movement in law*. London: Macmillan.

Jonsson, K. (1986). En nybadad renrasig svensk på… *I framtidens tjänst: Ur folkhemmets idé historia*. Stockholm: Gidlunds.

King, M. (2013). The radical sociology of Niklas Luhmann. In R. Banakar & M. Travers (Eds.), *Law and social theory* (pp. 59–74). Oxford: Hart.

Lane, C. (1989). From "welfare Capitalism" to "Market Capitalism": A comparative review of trends towards employment flexibility in the labour markets. *Sociology, 23*(4), 583–610.

Lee, R. L. M. (2005). Bauman, liquid modernity and dilemmas of development. *Thesis Eleven, 83*, 61–77.

Lessig, L. (1999). *Code: And other law of cyberspace*. New York: Basic.

Lessig, L. (2006). *Code: Version 2.0*. New York: Basic.

Llewellyn, K., & Hoebel, E. A. (1941). *The Cheyenne way: Conflict and case law in primitive jurisprudence*. Norman, OK: University of Oklahoma Press.

Luhmann, N. (2004). Law as a social system (trans: Ziegert KA). Oxford: Oxford University Press.

Malinowski, B. (1926). *Crime and custom in savage society*. London: Kegan Paul.

Marshall, T. H. (1965). *Social policy*. London: Hutchinson.

Menski, W. (2007). Beyond Europe. In E. Örücü & D. Nelken (Eds.), *Comparative law: A handbook* (pp. 189–216). Oxford: Hart.

Mided, J. (2000). The Internet and the public sphere: What kind of space is cyberspace? In L. Langel (Ed.), *Culture and technology in the new Europe* (pp. 63–75). Stamford, CT: Ablex.

Morrell, G. et al. (2011). *National riots in England: Understanding the involvement of young people*. London: NatCen. Ecopy at https://www.gov.uk/.

Nelken, D. (2009). *Beyond law in context*. Aldershot: Ashgate.

Norrie, A. (2005). *Law and the beautiful soul*. London: GlassHouse.

Paterson, J. (2006). Reflecting on reflexive law. In M. King & C. Tornhill (Eds.), *Luhmann on law and politics* (pp. 13–35). Oxford: Hart.

Ritzer, G. (1992). *Sociological theory* (3rd ed.). New York: McGraw-Hill.

Samuels, H. (2013). Feminist legal theory. In R. Banakar & M. Travers (Eds.), *Law and social theory* (pp. 129–146). Oxford: Hart.

Scharpf, F. W. (2000). *Globalization and the welfare state: Constraints, challenges and vulnerabilities*. Köln: Max-Planck-Institut für Gesellschaftsforschung. www.issa.int/pdf/helsinki2000/topic0/2scharpf.PDF.

Selznick, P. (1949). *TVA and the Grass Roots*. Berkley: University of California.

Shamir, R. (1996). Suspended in space: Bedouin under the law of Israel. *Law and Society, 30*, 231–257.

Slevin, J. (2000). *The Internet and society*. Cambridge: Polity.

Spektorowski, A., & Mizrachi, E. (2004). Eugenics and welfare state in Sweden. *Journal of Contemporary History, 39*(3), 333–352.

Strahilevitz, L. J. (2003a). Social norms from close-Knit groups to loose-Knit groups. *University of Chicago Law Review, 70*, 359–360.

Strahilevitz, L. J. (2003b). Charismatic code, social norms, and the emergence of cooperation on the file-swapping networks. *Virginia Law Review, 89*, 505–595.

Sun. (2011, August 8). *Roll up and loot: Rioting thugs use Twitter to boost their numbers in thieving store raid.* http://www.thesun.co.uk/sol/homepage/news/3738786/Tottenham-riot-thugs-use-twitter.html. Accessed 20 Mar 2014.

Susskind, R. (2010). *The end of Lawyers? Rethinking the nature of legal services*. Oxford: Oxford University Press.

Susskind, R. (2013). *Tomorrow's lawyers: An introduction to your future*. Oxford: Oxford University Press.

Teubner, G. (Ed.). (1987). *Juridification of social spheres*. Berlin: de Gruyter.

Teubner, G. (2009). Self-subversive Justice: Contingency or transcendence formula of law. *Modern Law Review, 72*(1), 1–23.

Thompson, J. B. (1995). *The media and modernity: A social theory of media*. Cambridge: Polity.

Treves, R., & Glastra van Loon, J. F. (Eds.). (1968). *Norms and actions: National reports on sociology of law*. The Hague: Martinus Nijhoff.

Trubek, D. M. (1990). Back to future: The short, happy life of law and society movement. *Florida State University Law Review, 18*(1), 4–54.

Twining, W. (2000). *Globalisation and legal theory*. London: Butterworths.

Twining, W. (2009). The implications of 'Globalisation' for law as a discipline. In A. Hapline & V. Roeben (Eds.), *Theorising the global legal order* (pp. 39–59). Oxford: Hart.

Urinboyev, R., & Svensson, M. (2013). Living law, legal pluralism, and corruption in post-Soviet Uzbekistan. *Journal of Legal Pluralism and Unofficial Law, 46*(3), 372–390.

Wall, D. (2000). Maintaining order and law on the Internet. In D. Wall (Ed.), *Crime and the Internet* (pp. 167–183). London: Routledge.

Weber, M. (1978). In G. Roth & C. Wittich (Eds.), *Economy and society: An outline of interpretive sociology*. Berkeley: University of California Press.

Wickham, G. (2013). Foucault and the law. In R. Banakar & M. Travers (Eds.), *Law and social theory* (pp. 217–232). Oxford: Hart.

Williams, C. (2000). Reinventing the welfare state: Neo-liberalism and beyond. In A. McMahon et al. (Eds.), *Understanding the Australian welfare state* (pp. 248–262). Croydon, VIC: Tertiary.

Young, J. (1999). *The exclusive society: Social exclusion, crime and difference in late modernity*. London: Sage.

Chapter 13
Law and Regulation in Late Modernity

Abstract This chapter examines how the law fares under socio-cultural conditions specific to late modern societies. Section 1 uses the financial global crisis of 2007–2008 as a backdrop against which to formulate a number of concerns regarding the limits of legal regulation in late modernity. Section 2 explores the formation and operations of the late modern state, asking if power is separated from politics and has moved to the level of global organisations. Section 3 asks what kind of law is emerging de facto in response to the fluidity of late modernity, and how legal imagination envisages the future of law.

Modernity, Marx and Engels (1848, p. 224) observed about a century and half ago, is the experience of time and space as '[a]ll fixed, fast-frozen relationships, with their train of venerable ideas and opinions, are swept away, all new-formed ones become obsolete before they can ossify. All that is solid melts into air...'. They meant that capitalism's insatiable need to create and dominate new markets compelled it to incessantly renew itself, thus endlessly revolutionising the social and economic conditions. This in turn liquefied society by not allowing relationships, forms of organisation or social institutions to remain solid or permanent over time. In this sense, the notion of 'liquefaction' is hardly new and was already envisaged by Marx and Engels as a form of life and employed to describe the stage when 'all that is solid melts into air'. Marx and Engels could not, however, have imagined how the advent of digital technology would take the liquefying properties of modernity to new heights. Nevertheless, what we experience as a novel or unprecedented shift is part of the unfolding of modernity and its unrelenting drive to change and renew itself.

In this final chapter of the book, we explore further the stage when the pace of social change has accelerated by globalisation, thus breaking down all social, cultural and geographical boundaries, and causing 'a maelstrom of perpetual disintegration and renewal, of struggle and contradiction, of ambiguity and anguish' (Berman 1991, p. 15). Under these conditions, both the individual and the collective face 'disembeddedness', i.e. they experience how 'culture and norms

This chapter is based on 'Law and Regulation in Late Modernity' in Banakar R, Travers M (eds) (2013) *Law and Social Theory*. Oxford: Hart, 305–324.

R. Banakar, *Normativity in Legal Sociology*, DOI 10.1007/978-3-319-09650-6_13

become loosened from their moorings in time and place: normative borders blur, shift, overlap, detach' (Young 2009, p. 3). Durkheim did, admittedly, conceptualise the breakdown of social norms, or *anomie* as he called it, and widespread individualism as a consequence of industrialisation, but for him *anomie* was a by-product rather than *the* product of modernity. It marked a pathological state brought about by exceptional societal developments, resulting in periods of social disruption and severe crisis. In contrast, the experience of disembeddedness we are concerned with in late modernity, constitutes a normal rather than an exceptional social condition. It is in this context that we shall explore how law, which crystallises values and norms by embedding them in institutional settings, thus ensuring durability and certitude in social relationships, fares in late modernity's increased liquefaction of social structures.

1 Regulating Global Corporations?

On the day that the UK government was warned by charities and campaigners against cutting welfare benefits to the poorest—an austerity measure aimed at reducing the country's deficit (*Independent* 3 December 2012)—a parliamentary report revealed that certain multinational corporations, which generated huge amounts of income by operating in the UK, had used 'secretive jurisdictions, royalties and complex company structures' (*Guardian* 3 December 2012) to avoid paying UK taxes (also see *HM Revenue and Customs* 2013). They had been enjoying the right to operate businesses in the country, unfettered by any sense of responsibility such as declaring their true taxable income to the UK authorities.[1] They were, however, not breaking any UK laws and had been simply making use of existing domestic rules and international agreements to move their profits to low-tax jurisdictions. Although these companies had not committed any illegal act, the revelation nonetheless provoked a barrage of public criticism followed by demands for new legislation aimed at curbing the tax avoidance practices of multinational corporations. Some argued that legislative intervention was the only way to ensure that these corporations reported their gross profits as well as their taxable income. Others argued that in order to introduce and enforce a regulatory regime capable of clamping down on this type of tax avoidance, one first needed to ensure international cooperation between various countries. There was therefore no point in the government of the UK legislating against global companies' tax avoidance strategies on its own. Vince Cable, the Business Secretary, summed up the situation in this way:

> Governments have been very fragmented. They are behind the curve. We operate national systems of business taxation and enforcement in a world where companies operate on a

[1] Although Starbucks briefed its shareholders that its UK business was making a 15 % profit, it reported to HM Revenue and Customs that 'it [had] made a loss for 14 of the 15 years it [had] been operating in the UK' (HM Revenue and Customs 2012).

> global scale, seeking out low tax jurisdictions. Governments are at a disadvantage. (Guardian 12 December 2012)

The news of global corporations' tax avoidance belongs to a long line of public scandals—including the irresponsible conduct of 'greedy bankers'[2] and their bonuses, the MPs' expense scandal[3] and more recently the News International hacking scandal[4]—in the UK. These 'scandals' raise a number of questions: why do growing numbers of politicians, journalists, bankers, global corporations and other professional and interest groups, who rely on legal rights to safeguard and promote their ideal and material interests, seem unconcerned with their responsibility towards the society in which they operate? Furthermore, why do governments appear either unwilling or unable to regulate the activities of these groups in a more stringent fashion? These questions can, admittedly, lure us into moralising on the conduct of bankers, politicians, journalists or global corporations. However, they are posed here, firstly, to examine how and why, in a society that is becoming progressively individualised and rights-based, rights are being gradually divorced from a sense of social responsibility and, secondly, to ask why the traditional forms of regulations have proved inadequate, or simply ineffective, in constraining what appears as socially irresponsible public conduct. Is it because the interests of global capitalism, people of wealth and the political elite coincide to such an extent that governments appear indecisive when regulating corporate activities? Has domestic politics been drained of power, while power has been moved to the global level of transnational organisations and corporations? Have the forces of globalisation created, as some have suggested, new 'law-free spaces' where the global elite and corporations may operate unencumbered by external regulation? Although any attempt to answer these questions would inevitably brush against ethics and politics, in the following pages we shall seek a better understanding of these concerns by exploring the social conditions generated by the unfolding of modernity. Following Zygmunt Bauman, it will be argued that in tandem with the move from industrialisation to late (or reflexive) modernity, social norms, relationships and structures, which were previously considered as enduring and stable over time, have become rapidly unstable—thus giving rise to new, short-lived social formations which do not generate or require ethical commitments. The aim of this chapter is to explore how law fares under these conditions.

Two issues should be stressed at the outset. Firstly, the idea of late modernity will be employed critically to tease out the novelty of ongoing social developments, but without endorsing the idea of liquid society as an adequate description of

---

[2] We shall discuss the banking scandal in the next section.

[3] In a series of articles published during 2009, the *Telegraph* revealed that a large number of MPs (members of parliament) across all parties had exploited their right to the second home allowance and misused the expense system for personal gains. For a discussion see Banakar (2010a, b).

[4] *News of the World* and other British newspapers published by News International, a subsidiary of News Corporation, were accused of engaging in extensive phone hacking, police bribery and exercising improper influence as part of their work to obtain stories. See the *Leveson Inquiry* (2012).

contemporary society. A point will be made that Bauman underestimates the power of domestic politics and the nation state; a flaw which is linked to his tendency to underrate the force of existing social structures and the continued 'solidity' of many institutional relationships. Secondly, this chapter will use recent events in the UK to advance its theoretical arguments, and thus it will first of all describe the unfolding of late modernity in a British context. Economic developments in Britain often echo events in the US, or are influenced by EU policies, regulations and directives, but they do not set the standard for assessing social change in other countries. In the same way that different forms of modernity have emerged in countries with different socio-political histories and economic preconditions (cf. Eisenstadt 2010, p. 3), different forms of late modernity will also appear in different parts of the world.

The following is divided into three sections. Section 1 uses the financial global crisis of 2007–2008 as a backdrop against which to formulate a number of concerns regarding the limits of legal regulation in late modernity. Section 2 explores the formation and operations of the late modern state, asking if power is separated from politics and has moved to the level of global organisations. Section 3 asks what kind of law is emerging de facto in response to the fluidity of late modernity, and how legal imagination envisages the future of law. The chapter concludes by discussing why late modernity, which marks the agency's heightened powers of reflexivity, appears paradoxically wanting in transcendental imagination and determination.

2 Reflexivity

2.1 When Controlling Risks Generates More Risks

The global financial crisis, which began in 2007–2008, was a multidimensional crisis brought on by the unfolding of new social and economic conditions driven by, to borrow from Castells et al. (2012, p. 2), 'the dynamics of a deregulated global capitalism, anchored in an unfettered financial market made up of global computer networks and fed by a relentless production of synthetic securities as the source of capital accumulation and capital lending'. Davies (2010) lists 38 separate macro and microeconomic factors which have been used to explore the causes of the crisis. These include the build-up of considerable global imbalances that generated a surplus of liquidity in the years before the crisis, growing income inequality among countries, flawed macroeconomic policies which financed the rising consumption trends by borrowing, the undisciplined financial markets which facilitated and encouraged this borrowing, and the failure of regulators to bring these markets under some form of control (Davies 2010). Although the crisis was systemic and caused by a combination of these factors, it was initially forced to the surface by 'the accumulation of small, and in themselves relatively harmless, decisions made by individual traders or bankers and banks', who were trying to refine the market

(Engelen et al. 2011, p. 9). Relatively harmless as these decisions arguably were, they concealed an irresponsible attitude towards excessive risk-taking at the expense of others, illustrated by the subprime mortgage scandal, where mortgages were sold on to another party who had no interest in whether or not they defaulted, and the private equity and hedge funds' so-called 'greed game' (Peston 2008).

In *Fool's Gold*, Tett (2009), a social anthropologist working as a financial journalist who was given access to the inner circles of elite bankers, describes how the 'tribe' of young traders at JP Morgan unleashed forces which caused the near collapse of the global financial system. This group of investment bankers, who were fervent believers in the efficiency and superiority of free markets, was largely responsible for engineering a sophisticated financial product known as a 'credit derivative'. This complex financial instrument disembedded and re-commodified loan transactions, creating a new and opaque culture of finance, which as Picciotto (2011, p. 159) explains, was 'underpinned by arcane techniques and mathematical modelling based upon calculations of relative volatility'. The young traders combined derivatives[5] with the process of 'securitisation', which involved a lender selling its loans to an investment bank. The amalgam enabled banks to turn the risk attached to their loans, i.e. repayment risks, into a financial product and sell it as if it were bonds or shares. This innovative use of derivatives reduced the capital reserves the banks required for lending more money to a larger number of investors. Put differently, derivatives allowed them to take risk off their books, package it as 'securities' and sell it on in the market for high fees. When employed conservatively, derivatives, according to Tett, were capable of bringing security to global finance and worked as a means of *controlling* risk. At the same time, Tett (2009, p. 15) admits that there were also many investors who used derivatives to 'make high-risk bets in the hope of windfall profit'. Once used in this way, derivatives not only generated more risk, but also dispersed the risk of investment bankers' excesses across the financial system and around the globe.

As the application of credit derivatives spread across the sector, and other banks such as Citigroup, USB, Deutsche Bank and Merrill Lynch also adopted them, they inevitably fell into the wrong hands and were perverted. The largest application of derivatives was in subprime mortgages, which allowed the repackaging of loans to homeowners, who failed to meet the usual requirements, into bonds for sale on an industrial scale. What had been started by a group of traders at JP Morgan as a financial innovation and an attempt to control risks gradually cascaded into a full-scale crisis of global dimensions, a crisis over which (we were told) no one had any control. The governments of the US and other countries could step in only once the international economic crisis was in full bloom to bailout investment banks with hundreds of billions of dollars of taxpayers' money to avoid a collapse of their national economies.

[5] Derivatives are contracts between two parties. Their value 'derives from credit risk attached to an underlying bond, loan or other financial asset' (see Tett 2009, p. 322). According to Alessandrini (2011, p. 445), this standard definition conceals derivatives' speculative property.

Tett worked on the assumption that complex derivatives were not responsible for the crisis, and if anyone was to be blamed, it was the few 'bad apples' within the banking community who exploited them. There are good reasons for paying attention to the actions and decisions of those individuals who acted recklessly, yet the forces which triggered the financial crisis were, as pointed out above, multi-layered, caused by macro and microeconomic factors, and cannot be reduced to the actions of one group of individuals. One cannot ignore that Tett's 'greedy bankers' operated within a system which lacked transparency and did not allow the external monitoring of the way derivatives were traded. The system was, moreover, driven by an insatiable appetite for profits and paid little heed to warnings about the spread of a speculative economy divorced from production.[6] When examining the financial crisis in terms of the actions of the few 'bad apples', we run the risk of overlooking the role of macroeconomic factors as well as the impact of laissez-faire capitalism that has been spreading in the UK and the United States since the 1980s.

With these points in mind, I use Tett's description of the financial crisis to articulate three sets of concerns at the levels of the individual (human agency or social action), social system (or social structure) and global economy (transnational relations). Focusing on individual bankers and mortgage brokers, the question begging an answer is how they could act in such an *unrestrained* fashion. How could they make highly risky decisions motivated by what appears to be their own short-term interest alone, as well as without a sense of responsibility to their investors, financial institutions upon which their livelihood depended and the larger society? To repeat, these questions are not meant as an invitation to moralise on the culture of banking, but to explore the limits of formal regulatory regimes under the normative conditions of late modernity. Notwithstanding Tett's attempt to blame 'greedy bankers', the actions of individual actors also need to be assessed in the context of the financial institutions in which they worked and in view of the imperatives of a financial system based on profitmaking and speculation. Although banking and finance are regulated domestically (e.g. the Banking Act in the UK and the Glass-Steagall Act in the US) and internationally (e.g. the Basel Accords), the story of the elite traders who manufactured these complex derivatives nevertheless suggests that there are social spaces within which the tribe of bankers may roam free, beyond the reach of the usual forms of regulation and undeterred by external monitoring. Thus, we are led to ask: how can public spaces and networks, such as those of elite bankers, exist beyond the reach of the formal (official) and informal (unofficial/extra-legal) regulatory mechanisms of early modernity? Do they exist because they are de facto out of reach of the public authorities, such as central banks and regulatory agencies, with the responsibility for the financial system, or because the liberal state is unwilling to interfere in the operations of the market economy for ideological reasons? Alternatively, could it be that a regulatory system, which has

[6] Financial derivatives allow both hedging against risks and speculation in pursuit of windfall profit, and it could be very difficult to differentiate between these two functions of derivatives. See Alessandrini (2011), p. 442.

been founded on the market economy's past performance and dysfunctions, is doomed to failure because its formal mechanisms cannot stay abreast of the continuously changing structures of the capitalist system? (cf. Hayek 1952). These questions will allow us to sharpen our focus on the role of the state, which is responsible for introducing and enforcing formal regulatory regimes, and ask: why were Western governments unable to prevent the crisis and could do so little after the event to redress its consequences?

2.2 *How Could They Act in Such an Unrestrained Fashion?*

To understand the constraints exerted on social action in late modern society we need to start with the cultural and political programme of modernity which, as argued by Eisenstadt, has 'entailed a shift in the conception of human agency, of autonomy, and of the place of the individual in the flow of time' (Eisenstadt 2010, p. 3). Many forms of modernity have developed in different parts of the world, but despite their differences they share a quest for emancipating human agency from the restraints of tradition. Modernity, liberally paraphrasing Giddens (1999, p. 39), replaced the claims of tradition by reason and conferred a durable appearance upon social institutions by transforming their authority from one based on traditional relationships to one based on legal bureaucracy, which facilitated the centralisation of institutional power. The combined power of modern institutions made the expansion of modernity unavoidable; yet this power, which reached its peak under industrialisation, could not totally dominate social developments because 'reflexivity', to borrow again from Giddens (1999, p. 39), subverted reason, 'where reason [was] understood as the gaining of certain knowledge'.

In its most basic form, reflexivity refers to people's ability to talk to themselves silently in their heads, or as Archer (2010, p. 5) explains, to have an 'internal conversation'. In its more recent sociological conceptualisation, it indicates a state of self-knowledge through self-dialogue, which allows the individual to reflect on herself in relation to her circumstances and vice versa, to observe herself as subject and object and devise a plan of action accordingly. In this sense, reflexivity links social action and social structures by throwing light on the process through which human agency becomes socially embedded. However, in its radical or late modern form, it highlights the disembeddedness of the agency, or the increasing ability of the agency to reflect on structures in order to emancipate oneself from the constraints of social institutions in a way which, although not new in the context of modernity (for modernity has, admittedly, been partly about the liberation of human agency from the fetters of traditional authority, practices and institutions), is nevertheless unprecedented in its scope and societal consequences (Archer 2007, p. 2).

The reflexivity inherent in modernity has been enhanced by globalisation, accelerating the rate of structural change and causing what Bauman (2000) calls the 'liquefaction' of the 'solid' structures and relations of early modernity. Taking this idea to its final conclusion, Bauman (2005, p. 1) describes contemporary society in terms of 'liquid modernity', which refers to a society where 'the conditions under which its members act change faster than it takes the ways of acting to consolidate into habits and routines'. Under these 'liquid' conditions, human agency becomes increasingly *disembedded*, i.e. independent of social structures and free from institutional and traditional ties which previously constrained social action at the level of social interaction. This also means that *flexibility*, i.e. 'a readiness to change tactics and style at short notice, to abandon commitments and royalties without regret', rather than 'conformity to rules' will serve the individual's interest more effectively (Bauman 2010, p. 4). As the reflexivity of the agency is enhanced and disembeddedness spreads across society, the moral contingency of social action grows rapidly, influencing the way social institutions and systems operate. As pointed out by Beck (1992), systems such as polity and law become less capable of responding to socio-cultural complexity and moral diversity in their environment through further functional differentiation.[7] Social forces, which could be evoked by law and polity to reshape society and mould behavioural patterns under the first stage of modernity, either become less effective or redundant, as formal regulation fails to keep pace with continuously evolving social structures.

To reiterate, 'the apparent solidity and timeless *appearance* of modernity offered an ostensibly durable foundation for building relationships based on trust, certitude, security and stability, which in turn provided a rational basis for social engineering and reform' (see Chap. 12). These solid structures are now undermined by late modernity's temporary assemblages of shifting and precarious positions, as well as transitory social spaces and forms of community. As we argued in the previous chapter, at the centre of this development we find the increased significance of agency vis-à-vis structures. To borrow from Martyn Denscombe again, this 'does not imply that 'structural' factors cease to exert any influence at all. But it does mean that there is a tendency for them to exert less influence than in the past and for greater significance to attach to individual choices in terms of the creation of self-identities' (Denscombe 2001, p. 160). This idea can tentatively explain the seemingly unrestrained conduct of the young bankers and other professionals we discussed above. The tribe of young bankers is increasingly 'emancipated' from the general social and moral constraints of the society in which they live and operate, and they belong to the mobile elite of well-to-do professionals who are not constrained by national borders and cannot be pinned down in any one locality or jurisdiction; consequently, their activities cannot be controlled through the traditional means of regulation external to their field of work. Their daily work provides a site (or a rudimentary type of 'habitus',[8] which we shall discuss below as a *technical habitat*) for knowledge-based collaboration, but is largely carried out at

[7] We shall discuss this point further in Sect. 2.

[8] 'Habitus' refers to 'the habitual, patterned ways of understanding, judging, and acting which arise from our particular position as members of one or several social fields, and from our particular trajectory in the social structure'. See Bourdieu (1987, p. 811).

the global—multi-jurisdictional[9]—level, where no single external normative system can effectively monitor or regulate individual conduct. For example, as soon as the UK government started considering a super-tax to regulate the bonus culture of investment bankers and brokers in the City, the Mayor of London warned that any such measure would only result in them moving to other centres of finance with more liberal tax regimes.[10] The chief executive of one of the state-backed banks warned a few months later that a large number of investment bankers were quitting the UK, causing a 'rapid exodus' as a result of the 'bonus fiasco' (*Evening Standard* 4 March 2010.).

Tett's use of the word 'tribe' to describe the young group of investment bankers at JP Morgan is significant in itself. In an unrelated study, Ethan Waters also employs the word to portray a group of college-educated young people in California, who being liberated from the structural (economic as well as cultural) pressures to which their parents were subjected choose not to form families, or they marry much later than their parents did (Watters 2004). At the same time, they are so driven by a culture of hyper-individualism that their lives, as described in Waters' *Urban Tribes*, appear as completely self-absorbed and egoistic.[11] Therefore, their heightened reflexivity, which emancipates them from certain constraining aspects of institutions, does not appear to empower them to look or step beyond modernity's epistemological premises. There is, however, more to this emerging trend than liquefaction. Instead of forming traditional families, the young adults in question are forming their own communities of friends, which Waters calls 'urban tribes'. Tett's tribe is different from Waters' in that it is created through the knowledge-based practices of traders: it requires of its members shared knowledge of how to trade in derivatives and other financial products, which temporarily joins them together in a collaborative network. However, Tett and Waters' tribes, different as they are, draw attention not only to the rise of new social formations, but also to the emergence of new forms of inequality and alienation. These tribes consist of well-educated, economically independent and socially successful young professionals, whose privileged backgrounds have granted them access to economic as well as cultural resources required for living flexibly and detached from local concerns and structural pressures. They do not, in other words, represent the whole of society, but a privileged group.

As Petersen (2010, pp. 333–347) explains, a widening gap is emerging between elite citizens, the successful high-flying global citizens who feel responsible for little more than their own wellbeing and interests, and a local underclass consisting of those who feel socio-economically vulnerable and culturally defenceless. This

[9] They might physically be based in one jurisdiction while operating in other jurisdictions.

[10] Boris Johnson, the Mayor of London, claimed that up to 9,000 bankers would leave London to avoid paying the taxes. *Evening Standard*, 1 January 2010.

[11] It should be noted that Waters' journalistic study (see above, n. 35) mainly concerns college-educated young people in California. The trend which Waters describes is, nevertheless, familiar to many Western and non-Western societies today (a few of the people Waters interviewed lived in Britain and other countries).

underclass does not live a liquid life, but takes on more than its share of anxiety and uncertainty, as it is culturally and economically undermined by social processes and political forces beyond its control. In response to late modernity's new forms of inequality, new kinds of social movements, such as the anti-globalisation movement, are born. Occupy Wall Street is an example of a new form of spontaneous social networking, which is organised in cyberspace as well as in urban space. This movement is also known as 'We are the 99%', which refers to the disparity in income and wellbeing between the majority of Americans and the 1 % who control the country's wealth.

2.3 From Community to Transitory Social Networks

The individual never totally submitted to the normativity of social structures, institutions, customs and traditions. A gap has always existed between injunctive norms, which prescribe what *ought* to be done, and descriptive norms, which reflect empirically ascertainable patterns of behaviour (or how people behave in actual fact).[12] Nonetheless, human agency's growing potential to free itself from the normative constraints of social structures is decisive for understanding the limits of formal regulation under late modernity. 'The central aspect of regulatory compliance', as Casey and Scott (2011, p. 77) explain, consists of 'institutionalisation and embedding of norms within some wider set of structures'. Employment law, which we shall discuss in Sect. 3, exemplifies how law was employed to embed certain values, such as fairness and equal treatment, in the structures of the labour market. This type of regulation requires the durable structural relations of *early* modernity capable of normatively influencing the agency. In the context of *late* modernity, however, the traditional form of regulation which employs law to ground values and norms in social structures and institutions loses its determinacy, as the agency's reflexivity grows vis-à-vis structures and institutions. Does this therefore mean that the late modern agency exists in a normative vacuum? The fact that Tett considers the young bankers as a 'tribe' suggests that although they might exist as 'nomadic individuals' (Lee 2010, p. 170), whose fleeting reality enables them to stay beyond the effective reach of formal (official) and informal (unofficial) regulatory mechanisms of early modernity, they nevertheless exist as a form of community. This late modern form of community is, admittedly, not the same as Ferdinand Tönnies' *Gemeinschaft* (1955), but is instead a temporary *network* created to facilitate collaboration between individual actors.

Gemeinschaft, or the traditional community, is based on tacit mutual understanding, interpersonal trust and care, and as such it has a more or less pronounced ethical dimension. According to Bauman (2001, p. 71), a traditional community generates inalienable rights, long-term commitments and obligations that bind

[12] For a discussion see Chap. 9.

together the participants of a community. It is therefore, historically speaking, the primary source of law and social order.[13] *Gemeinschaft* may be contrasted with late modern communities or networks based on the short-term association of groups of individuals brought together by a common specific interest, which might have been formed 'around "problems" with which individuals are struggling separately and on their own in their daily routine (for example weight-watching or inch-fighting)' (Bauman 2001, p. 71). 'Whatever the focal point of these communities', writes Bauman, their common feature is 'the superficial and perfunctory, as well as transient, nature of the bonds emerging between their participants' (Bauman 2001, p. 71). Most importantly, these communities do not unite their members by creating 'a web of ethical responsibilities' (Bauman 2001, p. 72), and they require neither long-term commitment nor geographic locality as their base. Instead, they spread a culture of hyperindividualism which, despite being excessively rights-based, understands rights as entitlements without obligations to others (Smith 2002; Banakar 2010a, b).

If the tribe of bankers, derivative traders and other global elites do not form a *Gemeinschaft* or cultivate long-term webs of ethical responsibility, then what holds them together as a 'tribe'? In her ethnographic study of Japanese derivative traders (which was conducted mainly before the global crisis between 1997 and 2001), Riles (2011, p. 41) provides a tentative answer to this question by focusing on the knowledge-based practices of traders. In Riles' account, derivative traders generate a technical (in contrast to a value-based) context for collaboration through their day-to-day standardised tasks and knowledge practices comprising a 'constellation of both theoretical and doctrinal manoeuvres and material documents' (Riles 2011, p. 38). Riles (2011, p. 232), who hopes to find a way of making financial regulation more 'stable, effective and democratic', suggests that the daily practices of traders involving the application of legal techniques associated with securing contractual obligations, more specifically collaterals, in the derivative markets provides a possible starting point for regulatory innovation. Her focus is on the *form* of the law itself—the hollow-cored form of regulation such as Japan's 'netting law', the content of which is unspecified—to which she attributes agency. Moreover, Riles contends that in the deployment and application of the law as a form, rather than substantive judgements, resides a commitment to democracy (this is reminiscent of Jürgen Habermas' idea of 'law as a medium' and Gunther Teubner's theory of reflexive law[14]), whilst 'private law doctrines and techniques can stand as a bulwark against the complexity and indeterminacy of the market' (Riles 2011, p. 164). Specialised technical knowledge and the practice of law in derivatives markets do not create a web of ethical commitment—or a 'habitus'—at the transnational level,

---

[13] For a discussion see Chap. 10.

[14] Reflexive law does not require the enforcement of particular substantive rules and does not set particular goals to be achieved in a regulated area. Instead of authoritatively determining the social function of sub-systems, or trying to regulate their input and output performances, reflexive law tries to establish norms of procedure, organisation, membership and competence that can '*further the development of reflexive structures within other social sub-systems*' (Teubner 1983, p. 275).

but they do generate a technical 'habitat' for traders, bankers and other financial actors to collaborate 'according to carefully scripted routines' (Riles 2011, p. 65). Transitory as this space might be, it provides a site for internal self-regulation, which according to Riles lends itself also to state intervention.

There are also forces external to global finance capable of exerting regulatory pressure on transnational corporations. The nation states remain the most powerful of these—the fact that they chose not to intervene in the markets is, however, another matter which we shall discussed in the next part. States aside, there are other forces in play. The moral condemnation which was triggered by revelations about MPs' expenses, bankers' bonuses or the tax avoidance strategies adopted by multinational corporations in the UK constitutes a normative force that compels not only corporations but also individual tribe members to take notice of how their actions are viewed from the outside. However, these normative forces, being dependent on the mass media's erratic reporting, lack durability and consistency. Public protests, for instance, against multinational corporations' tax avoidance in the UK lasted for 1 week and soon abated as new events made the headlines. Moreover, protests have a local dimension (although they are often in part organised in cyberspace, they still require action in urban spaces), while 'nomadic individuals' and the transnational corporations they work for are not committed to local concerns. The burgeoning literature on corporate social responsibility engages with the regulatory challenges that this type of detachment poses by suggesting new forms of self-regulation backed by law (Shamir 2011, p. 315; also see Black 2012). However, their primary assumptions—that through self-regulation norms of social responsibility can be implanted into corporate structures and cultures—appear incompatible with late modernity's postulate that structural conditions can change faster than it takes to consolidate norms of conduct. If true, then what is gained from transplanting norms of social responsibility in corporate structures whose durability is a function of transient networks which do not generate or require ethical commitments? Before we answer this question, we need to consider how the nation state is influenced by late modernity.

3 The Transformation of the State

Within the banking sector and among politicians there were those who knew that the risks to major financial institutions had been dangerously underestimated. For example, as early as 1992, the financier Felix Rohatyn described derivatives as 'financial hydrogen bombs built on personal computers by 26-year-olds with MBAs' (quoted in Manne and McKnight 2010, p. 24). Nevertheless, Western governments chose not to interfere in the way the banks were recasting the financial system. As Alan Greenspan, the former US Federal Reserve Chairman, admitted, they knew that the crisis was growing but did nothing, instead presuming that the banks could and would regulate themselves (Neate 2012). Greenspan's admission that they decided not to get involved could be described as primarily ideological and an indication of how the logic and representations of markets have been internalised by governments and turned into 'an optimum organizational principle for state and society as a whole' (Shamir 2011, p. 315). If true, then we still need to explain why the logic and representations of the market exercise such a hold over late modern states and society. Are states unable to intervene and regulate banks and transnational corporations because, as Vince Cable remarked (see the introduction), in a world where corporations operated globally, governments had become 'very fragmented' and could act only nationally? (*Guardian* 12 December 2012) Has power been split, as suggested by Lyon (2013: 5), from local politics, and thus from nation states, and moved to the level of global relations and transnational corporations?

Here we notice a tendency to underestimate the force of domestic politics. Although it is true that power is exercised globally among others by transnational corporations and, arguably, is outside the reach of national governments, it does not follow that domestic politics has been drained of all power in the way that theorists of late modernity, such as Lyon, argue. The nation state has not been dissolved by the forces of late modernity, and according to Centeno and Cohen (2010, p. 8) remains 'by far the most powerful force shaping economic life'. The global economy continues to rely on the state protection of property rights and 'the supposedly anachronistic notion of territorially defined authority' (Centeno and Cohen 2010, pp. 16–17). The late modern nation state 'functions with a fundamental governance paradox: policy and enforcement remain within the responsibility of individual states, yet transactions occur in a space policed by none of them' (Centeno and Cohen 2010, pp. 16–17). Following Centeno and Cohen, we may postulate that states and governments were unwilling to intervene when they were warned at an early stage of a pending financial crisis, because they saw the burgeoning global crisis as a problem outside their proper domain of action. This stance was motivated by the ideology of a free market economy and justified by the practical difficulties inherent in regulating private financial activities which take place outside the jurisdiction of the state. Thus, regulators in the US, UK and other countries relied on—and believed in—the ability and willingness of investment banks to regulate the financial sector's excessive risk-taking. To make matters more complicated, the regulators to whom the regulation of transactions had been delegated—and many regulators such as the credit rating agencies belonged to the private industry bodies—were part of the problem for, as Picciotto (2011, p. 161) points out, they had 'developed a vested interest in encouraging rather than controlling, the growth of markets' in complex financial instruments. Nonetheless, once the collapse of the sector became imminent, world states did step in to bail out the banks, demonstrating their ability to act. The policies implemented by national governments between 2007 and 2010, according to Davies, were instrumental in avoiding 'the recession turning into a depression', which in turn left many governments with huge fiscal deficits' (Davies 2010, p. 12). It is therefore more accurate to argue that the nation state has remained an important force under late modernity, although it has redefined its 'mission' in response to the intensification of reflexivity—it has reduced its social role, which required ethical commitment to improved welfare, while continuing to protect and promote the global economy. It is, at the same time, 'widening and strengthening its penal intervention' (Wacquant 2007, p. 18), as well as expanding its powers of surveillance, in order to manage risks more effectively.

3.1 A Shift to Risk Management

As the sphere of market economy took shape in the nineteenth and early twentieth century, wrote Karl Polanyi in *The Great Transformation*, economic relations which had previously been a function of social organisation—or embedded in social structures—were dislocated from their societal context and turned into an autonomous system (Polanyi 2001; also see Joerges and Falke 2011). This system possessed its own imperatives and did not exist to serve the society out of which it had been born. Moreover, it had the ability to impose its norms and form of rationality upon other spheres of action and reconstruct law and politics as well as everyday social relationships [a process which Habermas later described as system's colonisation of lifeworld (Habermas 1975)]. Much of the 'juridification' of the social sphere that was carried out during the 1960s and 1970s by the welfare state aimed at reversing this disembedding process, i.e. to re-embed the forces which had been unleashed by the market economy in the social context (Teubner 1987). The welfare state was in turn overtaken in the 1980s by profound transformative changes in the way the economic relations were organised. According to Edgeworth (2003, p. vi), these changes, which resulted from the rise of globalisation, included 'the dismantling of welfare safety nets; the greater reliance on markets to restructure regulatory frameworks; and the progressive withdrawal of the states from former areas of responsibility'.[15] The welfare state did not cease to exist and continued its stabilising social role, aimed partly at easing the socially dysfunctional effects of the expanding market economy, albeit with a severely weakened ideological conviction in its own ability to generate lasting social reform.

With the rise of transnational and global forces, we observe a move from the welfare-oriented social and legal policies of the 1960s and 1970s, to forms of regulation more concerned with managing risks than addressing the causes of social problems. The shift to risk management strategies is often explained by reference to the inability of late modern social systems and institutions (such as law, economy and polity) to respond fully to and control the increasing complexity of moral conflicts arising out of the 'unforeseen consequences of functional differentiation' through further functional differentiation (Beck 1999, p. 2). This does not imply

[15] Edgeworth (2003) contends that postmodernity generates its own specific forms of law. One form is reflected in the development of norms and institutions of global governance—the extension of which is the emergence of law without the state—and, the other, in replacing traditional public law regulations with contractual arrangements for the delivery of public services.

that early modern social systems responded *fully* to their environment. Instead, it is suggested here that early modern systems operated in a social environment which offered, relatively speaking, prolonged contextual continuity and structural stability, which in turn translated into dispositional durability in patterns of social action. This allowed social systems to respond, if not fully then at least in a seemingly meaningful fashion, to moral conflicts in their environment.

At the local level, late modernity marks the failure of social welfare ideology, which required an omnipotent nation state to realise its vision of a better society, i.e. a welfare society that guaranteed a minimum standard of living, education, health care and employment for all its citizens. Put simply, the modern welfare state was characterised by governmental *regulation*, often carried out by introducing legal measures aimed at enhancing *social integration* through a fair allocation of resources, duties and responsibilities. The state was seen as a potential force for good, capable of reorganising social conditions for the better, by legally regulating social and economic relationships. In contrast, late modernity is characterised by governmental *deregulation* (not to be confused with the reduction in the volume of laws and regulations)[16] and system integration through the market economy. In a western European context in general, but the UK in particular, this is achieved by facilitating two apparently separate, but on closer inspection interrelated, processes at global and local levels by: (1) promoting the rise of transnational networks in production, global finance and trade and (2) by passing on responsibility for the general welfare of citizens, i.e. for employment (benefits), health care, retirement, education, housing, etc., to individual citizens themselves. We also see a move from policies designed to promote social integration through participation and mutual recognition to ones based on cultural *assimilation* (for example, in respect to immigrants and ethnic and religious minorities), social *exclusion* (reflected, for example, in the emergence of criminal policies aimed at prevention, preferring to build more prisons to house an ever-growing number of inmates for longer periods instead of attempting to rehabilitate them)[17] and political *neutralisation* (for example, in respect to the way moral issues are politically marginalised (for a discussion see Banakar 2010a, b). Assimilation, exclusion and neutralisation provide the bases for developing forms of social control, which are exercised through an ever-increasing machinery of surveillance, ultimately motivated by the belief that the risk posed by various threats can be calculated and pre-empted.

[16] The notion of 'deregulation' refers here to the growing privatisation of public services and not to an overall reduction in the number of laws and regulations.

[17] In late modernity, rehabilitation—what Bauman calls the 'recycling of human waste'—is no longer taken seriously. Imprisonment—or 'waste disposal'—is considered too expensive, which means that the public must accept living with an ever-growing threat and fear of crime and must find their own ways of protecting themselves against it. See Bauman (2007), p. 22.

4 Late Modern Law

What kind of law and legality can respond to the increasing fluidity of late modernity's social structures? Here we should distinguish between at least three levels of law and regulation.[18] The first level concerns traditional areas such as contract, family, property and criminal justice, which uphold a particular type of social organisation (preserving the status quo). The second concerns public international law, which is of sovereign states but is created to regulate inter-state relationships. The third level is that of transnational law of supra-national agencies such as the EU, IMF, the World Bank and UNCITRAL. Since lack of space does not allow for a discussion on all of these levels separately, in the remaining part of this chapter I shall briefly touch on recent developments within family law and employment law to exemplify how traditional areas of law are influenced by the liquefaction of social structures, before discussing forms of law and regulations which are introduced to bring about social change under late modernity.

4.1 When Law Loses a Clear Concept of the Social

The family, once regarded as the bedrock of human society, has been undergoing dramatic transformation in recent decades. Baroness Deech, the Chairwoman of the Bar Standard Board in the UK, warned recently that the 'traditional Christian image of a lifelong marriage is no longer accurate because of the changing nature of relationships and the introduction of legal rights for same-sex couples' (*Telegraph* 2010). She also warned that human rights law in the UK 'may soon rule that it is discriminatory to ban homosexuals from marrying in the same way that heterosexual couples do' (*Telegraph* 2010). This not only highlights the changing constitution of the family in Britain, but also shows that local considerations on policy issues are no longer contained by the legal constraints of the national state. Legal deliberations, which are part of any such institutional change, place the national discourse on the family in a broader socio-legal context created by transnational forces. The Human Rights Act 1998, introduced to give further effect in UK law to the rights contained in the European Convention on Human Rights, brings transnational forces to bear on national developments. In addition, in Western Europe, attitudes to marriage, family formation and sexual relationships have changed over the last few decades, leaving their mark on EU law, which in turn influences all member states' legal systems (Antokolskaia 2007, p. 241).

These changes in attitude and practice can be suggestive of the expansion of a 'liquid society', which the 'solid' traditional bonds of family are melting away. The legal system cannot stay outside social transformations and has to observe, respond

[18] William Twining distinguishes between nine levels of legality, ranging from global and international to transnational, sub-state and non-state law. See Twining (2009).

to and in many cases accommodate emerging new values, attitudes and practices in the larger society. As a result, traditional institutions of the law can also appear as if losing their solidity and durability. To borrow a phrase from Baroness Deech, the legal system's attempts to accommodate changes in its environment reveal that 'English law has lost any clear concept of marriage' (*Telegraph* 2010). However, it would be misleading to ignore the fact that traditional family structures also persist, and the majority of families continue to consist of married heterosexual couples. More significantly, as argued by Wyn et al. (2011, p. 4), the fragmentation of institutional and traditional structures under late modernity does not necessarily lead to the dissolution of the family, but can instead heighten its significance, albeit in a new form. Once new family formations are normalised and allowed to coexist alongside traditional families, they subvert the normativity of traditional structures by constantly reminding us of the existing alternative models of social organisation and our options to act differently. This engenders greater normative uncertainty and institutional fragmentation, but it does not necessarily entail the liquefaction of all solid structures and relationships as Bauman suggests.

4.2 Using Law to Generate Uncertainty

Employment law establishes a general legal framework for terms and conditions of employment, which grounds certain legal standards or values—such as fairness, equal treatment and reasonableness—into the structure of a working relationship, thus safeguarding how employees are hired, treated in work and dismissed. In so doing, it regulates the behaviour of employers and their staff as well as their relationship, bringing continuity and certitude into the spheres of work and production. Viewed in this way, employment law helps to solidify the spheres of employment and labour relations, while embedding market relationships in a social context. But social embeddedness, permanence and stability, which were valued highly during early modernity, are no longer regarded as useful organisational qualities by many employers. To meet the challenges of rapidly shifting and perpetually evolving globalised markets, businesses have been increasingly adopting 'non-standard employment relations' based on temporary or short-term contingency work (Kalleberg 2000).

According to the UK government, businesses find current employment laws difficult to implement, which deter them from creating new jobs and employing more staff. This in turn, 'slows the growth of businesses and the economy' (*Gov.Uk* 2013). Subsequently, the government announced in January 2011 that it planned an overhaul of the law in order to allow employers to 'hire and fire at will' (*Evening Standard* 27 January 2011). The 'reform' was heavily criticised by unions and the opposition party, and the government was eventually forced to drop the proposal the following year. Instead, in the *Enterprise and Regulatory Reform Bill* (*www.parliament.uk*, 18 December 2012), the government provided provisions to grant employers new powers, including introducing a cap on unfair dismissal payouts (reducing the amount of compensation for unfair dismissal by two-thirds), making it more difficult to claim unfair dismissal (the employer requires 2 years' service instead of one before claiming unfair dismissal) and reducing the redundancy consultation time from 90 to 45 days. Finally, the government announced more recently that from April 2013 it will allow workers to forfeit some of their employment rights, such as the right to unfair dismissal and redundancy, in return for tax-free shares. This new employment contract will accomplish the initial idea of empowering employers to 'fire at will' (*Guardian* 8 October 2012).

The public political discourse on employment rights and the way the law is 'reformed' to satisfy the requirements of businesses demonstrate how certain areas of law might fare as the social structures and institutional settings (in this case companies, corporations and firms) which grounded law's normativity (they crystallised the legal standards and values of employment) adopt more flexible and transitory organisational arrangements. As the law struggles to respond to the needs of businesses, employment law starts to melt away, therefore generating flexibility for employers and uncertainty for employees. Employment law is no longer the normative framework for enhancing stability and certainty in the relationship between the employer and the employee; rather, it is an integral part of the organisational fluidity of late modernity.

4.3 The Possibility of Social Change

At the height of the welfare state, when legal measures were frequently employed for bringing about social change, law showed great regulatory limitations and proved not to be the effective instrument of social control and engineering many had hoped (see Chap. 12). Under late modern conditions, where law's normativity can no longer find a durable foothold in fleeting social structures, legal measures aimed at generating new patterns of behaviour or social change grow evermore ineffective. In contemporary Britain, law is therefore employed all the more for risk management purposes, i.e. to control the risk of threats which, paradoxically, do not lend themselves to rational assessments or calculations. This is achieved through enhanced methods of surveillance and measures devised to pre-empt threats, the best example of which is to be found in the UK's anti-terrorism legislation, which at best generates more and new risks (see Chap. 10).

Law and surveillance are becoming all the more interwoven. An era of modern surveillance, which began with Jeremy Bentham's 'panopticon', devised as a solid piece of 'moral architecture' (Lyon 2013, p. 11), is giving way to the 'post-panopticon' era. Lyon maintains that the solidity of panopticon, where neither the prisoners nor the invisible watchers could move physically, has been dissolved and replaced by the liquidity of new surveillance technologies:

> [N]ew surveillance practices, based on information processing rather than the discourse that Foucault had in mind, permit a new transparency in which not just citizens but all of us, across the range of roles we play in everyday life, are constantly checked, monitored,

> tested, assessed, valued and judged. But the converse is clearly not true. As the details of our daily lives become more transparent to the organizations surveilling us, their own activities become less and less easy to discern. (Lyon 2013, p. 12)

The Communications Data Bill, proposed recently by the UK government, exemplifies the rise of the 'post-panopticon' era. The Bill aims at expanding police and security services' powers to monitor the surfing and email activities of all those who live in Britain. This measure is, according to the government, part of the policy to tackle paedophilia, terrorism and other forms of crime (*BBC News* 11 December 2012). This demonstrates the gradual transformation of law, from an instrument of social change, a mechanism for ensuring continuity and upholding the status quo, into a tool for supporting sophisticated technologies of surveillance.[19]

The description of law as a formal instrument for managing risks does not offer a promising starting point for speculating on the future of the law. Understandably, legal imagination has turned to normative theories, such as those propagating corporate social responsibility and cosmopolitanism, in search of a law which can meet the challenges of the contemporary global society. Those who are concerned with the consequences of globalisation, but remain committed to the ideology of a market economy continue to search for methods of re-embedding the market forces. They either assume, as Riles did (2011), that law enshrines democratic potentials and the agency to realise social goods, or tend to resort to theories of corporate social responsibility in search of a form of law or regulation which can tame the power of transnational corporations and alleviate the dysfunctional consequences of global capitalism (Davis et al. 2012; Black 2012). Advocates of one strand of this approach maintain that corporations have to incorporate norms of social responsibility—in effect self-regulate themselves—because they operate in a 'world culture' which expects them to do so, i.e. this so-called 'world culture' constrains them normatively (Shamir 2011). One problem with this approach is that in order for corporations to devise self-regulatory mechanisms, they need durable structures as well as a sense of ethics, whereas they operate in a highly fluid environment which does not lend itself easily to internal or external monitoring and does not foster 'a web of ethical responsibilities' (Bauman 2001, p. 72). More importantly, the idea of a 'world culture' as a coherent and normatively forceful global entity is fraught with difficulties, for globalisation interconnects and produces unity as well as fragmentation (Held 2006, p. 688). Assuming that 'world culture' is an empirically discrete unit of analysis, we still have to take into account its interplay with transnational corporations. Moreover, as it interacts with and influences corporations, it is in return shaped normatively by the latter (Shamir 2011).

---

[19] Top secret documents leaked by Edward Snowden, a former US National Security Agency (NSA) contractor, revealed that the NSA had 'collected almost 200 million text messages a day from across the globe, using them to extract data including location, contact networks and credit card details'. The NSA had 'made extensive use of its vast text message database to extract information on people's travel plans, contact books, financial transactions and more – including of individuals under no suspicion of illegal activity'. See *Guardian* 16 January 2014.

There are, however, other universally inclined theories, such as cosmopolitanism, which articulate concerns with globalisation but draw inspiration from natural law by emphasising the moral duty of each person towards the rest of humanity. Cosmopolitanism consists, according to Jeremy Waldron, of several approaches:

> For some it is about the love of mankind, or about duties owed to every person in the world without national or ethnic differentiation. For others, the word 'cosmopolitanism' connotes the fluidity and the evanescence of culture…; and it anticipates a world of fractured and mingled identities. For still others… cosmopolitanism is about order and norms and not just culture and moral sentiment. It envisages a world order, and (in some views) a world government or world polity. According to the cosmopolitan, there are already many norms in the world which operate at a cosmopolitan level, including (for example) the principles that define human rights and crime against humanity, the laws that govern refuge, asylum, travel, and migration.… (Waldron 2008, p. 83)

Whereas Beck (2006, p. 2) asserts that cosmopolitanism has left the realm of philosophical castles in the air and has entered reality as 'the defining fixture of reflexive modernity', Fine (2007, pp. 133–134) adopts a more cautious approach by suggesting that it 'should be understood as a research agenda rather than a fixed idea or state to be achieved'. In contrast, Raymond Lee describes it as a 'fragile and incomplete political settlement' and 'a flawed attempt in promoting a new sense of liberal mindedness' (Lee 2010, p. 172). How cosmopolitanism can generate a universal sense of solidarity and belonging in the highly liquid conditions of late modernity remains a contested issue (Lee 2010).

Why should we entertain ideas such as corporate social responsibility and cosmopolitanism? The structures and relationships which create corporations are transitory and not disposed to grounding ethical responsibility through the force of law or moral pressure. Cosmopolitanism, on the other hand, appears as the desperate attempt of the liberal-minded intelligentsia to transcend the present impasse by resorting to ideas from the past. In this sense, both approaches arguably reinforce late modernity's sense of stalemate—that there is nothing beyond the culture of consumerism and a legal order based on risk management. In the same vein, late modernity—whether viewed as a theory or an empirically-based description of contemporary conditions—lacks imagination and the impetus to break with modernity's order of things. Human agency might be gaining heightened reflexivity vis-à-vis social structures, but individual imagination and transcendental determination remain constrained by the normativity of consumerism and the celebration of hyper-individualism, which is but a form of alienation and translates into a lack of responsibility for others. This should cause neither despair nor nihilism, for in the theoretical and empirical unoriginality of late modernity lies latent the promise of a paradigm shift. Anti-capitalist protesters occupying the square in front of St. Paul's Cathedral, in London in 2011, the Occupy Wall Street Movement in New York and similar movements in Spain, Italy, Portugal, Greece and Israel are examples of late modernity's 'networked social movements' in progress (for a discussion on new forms of social movements see Castells 2012). Theoretical constructs such as corporate social responsibility and cosmopolitanism can potentially contribute to the birth of a new 'state of being' by putting ethical conflicts inherent in the global market economy under the spotlight and demanding solutions. Their potential to generate social change can be preserved by employing them as normative standards for evaluating and challenging existing conditions, claims and disputes. Thus, they carry within them the seeds of future developments.

References

Alessandrini, D. (2011). Regulating financial derivatives: Risks, contested values, and uncertain futures. *Social & Legal Studies, 20*(4), 441–462.

Antokolskaia, M. (2007). Comparative family law: Moving with the times. In E. Örücü & D. Nelken (Eds.), *Comparative law: A handbook* (pp. 241–262). Oxford: Hart.

Archer, M. (2007). *Making our way through the world: Human reflexivity and social mobility*. Cambridge: Cambridge University Press.

Archer, M. (2010). Reflexivity. *Sociopedia.isa*. http://www.isa-sociology.org/publ/sociopedia-isa/.

Banakar, R. (Ed.). (2010a). *Law, rights and justice in late modern society: A tentative theoretical framework* (Rights in context). Farnham: Ashgate.

Banakar, R. (2010b). Law, rights and justice in late modern society: A tentative theoretical framework. In R. Banakar (Ed.), *Rights in context* (pp. 19–37). Farnham: Ashgate.

Bauman, Z. (2000). *Liquid modernity*. Cambridge: Polity.

Bauman, Z. (2001). *Community: Seeking safety in an insecure world*. Cambridge: Polity.

Bauman, Z. (2005). *Liquid life*. Cambridge: Polity.

Bauman, Z. (2007). Uncertainty and other liquid modern fears. In J. Priban (Ed.), *Liquid society and its law* (pp. 17–40). Farnham: Ashgate.

Bauman, Z. (2010). *Liquid times: Living in an age of certainty*. Cambridge: Polity.

Beck, U. (1992). *Risk society: Towards a new modernity*. London: Sage.

Beck, U. (1999). *World risk society*. Cambridge: Polity.

Beck, U. (2006). *Cosmopolitanism vision*. Cambridge: Polity.

Berman, M. (1991). *All that is solid melts into air: The experience of modernity*. London: Verso.

Black, J. (2012). Paradoxes and failures: "New Governance" techniques and the financial crisis. *Modern Law Review, 75*(6), 1037–1063.

Bourdieu, P. (1987). The force of law: Toward a sociology of the juridical field (trans: Terdiman R). *Hastings Law Journal, 38*, 805–853.

Casey, D., & Scott, C. (2011). Crystallization of regulatory norms. *Journal of Law and Society, 38* (1), 76–95.

Castells, M. (2012). *Networks of outrage and hope: Social movements in the internet age*. Cambridge: Polity.

Castells, M., et al. (2012). The culture of economic crisis. In M. Castells et al. (Eds.), *Aftermath: The culture of economic crisis* (pp. 1–14). Oxford: Oxford University Press.

Centeno, M. A., & Cohen, J. N. (2010). *Global capitalism: A sociological perspective*. Cambridge: Polity.

Davies, H. (2010). *The financial crisis: Who is to blame?* Cambridge: Polity.

Davis, K. E., et al. (2012). Indicators as a technology of global governance. *Law and Society Review, 46*(1), 71–104.

Denscombe, M. (2001). Uncertain identities and health-risking behaviour: The case of young people and smoking in late modernity. *British Journal of Sociology, 52*(1), 157–177.

Edgeworth, B. (2003). *Law modernity, postmodernity*. Aldershot: Ashgate.

Eisenstadt, S. N. (2010). Modernity and modernization. *Sociopedia.isa*. http://www.isa-sociology.org/publ/sociopedia-isa/.

Engelen, E., et al. (2011). *After the great complacence: Financial crisis and the politics of reform*. Oxford: Oxford University Press.
Fine, R. (2007). *Cosmopolitanism*. London: Routledge.
Giddens, A. (1999). *The consequences of modernity*. Cambridge: Polity.
Habermas, J. (1975). *Legitimation crisis*. Boston: Heinemann Education.
Hayek, F. A. (1952). *The counter-revolution of science: Studies on the abuse of reason*. New York: Free Press of Glencoe.
Held, D. (2006). Democracy: From city states to a cosmopolitan order? In R. E. Goodin & P. Pettit (Eds.), *Contemporary political philosophy*. Oxford: Blackwells.
Joerges, C., & Falke, J. (Eds.). (2011). *Karl Polanyi, Globalisation and potential of law in transnational markets*. Oxford: Hart.
Kalleberg, A. L. (2000). Nonstandard employment relations: Part-time, temporary and contract work. *Annual Review of Sociology, 26*, 341–365.
Lee, R. L. M. (2010). On the origins of belonging: Confronting cosmopolitanism in the late modern age. *Journal of Sociology, 46*(2), 169–186.
Lyon, D. (2013). Introduction. In Z. Bauman & D. Lyon (Eds.), *Liquid surveillance* (pp. 1–17). Cambridge: Polity.
Manne, R., & McKnight, D. (2010). *Goodbye to all that? On the failure of neo-liberalism and the urgency of change*. Melbourne: Black and Agenda.
Marx, K., & Engels, F. (1967). *The Communist manifesto*. Harmondsworth: Penguin (original publication 1848).
Neate, R. (2012, August 6) Financial crisis: 25 people at the heart of the meltdown – where are they now? *Guardian.ac.uk*.
Peston, R. (2008). We lose in Greed Games. Blog posted on the *BBC website*, 28 March 2008. http://www.bbc.co.uk/blogs/thereporters/robertpeston/2008/03/we_lose_in_greed_game.html.
Petersen, H. (2010). Rights and responsibility. In R. Banakar (Ed.), *Rights in context* (pp. 333–347). Aldershot: Ashgate.
Picciotto, S. (2011). Dis-embedding and regulation: The paradox of international finance. In C. Joerges & J. Falke (Eds.), *Karl Polanyi, Globalisation and potential of law in transnational markets* (pp. 157–180). Oxford: Hart.
Polanyi, K. (2001). *The great transformation: The political and economic origins of our time*. Boston, MA: Beacon (original publication 1944).
Riles, A. (2011). *Collateral knowledge: Legal reasoning in the global financial markets*. Chicago: University of Chicago Press.
Shamir, R. (2011). Social responsible private regulation: World culture or world capitalism? *Law and Society Review, 45*(2), 313–336.
Smith, C. (2002). The sequestration of experience: Rights, talk and moral thinking in "Late Modernity". *Sociology, 36*(1), 43–66.
Tett, G. (2009). *Fool's gold: How unrestrained greed corrupted a dream. Shattered global markets and unleashed a catastrophe*. London: Little Brown.
Teubner, G. (1983). Substantive and reflexive elements in modern law. *Law and Society Review, 17*(2), 239–285.
Teubner, G. (Ed.). (1987). *Juridification of social spheres*. Berlin: de Gruyter.
Tönnies, F. (1955). *Community and association (Gemeinschaft und Gesellschaft)*. London: Routledge and Kegan Paul.
Twining, W. (2009). The implications of "Globalisation" for law as a discipline. In A. Haplin & V. Roeben (Eds.), *Theorising the global legal order* (pp. 39–59). Oxford: Hart.
Wacquant, L. (2007). Comment la tolérance zéro vint à l'Europe Sociétés sous contrôle', *Manière de voir*, March–April. Quoted in: Z Bauman 'Uncertainty and other Liquid Modern Fears. In J. Priban (Ed.), *Liquid society and its law* (pp. 17–40). Farnham: Ashgate.
Waldron, J. (2008). Cosmopolitan norms. In S. Benhabib (Ed.), *Another cosmopolitanism* (pp. 83–101). Oxford: Oxford University Press.
Watters, E. (2004). *Urban tribes: Are friends the new family*. London: Bloomsbury.

Wyn, J., et al. (2011). Beyond transitions metaphor: Family relations and young people in late modernity. *Journal of Sociology, 48*(1), 3–22.
Young, J. (2009). *The vertigo of late modernity*. London: Sage.

Reports

HM Revenue and Customs (2012) 'Tax avoidance by multinational companies' at http://www.publications.parliament.uk/pa/cm201213/cmselect/cmpubacc/716/71605.htm#note19
Leveson Inquiry (2012) *AN Inquiry into the Culture, Practices and Ethics of the Press.* at http://www.official-documents.gov.uk/document/hc1213/hc07/0779/0779.pdf.
Gov.Uk (2013) 'Making the Labour market More Flexible, Efficient and Fair', posted at https://www.gov.uk/government/policies/making-the-labour-market-more-flexible-efficient-and-fair accessed on 9 January 2013
www.parliament.uk (2012) *Enterprise and Regulatory Reform Bill at* http://services.parliament.uk/bills/2012-13/enterpriseandregulatoryreform.html 18 December 2012

Newspaper Items

BBC News (11 December 2012) 'Draft Communication Bill to be Redrafted' at http://www.bbc.co.uk/news/uk-politics-20676284
Independent (3 December 2012) 'Cutting benefits to poorest "a tragedy": Campaigners warn Chancellor not to freeze welfare payments to balance budget'
Guardian (3 December 2012) 'MPs attack Amazon, Google and Starbucks over tax avoidance' at http://www.guardian.co.uk/business/2012/dec/03/amazon-google-starbucks-tax-avoidance
Guardian (12 December 2012) 'Vince Cable calls for international efforts on tax avoidance'
Guardian (8 October 2012) 'Workers can swap rights for company shares' at http://www.guardian.co.uk/politics/2012/oct/08/george-osborne-workers-rights-shares
Guardian 16 January 2014, 'NSA collects millions of text messages daily in 'untargeted' global sweep' at http://www.theguardian.com/world/2014/jan/16/nsa-collects-millions-text-messages-daily-untargeted-global-sweep
Evening Standard, 1 January 2010
Evening Standard, 4 March, 2010
Evening Standard (27 January 2011) 'Employment law "will let bosses hire and fire at will"' at http://www.standard.co.uk/news/employment-law-will-let-bosses-hire-and-fire-at-will-6560471.html
Telegraph.co.uk (16 March 2010) 'Baroness Deech: English law no longer has clear concept of marriage' http://www.telegraph.co.uk/news/uknews/law-and-order/7449696/Baroness-Deech-English-law-no-longer-has-clear-concept-of-marriage.html Accessed on 5 March 2014
Telegraph.co.uk (01 Jul 2009) 'MPs' expenses: scandal damage "cannot be underestimated" says Electoral Commission' at http://www.telegraph.co.uk/

Index

R. Banakar, *Normativity in Legal Sociology*, DOI 10.1007/978-3-319-09650-6

MIX
Papier aus verantwortungsvollen Quellen
Paper from responsible sources
FSC® C105338

If you have any concerns about our products,
you can contact us on
ProductSafety@springernature.com

In case Publisher is established outside the EU,
the EU authorized representative is:
Springer Nature Customer Service Center GmbH
Europaplatz 3, 69115 Heidelberg, Germany

Printed by Libri Plureos GmbH
in Hamburg, Germany